HUNTING
ERIC RUDOLPH

HUNTING ERIC RUDOLPH

HENRY SCHUSTER

with Charles Stone

BERKLEY BOOKS, NEW YORK

THE BERKLEY PUBLISHING GROUP
Published by the Penguin Group
Penguin Group (USA) Inc.
375 Hudson Street, New York, New York 10014, USA
Penguin Group (Canada), 10 Alcorn Avenue, Toronto, Ontario M4V 3B2, Canada
(a division of Pearson Penguin Canada Inc.)
Penguin Books Ltd., 80 Strand, London WC2R 0RL, England
Penguin Group Ireland, 25 St. Stephen's Green, Dublin 2, Ireland (a division of Penguin Books Ltd.)
Penguin Group (Australia), 250 Camberwell Road, Camberwell, Victoria 3124, Australia
(a division of Pearson Australia Group Pty. Ltd.)
Penguin Books India Pvt. Ltd., 11 Community Centre, Panchsheel Park, New Delhi – 110 017, India
Penguin Group (NZ), Cnr. Airborne and Rosedale Roads, Albany, Auckland 1310, New Zealand
(a division of Pearson New Zealand Ltd.)
Penguin Books (South Africa) (Pty.) Ltd., 24 Sturdee Avenue, Rosebank, Johannesburg 2196,
South Africa

Penguin Books Ltd., Registered Offices: 80 Strand, London WC2R 0RL, England

This book is an original publication of The Berkley Publishing Group.

Copyright © 2005 by Henry Schuster and Charles Stone.
Text design by Kristin del Rosario.

First edition: March 2005

Library of Congress Cataloging-in-Publication Data

Schuster, Henry.
    Hunting Eric Rudolph / Henry Schuster with Charles Stone.—1st ed.
       p. cm.
    Includes bibliographical references and index.
    ISBN 0-425-19936-3
    1. Rudolph, Eric. 2. Bombing investigation—United States—Case studies.
3. Bombings—United States—Case studies I. Stone, Charles, 1951– II. Title.

HV8079.B62S34 2004
364.152′3′0975—dc22   2004053711

PRINTED IN THE UNITED STATES OF AMERICA

10   9   8   7   6   5   4   3   2   1

ACKNOWLEDGMENTS

Charles Stone has been after me about writing a book together on the Rudolph case since 2001. I produced a documentary for CNN called *The Hunt for Eric Rudolph* in the summer of 2001, and Charles was a main character. We got serious about the book after Rudolph's capture. Charles, being one of the world's most optimistic people, just assumed success from the beginning. We'd come up with the right book proposal, find an agent and a publisher, then write a book! It was going to be that simple, Charles kept saying.

Not quite, but close. Every morning, after I spent another early session in front of the computer, writing for a couple of hours before heading into work at what Charles called my day job, we'd go through the latest addition to the manuscript, talk about any changes and what we needed to do the next day. Day by day, we watched in amazement as the book seemed to gain another thousand words or more and the story unfolded. But most of all we looked forward to those chats; I know I enoyed my daily dose of Charles's wit and wisdom—and most of all his encouragement.

We didn't do this alone. Writing the book was the culmination of the years that Charles spent investigating this case and I spent reporting on it. Throughout, between the two of us, we had plenty of help from colleagues and others who always had time for us. We know that despite the best of our intentions, we will leave some people out. Please accept our apologies for that. Others, because of their jobs, prefer that we not name them, but we are grateful nevertheless.

In the law enforcement community, we would like to thank, among others, Woody Johnson, Dave Maples, Roy Harris, Jack Daulton, Rich Kolko, Todd Letcher, John Behnke, Tracey North, Chris Gravelle, Tom Davis, Duke Blackburn, Chris Bellavita, John Bankhead, Dave Jordan, David Tsur, Jack Killorin, Jim Cavanaugh, Steve Gillis, Pat Curry, Phillip Russell, Tommy Mefferd, Woody Enderson, Terry Turchie, Don Bell, Les Burrell, and members of the SBTF. Former U.S. Attorneys Kent Alexander and Doug Jones were always generous with their time without overstepping their professional obligations. The same goes for Assistant U.S. Attorney Sally Yates. In North Carolina, Cherokee County Sheriff Jack Thompson and his successor, Sheriff Keith Lovin, were of great help, as were members of the department. In Murphy, Chief of Police Mark Thigpen and Mayor Bill Hughes were always ready to assist.

Folks in western North Carolina are nothing if not hospitable and we'd like to acknowledge their help over the years. Neither of us can think of a time when residents of the area were less than helpful to us. For the view below-ground, our thanks go to Cato Holler and Susan Holler, along with Darren Free, for helping us to understand the caves and mines that offered potential hiding places in the area.

Deborah Rudolph answered countless questions on countless occasions. John Hawthorne and Fallon Stubbs were gracious and forthcoming. The same is true for Emily Lyons and her husband, Jeff. Robert and Nancy Gee have also been helpful and encouraging through the years.

Any mention of the CNN team has to begin with Art Harris, who made covering the story, from the time we started covering Olympic security in early 1996 all the way through Rudolph's arrest, so much fun. Ditto for Mike Phelan, who always seemed to be in the right place at the right time. There are many others, past and present: Brian Cabell, Michael Heard, Leon Jobe, Andre Jones, Johnny Hutchens, Mike Calloway, Kimberly Babbit-Arp, Emily Probst, Sarah Fogel, Aram Roston, Graylian Young, Karen Nolan, and Meg Pearlstein. My colleagues and good friends covering the world of terrorism, Mike Boettcher and Ken Robinson, were always ready with advice and insight. Others supported and encouraged our work, including Vivian Schiller, who commissioned the Rudolph documentary, and Charles Hoff, who gave me the time to work on it.

Tom Johnson, Fuzz Hogan, Keith McAllister, and Nancy Lane were supportive managers, while Richard Griffiths, Rick Davis, Marianna Spicer, and Lee Rivera also offered their counsel.

Just as with law enforcement, there were others in the journalism community whom Charles and I found to be generous with their time and help during the years we worked on the case. These include Max McCoy, Don Plummer, Mark Winnie, and Ron Martz. Ben Selkow has been one of our biggest supporters and we're looking forward to seeing his documentary on the Rudolph story. Louis Ledford was generous with his photography. Jay Kaiman and Mark Pitcavage at the ADL, along with Mark Potok at the Southern Poverty Law Center, were always ready to help.

Special mention of two people must be made: Peter Bergen, a colleague and dear friend, strongly encouraged me to write this book and helped guide me through the process. His insights on terrorism have justly earned him the prominent reputation he has and strengthened this book. Mike Sager is one of the reasons I took up journalism in the first place. He is a writer's writer, a great friend and unstinting in his support.

There are others who read the manuscript and offered their suggestions or provided us with other forms of support. These include: Jim Hallman, James Moss, and Steve Schuster. Thanks to Paul Julian, George Rosenzweig, and Delia Crouch for representing our best legal interests, as always.

We would never have made it this far without our agent, Faye Bender of Anderson-Grinberg Literary Management, who was our biggest advocate and always ready with moral support. Natalee Rosenstein edited the book and introduced us to the world of publishing in the best of all fashions. John Pelosi helped us steer through the legal shoals. Brian Lipson of Endeavor looked out for us as well.

Finally, of course, are our families, who were always there to cheer us on even as we tested their patience with frequent absences. Our respective wives, Sandra Huckaby and Rhonda McClendon, were our best copyeditors and our true champions. We missed time with Ben, Van, and Misha, along with Parks, and want you to be proud of our efforts.

We are both natives of Georgia. This case began with an act of terrorism that was figuratively in our front yard. We hope we've done the story justice.

CONTENTS

1.

"YOU HAVE THIRTY MINUTES"

THE NIGHT WAS *hot and humid, about what you would expect for the South in the middle of the summer, but no one paid any attention to the goateed young man wearing a hooded sweatshirt and a watch cap. He was standing at a pay phone on a downtown Atlanta street corner, just a few feet from the entrance of a Days Inn motel. Normally on a Friday night in downtown Atlanta, these streets would be empty, except for the stray drunk conventioneer trying to make his way back to his hotel. But tonight, all around the man, there were people—laughing, shouting, crowding the streets, maybe a hundred thousand of them. As he dialed, he could hear the music from a few blocks over, a little of the highs, some of the bass, and crowd noise, lots of it, where a huge party was going on, another 60,000 people enjoying themselves, rocking to a world-class party in Atlanta's newly opened Centennial Park as the city celebrated the 1996 Summer Olympic Games.*

If the man was paying attention to the crowds that moved past him, he'd be hearing accents from places he never dreamed of, places that threatened him, from people who disgusted him. What were they doing here in his country? Who gave them the right? Who was going to stop this New World Order before it completely destroyed his America? No matter. The man was going to deliver a message, to this United Nations of crowds in and around downtown Atlanta, and to this Olympic-loving New World Order. He'd deliver it—just as soon as someone answered the phone. It was 12:58 A.M. on July 27, 1996. Friday night was becoming Saturday morning.

"Atlanta 911," said an operator.

"There is a bomb in Centennial Park," the goateed man said. His voice was flat, emotionless, as if he were reading a script, and none of the crowd noise came through on the call. "You have thirty minutes."[1] The entire call took just fifteen seconds. Then he hung up the phone and disappeared in the haze of a hot Georgia night.

Fallon Stubbs couldn't believe she was in Atlanta. It was her fourteenth birthday, and just this very afternoon, her mom had scored tickets to tomorrow's Dream Team game. She was on her way, Albany to Atlanta, a three-and-a-half-hour drive, going to see Charles Barkley, Karl Malone, and the guys whoop up on some hapless Third World team.

It was just like her mom. Fallon liked to say that she spent half her middle school career in this south Georgia town in time-out, courtesy of Alice Hawthorne's tough love. But Alice, a businesswoman with a weakness for Corvettes, would also indulge her daughter. So it was on to Atlanta.

Somewhere on the interstate, they passed her husband John, Fallon's stepdad, a former army guy who now owned a gas station and restaurant in Albany. He was headed the other way, back home after taking his son to Atlanta for some minor eye surgery. John wasn't aware of Alice and Fallon's trip until after they'd gone, but he knew they could look after themselves. When he'd met Alice, just a few years back, they'd been working together at Procter & Gamble, then really gotten to know each other through community activities like the Miss Black America Pageant. John was there the night at the local youth center, the Outer Limits, when things got out of hand out in the parking lot. The kids had guns and knives, but Alice just busted right in and sorted it all out, smiling and talking everyone out of their anger. No doubt in his mind that Alice and Fallon would do just fine in Atlanta that night.

They got in to Atlanta late, found a place to park, wandered the streets for a while, checking out Planet Hollywood, enjoying the crowds.

Alice had a small disposable camera with her, and they took some pictures along the way. Mother and daughter could hear music and decided to head over to the park, maybe get there in time to see Black Uhuru, a reggae band.[2]

Robert and Nancy Gee were also wandering through downtown Atlanta that night. The couple from Scottsdale, Arizona, was on an Olympic tour of sorts. They'd started in Washington, D.C., where they'd gone to see some relatives and Olympic soccer. Then they drove down to Atlanta, staying at a motel seventy-five miles north of the city, commuting in every day just to breathe in the Olympic spirit. The events were great—they'd seen women's basketball, team handball, and karate—but the people were even better.

Nancy and Robert had met one of the Norwegian athletes, a team handball player, while riding the subway. She wasn't some American superstar, just very nice and modest, still a student. After spending time with her, they found themselves hunting out a Norwegian church in Atlanta, where they bought a cowbell to take to the events (it was a Norwegian tradition). Nancy was wearing it that Friday, now that they were practically honorary Norwegians.

Robert had his video camera with him. He always had his video camera. He'd started taking pictures as a student at Berkeley in the early '80s and had gotten serious enough about photojournalism that he used to attend demonstrations there to learn how to handle himself in crowd situations. He was an engineer now, working for Motorola, but he still kept a camera with him. For the last three years, it had been a little Sony video camera. Nancy and Robert loved to travel and take plenty of pictures, stills and video, but didn't usually look at what they shot. Something for the grandkids, they would tell everyone, we'll look at them then.

They had seen a play about Muhammad Ali Friday night and should have been heading back to their car. The plan was to drive back to their motel, check out, and keep going up to the Georgia-Tennessee border overnight so they could see whitewater kayaking the next morning. That was the plan, but they didn't want to leave. They were looking for an excuse to stay, and the park was the best one they had. Nancy wanted to trade a few more pins, Robert wanted to take a few more pictures. Mostly, they just wanted to meet a few more people from a few more countries, and go listen to some music. They'd been to the park once already, and it made them feel like they were at the center of things, that they could meet anyone from anywhere. Not just from other countries; they were talking to Americans who would never give them a second glance even if they were visiting their hometowns. English helped, but sign language and a smile worked, too. This was once in a lifetime, they told each other, why not keep going for a couple more hours? Why not head back to the park? This was Atlanta, for goodness sake, if you couldn't say "tomorrow's another day" here, where could you?[3]

The Gees and the Hawthornes were doing just what Billy Payne had hoped. He was the former University of Georgia football player who had been the driving force behind Atlanta's improbable bid for the 1996 Olympic Games and its seemingly impossible victory. Ever since Juan Antonio Samaranch, the head of the International Olympic Committee (IOC), had uttered the unlikely words, "It's Atlanta," in 1990, it was Payne's job to get the city ready. After Barcelona had put on a 1992 Summer Games steeped in Catalonian charm and filled with spectacular venues, Payne was searching for ways to make Atlanta distinctive. Already critics were grumbling that these would be the Coca-Cola Olympics (the company, the Olympics' biggest sponsor, was based in Atlanta), sure to be tacky and underwhelming, that Atlanta was only world-class in its hustle, but had no style.

Centennial Park was Payne's answer. His office at the headquarters of ACOG, the Atlanta Committee for the Olympic Games, overlooked blocks of parking lots, homeless shelters, and small offices. But that's only what visitors saw; when Payne looked, he saw a grand plaza, an answer to Barcelona, a legacy for the Olympics. "What I think we need is a magnificent gathering place so our visitors can mix with Southerners and experience firsthand the friendliness of the American South," he announced.[4] There would be statues honoring Olympic history and in the middle, a grand fountain in the shape of the Olympic rings. Using the same charm and salesmanship that got Atlanta the Olympics, he convinced Georgia governor Zell Miller to put up $50 million; ACOG would get $15 million by selling commemorative bricks. Somehow, the leases were negotiated and the deals closed, and Centennial Park was born, after a frenetic and sometimes painful gestation.

It was urban America's first major park in three decades. But it was also a work in progress. This wasn't some wild space to be tamed and landscaped. This was demolition work, the brute force of bulldozers needed to knock down buildings and get to the red clay somewhere below the old sidewalks and foundations. The homeless were rousted, and the construction guys moved in. It was more plaza than park, at least for the Olympics. There was barely going to be a blade of grass until after the games (especially if they actually sold some of those commemorative bricks), but still it would be a place to go, a gathering spot to trade pins and listen to music, and to beat the heat by running through the fountain. That was the plan.

All was not Olympic joy, however. When ACOG's security chief, Bill Rathburn, mentioned in an interview in the Atlanta paper in September 1995 that "this will not be a public park," the Atlanta newspaper was quick to thunder back, "Let's hope Payne gets Rathburn straightened out. . . . It [the park] belongs to everyone."[5] Rathburn had been suggesting that the park would be an Olympic venue—and that just like any other Olympic venue, it would require a ticket to get in, only in this case the tickets would come from corporate sponsors, who would have tents and booths inside the park. There would be the Swatch Pavilion, Bud-World, and the AT&T Soundstage. There was also the issue of free speech. If Rathburn could close off the park somehow, make the public land private, then he could avoid the problem of demonstrators using the Park as a platform, hijacking it for their causes. The Atlanta paper did grudgingly accept the notion that Rathburn, who had handled security for the 1984 Olympic Games in Los Angeles, could build temporary fencing around the park to limit the number of people coming in.[6] But that was it.

Somewhere in all this, security was taking a backseat. It was already a sore issue between all parties concerned, which included an astonishing and bewildering number of local, state, and federal agencies. About the only thing they all had in common was they mistrusted ACOG and its motives. They thought ACOG was trying to balance its books at the expense of security.[7] The state and the Feds had been trying to plan security for the Games since they had been announced, while ACOG went out and hired Rathburn, who had left the LAPD and was police chief in Dallas. Never lacking in confidence, Rathburn would show you pictures of the pet tigers he owned within minutes of meeting you and the scratches they occasionally left on his hands and arms. He favored the high-tech approach, pointing to surveillance cameras and magnetometers as proof that his venues were going to be the safest in the world. There were also elaborate plans to use volunteer police officers from all over the world, to make up for an embarrassing experience that the L.A. Games had experienced by relying on rent-a-cops. Rathburn and ACOG also wanted to bring in the army, using soldiers to supplement security at the venues, even to drive buses containing Olympic athletes and IOC officials.

The world had changed since Bill Rathburn's Olympics in Los Angeles in 1984. There was Waco in 1993, but two events in 1995 were seismic. The bombing of the Murrah Building in Oklahoma City woke everyone up to the reality of domestic terrorism; and when a Japanese cult used sarin gas in the Tokyo subways, nerves, especially at the federal level, were on edge. So everyone trained.[8] There were hostage-taking exercises at the stadium and inside the subway, and plenty of what were known as tabletops, where different, scary scenarios were played out and responded to. There were committees to coordinate the dozens of agencies involved, but each one of these security edifices collapsed under its own weight because of personality problems or organizational confusion.

Finally, the White House stepped in. With President and Mrs. Clinton planning on attending Opening Ceremonies along with a number of other world leaders, the last thing they wanted was some sort of *Black Sunday* scenario (a novel and movie based on the premise that terrorists would crash a blimp into the stadium hosting the Super Bowl). But even getting the airspace over Atlanta restricted proved to be an exercise in bureaucratic agony.[9] Vice President Gore personally intervened. He summoned all the security officials to Washington and asked them point-blank, "Who is in charge?" When that question was met with mumbles and elaborate diagrams, the vice president made it clear that the situation had to change. The Justice Department sent one of its top prosecutors, who helped lead the case against the 1993 World Trade Center bombers, down to Atlanta as the eyes and ears of the deputy attorney general. The FBI, which was planning on having a thousand agents in Atlanta, was placed in charge, should any serious situation arise. That meant Woody Johnson, who was the head of the FBI's local field office and the former head of the Bureau's elite Hostage Rescue Team, was now effectively in charge. He immediately brought in a slew of senior agents, including Jim Bernazzani, who had investigated Middle Eastern terrorism and was placed in charge of intelligence efforts. Another two thousand federal agents from agencies as far-flung as the Fish and Wildlife Service would be drafted into the effort. Other responsibilities were doled out accordingly to Georgia's Emergency Management Agency, which was planning on using prison guards to supplement the Georgia Bureau of Investigation (GBI) and the Georgia State Patrol. The Atlanta Police Department, although seriously undermanned, also had a role. ACOG was effectively taken out of the mix, private security guards and volunteer police were still in the picture.

There was an Olympic ring drawn around downtown Atlanta, where most of the venues were located. In security lingo, those became hardened targets, particularly the Olympic Village. No one wanted a repeat of Munich in 1972, when Palestinian terrorists sneaked into an essentially unguarded Olympic Village and took Israeli athletes hostage. By the end of what was the worst day in Olympic history, eleven Israeli athletes were dead, killed by the Palestinians after a botched rescue attempt by the German government.[10] The Olympic Village, which was on the Georgia Tech campus, just a few hundred yards from a small experimental nuclear reactor, was locked down. So were the venues, like the Omni, the Georgia Dome, and the Georgia World Congress Center. Centennial Park, the gathering spot, the beacon right at the center of the ring, a place that could hold 60,000 people, wasn't. If the others were hardened targets, it was a soft target. Some security, but after the Rathburn PR fiasco of the previous year, it was going to be open to all, or almost all (you could still be stopped and searched, kicked out of the park if you were too rowdy).

Which was how Tom Davis came to be at the park. He had been there every evening even before the Olympics began. As a fifteen-year veteran of the Georgia Bureau of Investigation (GBI), Centennial Park was his assignment for the duration. Centennial Park was state property, since Billy Payne had talked Governor Miller into picking up the tab. GBI agents didn't normally walk a beat, but this was a good place to be, Davis thought. He made the rounds several times a night, sometimes stopping to chat with one of those private security guards, a guy named Richard Jewell, a former cop (they'd been introduced by a mutual friend, a GBI agent who knew Jewell from north Georgia and was also working the park). The word he liked to use was festive. This was a festive place. He liked the crowds, liked seeing folks have fun, and there weren't too many drunks to spoil the atmosphere. There were a few altercations, as he called them, but there weren't too many problems.

By choice, Davis was a small-town guy, a straight arrow, soft-spoken. Normally he was down in Perry, a couple of hours south of Atlanta, handling special investigations, the occasional homicide that was too tough for the locals. He was bunking with his in-laws, checking in with the wife and boys whenever he could. Davis was looking forward to having them come up to Atlanta, but he was also running on empty just a bit. This was day eight of the Games, and the hours and heat were getting a little old.

The park was every bit as popular as its designers hoped. Day and night, folks especially seemed attracted to the fountain, which was designed as a place they could get soaked and enjoy some relief from Atlanta's summer. Crowded as it was, people were always leaving something behind, especially by the fountain. A purse or a backpack, as parents would scoot off trying to catch up to their wandering kids. They had a protocol for those unattended packages and even one for bomb threats. If Tom Davis needed to, he could call in a two-man team that was stationed at the park, but that was only a first line of protection. Anything serious, and they would bring in a bomb disposal team that was housed miles away at Dobbins Air Reserve Base (where the army's Delta Force was also set up, just in case things got really ugly). So far, nothing like that was necessary.

Security was still very much an issue, even though the Games were by now into their second week. Just days before the Games opened, a TWA flight from New York to Paris went down shortly after takeoff, killing all 230 on board. No one knew what caused the crash, but eyewitnesses reported an explosion, and lots of people were assuming this was an act of Middle Eastern terrorism.[11] There had been persistent rumors of a threat from the Lebanese-based group Hezbollah to the Atlanta Games for months, so when TWA 800 went down, there were worries in Atlanta that the Games were the next target. There was an even more exotic threat. The president of the Indian field hockey federation had to be brought from New York to Atlanta on a specially guarded train because no domestic airline would fly him, due to threats against his life by Sikh militants. K.P.S. Gill wanted to do nothing more than watch his team play, visit local bookstores, and see one of Atlanta's famed strip clubs, but he was being kept under tight security at a secret location by more than two dozen State Department security agents.[12]

Homegrown terror also remained a concern. In April, an alleged plot by three Georgia militia members was uncovered south of Atlanta in rural Crawford County; a number of guns and explosives were confiscated. Depending on who you believed, it wasn't clear if the men were intending to blow up some government buildings or were preparing to defend themselves from all the federal lawmen who were about to flood into Georgia. While the government sought to put some daylight between these arrests and the Olympics, one of its informants would later testify that the men were stockpiling pipe bombs to use at the Olympics in Atlanta.[13]

Militia Web sites and newsletters were full of apocalyptic language; some on the far right feared Washington (the New World Order, as they called it, or the ZOG, the Zionist Occupation Government) was using the Olympics as a pretext to crack down on freedom-loving Christian Americans, that it was all part of a secret plot to put the black helicopters of the United Nations into their hometowns and turn America into a police state.

There was more than enough to worry about if you were a security official in Atlanta. Not just the domestic and international threats. There were snafus aplenty. Right before the Games opened, a security guard was shot near the Olympic Village. The night of Opening Ceremonies, despite the presence of all that security, including the Secret Service to look after the Clintons, a man managed to bring a gun into Olympic Stadium.[14] Those volunteer police who were supposed to supplement security at the venue were a problem as well: they didn't like their sleeping quarters, felt they were being housed in an unsafe neighborhood, and were threatening to call it quits. And the rent-a-cops who were running the magnetometers at some of the venues had apparently started turning them down and letting people walk through them, into Olympic events, without any real security check, after complaints about long lines and delays getting into various events. It seemed like ACOG security chief Rathburn and the Atlanta Police Chief Beverly Harvard were holding almost daily press conferences about one subject or another. But for FBI Special Agent-in-Charge Woody Johnson, a quiet ex-marine who preferred to be in his command post, rather than the public eye, things were going pretty smoothly. On Thursday, July 25, Johnson had a chance to review the numbers and was surprised that there were fewer bomb threats during the first week of the Games than he or his agents had expected.

The goateed man was just another face in the crowd as he slipped into the park. Everywhere he looked, everything he heard, everything he smelled, was foreign to him. It must have repulsed him. African voices, Asian smells, European accents. Blacks, Jews, Moslems. All walking the streets of Atlanta. Laughing, smiling, somehow their very presence taunting him. And at every corner, security. Not just police, but bereted Air Force enlisted men, helping to direct traffic. National Guardsmen at garage entrances, poking long mirrors under cars, checking for bombs. He'd heard the warnings that the Olympics were just a Trojan horse for the government and the United Nations to end the America he knew. That once these guys moved in, they would end becoming an occupying army.

He found a bench to sit on. It was on the top of a small rise about 150 feet from the soundstage and off to the side just a bit. If he hadn't been to the park before tonight, then he was busy surveiling the scene, figuring out vectors and explosive force, calculating the best place for doing maximum damage. With so many people moving around, leaving the pack under the bench was probably the best choice. It was dark under there, and not many people seemed to be sitting down, so no one would probably notice it. He left it upright, knowing that the steel plate inside the pack would force the blast in the opposite direction, toward the crowd that was in between the bench and the stage.

He got up and made his way out of the park. It was about 12:40 A.M. He had to go find a phone booth and make a call.

Robert and Nancy Gee finally made it into the park about 12:20 A.M., their video camera rolling almost continuously. Over the loudspeaker, as they entered, a voice was saying, "You are now entering Centennial Park. Please dispose of alcoholic beverages." Like so many others, their first stop was the fountain. There were five interlocking rings spread out across the bricks. Water jets would begin to bubble up from them every few minutes. If you timed it right, you could get inside a ring without getting too wet. That's what Nancy did, urging Robert to follow her. Laughing, she pointed down to her shoes. "Squish, squish," she said. They watched two men convince an unsuspecting woman to stand on one of the jets. Suddenly the water came shooting out, soaking her. Robert still couldn't figure out if she was in on it and just wanted to cool down.

After a few minutes at the fountain, they moved deeper into the park. They stopped by BudWorld, a beer garden run by Budweiser. Robert was mesmerized by a sort of high-tech piece of water engineering here. There was a thirty-foot rectangular frame, studded with lights. From the top, water would come out in shapes, spelling phrases and making shapes, as it fell into a pool below. Robert was figuring out the message. "B-U-D-W-E . . ." He and Nancy laughed. The Games had been sharply criticized for their commercialism, especially for all the vendors lining the streets near the park. But this, they thought, was a hoot, and they stared at it for several minutes.

They turned toward the stage, where there was another commercial message: "AT&T Welcomes the World." While you could barely make out the actual figures onstage, you couldn't miss them on the huge video wall behind them. The band, Jack Mack and the Heart Attack, was playing some good-time funk, just the right sort of thing for a late Friday night. "Are you having a good time?" shouted the lead singer after they finished a number, "ARE YOU HAVING A GOOD TIME?"

Nancy was. She was moving to the beat, a smile on her face. As Robert panned around, a twenty-something frat boy with a baseball cap put himself in front of the camera. "Where y'all from?" he asked. "California," Robert answered. "I'm from Atlanta, G-A. This is where the party's at." Then, just to make sure Robert understood the historical import of the night, he gleefully shouted, "THIS IS THE PARTY OF THE CENTURY, BABY!!!!"

Alice and Fallon were also inside the park by now. They moved down close to the stage. The band had returned from a break, and they were ready to listen to the music. Fallon couldn't have been happier. Great food, great music, great fun. She was thinking to herself, *This is a once-in-a-lifetime experience*. How many other kids in Albany, Georgia, were celebrating their fourteenth birthday at the Olympics? As they moved through the crowd, Alice was keeping an eye out for some friends from Albany. Fallon was just wide-eyed, trying to take it all in. She wasn't sure how long she was going to last—she'd been going since that morning—but she wanted to get down near the front, and Alice was letting her birthday girl take the lead.[15]

It was about twenty minutes to one. Tom Davis was walking up a sidewalk that led from the soundstage toward a lighting tower about two hundred feet away. The tower was a three-story makeshift structure used by the engineers and sound guys producing the concerts; so did some NBC crew members as well (they were televising the Olympics and also hosting a bunch of their local affiliates from around the country). It was on a very small hill that banked down toward the stage. On the side facing the stage, there were benches, just outside a fence that marked off the tower. Sometimes the sound crew would hang out on those benches, sometimes members of the public. As Davis made his rounds, slowly making his way toward the tower, that private security guard Richard Jewell came up to him and asked for some help.

This was supposed to be Davis's last pass through the park before checking out and going home. But Jewell had a problem. He said there was a group of drunk young men throwing beer cans inside the tower, and they were aggravating the crew members. Could Davis come over and help straighten out the situation? As they walked toward the front of the tower, Davis saw two men picking up beer cans and heading away, apparently toward a trash can. As Davis came around the front of the tower, Jewell told him those were two of the guys causing the fuss, but now everyone seemed to have gone.

Then Jewell looked down, under the benches, and motioned Davis over. There was a backpack, a green military-style pack, under there, and Jewell said it must have belonged to one of the rowdy young men who had just walked off. "How do you wanna handle the situation," he asked Davis. "Just like any other situation," Davis replied. They'd try to find the owner of the backpack. If they couldn't, then Davis would treat it as a suspicious package. Davis asked the two young men with the beer cans. Not ours, they said. So Davis and Jewell started asking folks around the bench, even folks inside the tower, if this was their pack, being careful not to move it.[16]

Even at this point, Davis wasn't worried. Still, he liked to go by the book, so at about 12:57 A.M., he radioed his command post and asked for a bomb assessment team to come check out the pack. It took the two men about five minutes to make their way across the park. Steve Zoeller and Bill Forsyth were dressed casually, wearing shorts, and as they met up with Davis, he filled them in. The bomb techs dropped down on the ground near the pack and crawled up under the bench for a look. Very carefully, one of them opened the pack, then they moved away, came back to Davis, this time asking if they could borrow his cell phone.[17]

The bomb techs had seen wires and a pipe inside the pack. It was time to call in the bomb disposal unit (in their lingo, it was the render safe team). But the team was at least twenty minutes away, assuming it could get on a helicopter and make its way to the park. Davis thought it was time to tell his boss the latest and get permission to begin moving people away from the area. They weren't talking about evacuating the park, at least not yet, not until his commander got on site, but they were going to try and get everybody fifty to one hundred feet away. Jewell went around to the other side of the lighting tower, out of sight of the others, and began to clear people from inside it.[18]

The goateed man had already made his phone call by the time the bomb techs arrived on the scene and started their examination. He'd hung up the phone about two minutes after Tom Davis first radioed in. But inside Atlanta's 911 headquarters, a combination of confusion and incompetence was about to take place—which would ensure no one at the park would get word of the bomb threat. For the next three minutes, the 911 operator got a busy signal when she tried to call the Atlanta Police Department's Command Center.

Finally, she reached someone and asked, "You know the address to Centennial Park?"

The dispatcher gave a laugh and said, "Girl, don't ask me to lie to you."

The operator, who couldn't send the alert out until she entered the right address in the computer system, said, ". . . I just got this man talking about there's a bomb set to go off in thirty minutes in Centennial Park."

The dispatcher said, "Oh, Lord, child. One minute, one minute . . . Uh, OK, wait a minute. Centennial Park. You put it in and it won't go in?"

"No, unless I'm spelling Centennial wrong. How are we spelling Centennial?" asked the operator.

"C-E-N-T-E-N-N-I—how do you spell Centennial?" asked the dispatcher back at her.

By now the 911 operator was frustrated: "I'm spelling it right, it ain't taking."[19]

The confusion continued. Finally, minutes later, the operator called the Centennial Park switchboard for the address, punched it into the system, and sent out a dispatch to Atlanta Police Department units. But because the park secu-

rity was being run by the state of Georgia, not the city of Atlanta, word never reached the Command Center at the park—at least not in time—nor did it get to Tom Davis at the scene.[20]

Robert and Nancy moved closer to the stage. They were handing the video camera back and forth. Their attention seemed to wander from the band onstage; instead, they kept looking to the crowd on their right. There were people clapping and singing along as Jack Mack and the Heart Attack launched into Al Greene's "Take Me to the River." Someone was waving a Brazilian flag, another person had the French tricolor. In the background, they could see the sound tower and the pink shells of the Swatch Pavilion behind it. But they were too far away to see the crowd being moved from the base of the tower. One thing was curious; a security guy seemed to be pushing some sort of big trash can through the crowd in the direction of the sound tower. That was odd, Nancy thought, but they turned their attention back to the music.

Fallon was ready to go. Alice still had a few pictures left on her disposable camera, so they decided to pose for a couple of snapshots as they were leaving the park. They saw a statue that looked like a big fan; as they got up closer, they noticed it showed three runners. This looked like a good place. There was a good-natured argument about who should take the picture. Neither of them noticed the commotion on the small rise at the base of the sound tower, even though they were less than a hundred feet away. As she stood in front of the statue, Alice was looking in that direction, smiling at her daughter. Fallon was actually closer to the backpack, but by now her back was turned as she faced away from the tower.[21]

Tom Davis still wasn't convinced there was a bomb inside the backpack, even at this point, but he was going to get permission to evacuate the area once his boss, a Georgia State Patrol captain, arrived at the scene. A number of other state police and GBI agents gathered near him to establish a perimeter and began to move outward, putting space between the crowd and the bench. But it wasn't easy going. The crowd was into the music, even over at this edge, and getting rowdy. A camera crew from KNBC in Los Angeles had been doing a live shot by the tower a few minutes earlier. While the cameraman was off using the bathroom, the sound tech overheard Jewell talking to someone about the suspicious bag. Now, their news instincts aroused, the cameraman and sound tech moved toward the bench to get a picture. The cameraman, Mark Field, was able to zoom in and get a shot of the green backpack still sitting under the bench.[22]

Fallon saw her mother through the viewfinder, pressed down to take the picture. There was a flash, then an explosion. That didn't make sense. She saw her mother turn, do a complete 360, then fall. *This is like a movie*, Fallon thought, *it can't be happening*. Then she was also knocked to the ground. She tried to get up, couldn't. She saw people scared and running. Fallon noticed cuts all over her body and couldn't believe it, but one of her fingers was almost cut off, dangling at some weird angle from her hand, looking ready to fall off if she moved. Alice was on the ground only a few yards away; there were people gathering around her mother, but Fallon didn't have the strength to get up and make her way to her.

Tom Davis was even closer to the bomb, about twenty paces from it, with his back turned. He was talking to his venue commander, briefing him on what he'd done so far, telling him how long it was going to take for the bomb disposal crew to get on site. Suddenly, there was a flash of heat, then it felt like all the air had been sucked out of the park. It was as if someone used both hands and shoved him facedown on the ground hard. There were screams and moans all around him, but his ears were ringing, filtering out most of the pain, replacing it with a roaring sound. Stunned, he got up, tried to help the people around him. The KNBC cameraman, who had shut off his camera moments before the blast, started rolling again, capturing the chaos around Davis. Somehow, the GBI agent had the presence of mind to radio in a report of the explosion to his command post. It was logged in at 1:18 A.M.[23]

Robert was not even looking through the viewfinder of the camera when the bomb went off, not realizing he had captured the explosion off to his right. "Wow" was his first reaction, caught forever on video. There was one large, sharp crack, as if the world's largest M-80 had gone off. That's what it sounded like, but his feet were telling him a different story. The asphalt rumbled like an earthquake. A California native, he knew what that felt like. Still, it might have been a car crash on the street just outside the park; that would explain the smoke. Then, people in the crowd started moving toward Nancy and him. The first wave was full of nervous laughter, not really knowing what had happened, but anxious to get away. What was surprising was how calm people were. They still didn't know it was a bomb, thought maybe it was just a prank. But more people started to move toward them. They noticed one man with a shredded T-shirt, heard others muttering, moaning. The message was beginning to reach them: this had been a bomb.

The emergency response was quick, a sign that all the disaster training would at least pay off after the fact. The radio call from Tom Davis wasn't the only trigger. Ironically, one of the APD patrol cars dispatched in the wake of the 911 call was just getting to the park and radioed in its own report at 1:20 A.M. Within minutes, the streets adjacent to the park were crowded with emergency vehicles—police cars, fire trucks, and especially ambulances—at the same time as the crowd was leaving the park.

There were by all estimates another 100,000 people in the immediate area, and they began to move toward the blinking lights, trying to find out what was happening. Emergency rooms at Atlanta's downtown hospitals quickly braced for a flood of casualties. In the initial confused reporting it became clear that there were going to be at least a hundred casualties; no one knew how many were already dead.

*   *   *

Fallon was on the ground. There were people—she didn't know who they were—telling her to lie down, get down. She thought she was saying, "my mother, my mother." It isn't clear anyone understood her. Fallon's sense of time was all off—the pain in her hand was beginning to register—but she thought it was ten or fifteen minutes before she was loaded up on an ambulance. She tried one last time with the paramedics. "Wait, wait, my mother!" Either they weren't listening, or the words weren't actually coming out, but they needed to get Fallon to the hospital and into surgery right away, or she would lose her finger.[24]

Tom Davis's senses were still scrambled. After radioing in the explosion, he tried to help. All around him were fellow officers, who had arrived to help set up the evacuation perimeter; many of them were now wounded. He had seen plenty of death in his GBI career, including some pretty gruesome traffic accidents, but nothing like this. Utter chaos. People wandering around bloodied, screaming. Davis walked over toward the statue to see if he could help out over there. He saw a woman on the ground. Instinctively, he knew she was gone, but he bent down and checked for a pulse. He couldn't find one.

Tom Davis didn't realize the woman was Alice Hawthorne. There was no time to check her ID. This was a triage situation; help those who might have a chance to make it. There was a man on the ground next to her, and he was screaming. Davis moved over to help him. He tried some first aid, anything to help ease the man's pain, then flagged down paramedics to take over. He never made it back to the body of the woman. There was just too much to do, and that was someone else's job by now.[25]

Nancy and Robert joined the exodus from the park, still not aware how serious the bomb had been. Someone, perhaps a vendor, even stopped them to offer a souvenir for whitewater rafting. They talked about picking up a newspaper the next morning to find out what really happened. Nancy turned around to get a shot of the park on her still camera. Robert told her he was sure that whatever happened, it must have been caught by a hundred other cameras closer to the scene. They were still wondering about the security man who had been wheeling the garbage can.

As they were heading toward the subway, Nancy suggested they might want to look at their own tape. When they did, they saw the smoke and realized this might be important evidence. But every time they tried to flag down a policeman, they were ignored. Robert remembered they were only a couple of blocks from CNN and thought if he called over there, they could get some help making a copy of the tape for the police. They finally found a phone and got connected to the CNN newsroom; by chance, the person who came down to meet them was Chris Cramer, the vice president of CNN's international network, who got them inside and into an edit room to look at the tape. Once they saw it, the CNN people wanted to get it and Robert on the air as quickly as possible. He agreed, but insisted that a copy be made for the police. Within two hours of the blast, Robert Gee was on the air with Judy Woodruff, telling a worldwide audience what he and his wife had seen unfold at the park.

It was hours before Tom Davis could unscramble his brain. He helped more of the wounded; then finally his colleagues insisted he stop. They wanted to debrief Davis, get his account while it was still fresh. This was going to be the mother of all investigations, and his contribution could be crucial. Hours later, he finally got back to his in-laws'. As he was getting undressed, unzipping his pants, Davis was stunned to discover pieces of shrapnel in his left rear pocket. That's where he kept his GBI credentials, the badge and ID that he would take out and flip open when he needed to prove who he was.

They were inside a hard case, which was dented by the shrapnel. He didn't think it would have been a bad wound, anyway, and he knew he was going to take some ribbing once he let everyone else know how he had been saved from getting his on the ass by flying metal (he was right; at a press conference later in the morning at GBI headquarters, Davis drew laughs when he described his almost-wound). All he could think at this point was that he had been just twenty paces away from the backpack; that the Lord had been looking out for him tonight.

John Hawthorne didn't make it back to Albany until about 8:30 that Friday night. The eye surgery for his son, then traffic, had taken longer than he anticipated. He hadn't heard from Alice and Fallon before going to sleep, but wasn't particularly worried. Then, about 1:30 in the morning, just a few minutes after the explosion, he got a call from Fallon's father, Alice's ex-husband. Had he heard about Fallon being injured? He turned on the TV, saw the initial reports, and got a number to call off the screen. Somebody at the Atlanta Police Department told him Fallon was being treated at a local hospital, Georgia Baptist, but no one could—or would—tell him where his wife was.

Several calls later, he was on the road back to Atlanta. Finally, someone suggested he might try Grady Hospital, Atlanta's main trauma center, where most of the victims from the bombing were being taken. When he showed up, the hospital didn't seem to have a record of Alice being there. Someone checked again. After ten minutes, she came back and said there was no record of Alice at any Atlanta hospital. John started fearing the worst, knowing from the radio reports as he was driving up that at least two people had died. Still, he couldn't believe that one of them might be his wife.

He drove a couple of miles over to Georgia Baptist to see Fallon; maybe someone else in the family was there and could tell him about Alice. He showed up at the Intensive Care Unit, but got sent up to the Pediatrics floor, where Fallon was in a room, sedated, recovering from some surgery to her hand. As he got off the elevator, Alice's sister Diane saw him and just sort of blurted it out. Alice was dead. John went numb, couldn't think, didn't want to believe it.

But the agony wasn't over. He went with his sister-in-law to Fallon's room, where her dad and a whole bunch of other family members were crowded around. When Fallon woke up, they were all in there. Like John, her first thought was, *This can't be good.* Everyone was looking at her, and she had that feeling that she was the last one to know that something wasn't right, but she was about to hear it. She thought it was her aunt who finally broke the silence and told her that her mother was dead.

John knew he was in shock, knew that he needed to be in there with Fallon. But he also needed to get out of that room, so he wandered down the hall and just stood there in a daze for what could have been an hour, his mind not accepting that Alice, the woman her daughter called "the total package," was dead. Someone from the coroner's office came to the hospital and said he had a photo, and could someone identify it? John wanted to but was afraid to look. He'd been a colonel in the artillery, he knew what a bomb could do to a person, and that's not what he wanted his last glimpse of Alice to be like. But when the man showed him the photograph, John was surprised. It was a head shot, and she looked peaceful, like she was sleeping. Remarkably, the only sign of any injury was a small wound over her eye. He would later learn that though her body had been hit several times, that one blemish over her eye was how she died. A nail from the bomb had pierced the skin, then the skull, lodging in her brain.[26]

There would be another death that night at the park. A Turkish photographer died of a heart attack as he rushed in to cover the aftermath of the bombing (his death would not become part of the criminal charges). There had been so many scenarios, so many preparations, against terrorism. Tens of millions of dollars had been spent. Thousands of police officers had been deployed. But that had not prevented one man, a goateed man with a hooded sweatshirt, from bringing terrorism back to the Olympic Games. Nor had it kept Alice Hawthorne alive. As prevention turned into investigation, the questions were mounting: Who was the bomber (or bombers)? Why did he or they do it? And could he (or they) be stopped before striking again?

No one knows where the goateed man disappeared to after he made his 911 call. His call came in at 12:58 A.M., when he warned the operator, "You have thirty minutes." Even if word had made it to Tom Davis in Centennial Park, the bomb went off less than twenty minutes after the call. The police and FBI would soon be wondering if they were the targets.

2.

EIGHTY-EIGHT DAYS OF HELL

IT WAS THE largest pipe bomb ever seen. More than forty pounds: three pipes packed with nails and powder, set off by a standard alarm clock. All carefully placed inside a green military-style backpack with a metal plate to direct the force of the blast. The goateed man's handiwork was strewn across Centennial Park. There were nails embedded in the statue that Alice Hawthorne had been posing in front of. There were even pieces of shrapnel found five stories up and across the street.

Investigators would soon understand that the bomber could have killed dozens, if not hundreds of people, if not for some unlikely heroes. They also began to realize they themselves were probably the intended targets. But it would be weeks, even months before they even knew about the goateed man and realized he was their prime suspect. But he was already long gone, off the grid, planning his next attacks, while many of them were busy chasing the wrong man.

Charles Stone had been looking forward to his bacon and egg sandwich all night. A longtime GBI agent, his piece of Olympic security was to run the undercover teams that worked outside the venues. These ID (Intelligence Detail) teams were all over town. One was up in Buckhead, Atlanta's nightclub district, which was packed this and every Friday night; another operated in and around Centennial Park, which on a non-Olympics Friday night would have been a ghost town. It was more than enough to keep him busy. He had been on the Olympics beat for years now, while still working major cases. One of his most recent had been that militia conspiracy down in Macon, so he knew just how paranoid the far Right was about having the Olympics in Georgia.

Stone was also the GBI's go-to hostage negotiator. He had an easygoing way about him that tended to quiet down squirrelly gunmen, part of his good old boy charm. Right now he was putting it to work. He was at a state-run office building about ten blocks from the park where a commissary had been set up for Olympic law enforcement officers. He was convincing—make that negotiating—with the state prisoners doing the cooking that, yes, while it was just after one A.M., it was the perfect time for breakfast, and he had something in mind, something that would speak to him in the language of food, keep him going until he signed off at three A.M. And that would have been his bacon and egg sandwich.

But it was not to be. One of his agents in the park called just as soon as the bomb went off, and Stone headed over there without hesitation. In all of the thousands of contingencies that the entire Olympic security team had run through, all of the scenarios of hostage crises and hijackings and even nuclear weapons, no one had talked about what to do if they had actually had to investigate a case. This was a bomb on state property, so Stone, along with dozens of other GBI folks who weren't already at the scene, went there immediately and got to work. He formed a team, and pretty soon agents were bringing him eyewitnesses to interview. It wasn't very comfortable for his team to talk to them with the crowds swirling around and the ambulances going back and forth, so he decided to set up shop across the street at CNN Center. His GBI boss was a college frat brother of CNN's CEO Tom Johnson, and he knew a couple of folks over there, so everything was arranged with some quick phone calls.

His interview room was in the hotel there, but Stone was also using the CNN green room, where CNN put guests who were about to go on the air. The network had people of its own out on the streets, grabbing eyewitnesses and bringing them in to put on the air. Every time one would get off the set, Stone would pull them aside and ask them what they saw. That's how he found Robert and Nancy Gee. They told him what they saw, showed him what they taped, and also how the officers from the Atlanta Police Department seemed to act as if they might be suspects.

Stone sent the witnesses down to a sketch artist the GBI used, a woman named Marla Lawson, and soon enough his folks did have one image. It was of a thin young man with blondish hair pulled back in a long ponytail. Not bad for a night's work. Stone agreed with an FBI request not to distribute the sketch for now and sent his team home for a short rest. When he woke up, he discovered that someone in his office had sent the sketch out anyway. The Feds had moved in and grabbed the case, declaring it an act of terrorism, and they were ballistic, demanding unsuccessfully that every copy be retrieved.[1] When he was later asked about it, the FBI's Dave Tubbs told reporters that there was no reason to believe the man in the sketch was a suspect. He was right; the young man turned out to be one of the rowdy young men who got into it with Richard Jewell, the security guard, and he ended up being an important witness.

Stone was now part of an ad hoc task force, watching in bemusement as the FBI and ATF started arm-wrestling for bureaucratic supremacy. Something like this had happened on the Macon militia case, and the ATF won. This time, FBI director Louis Freeh and Deputy Attorney General Jamie Gorelick made sure the FBI was in charge. Which Stone saw as OK, because the FBI's local special agent in charge, Woody Johnson, was someone he trusted. But with so much heat already coming from Washington, Stone was not alone in thinking the situation could get out of control pretty quickly.

The bomb happened after midnight, so most of Atlanta and America woke up to the news the next morning. The Games would go on. No one thought this was Munich revisited with a horrible sort of crisis playing out on the world stage over a long and agonizing day. Or rather, that's what they hoped—that this was a one-off event, the people behind it would be caught quickly, and everyone could pretend the Olympic spirit had triumphed. Except by midafternoon on Saturday, the bomb threats were pouring in. Everyone had the jitters, and every suspicious package was taken extra seriously. There were copycat callers, trying to get their own kicks by inciting panic.

But what almost sent everyone over the edge was a package that cleared out Underground Atlanta, a tourist area just a few blocks from Centennial Park, on Saturday afternoon. Tens of thousands of people, who could no longer gather at Centennial Park since it had been closed off by investigators (it would reopen in a big public ceremony days later), were drifting toward Underground. Now it was being evacuated, and a bomb robot was sent in. All this played out live on CNN, which intercepted an aerial shot from the police blimp flying overhead and broadcast it worldwide. The robot slowly moved in, secured the package . . . and blew up a toaster. Atlanta and the Olympics weren't going to be able to take much more of this. As calm as the crowd had been the night before when it evacuated Centennial Park, anxiety was replacing shock as the emotion of the day. Get it solved and do it now was the mood on the street—and it was also the message Woody Johnson and his FBI Task Force were getting from Washington and Olympic officials.

Investigators were moving ahead, trying to put two and two together, coming up with five. A car with an Alabama license plate was seen leaving the area of Centennial Park after the bombing; they had a sketch, even if they didn't want to use it; and they had almost immediately ruled out international terrorism. Remembering the Macon case, they started scanning their files for known militia members in the Southeast. By Sunday, they were already in Gadsden, Alabama, questioning a couple of men who had allegedly been seen in Macon, demonstrating their support for the men arrested there.[2] One of them, who turned out to be a bizarre mixture of militia member and Deadhead, even looked remarkably similar to the sketch. But that lead evaporated after a day when it turned out the men had been nowhere near Atlanta. By then, however, there were many within the FBI who believed they already had their suspect.[3]

Which was just as well. There were some 15,000 members of the media covering the Olympics, and this was the story du jour for the world press. And the pressure from Washington was intense. FBI agents on the ground were getting the message loud and clear: solve this before the Closing Ceremonies the following Sunday.[4] Later, when it was all over—or at least the worst of it—the Justice Department would publish the results of its own internal investigation, done by its Office of Professional Responsibility.[5] While many of those involved would dispute its findings, saying they were slanted to whitewash just how hard the FBI and Justice Department's higher-ups were pushing for a quick solution to the investigation, the chronology in the report lays out a story that would add to the litany of high-profile embarrassments for the FBI in the 1990s, and often be quoted in the same breath as Ruby Ridge and Waco.[6]

The first time Richard Jewell's name was mentioned publicly, it was only his first name. Tom Davis and a fellow GBI agent from the park, Steve Blackwell, were made available to the media Saturday morning, and during the course of describing what happened, Davis mentioned the actions of a security guard named Richard who spotted the suspicious package and alerted him. Sensing a hero in the making, CNN spent hours tracking him down and finally with the active help of his boss at AT&T security, Anthony Davis, they got Jewell to agree to come into their Atlanta headquarters for an interview on Saturday night.[7]

Jewell seemed awed by his visit to CNN. Before and after the interview, he was taken around the studio, introduced to Senator Sam Nunn and Speaker of the House Newt Gingrich, both of whom stunned him by congratulating him and shaking his hand. Twice that day he had already made statements about the events in the park for investigators. Now he was just beginning to get caught in the media glare.

The interview seemed innocent enough, but in many ways it would become the triggering event for the whirlwind that would soon engulf an innocent man. Anchor Jeanne Meserve's questions were straightforward: what did he see, what did he do (at that point, neither she nor he was aware of the 911 call). Jewell was slightly nervous and very deferential, expressing concern for the victims and answering in cop-speak, which while unusual for a security guard, might have been explained by his own answer to the last question about whether he was adequately trained for such a crisis. "I was in law enforcement before I got this job. I've been in law enforcement for six years in Georgia and uh I just came down to Atlanta to do the Games and then I'm going to try to get on with an agency here in Atlanta," he said when asked if he was properly trained for the job. Jewell went home to his mother's apartment, wondering whether he was supposed to go back to work, since the park was still closed off by investigators.

It wasn't as much what Richard said as who was watching the interview that started the problems. Among them was Ray Cleere, the president of Piedmont College, a small liberal arts school in north Georgia. He certainly knew Richard Jewell, and he had a story to tell the FBI. Which he did the next afternoon, calling the Atlanta office. "He expressed concern that Jewell may have been involved in the bombing and related that Jewell was a former security guard at Piedmont College and that the college had information concerning improper conduct by Jewell," would be the way it was later phrased in the OPR report.[8]

A perfect storm was gathering that Sunday, and Richard still didn't realize it was headed his way. Someone at the FBI recalled what had happened during the 1984 Olympics when a Los Angeles police officer named Jimmy Pearson became an instant hero by claiming to have discovered and disarmed a bomb he found on board a bus full of Turkish athletes. Pearson was soon unmasked as being responsible for the bomb, which turned out to be fake. By 5:00 P.M. on Sunday, the day after the bombing, Jewell's name was already being kicked around as a possible suspect. By that evening, more dirt was uncovered about Jewell: "that he had been arrested for impersonating a police officer in 1990; had employment problems in a previous law enforcement position" and a couple of "may haves" which would lead the FBI further down the wrong road—"that he may have had access to a bomb-making 'cookbook' " and that he "may have started to clear people away from the area before the backpack was found to contain a bomb."[9]

A team of FBI profilers had already been on the case less than two hours after the bombing. Now, agents were assigned to go back and watch Jewell's CNN interview, while other agents were to head up to north Georgia the next day to learn more about his past. When they watched the tape, they were struck by Jewell's use of language, thought that in spite of his remarks expressing concern for the victims that he somehow was emotionless and didn't really care for them.[10]

An FBI agent who went up to north Georgia on Monday returned home with even more seemingly damning evidence—that Jewell might have had a green backpack similar to the one used to hold the bomb, and the agent got information that seemed to corroborate the charges about access to the bomb-making book and his troubled employment history. Worse still, was the claim, "He had told friends that he wanted to 'be in the middle' of anything that might happen at the Olympics."[11] A series of unrelated and possibly innocent events were becoming, in the minds of some investigators, items for a bill of indictment (they would certainly be used that way in an application for a search warrant on the Jewell apartment and at least one other court document).

By Monday night, suspicions about Jewell were high, though it was all still seemingly based on a profile and some interviews at Piedmont College, rather than a single bit of actual evidence. Hoping to get a telling admission, the FBI upped the ante. They asked a GBI agent (the one who introduced Tom Davis to Jewell a few days earlier in the park) who was going to see Richard that night for dinner to wear a wire and record what was said as Richard and he ate a late lasagna dinner. Jewell himself seemed to have some understanding that he might be a suspect, although not a serious one, if only because of where he was when the bomb went off. When the agent called him to say he was on his way over, Richard asked him if he was under suspicion and if he might be arrested. The day before, after doing a taped interview with CNN, Jewell mentioned to correspondent Art Harris that based on his own law enforcement experience, he would be surprised if he wasn't treated as a suspect because everyone involved should be checked out.[12]

There was no way this was going to stay a secret. Not with 15,000 reporters in town, not with hundreds of law enforcement officials in Atlanta and Washington, from street cops to high-level bureaucrats, working the case for a dozen different agencies. The *Atlanta Journal-Constitution* was the first to break the story with a huge headline and some phrases that would soon place it on the receiving end of a libel suit. CNN reporters were discussing how to handle the Jewell situation when

CNN executive Tom Johnson got a call from an editor at the newspaper informing him they were about to go with the story in a special edition. He had a copy sent over and ordered a news anchor to hold up the front page and read part of it on the air. Later, Tom Johnson would call a high-ranking FBI official who assured him Jewell "was our man."[13]

By the time FBI agents actually arrived to do an interview with Jewell, the parking lot next to his mother's apartment was jammed with reporters, cameramen, and satellite trucks. He agreed to go over to the FBI building (which was nearby) to be questioned, but had to fend off a journalistic horde peppering him with questions about his possible role in the bombing as he got into his pickup truck. The media circus had arrived at Jewell's doorstep, and for the next several weeks he was unable to go anywhere without the FBI and media following him.[14]

It just kept getting worse. A team of FBI profilers was headed to Atlanta but would not make it there in time for the interview, so they asked that a videotape be made for them; they wanted to see how Jewell would react. There was a cameraman from FBI headquarters already in the building doing an in-house video about the Olympics who said he'd like to tape the interview as part of a piece on first responders, not realizing that the agents conducting the interview had another reason altogether for taping. FBI Director Freeh had already come up with a question of his own for Jewell, about whether the bomb was intended to ambush police officers and first responders, and the agents were directed to ask that.[15] In fact, Freeh was so involved that some federal agents were snickering and calling him the case agent for the Centennial Park bombing, effectively overshadowing not only Woody Johnson but also the newly appointed supervisors of the case.

The interview began, and so did the taping. But soon afterward, the two agents, Don Johnson and Dee Rosario, were told that Director Freeh had called again, and this time he wanted Jewell to be given his Miranda rights, just in case the interview yielded important information (Freeh was already unhappy that the media was reporting the Jewell story). The agents weren't happy about Freeh's request, but then Johnson made what might have been the worst of many FBI decisions when it came to Jewell.

Johnson decided he would tell Jewell that he was only reading him his rights because it would make the video look more realistic: "So what I'm going to do is I'm gonna . . . walk up and introduce myself to you, basically, tell you who I am, show you my credentials, just like we're doing a professional interview. Okay? And then I'll just ask you a couple of questions like your name and your age, and . . . I'm even gonna go as far as to advise you of your rights."[16] Jewell first refused then agreed to waive his rights—he had been trying to get in touch with an attorney friend of his for at least a day because he had a question when someone approached him about selling book rights, but the attorney hadn't gotten back in touch. He left another message, then the interview picked up. They went on for a while, until Richard asked if he could call his mother, to let her know everything was OK.

The legal cavalry finally arrived for Jewell about an hour later. His attorney friend, a man named Watson Bryant (they hadn't actually talked in years but used to play video games together during lunch breaks when both worked at the U.S. Courthouse in Atlanta), had been downtown, attending some Olympic events, when he saw the Atlanta newspaper's article about Jewell. He remembered that Richard had been trying to reach him, checked and found another message from Richard, and tried calling the FBI. After one unsuccessful attempt, he finally was patched through to Jewell. After speaking with him, Bryant told the FBI agents the interview was over and ordered Richard to get the hell out of there.

The worst wasn't over for Jewell. He had gone from hero to zero—and worse—in a media nanosecond. The satellite trucks were there when the FBI showed up to serve a search warrant and took his mother's Tupperware to the lab for analysis. They were there when he walked the dog, washed the truck, just stepped outside, forgetting for a brief instant that he was trapped inside this hell. It was Camp Jewell for cameramen and reporters outside the apartment complex with savvy neighbors selling location rights and cashing in on the media frenzy. But the media was there, it should be remembered, because the FBI was there. Whenever Jewell went anywhere, the convoy included at least one car with agents on surveillance duty. Sometimes there was also an FBI plane flying overhead, as if Jewell was somehow going to pull a fast one and shake the line of cars behind him.

Without realizing it, Richard Jewell had made one brilliant move that would eventually help mitigate, if not end, his nightmare. Watson Bryant wasn't a criminal attorney, and he knew it. The only reason Richard had called him was because he used to give Jewell the occasional ride home from work years earlier and they shared a few beers in their time. But Bryant did have a bone to pick with the federal government, feeling that he had been unfairly treated years before during an investigation about some Small Business Administration loans that he was involved in and that made him identify personally with Richard's plight. Bryant knew how to raise hell, and he began doing so immediately, in the same court of public opinion where Jewell was being pilloried as a suspect, in plain, unlawyer-like language that began to strike a chord. And Bryant helped Jewell assemble a legal team, first bringing on a highly respected criminal lawyer, Jack Martin, then civil attorneys Lin Wood and Wade Grant.

The lawyers mounted a stunning counterattack that would become a model for those who felt they were being victimized by the Feds and the media. At every turn, Jewell's attorneys turned the debate back on to the government, exposing its case and questioning its motives. Even as the FBI was very publicly visiting hardware stores near Jewell's apartment, looking for signs he had been there and might have purchased a certain type of metal pipe that was used in the bomb, Jack Martin was walking the streets of downtown Atlanta, CNN camera in tow, from the bomb site to the phone booth where the 911 call was made, dramatically showing that Richard Jewell couldn't have had the time to sneak out and make the call. That worked so well, he did it the next day for the rest of the media.

Lin Wood and his partner had never tried a libel case before, but the ultraconfident Wood began very publicly serving notice to NBC, CNN, the *Atlanta Journal-Constitution*, and others that they were going to clear Richard's name and then come looking for damages. At the same time he was threatening the media barons, he was appearing on their air, castigating the government. Jewell was the big "get" that fall season for TV news magazines, and Wood went with *60 Minutes*, and Mike Wallace not only talked to Jewell, but he put NBC news anchor Tom Brokaw on the spot, questioning some of the comments he made on air about Jewell. The attorneys got a former FBI polygraph expert to give Jewell a lie detector test; when he passed with flying colors, they announced the results at a news conference on the steps of the federal courthouse—and it was carried live on CNN.

Investigators were livid. To a man, they loathed Lin Wood, who was charming in public but seemed to have unlimited reservoirs of aggression in private. They thought he was all about the media (and he did use the Jewell case as a stepping-stone to even bigger things). But they didn't get that this wasn't for show, that Wood and the others believed passionately that their client was not only innocent, and a victim, but that he should have been treated as a hero for his actions. Many agents were still suspicious of Jewell, thought his story about what he had done before, during, and after the package was spotted didn't add up and would cling to that belief until events proved they were flat-out wrong.[17] Some were also still smarting that the attorneys publicly questioned their tactics, including the Miranda warning ploy they tried on Jewell. In an FBI increasingly beset by self-inflicted wounds, headquarters was in a cover-your-ass mode, ordering up an internal investigation and trying to distance itself from the whole fiasco.

U.S. Attorney Kent Alexander finally decided someone needed to cut the government's losses. The FBI wasn't willing to do it, nor were his superiors at the Justice Department (up until the end, Attorney General Janet Reno refused to state publicly that Jewell was not a suspect). Alexander was no stranger to criminal cases nor to playing hardball with suspects, but he also knew that the evidence against Jewell simply wasn't there, and the real investigation was going to keep getting bogged down until someone cut the cord. He made a deal: Jewell would come in for an informational interview, so investigators could see if he had any important leads to offer about suspects he might have seen in the park; if nothing else turned up on him in three weeks, his attorneys would get a letter saying he was not a target of the investigation. Jewell did the interview, which for the most part went quietly. Three weeks later, Alexander and Martin went for coffee on a Saturday morning, and Jewell got his letter—without an apology. By Monday afternoon, Jewell and his attorneys were holding a news conference, again carried live on CNN and local Atlanta stations, talking about his eighty-eight-day nightmare. In the end, Jewell would get settlements from NBC, CNN, and Piedmont College; the *Atlanta Journal-Constitution* fought him in court, and the case is still pending.

The Jewell affair was not the only embarrassment growing out of the Centennial Park bombing. There was the effect on the Olympics themselves. Although the Games continued, many in the international media heaped the bombing on top of complaints about traffic, bad computer systems (writers weren't getting results about the winners in timely fashion), and the general tackiness of the street vendors, and concluded Atlanta wasn't ready to host something like the Olympics. IOC president Juan Antonio Samaranch seemed to agree and at the Closing Ceremonies didn't give Atlanta his usual blessing by calling it "the greatest Games ever"; instead Atlanta got damned with the faint praise of putting on a "most exceptional" Olympics.

From the day after the bombing, Atlanta's Police Chief Beverly Harvard was also under fire, when word leaked out about the 911 problems. She tried to spin the incident, first saying protocol was being followed, then blaming the screw-up on her Public Works Department. Others in the law enforcement community who already had a low opinion of her held their tongues in public, but privately they were disgusted that word never reached the park. The officers at the scene were diplomatic but made it clear that if they had known of the telephone warning, they would have moved the crowd back farther and more quickly, possibly reducing the death and injuries from the blast. And because of the fixation on Jewell—including trying to get him to say the 911 message so FBI agents could do a voice analysis—it would not be until early December, more than four months after the bombing, before the public heard the chilling message.[18]

There was at least one more embarrassment that was kept quieter. Before the Olympics, ACOG Security Chief Rathburn had boasted of the surveillance cameras that were all around Centennial Park, disguised as streetlights (the cameras were part of a sponsorship deal with Sensormatic). Charles Stone, who was by now working as part of the Investigative Task Force—the case was dubbed CENTBOMB—discovered that the cameras were virtually useless for providing evidence. No one had budgeted for VHS tapes, so one of the supervisors had to pay for them out of his pocket. The cameras were being operated by some of the soldiers brought in to supplement security. But Stone discovered that when they did bother to record the output from the cameras, which wasn't very often, they were often filled with shots of attractive women frolicking in the park!

ACOG was giving investigators fits on another score. Stone got a phone call from a former police buddy, who had gone to work for ACOG before the Olympics, warning him that the group was about to shred all its accreditation documents, thousands of files. At that point, no one knew if the bomber might have had any sort of Olympic affiliation, but if he did, it would have been in those files. Stone went to an assistant U.S. attorney, Sally Yates, and she got a court order preventing the destruction of the files.

The CENTBOMB Task Force was making some progress, although it was obscured by the fallout from Jewell. The various agencies were for the most part playing well together, although Stone found himself trying to soothe over some ruffled feathers. One of his GBI colleagues had managed to anger the FBI and others when she kept demanding that she have an office as big as her federal counterparts. And Stone was stunned by the sheer number of meetings that took place every day; to borrow a phrase that the Treasury secretary had used about the Clinton White House, these were the "meetingest people" he had ever met. But now they were going to go about investigating the old-fashioned way.

FBI and Bureau of Alcohol, Tobacco, Firearms and Explosives (ATF) technicians began to reconstruct the bomb. It was clear this was the work of someone who intended to kill dozens of people. The lab techs were shocked to discover that this was the largest pipe bomb in their files, weighing more than forty pounds. Whoever built it must have either been well read or had military experience, because there was an eighth-inch steel plate in back of the pack that was there to direct the force of the blast in a specific direction, something you would see on a Claymore mine.

They analyzed the pipe (two-inch-diameter metal pipes with metal end caps); the type of gunpowder (Accurate Arms # 7 or #9 smokeless); the cut masonry nails (8d). They made lists of the stores that sold the Westclox Big Ben windup alarm clock and the twelve-volt Evcready lantern battery that powered the fuse, checking out leads in places like south Florida. Military surplus stores that sold the backpack (it was called an ALICE pack) were visited. They even tried to track down the gray duct tape and black plastic electrical tape. It was forensic work that was time-consuming and used up thousands of man-hours.

There was something else about the bomb, and it had to do with those rowdy young men that first led Richard Jewell to the bench where he would spot the backpack. Investigators would dub them the Speedo boys, because several of them had been working at a pavilion run by the swimwear manufacturer up the road near the Olympic Aquatic Center. The Speedo boys had come to the park to party, and they were the first to admit they had their share of beer. It turned out that the initial sketch that Charles Stone's GBI crew made was of one of them.

The Speedo boys had a lot to say. Three of them—Steve Schmitz, Jason Fishburn, and David Szabo—described a man who sat by himself on a bench. He glared at them, wouldn't respond to their well-lubricated sense of humor. He had a goatee, intense eyes, and they could swear he was wearing a dark watch cap as well as a hooded sweatshirt. They didn't notice the pack until he got up and left. By that time, there were other things going on. One of their group, Larry Coune, was getting into it with Jewell, and Szabo pulled him away.

The Speedo boys decided they had enough of the park. They thought a band called Steel Pulse was going to play, and when they found out otherwise, they decided to leave the park and go across the street to the House of Blues. Besides, who needed the hassle from the security guard, who had gone off to get a GBI agent. They began to pick up their beer cans, hoping to avoid any more hassle. That's when they saw the pack. Was it one of theirs? They wouldn't quite come out and admit it, but maybe they were thinking of taking the pack into the crowded club.

Coune went over and gave it a nudge, asked if it belonged to one of his friends. Szabo did the same. It was heavy, very heavy. No need to weigh themselves down, especially if it wasn't beer. But while they were looking at the pack, they had tipped it over on its back. Now the steel plate was on the ground, meaning the force of the blast would be directed straight up, instead of into the crowd. The Speedo boys were inadvertent heroes (Stone would later shudder at the thought of them, unsuspecting, carrying the pack into the House of Blues). No less than the deputy director of the FBI would later pay homage to what the Speedo boys had done during a press conference, saying, "no doubt that movement saved a lot of lives."[19]

Profiling had gotten the FBI into the Richard Jewell mess. Now, a new group of case agents hoped that profiling would help them find the bomber or bombers. After the Jewell debacle, the man who ran intelligence operations during the Games, Jim Bernazzani, was brought in to supervise the investigation. In turn, he made John Behnke one of the case agents, since he had experience on another high-profile bombing case. Although Behnke had strong political clout, being a protégé of Director Freeh (in Bureau parlance, he was an FOL, friend of Louis), he liked to keep a low profile, preferring life as a street agent rather than as an executive. Tracey North, who happened to be another FOL, was also assigned by the FBI to run the case. They wanted to give profiling a second chance, but this time they bypassed the Bureau's Behavioral Sciences Unit and went outside to Dr. Park Dietz. Dietz, once dubbed "the world's most famous forensic psychiatrist" by the *Los Angeles Times*, had examined would-be presidential assassin John Hinckley and serial killer Jeffrey Dahmer. But more importantly for Behnke, North, Stone, and the rest of the Task Force, Dietz had helped investigators build a profile in a previous bombing case that ultimately led them to their man. And he was willing to work for less than his usual fee, which was once put at $3,000 per day.[20]

Dietz had a few clues to start building his profile. The military-style backpack and the type of bomb led him to believe the bomber had military training. Then there was the puzzling issue of timing; the bomber called at 12:58 A.M. with his warning that "you have thirty minutes"; the bomb went off some twenty minutes later. So who was the real target? Was it the crowd, or the law enforcement officers, the first responders to any such warning? The bomber had planned that the warning would be relayed to the officers in the park. Even though it wasn't, the backpack was still found, and the closest people to the blast were police. Dietz, along with many in the 'Task Force, believed that law enforcement was the target—and this was an indication of militia-type leanings. An even more basic question: Was this the work of one man or several? Dietz leaned toward the loner theory, and again many in the Task Force agreed with him.

A profile was only going to take the CENTBOMB team so far. So was their dogged forensic work. The Task Force set up an 800 number, and people were calling in, hundreds a day. But these soon began to fall into a familiar pattern: wackos; well-meaning but misinformed people; and an unusual number of women who seemed to be ratting out boyfriends after a fight. The Task Force also began to build a time line of what happened in the park from their interviews with the Speedo boys and others (including Richard Jewell, during that October interview). They took a unique approach, starting with what was happening onstage. They got the tapes of the concert performances from NBC and its affiliates. Then they began to match up home videos, photographs, and witness statements. If, for example, a witness had a video that had "Take Me to the River" playing in the background, they knew it was shot just after 1:00 A.M. but before the bombing.

They found shots which showed the Speedo boys sitting on the bench. Slowly, on a wall in an FBI office, they were able to begin piecing together their time line. By early December, they were ready for another public plea. This time, they added in 500,000 reasons for the public to care. Deputy Director Kennedy played the 911 tape, showed a replica of what the backpack containing the bomb looked like, and talked up the new, half million dollar reward that was being offered.

At the end of the news conference, Kennedy handed out a sheet with four photos and a sketch, asking for them to be shown by the media. These were the people who couldn't be identified as investigators built their time line. The first showed young men, one of them appearing to carry a bag. The second showed two women sitting near the base of the sound tower. The third, a young man with a backpack near the metal fencing surrounding the tower. But it was number four that they were really interested in: a heavyset blond-haired man in a dark shirt. One of the few surveillance camera tapes that actually had something on it appeared to show this man carrying a military-style pack, and the Task Force was terribly interested in talking with him. As for the sketch, it was the young goateed man described by the Speedo boys. Investigators thought it was worth including in their public appeal, but the person they really wanted to talk to was the blond man in the dark shirt.

If the blond man was their best lead, they were thrilled when they got a quick response. This could be the break, it had to be. That same evening, the Task Force got a call from a man who said he was the person in the picture. He was a corporate headhunter from Atlanta who happened at that very moment to be out in Arizona visiting the New Age town of Sedona. Friends had seen his picture that night on the news and called him, then he phoned the 800 number for the Task Force. Agents from the Arizona field office were immediately dispatched to talk with him, the Task Force hoping they had an answer. Yes, he had been in Centennial Park and, yes, he had a backpack. In fact it was sitting in the closet of his apartment back in Atlanta, and his girlfriend would be happy to show it to agents that night if they wanted to come over. They did, interviewed her, and realized he was just another Olympic spectator—and he couldn't even offer them much help in describing any suspicious-looking people from the park. While they were thrilled at the quick response, they were incredibly disappointed. They wanted to rule someone in, not out, make the arrest, and get everyone to forget all about Richard Jewell.

Six months had passed since the Centennial Park bombing. An innocent man had been the focus of the investigation for almost half that time. The Task Force was finally making some progress, both with forensics and with their profile. They put on a game face in public, but in private, some in the FBI were talking about a silver bullet, that one lucky break that would lead them to the bomber. But it hadn't happened yet, not even with the offer of a half million dollar reward nor when the public finally heard the voice on the 911 tape. They knew what the bomb looked like. They knew what the backpack looked like. They were sure their man had military experience, exposure to the extreme Right, and that he viewed them as his real target. What they didn't realize is they already knew what the bomber looked like, too.

The goateed man may not have even seen the sketch of himself on TV or in the newspaper after that news conference in December. There was no reason to suspect anyone knew who he was. If he was paying attention, he saw what others saw, an investigation that appeared to be troubled, not one that seemed to be hot on his trail. Besides, he had probably already shaven the goatee, just to be on the safe side.

But he was busy making plans and experimenting. Bomb technicians liked to talk about how a bomber has a profile, that he will use certain ingredients and certain techniques. The goateed man, if he could still be called that, was still learning his trade, and he had some surprises he was getting ready to reveal to the world.

3.
ARMY OF GOD

HE WASN'T THE goateed man this morning. He was changing his look, ever so slightly, and changing his profile, too. The location was different. So was the time of day. He was using dynamite instead of gunpowder, different nails, even a different container. But these were minor changes. He had something else in mind this morning, something that would make it clear just who he was after. If they thought Centennial Park was the end of it, they were wrong. He had been watching, waiting, learning.

Adam Scott* needed his methadone. He was a recovering addict, but he also had a tree-cutting job, so he wanted to get his fix early in the morning. Sometime between 6 A.M. and 6:30 A.M. on January 16, 1997, he couldn't exactly remember, Scott pulled his pickup truck into the parking lot of the Sandy Springs Professional Building, which housed the Apollo Clinic, where he was being treated.[1] It was a three-story concrete structure, just your basic suburban office, late sixties style, too plain to be

---

*A pseudonym

ugly, tucked on a side street just off the main artery of this north Atlanta suburb. Traffic wasn't bad this early in the morning. Scott could
hear the noise as cars raced along the nearby interstate, which was less
than a hundred yards away. It was easy to get here, and once he got his
medicine, it would take him less than a minute to hop back in the pickup,
get on the highway, and head out to anywhere he needed to go in the
metro area.

Scott noticed the man as he was parking. This wasn't a place where
you saw much foot traffic, especially not this early in the morning. Even
though dawn was still some time away, the sky was lightening up, and he
caught the man in the beam of his headlights. The man was about six feet
tall, maybe more, with a slight to medium build. Scott thought he might
be about 180 to 190 pounds and somewhere between thirty to forty-five
years old. The man was wearing a black cotton jogging suit with a hood.
He was clean shaven, no beard, but there might have been some stubble
on his chin. He was standing along the tree line that bordered the parking lot, separating it from other businesses and the main street just beyond. There was a Dumpster nearby, at the top of the parking lot just
where Scott had turned in.

What caught Scott's eye was what the man was carrying—it looked
like he had one of those duffel or sea bags in one hand, and attached to
it was a fold-up military-style shovel (they were called entrenching tools).
Scott wondered if the man might be homeless. It didn't seem like the
man had any sort of car, at least nearby. He was also worried the man
might try to steal some of the equipment from the bed of his pickup.
That had happened before, and this stranger on foot, at this hour, there
was something about him that stuck in Scott's head.

Scott went inside and got his medication. About ten minutes later, he
was back out at his truck. The man was still hanging around and seemed
to have moved closer to the Dumpster. Now he had the duffel-style bag
in one hand and was gripping it by the handle in the middle. It must have
only been half full, because the man didn't seen to have much trouble
carrying it. The folded shovel, that entrenching tool, was hanging off the
back of the man's waistband. Scott eyeballed the back of his truck. Everything still seemed to be there. He asked the man if he needed help or a

ride. No, said the hooded man, and he looked away. *I asked*, thought Scott as he got in his truck, leaving the man in his rearview mirror as he headed off for a cold day's work cutting trees.[2]

The parking lot of the Sandy Springs building was still fairly empty three hours later, many of the businesses inside just opening up. There were a variety of offices, a few lawyers, the Apollo Clinic, and around the back of the building on the south side on the first floor was an abortion clinic called Northside Family Planning Services. Today was not a clinic day for Northside Family Planning, so there were only three people inside, all of them staff. No one spotted a green, military-style ammunition canister, the sort of thing you might get at an army surplus store and use as a toolbox. It was outside the building, just by one of the windows of the clinic, seemingly left there by accident.

There wasn't any security to speak of at the Sandy Springs Professional Building, certainly no surveillance camera, and it had never seemed necessary. There was another abortion clinic down in the center of Atlanta in the Midtown neighborhood, and that seemed to attract the picketers from Operation Rescue and get all the bomb threats. Nobody paid much attention to this building out in suburban Sandy Springs. But just after 9:30 A.M., that changed in one explosive instant. There was a sharp percussive blast as the air was being sucked up and then hurtled toward the building. The force shattered more than sixty windows and ripped into the side of the building. But this was a reinforced concrete structure, and it was sturdy, absorbing most of the explosion and the shrapnel. The clinic took the worst of it. One minute, it was a functioning medical facility, the next it was soot and torn drywall, equipment tossed around haphazardly by the blast. If the bomber intended casualties, he was going to be disappointed. The three people inside the clinic were stunned, then angry, realizing quickly that they were the intended targets, but they were otherwise unhurt. As they wandered outside, they saw a big soot mark streaking up the side of the building above and around where the explosion had gone off.[3]

The county police were there quickly; there was a station a couple of miles up the road. Pretty soon, the Feds showed up as well. If this was an abortion clinic bombing, Washington was going to want them out in force. The U.S. attorney asked the FBI to check it out, and the ATF already had its response squad on the way. Sure, there had been the bombing in Centennial Park six months earlier, but at first glance this seemed to be something different.

Mike Rising caught the call at the FBI. He was the civil rights coordinator at the Bureau, working out of the public corruption squad. Rising got there pretty quickly, less than a half hour after the blast, intending to walk the site and call back to the U.S. Attorney's Office to give them a fill. He hooked up with another agent, and they checked in with the Fulton County police on the scene.

The media was showing up as well. Alan Duke was a CNN producer and sometime reporter. He happened to be on another job near there, some part-time work as a traffic reporter, when the report came over the scanner. He got there even before the FBI and began phoning in reports live to CNN while waiting for a crew and satellite truck. The local stations began showing up, too, setting up their trucks and getting ready to break in to programming if they needed to.

The police started moving cars away from the south end of the building, clearing folks out of the parking lot so the GBI, ATF, and FBI could get ready to start searching for evidence, including bomb fragments. They set up a command post up around the other side of the building at the other end of the parking lot, just where it hit the street, and cordoned everything off with the ubiquitous bright yellow crime-scene tape. No one paid much attention to the Dumpster that was over in the corner. In fact, one person moved her Nissan Pulsar just up by the Dumpster. Another person coming in also parked a BMW convertible there. The real work was going on down on the other side of the building.

Mike Rising needed to move away from the knot of police officers and bomb techs. It was about an hour after the bomb had gone off, thirty minutes since he got there, and he had to call in, brief his contact at the U.S. Attorney's Office. With some three dozen people right there near the blast site, he couldn't hear himself talk. It looked quieter up by the Dumpster, so he walked over there and leaned up against the side of one of the two parked cars. The attorneys back in the office put him on a speakerphone so they could all get a fill.[4]

The lawyers at the other end of the line heard a horrendous explosion, then Mike started yelling and cussing and he said, another bomb's gone off, I've got to go. Rising had been through this before, knew the sound and feel of an attack. He'd been wounded before in a rocket attack serving in Vietnam in 1969. This time, he'd been struck on the side of the head with what felt like a shotgun blast of nails and wire. He had three puncture wounds in his back and two in the foot, lost a chunk off his right ankle, and was knocked about four feet to the right. The bomb had gone off not thirteen steps away, just on the other side of the Pulsar and BMW. The force of the explosion was mostly absorbed by the two cars, but there was enough kinetic energy that it came up and over and whomped him.

Just like that, he was no longer Mike Rising, investigator. He was Mike Rising, victim. He didn't pass out, tried to keep himself from going into shock. Two fellow agents, buddies, grabbed him and sat him down over by a bush until the paramedics could take him to the hospital. Six others were injured badly enough to be taken to the emergency room; the rest of the crowd of police, media, and onlookers were stunned.

Leon Jobe happened to be rolling on his camera when the blast occurred. He was getting footage for his TV station, WSB. His tripod was down near the Dumpster, right near Rising, but he had spotted a couple hugging each other, trying to recover from the shock of the first blast. He could have just panned his camera over and stayed by the Dumpster. But he decided to move closer to the couple. Jobe thought he needed to get some emotion on tape, so he took his camera off the tripod and moved away about forty feet. Another cameraman set up next to him followed. Both were focused on the couple when the bomb went off. The woman's hair was literally pulled on end by the shock wave. Jobe's camera jumped from the force of the blast, tilted up crazily toward the sky. Then he had the presence of mind to turn around and shoot toward the Dumpster. His camera blocked the worst of the sound wave, so he only had a slight problem with his hearing.

The other cameraman would fall to the ground, both eardrums blown out by the explosion (one of them would also get shots of Mike Rising as he staggered crazily away from the blast, before collapsing).

Minutes later, after he got his tape to a live truck and saw it go out locally (and then worldwide on CNN), Jobe went back and got his tripod. It was knocked over, scarred and pitted by bomb fragments, a reminder that he just missed serious injury—or worse.

It was an old IRA trick, not something seen here in the United States before. The Irish Republican Army would plant two bombs. The first would go off, and the British Army and Royal Ulster Constabulary would rush to the scene. Then a second blast somewhere out on the perimeter to catch the real target, the authorities who responded to the scene. The British would eventually catch on, become much more wary, knowing they were the targets. Palestinian suicide bombers also picked up on the technique and sometimes also began going out in pairs, hoping to double their terrorist impact. Whoever had struck in Sandy Springs had put a lot of thought into this one. He had cased the scene, chosen the high ground up and away from the first bomb to plant the second one, which was buried at the base of the Dumpster but facing the building. If not for those two parked cars, he would have killed a number of police officers. Instead, the vehicles took the brunt of the blast so that, even though Mike Rising was just a few feet away, he survived the explosion.

Charles Stone had not had time to get to the scene. His other job, even though he was assigned to the CENTBOMB Task Force, was to oversee the GBI bomb techs, and there were a couple of his guys at the scene. It didn't take long for him and some of the other investigators to conclude this was the same guy as Centennial Park. Different technique but same MO (modus operandi). Sucker in law enforcement, then hit them with a bomb. Maybe the bomber used the 911 call the first time and a decoy bomb the second time. Sure, nobody had time to do the forensics, and that would really tell them one way or the other. But Stone had spent more than two decades working this sort of thing in Georgia. No bombs aimed at the police for years, then two in six months? His read was they had a serial bomber, plain and simple.

That sort of common sense quickly collided with bureaucratic politics. The FBI had grabbed the lead on the last blast. This time, the ATF was determined to be in charge. The two agencies had been at each other's throats for years. It was a cultural thing—white-collar FBI, blue-collar ATF—and a money thing. They were both scrapping for the same dollars out of Congress. For journalists, it was great sport and a great opportunity. All you needed to do if you were working a story was call one agency, mention the other, and the leaks would start flowing. Both agencies were still recovering from their share of scandals: the ATF had almost been put out of business after the initial fiasco at Waco; the FBI had Waco, Ruby Ridge, and now Richard Jewell to deal with.

Today was going to be no different. That was obvious to U.S. Attorney Kent Alexander when he got out to the scene. He went into the forward command post set up a block away from the bomb sites. The local heads of the FBI and ATF, both good men, were in the trailer, each on the phone to his respective boss back in Washington, each hearing the same thing: cooperate, but remember you are in charge. Alexander had witnessed dozens of turf fights during the whole run-up to the Olympics, so he could read this one in a bureaucratic heartbeat. He realized this could get ugly and public with a whole bunch of media just outside ready to take it all live, so he called his boss, Attorney General Janet Reno, and told her he was going to take the lead. After all, this started out as what seemed to be an abortion clinic bombing, so he was going to use the attorney general's authorization and put himself in charge.

That got everybody through the press conference, although the ATF's new Atlanta boss, Jack Killorin, still managed to steal even Alexander's thunder (the FBI boss, Woody Johnson, viewed talking to the press as somewhat less fun than a root canal). Killorin had been the ATF national spokesman post-Waco, and the agency had skated in no small part because of his public relations savvy. Questions about the real target of the blast and possible links to Centennial Park were fended off with artful phrases. But Atlantans didn't need much to convince themselves that either their city was becoming the bombing capital of the U.S. or there was someone out there on the loose, and he was likely to strike again.

Despite Alexander's play, the bureaucracies still went at it. By the end of the day, there was a separate Task Force for this case, a separate headquarters (the FBI and ATF were actually in the same office complex in northeast Atlanta, but of course they were in different buildings), and a separate lab doing the forensic work. The new investigation even had its own name: TWINBOMB (because two bombs were involved). To Charles Stone, it defied logic, but the ATF and even some in the FBI argued that until they could prove the bombs were done by the same person, then the better part of common sense was to keep the investigations on separate tracks. After all, a rush to judgment got them Richard Jewell, so maybe doing it this way wasn't such a bad idea after all. And if this meant everyone got a chance to play, then maybe that would mean fewer interagency games.

Almost immediately, folks in the ATF detected an important difference: the Sandy Springs bombs used dynamite. Pretty soon they picked up some other differences: a slightly different type of clock, and different nails. They were also packed inside those military-style metal ammunition cans; there were no metal pipes. What the ATF did in cases like this was both science and art. They'd trace the components, just like the FBI, but they'd also do some profiling of their own by going back through case files and looking for similar bombs. They liked to talk about how a bomber had a signature, and so far they weren't convinced the Sandy Springs bomber had the same signature as the Centennial Park bomber.

Of course, you could also turn that sort of logic on its head, because some bombers did evolve. Sure the components might be different, dynamite instead of powder, cans instead of pipes, two bombs instead of one. But the clocks used as timers weren't that different, they were still timers, and nails were nails. Most importantly for Charles Stone was that a bomber's signature was his choice of targets, and this guy seemed to be after law enforcement. And he noted one more sign, one that was pretty telling for him. Although the bomber used a different type of battery, he filed off the lot numbers, just in case. He had probably seen those news reports about how they were hunting in stores down in Florida, looking for batteries, and up in Atlanta, looking for pipe. That's how a bomber learned, by paying attention, changing his tactics, not his target.

Two task forces meant two ways of doing things. And that included sketch artists. The CENTBOMB folks had Marla Lawson (she liked to sign her work with her first name); TWINBOMB had an ATF artist known as Dr. Etch-a-Sketch, who preferred to work on a computer. Dr. Etch-a-Sketch and the ATF worked with the eyewitness, Adam Scott, and they came up with a sketch of a hooded man, a young white male, but his features were bland. More than a year later, when Task Force agents revisited Scott, he would tell them their sketch was only 70 percent accurate. No one thought to bring in the same artist who had drawn the goateed man. Then again, the CENTBOMB Task Force still hadn't focused in on the goateed man.

The hooded man wasn't through. In fact, he was just hitting his stride. He had chosen another target much like the last. It was just seconds away from the interstate. It was another place, like the abortion clinic, full of people to hate. He was able to edge around the perimeter, never actually getting close. Once again, he had two bombs. Maybe this time, his plan would work. Maybe this time, no one would park their car in the wrong place, foiling his carefully planned ambush.

Friday night was lesbian night at the Otherside Lounge. The bar and dance club had different theme nights—gay, lesbian, even straight—but Friday was when they aimed to get their biggest crowd. Atlanta had a surprisingly large gay population, and many lived in the Midtown area, just a few blocks south of the Otherside. It was a strange-looking place, white faux Tudor with a green-shingled roof, a regrettable early seventies style of architecture that resembled nothing so much as a painted over and stretched out Steak and Ale restaurant. It was along a strip of road that was lined with strip bars and a few other businesses. There was a Denny's just down the road, an animal clinic behind it and one building over. All-night restaurants and pizza places were scattered through there. It fronted on Piedmont Road, which was six lanes wide and just off the interstate. Another street ran behind it, so you could get into the club's parking lot from front or back. The exit and entrance ramps to I-85 were a block away, which meant you could be on the highway in seconds.

It was February 21, 1997, barely five weeks after the Sandy Springs bombing. Charles Stone was at home that night when he got a call from the GBI communications center. His bomb techs were on the scene at the Otherside Lounge, and they thought he might want to come on up there (he lived about forty-five minutes south). There had been an explosion, and it looked like they had found a second device. By the time he got to the club, all the folks from the Task Force he thought he'd left behind for the weekend were gathered out on the street, doing the same thing he was, trying to figure out what was going on. Barricades had been set up blocking off a stretch of Piedmont Road, and the Atlanta Police Department had its bomb squad robot deployed in the parking lot. Stone had a chance to speak with the APD folks who had responded first to the scene. When the officers got to the club, there were several people wounded. The most serious casualty had a nail in her arm. None of the customers were exactly sure what had happened. There was a large crack like a gunshot that seemed to come from somewhere out back, then the woman was clutching her arm, and a few others realized they were hit. It might have been a shotgun, but when the officer saw the nail in the woman's arm, his first thought was bomb.

It looked like the bomb was set on the top of a retaining wall out back, near a covered outdoor patio. It was February, and although the night was fairly mild, there weren't too many people outside. Ever since the Sandy Springs bombing the month before, there had been an intense amount of training for public safety officers on how to respond to bombs. In particular, officers were on the lookout for secondary devices. The training paid off. In fairly short order, the first cops on the scene spotted another package in what looked like a green backpack. This one was on the top of a different retaining wall, one that ran along the side border of the parking lot about sixty feet from the street and only about ten feet from the side of the club. That's when the officers called in reinforcements. By the time Stone got there, you had the whole alphabet soup: FBI, ATF, GBI, APD . . . not to mention WSB, WAGA, WXIA, and even CNN.

The folks from the Task Force had an impromptu huddle in the parking lot of a strip bar across the street. When you had a potential live bomb, the techs ran the show, but everyone agreed on a plan. The robot would try to pull the pack off the wall and bring it out away from the club. Then the bomb squad would use another of their fancy gizmos, something called a disruptor, which was basically sort of a high-speed water cannon, that was supposed to disable the device. The Task Force folks realized this could be a huge break if they could get their hands on a disabled bomb. There might be hair, fibers, even some DNA, not to mention it would be a hell of a lot easier to trace the components if they weren't scraping them off the side of buildings two blocks away.

As Stone and the others watched, the robot slowly rolled in. It was controlled by a long tether that ran back to the bomb squad's truck, and it had a small camera perched on top that provided a video feed. The robot turned up toward the wall, and one of its mechanical pincers closed around the strap of the pack. As it pulled back away from the wall, the pack came loose and hit the asphalt in the parking lot before anyone had a chance to react. Nothing happened! The robot was able to pick up the device and move it a few feet farther away from the wall, out toward the street. It wasn't able to provide much of a view inside, but there wasn't anyone out there who thought this might be some pack full of dirty clothes. It was too heavy, for a start.

They set up the disruptor at what seemed like a safe distance. Some-one yelled, "FIRE IN THE HOLE" and gave everyone enough time to take cover (the media were several hundred feet away, over near the Denny's). Stone was across the street in the strip club parking lot and ducked down behind some cars. The disruptor fired off its water charge and hit the pack. Again . . . nothing happened.

By now the green polyester pack was a bit messed up. It had been dropped and shot. Stone went over to take a look at the video feed inside the bomb squad truck, but you couldn't really tell much from the small camera. The techs decided to take another shot with the disruptor. This time, when someone started the "FIRE IN THE HOLE" cry, some of the officers were a bit lackadaisical about taking cover. Stone was about 150 feet away, back over at the strip club. This time the disruptor worked too well, and the bomb went off, startling the officers who had been slow to take cover. Fortunately, no one was hurt, but their best chance at evi-dence had just been blown to bits, which meant they were going to spend the next two days scouring the neighborhood for fragments (two days later, a real estate agent found part of the metal plate inside a nearby house she was showing to some prospective buyers).

Charles Stone had a theory about the Otherside bombing, one that was at odds with most everyone else. He thought they were looking at the bombs in the wrong order, that the one that went off was actually supposed to be the second bomb, and the one they found and set off was supposed to be the initial blast. The way he read the scene, the bomb they found had somehow malfunctioned. If it had gone off first, over near the front and side of the club by the main entrance, then it would have caused more casualties but also driven everyone outside. When police got to the scene, they would have looked for high ground to set up their investigation, which meant going around back, where they had a good view of the entire area. That's where the other bomb, the one that actually went off, was hidden. Stone couldn't figure out why the first bomb to go off was in a place where it did little actual damage. What he took away from the scene confirmed what he had seen by studying the Sandy Springs bombing—that this guy had some military training, because this looked like a classic ambush scenario.

The FBI's Woody Johnson had been talking to his behavioral people and realized there was something else at play here. The bomber had hit an abortion clinic and a gay lesbian nightclub in just over a month. Over the weekend, he started calling community leaders, the heads of civil rights groups and synagogues among them, urging extra caution and security. There was no telling what the next target might be, but anyone who read the newspapers knew that less than two months from now, black college students from around the country were going to descend on Atlanta for their spring break party known as Freaknik. There would be tens of thousands of students, cruising, holding street parties, offering a series of choice targets for the bomber.

Hooded man had something else to say. Maybe he hadn't made his message clear enough, maybe he wanted to indulge in a little misdirection. It was time to start talking. It was time to make everyone understand why he was setting off his bombs, why he was doing what he did.

The letters began arriving a couple of days after the bombing. There were four of them, all written and addressed in big block letters, using a felt tip pen, each looking something like a ransom note you would see in a movie, where the author is taking care to disguise their handwriting. The block letters, all in uppercase, slanted slightly to the right. One was addressed to WSB Television CH. 2, the leading local news station, with the words NEWS TIP added and underlined. The others were labeled and sent to A.J.A.C. NEWS TIP (that went to the *Atlanta Journal-Atlanta Constitution*, the local daily newspapers, which were essentially a single edition); NBC NEWS BUREAU (the network, which carried the Olympics, had a bureau in Atlanta); and REUTERS AMERICA NEWS TIP (the London-based wire service also had an Atlanta operation, although this choice would strike investigators as odd; it wasn't nearly as well-known, especially in America or Atlanta, as the other choices). Only the letter to WSB had a zip code. Each letter had the same return address: 170 8th St. Atlanta, GA 30309. There was such an address, and it would have been in the midtown area, but the zip code was wrong.

Each of the letters also bore the same postmark, NORTH METRO GA 30153, and all said PM 23 FEB 1997, the day after the bombings. The Task Force hoped that would help narrow down when and where the letters were sent, but U.S. postal inspectors looked into that lead and had some disappointing news. On weekends, any letter dropped into a mailbox from the city of Macon (ninety miles south of Atlanta) all the way up to the Georgia-Tennessee border would have that postmark. As for the P.M. stamp, if the letter went into a mailbox any time the night of the bombing, it would have been processed the next afternoon and gotten that mark. There was a post office with drive-through mailboxes a block over from the Otherside Lounge. Charles Stone figured that the letters were sent from there, either before the bomber planted his devices or as he was headed out of town. Investigators had collected the letters when they started getting calls from news organizations. They were paying such careful attention because they realized the letters, especially if they were mailed out around the time of the bombing, had to be the real deal, given what the writer knew about the bomb components.

All four were essentially the same. They began by declaring, "THE BOMBINGS IN SANDY SPRINGS AND MIDTOWN WERE CARRIED OUT BY UNITS OF THE ARMY OF GOD." Then came the part that investigators believed only the bomber would know, especially at the time the letter was sent out. The Task Force itself was still collecting evidence, trying to reconstruct the bombs, especially the ones that had just gone off at the Otherside: "YOU MAY CONFIRM WITH THE F.B.I.. THE SANDY SPRINGS DEVICE'S GELATIN-DYNAMITE-POWER SOURCE 6 VOLT D BATTERY BOX DURACELL BRAND, CLOCK TIMERS. THE MIDTOWN DEVICES ARE SIMILAR EXCEPT NO AMMO CANS, TUPPERWARE CONTAINERS INSTEAD—POWER SOURCE SINGLE 6 VOLT LANTERN BATTERIES DIFFERENT SHRAPNEL, REGULAR NAILS INSTEAD OF CUT NAILS."

The letters continued: "THE ABORTION WAS tHE TARGET OF THE FIRST DEVICE. THE MURDER IF 3.5 MILLION CHILDREN EVERY YEAR WILL NOT BE 'TOLERATED'. THOSE WHO PARTICIPATE IN ANYWAY IN THE MURDER OF CHILDREN MAY BE TARGETED FOR ATTACK. THE ATTACK THEREFORE SERVES AS A WARNING: ANYONE IN OR AROUND FACILITIES THAT MURDER CHILDREN MAY BECOME VICTIMS OF RETRIBUTION. THE NEXT FACILITY TARGETED MAY NOT BE EMPTY.

"THE SECOND DEVICE WAS AIMED AT AGENT OF THE SO-CALLED FEDERAL GOVERNMENT I.E. A.T.F. F.B.I. MARSHALLS'S ETC. WE DECLARE AND WILL WAGE TOTAL WAR ON THE UNGODLY COMMUNIST REGIME IN NEW YORK AND YOUR LEGISLATIVE—BUREAUCRATIC LACKEY'S IN WASHINGTON. IT IS YOU WHO ARE RESPONSIBLE AND PRESIDE OVER tHE MURDER OF CHILDREN AND ISSUE THE POLICY OF UNGODLY PREVERSION THAT'S DESTROY-

ING OUR PEOPL.E. WE WILL TARGET ALL FACILITIES AND PERSONell OF THE FEDERAL GOVERNMENT.

"THE ATTACK IN MIDTOWN WAS AIMED AT THE SODOMITE BAR (THE OTHERSIDE). WE WILL TARGET SODOMITES, THERE ORGANIZATIONS, AND ALL THOSE WHO PUSH THERE AGENDA.

"IN THE FUTURE WHERE INNOCENT PEOPLE MAY BE-COME THE PRIMARY CASUALTIES, A WARNING PHONE CALL WILL BE PLACED TO ONE OF THE NEWS BUREAU'S OR 911. GENERALLY A 40 MINUTE WARNING WILL BE GIVEN. TO CONFIRM THE AUTHENTICITY OF THE WARN-ING A CODE WILL BE GIVEN WITH THE WARN AND STATE-MENT."

The Task Force tried to make sure the next line was *not* made public, something they were able to do with one exception—when a Fox News reporter said it over the air during a broadcast. "THE CODE FOR OUR UNIT IS <u>4-1-9-9-3</u>." The writer skipped a line and added, as if it were a signature, the phrase, "DEATH TO THE NEW WORLD ORDER." That was how all four letters ended.

This was a windfall for investigators. The letter writer may have aimed his message at the media, but he was really talking to the Task Force. Park Dietz had paid one visit to Atlanta back in October to help agents begin to draw up a profile, but now he had so much more to go on. When he wasn't talking to the Jeffrey Dahmers and John Hinckleys of the world, this was the way he made his living, trying to build a mental and physical picture of an UNSUB, an unknown subject. He took the words from the letter apart, put them back together, looked over the physical evidence, got briefed by agents on their working theories. Then he came up with a profile. It took him the better part of six weeks, but his seven pages of findings and recommendations would provide the Task Force with the best road map they had and later be proven startlingly prescient.

The first point Dietz made was obvious and one that the Task Force had already confirmed through its lab work, that the letters were written by the person responsible for the clinic and nightclub bombings. The writer knew about the Tupperware and the other components of the Otherside bomb before they had been made public, before even investigators had figured some of them out. That matter having been laid to rest, Dietz then went on to say that the letter writer was also responsible for the Centennial Park bombing. But why then didn't the letter writer claim credit? Dietz argued that there could be a number of causes—he was ashamed, didn't want to tip his hand for a similar type of attack in the future, or might have been surprised that there was such strong public reaction to the event. But Dietz felt the bomber's tagline, "Death to the New World Order" was a tip-off about the Olympics. What, after all, was more representative of the "one-worldism," to use the psychiatrist's phrase, than the Olympics? All that talk of New York and Communism sounded to Dietz like a clear indication the writer was also anti–United Nations and anti–Council of Foreign Relations, both bugbears of the conspiracy-minded ilk that were on the extreme Right. If you hated those folks, then you weren't going to be happy about the Olympics, especially if it was showing up on your doorstep.[5]

Oh, and one more thing, noted Dietz. Despite the opening line claiming credit on behalf of the Army of God, Dietz was unequivocal. All three bombings, he wrote, are the work of an individual, not a group. The Army of God had been a name that had been around for years, and as best as investigators could tell, it was a catch-all name for a loosely knit, if that, group of violent antiabortion protestors. There even was a manual floating around, claiming to be in the group's name, offering advice on how to attack abortion clinics. Maybe, Dietz thought, the bomber had some accomplices or used to belong to a similar-style group, but a shrink's job was to sniff out paranoia, and Dietz found it in large doses in these letters. That much paranoia meant someone who would be extraordinarily wary about trusting others. Dietz thought the bomber was deeply immersed in militia propaganda but that ultimately, he was a lone wolf. Taking note of the paranoia in the milita movement about the Olympics being used as an excuse to crack down on its members, Dietz wondered if the bomber's first action had been triggered by the bust of the Macon militia members arrested a few months before the Games.[6]

"Death to the New World Order" was an awfully elastic concept, thought Dietz. It could easily expand to cover abortion clinics, gays and lesbians, just about any sort of liberal—and all those groups needed to be extremely careful, because the bomber was making it quite clear he was going to strike again. But the New World Order also included federal agents—what the letter writer referred to as the FBI, ATF, and U.S. marshals—and Dietz was quite clear both in his report and in private conversations with the Task Force that they were who the bomber was really after, who he most wanted to kill. If you had any exposure to the militia culture, the FBI and ATF were anathema, being jackbooted thugs and all, the foot soldiers of those one-world New Yorkers. Dietz even wondered if the next time the bomber struck, he might use three devices, including one at the site of a 911 call, in his quest to murder federal agents.[7] If the bomber were ever caught, Dietz recommended that he be interviewed by someone who wasn't a Fed, which later on would have just about everyone looking to Charles Stone as their designated good ole boy.

Dietz was sure the bomber was going to strike again, and he thought the secret code was a tip-off— that the next likely date of an attack was April 19, which just happened to be when Freaknik was in town. The code itself was telling; 4-19-93 was not a date anyone on the far Right nor anyone in the federal government was likely to forget. That was the day the FBI stormed the Branch Davidian compound near Waco, Texas; the day that David Koresh and some of his followers set fire to their compound and others committed mass suicide, killing some eighty-one people. The images of the burning compound were still etched on the public psyche, as well as the belief by many, not just on the far Right, that the government's actions led to both the siege and the deaths.

April 19 was also the date Timothy McVeigh chose two years later for his own personal revenge against the government, bombing the Murrah Federal Office Building in Oklahoma City. Using 4-19 as a code meant the far Right, as if that wasn't already clear enough. Dietz noted that Freaknik, with its crowds of black students, would be in Atlanta during April 19, and he redoubled Woody Johnson's earlier warning that this was a likely target (it would ultimately pass off peacefully, at least from the standpoint of a bombing, although it brought traffic in parts of Atlanta to a standstill for a few days; the students were unaware of the perceived threat against them from the bomber).

Dietz offered a rough sketch of his bomber: white, adult male. Strong enough to carry the Centennial Park bomb a long distance. A blue-collar worker, probably a marginal employee, likely an Atlanta native (given the familiarity with its neighborhoods), had spent time around bombs, possibly through military training. His paranoia meant he was probably not a drug user, since he would be loathe to give up control of his body and mind.[8] For all the detailed analysis, even Park Dietz realized the limits of a profile. When Charles Stone would later mention they were looking at a particular suspect, but that he didn't seem to fit the description laid out in the report, Dietz told him to follow the evidence and ignore the profile if necessary.

Science and one angry prosecutor were about to prove at least one part of Dietz's profile right—that all three bombings were the work of the same man. Nobody out there that night at the Otherside Lounge had to be convinced this was the same guy as the Sandy Springs bomber. That much was pretty obvious, what with the decoy bombs and the choice of targets. But there were still two separate investigations going on, CENTBOMB and TWINBOMB, one run by the FBI and the other by the ATF, and the Task Forces weren't always working well together. The CENTBOMB folks were sure all the bombs were the work of one person; the TWINBOMB team felt differently. Where you sat bureaucratically tended to influence where you stood on the investigation; it was only natural.

U.S Attorney Kent Alexander wanted to settle the matter once and for all. Even though it was highly unusual for him to keep intervening like this, he couldn't see the point of two completely different labs working two different investigations without ever comparing the results. Tired of trying to resolve the FBI-ATF conflict all by himself, he decided to bypass it. His staff had done some research and discovered that the Oak Ridge National Laboratory in Tennessee, just a few hours away, had a sophisticated metallurgical lab that could analyze pieces of steel and with almost DNA-like quality, tell if they came from the same batch. It was something neither the FBI nor ATF labs could do—and they both resisted giving up samples of the steel plate for testing—but it looked like a way to tell whether this common element could link all the bombs and resolve this issue. Interestingly, the ATF had already searched its own records (they had a database called the Explosives Incidents System) and discovered that out of 40,000 comparable bombs, only 20 had employed a metal plate of any kind, something that struck the prosecutors as pretty significant.[9] Alexander ordered that some of the evidence be sent to Oak Ridge for analysis.

The move paid off. The results indicated that the steel plates used in the Centennial Park and Sandy Springs bombings were from the same batch. When some of the Task Force members, including Stone, Behnke, and North, took the findings to the FBI lab, they met with a metallurgist there. Lead prosecutor Sally Yates was also there, and she tried to find out how the scientist would characterize the results if he ever had a chance to take the stand. She kept asking him, can you testify that these plates are an exact match? The metallurgist kept hedging. Finally, when Yates was nearing the point of exasperation, he told her there was something he could say in court—that if anyone tried to go out and find pieces of eleven-gauge steel that were as alike as the plates from the Centennial Park and abortion clinic bombs, they could get a piece a day for a thousand years and still wouldn't find one! Those sorts of odds would work just fine for Yates.

The Task Force was going to another unlikely place for scientific assistance. They had kept working on that time line from Centennial Park, and they thought they had a photo of the bomber, sitting on the bench in front of the sound tower, a hood over his head. The timing was right, and it looked like there was something on his back, probably a pack. Each time they tried to magnify the photo, all they were left with was a blurred-out face. Folks started calling him Blobman, and they even made a wanted poster with his image that hung in the office. Someone had the idea to call in NASA and see if the space agency could work some magic. This time, there was only limited success. No matter how much resolution was added to the photo, Blobman was still . . . Blobman. But the NASA scientists were convinced that it was indeed a pack on Blobman's back.

There was something else that the Task Force became convinced about Blobman—that he was goatee man. By matching up the times, they realized the photo of the hooded man had to be the same man that the Speedo boys had described for Marla's sketch. It had taken them a year, but now they were sure this was their bomber. They weren't doing too well with eyewitnesses from the Otherside, however. It seemed the bomber had learned how not to be spotted after his run-in with Adam Scott in the Sandy Springs parking lot. Some of the investigators had a bit of fun interviewing patrons and, especially, employees of the strip bar across the street, but in the end, what they got was another vague computerized drawing that showed an older bearded man. Like the sketch from Sandy Springs, it was an ATF job, and it was fairly generic. Goatee man aka Blobman was as good as it was going to get.

By November of 1997, the Task Force decided to go public again, showing off all the components from the three bombings. Earlier in the year, in June, they had tried something similar, finally releasing excerpts from the letters, showing the distinctive handwriting. When the FBI had gotten a couple of newspapers to publish the Unabomber's manifesto, someone had recognized it—Ted Kaczynski' s brother—and his tip led them to their man, ending an eighteen-year search. What worked there might work in Atlanta, they thought, but it didn't. Neither did the news conference about the bomb components, no matter how many replica clocks and ammo cans and batteries agents showed to the public. Truth was, the Task Force was running out of leads. It had been almost a year and a half since that night in Centennial Park and getting on ten months since the Sandy Springs bombing, and they were reduced to playing show-and-tell with the media.

Charles Stone knew what might work, what might give them a real shot at catching the bomber, but it was not something you could say out loud, certainly not in earshot of the media. He had learned this lesson the worst way possible years before, working a serial murder case, looking for someone called the Columbus Strangler. Sometimes you reached the point where the only way to catch a serial killer was to wait for him to murder again and hope this time he made a mistake. That's where they had gotten to with the Atlanta bomber.

4.
KND1117

HE HAD GONE dark for almost a year. They had profiled him, tried to give him a name, and somehow bring him to justice. He had never met Park Dietz nor would he have read his profile, so he did not realize how accurately the psychiatrist had pegged him—as an evidence-conscious bomber, although not necessarily a sophisticated one. Someone who was learning as he went, ready to try new things.

This morning there were lots of new things he was ready to try out. He was in a new city, a place that had a long and sad experience with what he was about to do. He had been experimenting again, and this time he was determined not to let a parked car or a malfunction or anything else keep him from killing.

He must have spent some time doing his surveillance, figuring his route in and out of town. This was going to be a lot more complicated than just walking away, getting in his vehicle, and being on the interstate in a matter of minutes. First you infiltrated, got to the scene; then, after you were done, you exfiltrated. He had already infiltrated, a long and careful process that he could do under the cover of night (although you didn't want anyone spotting you and calling the police because they thought you were a prowler).

This one was going to be more involved, more time-consuming, and with a greater chance of screwing up. This would take what was called E&E—escape

and evasion. There were some rules: don't overdo it, don't draw attention to yourself, and don't be too obvious.

He had a couple of close calls back in Atlanta. That first sketch from Centennial Park might have been too close for comfort. This morning he wasn't going to be goatee man or hooded man. He was wig man; if he played this right and happened to be spotted, then the police and Feds would be looking for someone with long brown hair and a long coat. A little bit of a disguise could go a long way, help you get out of town. Misdirection. Keep your pursuers off balance.

Sometime during the night, he had sneaked up to the building and planted his bomb. If you spent any time at all watching the building, you quickly realized a couple of things: there was no surveillance camera, which made it different from the other possible target a few blocks away; and nobody really showed up until right around 7:30 A.M., maybe a few minutes earlier. There was no overnight guard, just the occasional patrol from the university or city police.

He was ready. His bomb was ready. His letters were ready. Drop them in a mailbox on his way out, and then the world would realize he was back.

He stood behind the tree and waited. Today, he was going to kill the right target. Today, a year of planning, of learning new tricks, was going to pay off. Today, everything was going to go according to plan. Today, there weren't going to be any fuckups.

That's what he thought.

He was wrong.

It wasn't Emily Lyons's job to open the clinic. There was usually another nurse who did that, showing up at about 7:30 A.M. to go in, turn on the equipment, fire up the computers, and start waking up the building. Emily would come in a little later, scrub up, and help get the operating rooms ready, especially if it was a day they were doing procedures. But the other nurse was on maternity leave, so on the morning of January 29, 1998, Lyons was the first one scheduled in. She was already dressed in her pink scrubs when she got into her car and headed over to the New Woman, All Women Health Care Clinic on Birmingham's Southside.

There was a rhythm to the Lyons household most mornings. Emily tried to spend some time with her husband Jeff before they went their separate ways, maybe a quiet breakfast. It was just the two of them—her daughters lived with Emily's first husband—and Jeff was usually the first one out the door, headed to his job as a software developer. This was their morning routine, and there was still something fresh about it after four years. That's how long the forty-one-year-old Emily had been working as a nurse at New Woman. And that's how long she had been married to Jeff.[1]

They were coming up on their fourth wedding anniversary, just a little over two weeks away. Emily and Jeff had known each other in college, gone out for a couple of years. He liked to say he proposed to her back then, but it took her fifteen years to accept. They had gotten married, just to different people, and when that didn't work out for either of them, they got back together and started dating again in 1993. They got married a year later, on Valentine's Day. Jeff knew it sounded romantic, but he suspected that Emily preferred that date because she wanted to make sure he wouldn't forget their anniversary.[2]

If you were the early bird at the clinic, you would pull into the parking lot next to the building and wait for the security guard, an off-duty policeman, to get there. Just common sense really, since New Woman was an abortion clinic; doctors and nurses, even patients at the clinic got hassled from time to time. Emily Lyons was a strong supporter of abortion rights, this wasn't just a job to her, and she was often the one who found the mangled baby dolls and other packages that were left on the front steps.[3] It couldn't be called one of the highlights of her four years at the clinic, but Emily was there the day they got a suspicious package and had it X-rayed. Inside was a box of chocolates, and plastic fetuses were attached to them.

But what they got most at the clinic were protestors. Sometimes things got out of hand, and instead of the normal level of shouting and cursing and praying from the sidewalk across the street, you had people getting into the parking lot and slashing your tires or pouring fake blood on you or throwing paint on your car. So, if you were first in, you waited for the guard to get there first, and let him check things out.

The building stood just off Tenth Avenue South, right at the edge of the medical complex for the University of Alabama at Birmingham (UAB).

New Woman, All Women had been there for ten years, a white two-story building with a little burgundy awning over the front entrance. The parking lot was actually what fronted on Tenth Avenue. The building was next to it, up a couple of steps, facing on to a side street called Seventeenth Street. Across the street from the parking lot was a little eatery called the Purple Onion, and then up Seventeenth was another brick one-story medical building. Between those two buildings was another little parking area with a big oak tree that had a thick trunk, wide enough for someone to hide behind. Behind there was an open area, Rast Park, which had a couple of UAB dormitories along its edge.

There was sort of a grid, except that Seventeenth Street, which ran southeast and perpendicular from Tenth Avenue, began to rise, then leveled off a couple of blocks later, and then ran down along the base of what dominated the whole south side of the city, Red Mountain. It was hard to see from the clinic itself, but if you moved up to Rast Park, you could look up and see the side of Red Mountain, see the towers from the TV stations perched up there and see Birmingham's most famous statue, *Vulcan*, the god of fire. This was a steel town, at least it had been, infamous for its smog until the EPA came in and cleaned it up in the mid-'70s, and *Vulcan* was its proud symbol. The streets ran a little crazy as they got closer to the base of the mountain. The only way you could get up there was either climb on foot through Vulcan Park or snake around on another street, Twenty-First.

There had been a protest march the week before to mark the twenty-fifth anniversary of *Roe v. Wade*. A few hundred antiabortion demonstrators had marched by the building and also past another clinic, the Summit Women's Clinic, which was a block away (some investigators would later wonder if the protest march is what had caught the bomber's attention, made him choose Birmingham).[4]

That had been peaceful enough, although security was always an issue. A handful of clinics scattered throughout the state performed abortions, something of a risky proposition this deep in the Bible Belt. One of the clinics, the West Alabama Women's Center in Tuscaloosa, had been firebombed just six months earlier; no one was hurt, but the arsonist did a quarter million dollars' worth of damage.[5] Then there was the bombing six months before at the Sandy Springs Clinic—and no one was likely to forget they weren't that far from Pensacola, where abortion doctors had been murdered in 1993 and 1994. New Woman and Summit may have seemed like they were in a relative cocoon of safety, both being so close to the UAB campus. Still, Summit had gotten a surveillance camera and installed it, even though it wasn't fully operational yet. New Woman had its security guard, but no camera.

The guard this morning was Robert Sanderson, known as Sande to his family and friends. The thirty-four-year-old Sanderson had worked the night shift at the Birmingham Police Department, coming on at 11 P.M. Wednesday. He had spent the evening with a rookie partner, Calvin Crow, because that was his thing, helping to break in the rookies. Everyone expected him to take the sergeant's exam, he was certainly qualified, but they were also grateful he chose not to, because in many ways he was more valuable as a one-on-one real-life tutor. Sanderson and Crow had made a few marijuana busts overnight and talked some football. They were still chewing over the Super Bowl that past Sunday, when Green Bay had stuck it to the New England Patriots. They got off shift at 7A.M., said their good-byes, and Sanderson headed over to the clinic.[6]

Sanderson had taken the job at New Woman because he was trying to make enough money to get his stepson Nick a car. Robert was thinking now that Nick was finishing up high school, it might be time for a family move down to Sarasota, near where his mother-in-law lived. It was certainly a lot warmer on the Florida coast than it was out at the clinic this morning. And Sande had gotten some job offers from police departments down there.[7]

Funny thing was that neither Robert Sanderson nor his wife Felecia was pro-choice.[8] But Sande's personal opinions about abortion didn't matter. He was a police officer, sworn to uphold the law, and that's what he would do during his regular job and during his shifts at the clinic. It sounded corny, but in a way Sanderson was the prototypical Officer Friendly. He volunteered a lot—Explorers, the Diabetes Foundation—and was recognized for his community work by being chosen as an Olympic Torch Bearer in 1996, when the flame was being brought through Alabama on its way to Atlanta. One family would recount how its five-year-old boy met Officer Sanderson at the coffee shop of the Children's Hospital. The boy, who was being treated for leukemia, came up to Officer Sanderson and asked him about his gun. They had a brief talk. Several hours later, when he was off duty, Sanderson showed back up at the hospital with a toy police badge and a teddy bear for the boy.[9]

It was the same way at the clinic. Sanderson was civil to everybody, whether they were an employee of the clinic, a scared first-time visitor, or one of the protestors who showed up on a regular basis. Minzor Chadwick fell into that last category. He spent more time at the clinic than most of the employees. He liked to call himself a "sidewalk counselor," which meant that most mornings during the week, he would arrive at 7:30 A.M. and set up shop on the sidewalk across the street.[10] Chadwick was a retiree in his late fifties who kept a trunk full of brochures about the evils of abortion that he had at the ready, along with a sign that had a baby's picture on it and a big message written across it saying, "MAMA DON'T." Chadwick said he was there to persuade the women not to have an abortion, to find an alternative, and claimed he was ready to help. But he would also shout at them, "One slip and you could die, Mama! Think about it. We don't just say don't do this. We'll help you."[11] There was one thing that you noticed about Chadwick right away: those triple-thick glasses in their wire-rim frames. The man was legally blind and could barely see twenty-five feet away; everything beyond that was just images (which made you wonder, of course, why he had a car).

Chadwick liked Sanderson. He liked the way Sanderson treated him with respect. He liked the way that Sanderson would talk not just to him, but with him. How Sanderson took the time to tell him about his wife and how she stood by him when he got hurt. Chadwick admired that, and he appreciated how Sanderson also protected him. One day outside the clinic it was getting ugly; someone took offense at Minzor's sidewalk harangues, but Officer Sanderson quickly moved in and got the guy out of there, making sure that Minzor was unharmed.[12]

That was the cast of characters at the clinic that January morning. It would start getting crowded in about a half hour, when everybody else started arriving. There were eight patients scheduled, which meant by

8:00 A.M. you might find a dozen or more people either crowded into the lobby just inside the front door or waiting right there outside on the front stoop. But right now, it was the three of them: Emily Lyons, Minzor Chadwick, and Robert Sanderson.

Nobody saw the wigged man behind the oak tree. He had on blue jeans and a long coat. They couldn't see him, but he had the high ground and was just about one hundred feet away, at the most. It was light by now, and soon there would be a clinic full of people. He was ready. The device in his hand was just another remote control when you thought about it, something to turn on a TV or VCR.
    Or a bomb.

Officer Sanderson must have been the first to arrive, sometime before 7:30 A.M. Minzor Chadwick saw him, probably as much by instinct as by actual vision, when he got there around 7:30 A.M. and began getting prepped for his day on the sidewalk. They traded unspoken greetings. Emily Lyons doesn't really remember her actions that morning. What she has pieced together comes from others, including Chadwick, and from the forensics reports and crime-scene analysis.

    Emily was getting out of her car. As she made her way up the short steps from the parking lot to the front door of the building, Officer Sanderson spotted something over near the clinic entrance. Or maybe Emily saw it and said something to Sanderson. There was a little walkway that ran parallel to the front of the building, just a couple of feet from it, with some greenery in between. One of the flowerpots or something next to it was askew. It looked curious enough for Sanderson to want to examine it more closely. Emily might have been exchanging some words with him, your average morning greeting, as she was getting out her keys to the clinic front door. Or she might have paused to watch as he was examining the area. There was a toolbox, half buried in the dirt, tilted up toward the front of the building.

    It was coming up to 7:33 A.M. on Thursday morning.

    Officer Sanderson had one of those retractable police batons. He must have gotten it out and fully extended it, because now he was using it to have a nudge over at the flowerpot, to see what might be there. It wasn't the right procedure, especially if there were a bomb or a booby trap, but it would help him try and figure out what was down there. Then he could call it in if he needed to. Besides, he had been working all night. It was probably nothing, but he was paid to check, and that's what he was doing. It wouldn't have mattered anyway; tipping this thing or poking at it might have actually helped, jostling it, messing up a connection. Officer Sanderson didn't realize there was a device inside the toolbox—that there were dynamite, nails, and a small receiver all packed together, ready to detonate just as soon as someone nearby pressed a button. Of course Sanderson didn't realize any of that, or he would have backed himself out of there and Emily Lyons along with him, and yelled for Minzor Chadwick across the street to get away while he called for help.

Emily Lyons was standing over by the door. Officer Sanderson was five or six steps away, in between her and whatever he was looking at along that front little walk of the clinic. His baton was out, and he was leaning toward that flowerpot, using the baton as a pointer. Imagine how it must have looked to Minzor Chadwick, a couple of dim images in some sort of tableau, people he recognized more by instinct than by actual sight.

Now imagine how it looked to the bomber as he peered out from behind the tree. He was really the best eyewitness of all. Fifteen, twenty, even thirty minutes later he would have a full house, maybe a dozen targets. He had set up the bomb so the blast would go toward the front door and the waiting area just beyond. That was his intended kill zone.

Instead, once again, something was going to go wrong, something was going to keep him from upping the body count. That policeman was looking at his device, and sooner or later he was going to figure this out.

It was decision time.

The bomber, the wigged man, decided to cut his losses, take what he could get. And he could get a policeman, not to mention the woman in the pink scrubs.

He had warned them, hadn't he, in his Atlanta letters? They couldn't say they weren't told.

He pressed the button and set off the bomb.

There were no parked cars between the bomb and Robert Sanderson when it went off, the very thing that saved Mike Rising's life outside the Sandy Springs Professional Building. Standing right over the bomb, Sanderson never had a chance. His arm was blown off, his leg knocked out behind him. Metal from the bomb ripped into his head. The blast vaporized much of his uniform, blew it right off him, leaving his gun belt. One can only hope that his death took place in a merciful instant. Robert Sanderson's body lay back and away from the building, thrown over by the force of the explosion. But he had been standing at least partially between Emily Lyons and the bomb, and he acted as a shield, absorbing and protecting her from the deepest fury.

Nevertheless, stunning and swift violence was visited upon Emily Lyons's body. A partial inventory—the bomb tore her eyelids off; ripped up her lip. An inch-and-a-half piece of metal pierced her right eye, blinding her. Hundreds of nails shredded her face, torso, and legs. A tooth was broken; she had a hole in her abdomen and her intestines were ripped up. A piece of circuit board was lodged at the top of her liver. And yet, she was still alive despite the incredible trauma.

Emily had a gift for understatement. Since she had no memory of that day, later she would simply say she got up, went to work, and came home eight weeks later—after having a bad hair day. A photo taken minutes after the explosion shows her body in a heap, framed by the clinic door. When her husband was finally allowed to get close enough to the clinic several days later, he would see the building gouged with nails, except for one human-shaped silhouette, where the wall was relatively unmarked. That had been where Emily was standing when the nails embedded themselves into her flesh at high velocity.[13]

*   *   *

Jeff Lyons was just getting out of the shower that morning when the phone rang. One of Emily's colleagues had just made it to the scene and heard about the bomb. She told Jeff what had happened and said she was trying to do a head count, to see who was where. He told her that Emily had left for work a while before, that she was opening up the clinic today. Jeff hurriedly got dressed, waiting for the phone to ring, willing it to ring, wanting Emily to be on the other end.

But when he didn't hear anything after fifteen minutes of pacing, he did the only thing he knew to do and drove down toward the clinic. He couldn't get anywhere near it, of course, because the police had already backed people out of the area. He was frantic, by now fearing that his wife was either dead or badly hurt. Then his pager started vibrating, and he recognized the prefix as being from the UAB Hospital, which was less than two minutes from the clinic. Emily must be alive, otherwise they wouldn't be paging him! He made his way to the emergency room, where someone began telling him about Emily's injuries. Jeff may have been dazed, but he knew what to be worried about. A perforated liver could kill her, he knew, so he was listening for that. One of the doctors told him they might have to amputate one of Emily's legs, maybe both. What he couldn't figure out was if her injuries were that bad, how was she still alive?[14]

Across the street from the clinic, Minzor Chadwick thought he saw two people by the door, knew that one of them was likely to be his friend, Officer Sanderson. Then he felt a sharp rush of wind, heard a loud crack, and was showered by dirt from the blast. He couldn't think straight and wasn't sure what was going on. It was like waking from a deep sleep. Chadwick thought someone might be targeting him, so he began to walk away. He heard a scream and a cry of, "Oh my God!" When he looked over at the clinic, he realized there was something on the ground, something that might be a body. Whatever it was lay in a heap.[15]

Chadwick wasn't aware there had been someone behind him, back up by the tree. Even if he had turned, even if he had regular vision instead of being legally blind, it would not have been in time to see the man turn around and walk away. Chadwick barely had his wits about him and didn't realize that his very presence in front of the clinic was going to make a lot of people suspicious. They didn't know that he considered Officer Sanderson a friend. The police would have plenty to ask Chadwick that day, and they would spend six hours doing it before they released him—What did he see? Why was he out by the clinic that time of morning? Just how much did he hate abortion—enough to bomb the clinic and kill Officer Sanderson? Chadwick would cry when he found out that Sande was dead. There were antiabortion protestors who would not condemn the murder of abortion doctors. But Chadwick wanted the police and everyone else to be clear how he felt. Abortion was murder, as far as he was concerned, but so was this.[16]

The bomber might have paused for a minute to check out his handiwork. Was he admiring it, or was he already trying to figure out what to do differently next time? This was where preparation came in. He had a hike ahead of him, and he wasn't used to doing it in daylight. Time to get going.

He turned and walked away from the clinic. He may not have even known the name of the park he was cutting through. Rast Park.

He didn't realize someone was watching.

In legal parlance, the student would become known as WN-1, witness one. To many, including Officer Robert Sanderson's friends and colleagues, and to members of the Task Force in Atlanta, they had another word: hero. WN-1 was an African-American medical student at UAB who lived in Rast Hall, one of the dorms that lined Rast Park. Like so many in the neighborhood, he heard the blast and felt the windows shake. They didn't blow out here, but even at sorority houses blocks away, the blast shattered glass. He didn't call 911, not yet at least, but several people were already doing that.

WN-1 was doing his laundry in a room on the ground floor when the bomb went off. He said he looked out the window, and saw bluish white smoke rising near the Domino's Pizza a block away (it was across the street from the clinic). He wasn't exactly sure what was going on, but the noise and the plume made it pretty clear this wasn't anything good. What really seemed odd was that as everyone outside seemed to be walking or running toward the blast, there was this guy walking away from it, calm as you please. That was enough to catch his attention. Unconsciously, he was already beginning to assimilate the man's features. You got pretty good at that sort of thing in medical school—height, weight, age, features. What he saw was a white male about six foot one and 175 pounds, maybe in his mid-thirties with shoulder-length brown hair. The man was wearing dark pants and a long coat, one that reached down to his thighs. He had on a black baseball cap and a black backpack, which didn't look like there was anything in it.[17]

Noticing the guy wasn't what made the medical student a hero. He could have easily left it there, turned around from the window in the laundry room, and called 911. What he did next might be called the better part of stupidity or bravery, but it is what changed the course of the investigation and provided the silver bullet that investigators in Atlanta had been talking about and hoping for since July 27, 1996. The medical student decided he wanted a closer look at this man. He thought there was something too suspicious about the way he was walking away from the scene. So the medical student ran downstairs and got in his car, ready to give chase. He didn't have a cell phone with him.

The medical student headed in the direction that he thought the man was walking and pretty soon spotted him again. Now he was on Sixteenth Street South, continuing to walk away from the scene and making his way toward the base of Red Mountain. As the student slowly drove, he saw the man duck into an alleyway between Fourteenth and Fifteenth Street South, about five blocks from the clinic. He saw the man reach with his right hand into his right pocket and pull out something that appeared to be balled up. Now the last thing in the world the medical student was going to do was drive into the alley after the guy, so he pulled his vehicle around in front of an apartment complex on Fifteenth Avenue South and waited.

His instincts paid off. Moments later, a white man came walking out from around the apartments, where the alley had been, and began walking down the street eastbound. The man had changed his appearance in several ways: he had lost the hat and the coat; now he was wearing what seemed to be a light-colored shirt. The man's hair was still dark, but much shorter and pressed down, and now he was wearing sunglasses. He was still carrying a backpack, and it still appeared to be empty, but he had a blue plastic shopping bag in his hand, one of those Wal-Mart type carrier bags, and it seemed like it was full. Despite these superficial changes, the medical student was sure this was his man. Same backpack, same general features, same guy. He seemed to have hat hair, as if he had just removed something from his head.

The man turned out of the alley and headed up the street. The student, WN-1, wanted another look at the man, so he said he did something else that in retrospect seems foolhardy or out of a bad TV show. He drove his car down the street and stopped—as if his car was having mechanical trouble. Then WN-1 waited for the suspicious man to walk by. As he got out of the car, he noticed the man was wearing aviator-style sunglasses.

It was time to call for help. The student was trying not to let the other man know he was following him, but at the same time he was trying to flag someone down and have them call the police. There were a few people outside, maybe because they had heard the bomb blast and now the sirens, maybe because it was time to go to work. The student tried to flag down some motorists and find one with a cell phone. The first person he asked for help was a fellow black male student driving a silver car, but this guy blew him off, saying he had to get to class. Finally, after seeing the man walk off, still carrying the blue plastic bag, he got the attention of a woman in the neighborhood. Call the police, he told her, tell them where I am and tell them I'm following a guy who might have something to do with the explosion. By the time he got all this out, he realized he had lost track of his guy.

This is where it got strange. The medical student got back in his vehicle and drove around looking for the suspicious man, maybe twenty-five or thirty minutes, he thought. The way the streets are around that neighborhood, eventually you are going to either run right into the base of Red Mountain or you have to go over to Twentieth South, which wiggles around and starts climbing in a couple of switchbacks. That's what WN-1 did, still looking for his suspect. Eventually, Twentieth tops out and then starts to come back down the other side. If you are driving it fast, it takes fewer than five minutes, but if you are going slow, keeping a lookout, it can take much longer.

The medical student was looking for a place to stop and make a phone call, so he pulled into a McDonald's on Twentieth. It was on the other side of the street from Vulcan Park, which ran up one side of Red Mountain and down the other. He asked someone at the counter, who asked the manager, if he could use the phone there and call 911 because he had seen someone who he thought might be responsible for a bombing. Imagine the odds of this. He is on the phone, telling the 911 operator what he saw and why he thinks this man is who he saw walking away from the bombing—and then he looks out the window. Across the street, coming down along the sidewalk that borders the park and mountain, is his man! He looked a little bit different now than how he had just described him, but that was him, that was the guy he followed.

WN-1, the medical student, was so excited that he was talking loud enough to attract the attention of a customer in McDonald's. This man, who would become known as WN-2, the second witness, was a lawyer. He looked out the window, spotted the man that WN-1 was talking about, and started calling out his own description of the man back to WN-1, who repeated it to the 911 operator. WN-2 said the man was a white male, around six feet tall, approximately 180 pounds, with shoulder-length dark hair. He was wearing a black baseball cap, a green and black plaid shirt over a long-sleeve black shirt and had a black backpack that seemed full. WN-2, the lawyer, thought the man he was describing must be trying to hide his face because he was wearing sunglasses on what was an overcast morning—and he had his hat pulled low in the front.

Both witnesses, the medical student and the lawyer, watched as the man turned right from the sidewalk and began climbing back into the woods on some sort of trail. The lawyer thought the man must have known where he was going, since the trail didn't seem well marked. A Birmingham police cruiser was actually on the scene quickly, and WN-2 described the man again, then pointed out where he had vanished into the woods. The officers went across the street and began to search.

Neither the medical student nor the lawyer was going to quit now. They were both too invested in finding this guy. They got into their respective cars and started looking for their man again. When you turn left out of the McDonald's, back onto Twentieth Street South, you almost immediately hit a traffic light. The street that intersects Twentieth at a right angle is Valley Avenue, and when you turn right, you are tracking a parallel course to where the man disappeared into the woods. Hoping to get lucky yet again, that's what they each did.

The lawyer, WN-2, was the first one to drive down Valley Avenue. He didn't see the man out his right window, so after a short distance he pulled down a side street that ran back behind some apartments. There was a very small parking area and beyond it a wooded area that ran up into Vulcan Park. As luck would have it, he noticed a white man wearing a baseball cap standing next to a gray Nissan pickup truck that had a camper shell on the back. The lawyer pulled up alongside. The man moved over to the opposite side of the truck. WN-2 thought it was the same man he had seen near the McDonald's, and now it looked like the man was putting something in the back of the truck. He noticed the truck was parked with its nose toward Valley Avenue, so he took his own car and drove around the other side of the parking lot where he did a U-turn. A few seconds later, he was pulled up right behind the gray Nissan, both waiting for the light to turn green and take them back out onto Valley Avenue. The lawyer had a chance to see the license plate of the pickup as they waited. On a coffee cup, he wrote down a North Carolina plate number, KND1117.

When the light changed, WN-2 followed the truck as it turned left on Valley. They were headed back to the intersection of Twentieth, just below where the McDonald's was. The lawyer didn't even stop to think he might be putting himself in any sort of danger; if he had thought that, he probably never would have given chase a few minutes earlier. What the lawyer did next was pull up alongside the pickup, on his left. He looked over through his passenger window and tried to make eye contact with the guy, who wasn't wearing sunglasses anymore. He got a good look of the man's profile, but no eye contact. They were coming back up to the intersection. The lawyer noticed on his other side that the police officers were coming out of a little road that led up into Vulcan Park, so he broke off, turned to the left in order to tell them what he had seen. He noticed that the man in the gray pickup was turning right on Twentieth Street, away from the McDonald's, toward a road that would take him to the highway. That was the last time he saw the man, but just a few days later he would see a man's picture in the newspaper and tell agents that was who he saw drive away in the gray Nissan.

The medical student was still in the hunt. No way was he going to give up, not after he had found the man again at the McDonald's. Maybe it was adrenaline, but he was now also back in his car. First he turned up into Vulcan Park, but didn't see anything and quickly turned around. Then he drove down Valley Avenue, trying to spot the guy with the backpack. He was a couple of minutes behind the lawyer but following the same route. As he headed slowly down Valley, just coming up to that little side street where the lawyer had turned down (though he had no way of knowing that), he was scanning both sides of the street. The medical student said he saw a gray Nissan pickup coming toward him from the opposite direction. He thought the driver was the man he had been following, because he was wearing similar clothes. The same man he had seen walk away from the clinic, the man he saw turn down the alley and come out again, without a coat or a wig. The man he had seen outside McDonald's after he lost him at the base of Red Mountain.

Now the medical student thought he was in that pickup truck, headed the other way, and he was going to lose him again. So he did a quick U-turn and came up behind him. The med student read off the front plate to himself, then wrote it down: North Carolina, KND1117. At this point, WN-1 was stuck in his own lane by traffic and had to turn. That's when he lost contact with the pickup as he saw it continue through the intersection.

Wigged, baseball capped, short-haired man most likely didn't realize he had been spotted. Why should he? Not with his various feints. Who could have followed his path across the park, through the side streets, into the other park, up the side of a mountain, back out onto the sidewalk, into the woods, and to his truck. A wig, no wig, a cap, no cap, sunglasses, no sunglasses, a coat, no coat. He knew what he was doing. Now all he had to do was find a mailbox and drop off his letters, then head out of town. Head home, nobody the wiser.

A federal prosecutor isn't supposed to be one of the first people on the scene. Doug Jones was four months into his job as U.S. attorney for Birmingham and northern Alabama. He was on his way that morning to breakfast with a reporter when he heard on the radio first about a traffic jam over near UAB, then the bombing. Like his colleague Kent Alexander in Atlanta, Jones knew that abortion clinic bombings were right there near the top of your responsibility as a U.S. attorney these days. He called his office, told them to call Washington, and then headed over to the site, which happened to be near where he was. By the time he got there, the university police had been joined by the Birmingham police. Emily Lyons was being taken to the nearby emergency room at UAB, but Officer Sanderson's body was still out in front of the clinic.

Jones knew all about Birmingham's past. How back in the early '60s, it had earned the ignominious title of "Bombingham" because the Klan and others blew up a church and other places in the city. Jones had a personal connection to that era; as a law student, he spent time in the courtroom watching prosecutors finally win a conviction for the infamous Sixteenth Street Baptist Church bombing that killed four little girls (Jones would later take on the prosecution of the other church bombers and finally bring them to justice). But this morning, Jones was seeing the return of Bombingham firsthand.[18]

There was a problem at the scene. Shortly after Jones got to the clinic, the bomb dogs showed up. Atlanta had made everyone aware of the danger of a secondary device, and now one of the dogs smelled explosives. Everyone was pulled back immediately, and a perimeter was established. A bomb robot was brought in. But no one had a chance to remove Officer Sanderson's body. It lay there, exposed to the elements, exposed to the news helicopters flying overhead, and exposed to the curious who were watching from the surrounding buildings. They weren't even sure if there was another bomb right near him, ready to explode, when emergency workers moved in to get his body. This went on for what seemed like hours. One senior FBI official on the scene would have nightmares about that time for years to come. Everyone standing at the edge of the scene felt helpless until they got an all clear from the bomb techs. Finally, they were able to move in and remove Officer Sanderson's body and begin to work the scene.

Robert Sanderson was the sixth person killed in abortion clinic violence in America. The others—usually doctors or their escorts—had been shot. There had been many bombings at clinics all over the country, but Officer Sanderson was the first person to die during one. When he was buried several days later, his fellow police officers from the city, state, and indeed all over the country showed up. It was a sign of respect for the man and how he died that this was one of the largest funeral processions in Alabama history. Locals would say the cortege was as long as the one when perhaps the most famous of all Alabamians, football coach Paul "Bear" Bryant, was laid to rest a few years earlier.

Charles Stone wasn't thinking silver bullet when he got word of the Birmingham bombing. It was too early for that. It was just after 8:30 A.M. in Atlanta (they were in a different time zone, even though the two cities were only 140 miles apart), right after the bombing, when word began making it to what was now known as the Southeast Bomb Task Force. Stone didn't wait for this to come up in discussion at the morning meeting he was about to attend. He didn't have to, since the GBI bomb techs were his guys. What he knew at that point was that an abortion clinic in Birmingham had been bombed, and the last time there had been a clinic bombing like that, not a firebombing, was in Sandy Springs. If he got one of his guys over there quick, maybe they could help out with any secondary devices. And maybe they could turn up a crucial piece of evidence. All the protocol stuff, the interagency, interstate stuff could wait. Of course, it didn't hurt that the guy he sent over, Joel Criswell, was from Alabama (it turned out his brother had also grown up with the Birmingham police chief) and had been trained in a new way of handling secondary devices.[19]

By lunchtime, in between what he was hearing from his man in Birmingham and what was coming over the teletype, Stone was starting to think they might have finally gotten their break in the case, although at a terrible cost. The Birmingham Police Department and the Alabama State Troopers had put out a BOLO—Be On the Lookout—for a 1989 gray Nissan pickup truck with North Carolina tag number KND1117. There was even a description of a possible suspect, a man wearing a green plaid shirt, jeans, and boots, who had last been seen wearing a brown wig. He was to be considered armed and dangerous.

At the Task Force, they were doing what the Alabama State Police and by now the North Carolina folks were doing. Everyone was searching through any database they could find, trying to figure out who the truck was registered to, where did he live, and just who in the hell he was. The Task Force had something called TAG, the Technical Assessment Group, and it was working at high speed, now that it seemed like they finally had a live lead.

Everybody started getting the same hits on their computers. The truck was registered to someone named Eric Robert Rudolph. His address, at least when he got his driver's license in 1991, was 30 Allen Avenue in Asheville, North Carolina. Asheville was a beautiful city set in the Blue Ridge Mountains, up near Tennessee, Alabama, and Georgia. Its claim to fame was as the birthplace of author Thomas Wolfe. Or if you had ever seen the movie, *Being There*, with Peter Sellers, then you would have seen a big mansion. That was the Biltmore Estate, Asheville's most recognizable landmark, built by one of the Vanderbilts as a getaway. This afternoon, a whole bunch of Feds were about to converge on Asheville, but not to sightsee.

Charles Stone's boss decided that Stone should go up to Asheville on behalf of the Task Force. Already this thing involved the FBI, the ATF, and the Alabama police, and now they were talking about North Carolina. Which meant, in addition to more locals, a different FBI field office and a different ATF field office. It was hard enough getting these guys to share with the state guys, the local guys, and each other. But even worse, they wouldn't always share with themselves—one FBI field office to another. The head of the Task Force these days was a guy named

Woody Enderson, who had coincidentally just come from being the number two at the FBI's North Carolina field office. Now here he was sending Stone, a GBI agent, up to this meeting in Asheville as if he expected that it might be easier for his resident good old boy, rather than another Fed, to handle this tricky diplomatic situation. Especially if this turned out to be their guy as well. The politics were getting to be more complicated than the actual investigation!

By the time Stone got up to Asheville and joined the Fed fest at a local hotel, there was a picture of Rudolph waiting for him. It sure looked like the description that had been put out in the BOLO, and the height and weight listed on his license also were a close fit. But finding Rudolph was not proving to be as easy as finding his picture. He wasn't at the Allen Avenue address. There was another possible location in Nashville, Tennessee, that came up on a trace, but that one was also out of date. The North Carolina State Bureau of Investigations (NCSBI) was working on coming up with other possible locations, but it was hard going. They got a hit on a possible location in Topton, which was two hours away from Asheville, down in the western corner of the state in Macon County. But Rudolph didn't live there either; he had moved from that address awhile back. There seemed to be another address, a trailer in Marble, which was in neighboring Cherokee County, which also failed to check out. Whoever this Rudolph was, he moved around and he didn't seem to leave a very easy trail to follow.

This went on through the night and into the next day. On the morning of January 30, Charles Stone decided to return to Atlanta with the picture of Eric Robert Rudolph. He left behind one of his GBI agents to keep an eye on things up there, be a pipeline for information that the Task Force needed to know about, just in case the Feds in North Carolina were slow to keep everyone else in the loop. The local sheriffs in Macon and Cherokee County were seeing all the bulletins coming out from the FBI and NCSBI, and they started looking for Rudolph as well, since there was a chance he was still in the vicinity. But so far, the feds had not called the local sheriffs.

Rudolph's identity hadn't leaked out to the media yet, but it was only a matter of time. The day before, when the BOLO was broadcast, a number of news organizations picked up the information off their police scanners. They knew about the license plate number and the description of the truck. There was no way to keep a lid on this, and the U.S. attorney didn't want to; he was ready to go public. At this point, the ATF and FBI were still in the very first stages of the investigation; they were at the bomb site picking up fragments, just beginning to figure out the device. They had already picked up one important piece of information that at first blush suggested this might not be the same bomber as Atlanta. The bomber had used what they called "command detonation," or what we would call remote control, instead of a timer. The FBI and Birmingham Police Department were busy doing thousands of interviews, stopping cars and pedestrians in the vicinity of the clinic the morning after the bombing, to see if anyone had noticed anything unusual the day before. The most that was going to be said about Rudolph at this point was that he was a material witness, which meant he could be held in custody if he was found, but he wasn't officially a suspect.

Doug Jones decided to go public. That afternoon, Jones had a news conference, along with the local heads of the FBI and ATF.[20] He revealed the identity of the man who owned the truck that was seen leaving the scene after the clinic bombings and said that he was wanted for questioning. His name was Eric Robert Rudolph, and his last known address was in Marble, North Carolina, but that had turned out to be wrong. "Don't draw any conclusions," Jones said, "Rudolph is only a material witness." He hoped that Rudolph would come forward and talk with the police, but in the meantime there was a material witness warrant for Rudolph.

Some of the investigators were already sure that Rudolph was their man, or at least they were hoping he was. Not just for Birmingham but also for the bombings in Atlanta. They had waited a long time to catch a break, and now it looked like they had. All they needed to do was work the evidence and talk to this Rudolph character. That part should be easy. Someone was bound to have his address, and maybe he would turn himself in. Then they could clear all this up. No problem.

5.
HIDE-AND-SEEK

IT WAS THURSDAY afternoon around 5:30 P.M., and Eric Rudolph wanted a movie. That wasn't unusual. He was a regular at Plaza Video, a small independent video store in a little strip shopping center in Murphy, North Carolina, a town not big enough to rate its own Blockbuster franchise. Eric would hit the store several times a week. He didn't talk much, but he was in there enough that store workers got a sense of him anyway. One thing they knew, he was prompt. Video stores make a good chunk of change off of late fees, but Rudolph had never been tardy with a video before.[1]

The clerk noticed that Eric was clean-shaven and his hair was wet, like he had just gotten out of the shower. It must have been a fairly quick turnaround, since one of Rudolph's neighbors had noticed his gray Nissan truck arrive at his trailer about thirty minutes before.[2] The clean-shaven look was a change. Someone who had seen Eric days before was struck by his rough-looking appearance and one-quarter-inch beard. When Rudolph had been in the store earlier in the week, either on Sunday or Monday, the clerk had noticed he had shaved his scruffy beard into a Fu Manchu look. But this afternoon, on Thursday January 29, all of the facial hair was gone.

Rudolph didn't linger. Today's choice was *City of Industry*, a hard-edged heist film starring Harvey Keitel and Timothy Hutton. Keitel is a retired criminal who gets lured back into the action by his brother, played by Hutton. But after they knock off a score in Palm Springs, another of their partners, played by Stephen Dorff, kills Hutton and the fourth member of the crew, and runs off to L.A. with the loot. Harvey Keitel does what he often does, which is to say he does more killing than talking, and it all ends up bloody and noirish. Rudolph had already rented and watched two other videos this week. On Sunday, he had rented *The Game*, a Michael Douglas–Sean Penn film where Douglas is a rich businessman who is caught up in a virtual reality game (Penn is his brother) and suddenly finds himself on the lam. That one was part mystery, part science fiction, and quite a change from Monday's choice, *Picture Perfect*, a romantic comedy starring Jennifer Anniston, which had been pretty much trashed by reviewers.

It was 5:31 P.M. EST on January 29, 1998, when Rudolph rented *City of Industry* for the night and walked out the door of Plaza Video.[3] If he was aware that his truck had been spotted in Birmingham or that he was about to be named a material witness in the clinic bombing, it certainly didn't appear that way. By the time he left Plaza Video, it had been nine hours since the New Woman clinic bombing (the distance between Birmingham and Murphy is about 240 miles, mostly interstate, and you can do it easily in five hours without getting near the speed limit). The BOLO on Eric's truck had been out for hours. The meeting of federal agents was just getting under way in a hotel in Asheville, which is two hours' drive from Murphy. They were about to get a copy of Eric Robert Rudolph's driver's license and run down the address in Asheville. Eric, on the other hand, was making the short, ten-minute drive home to his trailer from Plaza Video, ready to settle in for the night and watch Harvey Keitel shoot his way through the L.A. underworld.

Rudolph was back at Plaza Video the next morning, just as it was opening up, returning *City of Industry* and grabbing another video. This one was *Kull the Conqueror*, a bad knockoff of *Conan the Barbarian*. Which made sense because they were both based on stories from the same author, Robert E. Howard, and Kull was supposed to be Conan's son. This one didn't have Arnold Schwarzenegger, it had Kevin Sorbo, whose claim to fame was starring in *Hercules: The Legendary Journeys* on TV, and the video resembled nothing so much as one of those Son of Hercules movies that came out in the '50s and '60s. Eric didn't dally inside the video store. He rented the movie at 10:05 A.M. EST on January 30, 1998. Several hours later, at 2:40 P.M. EST, he went grocery shopping at a local supermarket called Ingle's.

Jim Russell, an FBI agent based in Asheville, had been on Rudolph's trail since a few hours after the bombing. He was the one who had gone out to Allen Avenue, the address on Rudolph's driver's license, and discovered it was an apartment complex. There were no Rudolphs living there and the only Rudolph who *had* lived there was named Patricia. She had left a forwarding address and number in Hendersonville, which was a town about twenty-five miles south of there. Russell called that number and reached a man who said his name was Keith Rhodes and, yes, he knew Eric Rudolph, that was his brother-in-law.

Keith and his wife, Maura, agreed to come up to Asheville for an interview with Russell later that same day. They told Russell they had seen Eric a week earlier, when he came to their house on Saturday in his pickup truck, hoping to see their son's basketball game (he got there too late and missed it). The couple gave the agent a bit of background about Eric: he was a former paratrooper who had tried and failed to make it in the Army Special Forces. His mother's name was Patricia, which cleared up the link to the address in Asheville, and she currently lived in Florida. Neither Keith nor Maura, who was Eric's sister, knew where Eric lived—he had told them Tennessee but never gave them an address. He was always secretive when he called them, claiming he was using a pay phone. Eric could be there, but they also thought he might live around a small town called Topton, since that's where the family used to live. They explained Topton was about two hours away, closer to the North Carolina–Georgia border, right on the line between Macon and Cherokee Counties. It was real mountain country.

The Feds decided it was time to reach out to the locals and here is where they began wrong-footing themselves, setting the tone for what would be years of hard feelings. The ATF wasn't so bad at dealing with state and local police; many of its agents had started out in those ranks and worked their way up to the federal level. But the FBI played things a bit differently. It had one program where it brought state and local police to its National Academy in Quantico and trained them in the finer arts of investigation. Aside from that it was usually all take and no give. Flash the credentials and expect awe and obedience, even if it was some twenty-eight year old with little real investigative work talking to an experienced local cop. They could be good and they could be great working a case, but the FBI wasn't going to win any popularity contests and they weren't going to share more information than they had to with the locals.

That's the way it was shaping up in the hunt for Rudolph. When Charles Stone was up in Asheville picking up the picture of Rudolph, he suggested it might be a good idea to call the sheriffs out in those counties. Instead, Russell called the North Carolina State Bureau of Investigation agent who lived in Andrews, which was the closest town to Topton. Russell told Tom Frye, the local SBI agent, that he would come over there the next morning. In the meantime, he asked him to run some checks with the local utilities and see if he could come up with an address for Eric Rudolph.

By the time Russell arrived in Andrews the next morning, Frye had already run the utilities checks and come up empty. Russell and Frye decided their next step was to visit local post offices in Andrews, Topton, and Marble (another nearby hamlet). They got a lead at the Topton Post Office. The postmaster didn't have a current address for Rudolph, but an employee remembered that Eric had grown up there and that he had a friend from high school named Randy Cochran. Only there was no address for Randy Cochran, so they spent several hours driving around, looking for him. This was no easy task, since Topton was less a town and more a collection of isolated mountain roads on the border of Cherokee and Macon Counties.

Russell and Frye finally pulled into Randy Cochran's driveway after dark, certainly past 6:00 P.M. Cochran must have seen their headlights, because he came out to meet them. Russell was certainly surprised by the first words out of Cochran's mouth. You're looking for Eric Rudolph, aren't you? Come on in, it's all over the news, he told the startled agents. Sure enough, when they came inside Cochran showed them CNN, which had already carried the announcement about Eric from U.S. Attorney Doug Jones in Birmingham. No one had told them that Jones was going public. Russell thought this was supposed to be done quietly and that the arrest warrant, which had been issued earlier that afternoon, would remain sealed.

Randy Cochran did have some information for them. He thought Eric was living near Murphy, a larger town just a few miles away. At that point, Russell got a second unwelcome surprise. Frye pulled him aside and explained a little bit about the geography of the area. Andrews and Topton were on the eastern end of Cherokee County (Topton was actually just over the line in Macon County) and that's where he had checked with the utility companies. But Murphy was big enough to have its own post office and power company; Frye hadn't checked there. He'd better go call the sheriff and see if he could help them out.

Which was how Jack Thompson came to find out the Feds were interested in Eric.[4] Not that they told him much—only that Rudolph was wanted for questioning. Thompson grumbled a bit, as he was wont to do. It would have probably been easy for some agent to mistake Thompson for a local yahoo. Sure, he was a native of Cherokee County, you could hear it in the Southern twang of his voice. But that didn't mean he hadn't spent thirty years of his life as a federal employee before getting elected sheriff in 1986; he was off fighting fires and enforcing the law for the U.S. Forest Service (not to say that he was dumb or crazy enough to be one of those smokejumpers; anyone who jumped out of a plane that was flying perfectly well was nuts in his book). Thompson had more miles on him than any of these FBI agents, because you couldn't spend your time fighting the big fires back East; that meant places like Montana and Colorado and Wyoming. He also knew the woods around Cherokee County better than just about anyone (except perhaps Eric Rudolph), something that the Feds would spend the next few years forgetting to take advantage of. But that's getting ahead of the story.

Sheriff Thompson knew Investigating 101. He rustled up someone from the post office in Murphy. It turned out there was an Eric Rudolph who rented a box there, but he had used the driver's license with the Asheville address. Rudolph wasn't in the phone book, that would have been too easy. It was after hours, but he also got to someone at Murphy Power and pretty soon they got back to him. Yes, there was an Eric Rudolph on their books; they showed him paying for electricity on a trailer out on Caney Creek Road (it was actually Cane Creek Road until someone at the Highway Department had added an extra letter; now you called it either Cane or Caney Creek).

It could have, might have, all ended there, everything that was to follow. When Sheriff Thompson made his call back to the Feds a few minutes later, he told them about the address for Rudolph and advised them that it was a just a few minutes from Murphy. Should he go get the guy? Just wait, we'll send some of our folks over and check it out, he was told. That was about 6:30 P.M. EST, according to Russell, earlier according to Thompson. Nobody told Thompson to put some surveillance on the trailer, nobody said go on ahead and pick him up.

All the Feds said was wait, because we want to handle this, we want to talk with him, not much more than that. Playing it close to the vest was their style, though later on some of the more pissed-off locals would wonder whether they just wanted to hog the glory and make the arrest, overlooking the fact that Rudolph was still only wanted as a material witness at this point. Russell made plans to meet up with Thompson's folks at the Ford dealership, a mile or so down the road from this Caney Creek place. They would get directions from there. The rendezvous was set for 8:00 P.M. EST.

The clock was already running. It had been since Doug Jones held his news conference at 5:00 P.M. CST (that was 6:00 P.M. in North Carolina) and went public with Rudolph's ID. At that time, all investigators had was another address, the one that Jones mentioned in Marble, North Carolina, that hadn't checked out. Jones was worried that Rudolph's name was about to leak, and he wanted to get out in front on this one, at least make sure the media got the name and the information right. If reporters started going to air with the news that Rudolph was a suspect, it could get ugly à la Richard Jewell. Jones laid it all out during the news conference—they wanted to question a man named Eric Robert

Rudolph, last known address Marble, North Carolina, but they didn't know where he was. They just wanted to talk with him, but they were issuing a warrant for something known as a material witness. No, he wasn't a suspect, so they were hoping Rudolph or someone else would help them out by coming forward with some information.

Just when and how Eric heard his name is something only he knows, but it was certainly on the Atlanta TV stations, which you could see in Murphy if you didn't have CNN, just as soon as Jones made his announcement. Here's what we know. Just before 7:00 P.M.—6:56 P.M. EST, to be exact—Rudolph stopped at the Burger King on Highway 19 in Murphy and paid $4.65 for a Meal Deal #2: a double Whopper, fries, and Coke. Then it was on to a grocery store, the BI-LO supermarket, across the adjoining parking lot.

Rudolph certainly shopped like a man who was about to take off, not someone who was laying in supplies for a party with the guys. Remember that he had already been shopping once that day, before his name hit the airwaves. He moved quickly around the BI-LO and was done less than fifteen minutes after he paid for his meal at Burger King. Had he known that this day might someday come? Did he already have a shopping list and was he just topping off his supply list? Or was he doing this all on the fly?

What we know is what Eric bought that evening and when he bought it:

- 14 cans of BI-LO oatmeal

- 8 containers of BI-LO raisins

- 8 cans of BI-LO green beans

- 8 cans of StarKist tuna fish

- 5 cans of Planters cocktail peanuts

- 3 jars of Planters dry-roasted nuts

- 1 four-pack of Ivory soap

- 3 two-packs of D-Cell batteries

- 4 four-packs of AA Energizer batteries

The bill was $109.06. Eric paid cash. Later. the FBI would calculate the weight of the groceries, put it at seventy-two pounds. And they would bring in nutritionists, who said it was enough to last a man six months— six months!—if he was strict about rationing his food. Assuming of course that he had a can opener, used his flashlight sparingly, and had a supply of fresh water.

The receipt from BI-LO had a time stamp on it: 19:11, or 7:11 P.M. EST. Whatever exit strategy Eric Rudolph had, he was moving quickly. It could have played out a couple of different ways. He could have seen the news about himself at home, gotten out of there in a hurry, grabbing what he could, then headed out for his Whopper and six-month shopping trip, hoping that word had not spread around town and that even if it had, no one would recognize him.

Or he could have heard when he was in his truck, maybe even as he was pulling into Burger King. It does take a lot of cool to hear your name mentioned on the radio, then walk in to a fast-food reataurant and have it your way. (Charles Stone thought that if this was the same guy that hauled a forty-pound bomb on his back through Centennial Park without giving up the ghost, then he had already shown his poise and that he wouldn't lose it in a Burger King.) He had to have known by the time he went to the BI-LO, because of what was on his shopping list for a guy living in a trailer.

However he heard, Rudolph chose to run, and he had to know time was running out. It isn't clear if he went back to his trailer to grab some gear after he did his grocery shopping. Eric might have made one stop along the way, even before going back, and that would be to dump off the groceries, setting up a cache of supplies wherever he had a place out in the woods, what deer hunters called a hide. Then he could have gone back to the trailer, casing it out first, making sure no one was ready to spring a trap on him (that was Stone's theory). He must have gone through the trailer in a hurry, because he left behind some guns that would certainly have proven useful. There was a shotgun and a couple of .22 rifles, which might have slowed him down, as well as a .38 Smith & Wesson pistol still in the trailer. But the SIG Sauer .45 pistol, that was a nice gun and might have come in handy wherever he was headed. Maybe he thought it was already in the truck and just made a mistake. There were also a couple of empty boxes for a stove and a lantern that looked pretty new still in the trailer, so he might have had those sitting in the corner, on stand-by, just in case. Whether that's the way it happened, that he returned to the trailer after the BI-LO or took off straight from the grocery store, he got the hell out of Dodge—and Caney Creek.

It was 8:00 P.M. EST before the Feds met up with Sheriff Thompson and his folks at the rendezvous point near the Caney Creek trailer. FBI Agent Russell had John Felton of the ATF with him. They didn't take any of the deputies with them; they just got directions and headed out. It was about 8:30 P.M. EST, clear and cold, around freezing, as Russell and Felton made their way down the gravel and dirt drive leading off Caney Creek to the one-bedroom trailer. There was a streetlight near the top of the driveway, but they had to go down a short way before they could tell that Rudolph's truck wasn't parked there. They could see a light on inside. The storm door at the front was shut, but it was clear and through it you could see that the real front door, which should have been closed, was wide open, giving them a view into the trailer. Russell and Felton made their way around the perimeter of the trailer and the property, checking around back. Russell thought it took them about a half-hour before they returned to the top of the driveway, where they were met by FBI Agent Tom Frye.

Russell was hoping that Rudolph would return. He set up surveillance across the road and stayed on post until someone came to relieve him at 10 A.M. the next morning. Agents would maintain surveillance around the trailer for several days. But it was too late. The agents had missed their man, presumably after he heard on the news that he was wanted. After they told Sheriff Thompson not to go pick him up or put him under surveillance. Before they got there. Before they discovered the lights were on and nobody was home.

The bottom line was this: two and a half hours after Doug Jones made his announcement, with time enough to spare to grab a burger and fries at Burger King and go grocery shopping for six months' worth of food, Eric Rudolph was gone.

Now, it was a manhunt. And a truck hunt, because the gray Nissan was also gone. Which meant the FBI and ATF—and the NCSBI (though that didn't last, they got torqued off at the Feds within a couple of weeks) had a few jobs on their hands. They had to find Rudolph. They also had to learn more about him, who he was, whether he had any known hideouts, places where he might run. And they had to figure out if he was their man, if he really was the guy who was seen leaving Birmingham and the scene of the bombing Thursday morning, if he was the bomber. The Task Force folks in Atlanta also wanted to play, because they were hoping that Rudolph might turn out to be their guy, too. Wouldn't it be nice to wrap all this up quickly, find the string, tie it up, and present it to the public and the U.S. attorneys in Birmingham and Atlanta. It wasn't about glory, either, because back in Birmingham they were getting ready to bury a police officer, and a nurse was still in intensive care, fighting for her life. And it had been a year and a half since Alice Hawthorne had been buried, too, after what happened in Centennial Park. So the Task Force wanted in, to clear the books on this one. Find the evidence and find their man.

One possible clue arrived in the mail four days after the bombing. Two envelopes, postmarked from Birmingham on January 29, the day of the bombings. They were addressed to the *Atlanta Journal-Constitution* and the Reuters bureau in Atlanta, two of the four news organizations that got letters after the Otherside Lounge bombing. The envelopes were addressed in block printing similar to the Atlanta letters. The return address read: A.O.G. 17th ST S.; BIRMINGHAM, AL. 35203—the street where the New Woman, All Women Health Care Clinic was located.

The letters themselves were almost identical, even down to the misspelling and misplaced punctuation: "THE BOMBING IN BIRMINGHAM WAS CARRIED OUT BY THE ARMY OF GOD. LET THOSE WHO WORK IN THE MURDER MILL'S AROUND THE NATION BE WARNED ONCE MORE—YOU WILL BE TARGETED WITHOUT QUARTER—YOU ARE NOT IMMUNE FOM RETALIATION. YOUR COMMISAR'S IN WASHINGTON CAN'T PROTECT YOU!

"WITH THE DISTRIBUTION OF THE GENOCIDAL PILL RU-486 IT IS HOPED THE RESISTANCE WILL END. WE WILL

TARGET ANYONE WHO MANUFACTURES, MARKET, SELLS AND DISTROBTES THE PILL. 'DEATH TO THE NEW WORLD ORDER.' "

There was no inside information on bomb components this time. But to investigators there was something equally important: the last line at the bottom of each letter, where the author had written, "FBI NUM-BER: 4-1-9-9-3." Remember, this was the secret code, the one from the previous letters that had not been made public (except for that one time) and while it would take a lot of forensic work to make a connection, this was a pretty strong indicator to the Atlanta Task Force, at least, that the Birmingham bomber was also their bomber—goatee man, hooded man, Blobman. They couldn't tie those letters to Eric Rudolph, not yet, but their thinking was pretty straightforward: if the Birmingham bomber was probably the Atlanta bomber, based on the letters, and Rudolph was the leading candidate (although still a material witness at this point, for the Birmingham bombings), then they wanted to be in on what was happening in North Carolina.

What was happening in North Carolina was this. While the FBI and ATF were looking for Eric and his truck, they were beginning to search through his things, look for evidence and hints where he might have been. They started at the trailer, of course, spending the better part of that first night there, mostly eyeballing everything. You can not only enter a place but also do that sort of visual search if you have probable cause—and there isn't any practical difference between looking for a material witness and an actual suspect when it comes to the law and searches.

You might even do a bit more, but at this point, the only information that the trailer was where Eric lived came from Sheriff Thompson's check of the utility records, so they had to make sure of that the next morning. The agents checked property records and interviewed the landlord, who showed them a copy of the rental agreement Eric had signed. Only thing was, when he signed the agreement on November 11, 1997, less than three months earlier, he said his name was Bob Randolph, or Rudolph; the landlord was never quite sure. Randolph/Rudolph had paid in cash, $250 for a security deposit and $275 in rent (the identity issue was cleared up pretty quickly when the Feds showed the landlord pictures of Eric Robert Rudolph). The agents also learned Rudolph had been spotted in his truck, returning to his trailer about 5:00 P.M. the night of the bombing, which would have been about a half hour before he showed up freshly showered at Plaza Video.[5]

The Feds set up surveillance on the trailer, watching the driveway and periodically checking the trailer itself to make sure that Rudolph didn't return. But before they could do a proper search of the trailer, they were diverted by a phone call. Cal Stiles, the owner of Cal's Mini-Storage, one of those store-your-own places, got in touch with the FBI. He had heard the news and wanted to let them know an Eric Rudolph had rented a storage unit from him, #91, at his business just outside the nearby town of Marble.[6] Cal's was the sort of place where you had to provide ID, so Rudolph used his driver's license and proper name. Yes, said Cal, when he was shown Rudolph's picture, that's him. A check of his records showed that Rudolph had rented the unit around the same time he moved into the Caney Creek trailer. The last time he had paid Stiles was back in December; that covered him through January, but now it was February, and Eric's money was due.

If you are going to look for someone you think might be a bomber, one of the quickest ways of doing that is to look for explosives. Bombers have labs, usually makeshift places, but places where they store and put together their devices. Any bomb lab would be dangerous enough, given the presence of explosive material. And if you have someone you are looking for who might not just be a bomber but someone who has set off secondary devices, then you are going to be extra careful when you go in to make sure there are no booby traps.

Eric Rudolph may still have only been a material witness, but the agents searching for him were still going to be extremely cautious. Since they hadn't seen any overt signs of bomb making at the trailer during their initial visit, no Bunsen burners or anything like that, Cal's might just be the ticket. Even before they went off to get a search warrant for Unit #91, they brought in a member of the search team who would perhaps be the busiest—not to mention most important—member of the group over the next several days.

His name was Garrett, and he was a yellow Labrador retriever, specially trained at the ATF's Canine Explosive Detection School in Front Royal, Virginia. This was really a six-legged affair, since ATF Special Agent Ray Neely, Jr., had been to school with Garrett. They had worked together exclusively since the previous June.[7] Even before bomb school, Garrett had six weeks of what was called explosive odor imprintation training. In other words, bomb sniffing. There are 19,000 types of explosives, but they fall roughly into five families. Garrett was trained to sit at alert when he smelled one of these explosive odors; his reward was food. He did this over and over, between eighty and one hundred times a day. By the time he showed up at Cal's Mini-Storage, Garrett had done this sniff-alert-reward repetition more than 24,000 times. That was the only way he ate, so he had to do it every day, even when he was in North Carolina.

Before the Feds got a warrant, they brought Garrett and Neely to the shed which contained Rudolph's storage unit and the ones adjacent to it. Garrett sniffed around the handles, then stopped and sat in front of Unit #91. They had him do it again, and the same thing happened. Garrett had smelled explosive residue on the lower handle and lock on Rudolph's unit. When they immediately stopped and applied for a search warrant to get inside the unit, agents told the federal magistrate that it was likely that someone handling explosives had left traces of them when they were opening and closing Unit #91.

Garrett was just getting going. Rudolph's storage unit was going to be searched the next day, after all the paperwork got done, but the next stop that Sunday was Plaza Video. The box for *Kull the Conqueror* had been sitting out in plain sight when they had entered the trailer two nights before, so they knew where to go. Once the agents realized Eric was a frequent customer and had been in four times that week, the agents decided to test the videos he rented. They got *The Game, Picture Perfect,* and *City of Industry,* along with nine other videos, all unused, and took them out of their boxes. All the videos were spread out for Garrett, who sniffed his way through them. He alerted, to use the ATF lingo, on *The Game.* They ran the test again with the same result. To Agent Neely, this meant that the video, which Rudolph had rented on January 25 and returned the next day, just three days before the Birmingham bombing, contained explosive residue.[8]

Garrett and his crew were back at Cal's the next day to sniff and search Eric's storage unit. They didn't find any explosives, which put the public safety fears to rest, but as the dog was sniffing around, he indicated there was explosive residue on a container holding nails. The nails were interesting; they couldn't tell by eyeballing them whether they were the same sort as the ones in any of the bombs, but they were certainly going to send them to the lab for comparison. The agents also took away three spent cartridge cases that were also inside the same box holding the nails. Again, the idea was to check any powder that might have been left as residue from the cases. Maybe they could get enough to match it with that Accurate Arms smokeless powder that was found in the Centennial Park bomb. Otherwise, the agents took a few swabs—particularly from the door handle and the lock that Garrett had alerted them to the day before.[9]

Unit #91 would be the gift that kept on giving over the next few days and weeks, as agents became more refined in their searches (and with their search warrants). Three days after their first search, the Chevy Suburbans pulled back up to Cal's, and agents went back through Rudolph's belongings.[10] The last time they were at Cal's, they had seen some things that intrigued them, including an address book; a military training manual; and a book relating to Tim McVeigh, the Oklahoma City bomber. But their original warrant only related to explosives, so this time they got a much more flexible search warrant. They took away not only those items, but more nails, black duct tape, assorted clothing, some PVC pipe, an American flag, a Confederate flag, some more nails, and parts for a .22 caliber rifle. They found Rudolph's passport and birth certificate, a map of France, a folder labeled "Military Personnel Record," and a GED certificate from someplace called the Tri-County Community College. There was also a copy of the U.S. Constitution and dozens upon dozens of other books and magazines that would need to be gone through. They also found three unlabeled videotapes. When they later watched them, one had a recording of a newscast about the first anniversary of the Olympic park bombing.[11]

Garrett had another busy day when they searched Rudolph's trailer at Caney Creek. He sniffed explosives on several items: a red toolbox, a turquoise baseball cap, a cushion from a rocking chair, a pair of sunglasses, some clothing, and a towel that was taped to the bottom of the door in the master bedroom. That was just part of the haul agents took away from the trailer. The *Kull the Conqueror* video was there, of course, and the firearms (four rifles and two pistols). There was also a brown wig and a black baseball cap, along with some shoes, jeans, and a shirt, all of which resembled the clothes described by the witnesses in Birmingham. And there was a blue Wal-Mart plastic bag, which was also mentioned by the first Birmingham witness, although you could probably find one of those in a significant portion of homes across America. Then there were some other items that seemed to resemble bomb components from Atlanta: red copper wire; gray duct tape; a plastic, fourteen-ounce, Serving Saver bowl (all of the Atlanta bombs used plastic containers and at least one used the same size and brand); various batteries; and a Westclox travel clock. The agents took swabs, carpet samples, lots of clothing, several pairs of shoes, and a Bible. There were more books and an audiotape. Wedged into one picture frame, they found and confiscated $1,600 in cash.[12]

For all the material they were finding at Cal's and the trailer, it wasn't getting them any closer to finding Rudolph or his truck. There were certainly some promising leads that might link Rudolph to one or all of the bombings, although that would take some careful lab work. But the fact was they still had no idea whether Rudolph was two miles or two thousand miles away. Even getting ahold of his passport didn't mean that much. Rudolph could have another one, a fake or forged one, maybe even in the Bob Randolph name, that he kept at the ready in case he had to run. If he left behind $1,600 in cash that was that easily at hand, how much had he already taken? The agents had no idea at this point that Eric had been either to the Burger King or BI-LO in the hours before they showed up at his trailer on January 30, let alone the sorts of things he bought on his last-minute visit to the grocery. As far as they were concerned, Rudolph could be anywhere.

That would change a few days later. If you are going hunting for coons—raccoons for non-Southerners—you usually do it at night, since it is a lot easier to see those glowing little eyes when it's dark. On Saturday night, February 7, eight days since Rudolph had disappeared, Sheriff Thompson's office got a call from two coon hunters. They were out in an area called Martins Creek, and they had seen that gray Nissan truck that everybody in Cherokee County seemed to want to find real bad. As the crow flies, the truck was not that far from the trailer, considering how big Cherokee County was, only about four miles. If you wanted to, you could walk back into town in about three to four hours from where they found the truck. FBI and ATF agents went out that night and took a look. It was about a quarter mile off Martins Creek Road, down an old logging road. When they got there and shone their flashlights through the windows and into the camper shell, the gray Nissan looked abandoned—and it also looked like it might be stuck.

They couldn't do much that night except make a few calls. The next day, a Sunday, was spent rounding up their evidence techs and getting the paperwork in order for a search warrant. It was actually Monday before agents were ready to start searching the truck. This time, Charles Stone was up there for the whole spectacle. So was a good portion of the Atlanta and national media. Word about the Nissan's discovery had spread on Sunday, and come Monday, there were satellite trucks, even news helicopters, from the Atlanta stations, not to mention CNN. This was all going to play out in front of the cameras. The media had come and gone during the week, but they were mostly running up and down the roads near Murphy until the weekend hit and most everyone went back to Atlanta to wait for the next development. Now, the invasion of Cherokee County was officially under way.

What brought Stone up there was this: his boss at the Task Force, Woody Enderson, wanted to bring in a team of bloodhounds and handlers from Texas that the FBI's Hostage Rescue Team had worked with before. Stone had a pickup truck with a camper shell so he was the likeliest candidate to meet these folks when they came into Atlanta and take them up to the truck. If the hounds could pick up a good scent, who knows, maybe they would get this thing wrapped up quickly. For Stone, it was another Forrest Gump moment. Somehow, since the start of this thing at Centennial Park, he kept getting thrust right into the middle of this thing, sometimes for the oddest of reasons. And these next couple of days would certainly prove interesting.

The plan was to bring in a wrecker and haul the truck out to a place where agents could do a proper search. Before that, however, they needed to make sure the truck wasn't booby-trapped or otherwise full of explosives. You didn't really want to be hauling this thing on the bed of a wrecker if it was full of dynamite. So they opened up the doors and the hood by remote control. At least that's what they called it. No one had a key and a remote that would pop the locks, so they brought in some hooks and ropes and moved back quite a ways and yanked open the doors. Garrett was there, of course, and sniffed some explosive residue, but after a careful search, it was apparent the truck wasn't wired.

The next step was to bring in the wrecker. Of course, if you are going to be that close to a town named Murphy, then Murphy's Law was going to rule. The wrecker couldn't get in close enough to get to the Nissan— hadn't the agents who went out on Saturday night already said they thought Rudolph's truck was stuck? So they brought in a tractor, which hauled the Nissan out far enough for them to get it loaded up on the back of the wrecker. All of this made for great TV, especially if you were shooting from the helicopter. And all the crews that were being held back away from the truck were able to get their pictures of it being loaded up and hauled away once the trailer brought it out.

Once the truck was on its way, the bloodhounds went to work. Their handlers had them on long leads, ready to go as soon as they picked up a scent. The dogs made one circle around the truck and took off up the side of a nearby hill. Behind them, strung out in a ragtag line, was a makeshift FBI SWAT team. It was a group of heavily armed men (and one woman), wearing camouflage and bulletproof vests, carrying M-16s and Heckler & Koch MP5s. They tromped across yards, running in and around the houses that made up the little community of Martins Creek. All the while, there were helicopters overhead, trying to offer some visual support to the SWAT team chasing the dogs. Needless to say, residents weren't exactly thrilled about the new army of federal agents that was tromping through flower beds. One of them sidled up to Charles Stone, who wasn't running with the pack, and observed with a bit of country-fried wisdom that if that was the way they went after a witness, he was sure curious to see what they would do if they had an actual suspect.

The law enforcement term for what was happening is "clusterfuck," and that's exactly what Stone thought was going on at Martins Creek. After all, the truck had probably been abandoned the night that Rudolph started running, so the dogs were trying to run down a week-old odor. And it wasn't a good idea to start losing the hearts and minds of the locals so quickly into a fugitive hunt. Instead of getting out and doing a little public relations, the FBI and ATF guys not directly involved in the chase were off on their own, in little groups, talking. Well before dusk, the dogs lost the scent, and their handlers got ready to pack it in and check into a local motel. Before leaving with them, Stone asked the FBI agent heading the search if he was going to set up a perimeter, just to make sure that Rudolph didn't leave the area. After all, if they actually flushed out Rudolph and didn't have any way of keeping him from getting away, what was the point? No way, was the answer he got, the FBI was going to shut down at dark; they didn't like to do night operations out in the woods.

They were back at it the next morning. The dogs and their handlers were out walking the roads around Martins Creek, with the SWAT team in full battle gear behind them. Stone thought he didn't want to be around when they started angering even more of the locals, so he headed over to a temporary command post in Murphy to get filled in on what was pulled out of Eric's truck. He left behind a couple of his GBI agents, Dave Bartlett and Tommy Mefferd, with some pretty specific instructions. If the dog and SWAT show looked like they were headed toward the Georgia border, which was only ten miles from Murphy, he wanted fair warning. No way was it going to go like this if they crossed the border.

Stone had barely made it back to Murphy when his pager went off. The alphanumeric message said, "HEADED TO BLAIRSVILLE," which was a town a few more miles into north Georgia. *Oh shit*, thought Stone, and he headed to Blairsville himself. He was just pulling into town when his pager went off again. "IN BLAIRSVILLE," it said. By now he could see that with his own eyes. Up ahead at the main intersection in town, Stone saw a commotion outside a convenience store. There were unmarked police cars and a couple of TV satellite trucks, their dishes already pointing skyward as their reporters were preparing for live shots. Stone pulled out his binoculars and took a closer look. He saw his agent, Tommy Mefferd, standing off to the side of the parking lot with a big grin, maybe more of a smirk, on his face.

Stone was flabbergasted at what Mefferd told him next. Tommy said, Charles you won't believe how they are tracking. They put the dogs in the truck, let them out at each intersection they come to, and let them circle around. Whichever road the dog takes off, that's the way they take off. They swear this worked during some abduction case, and they've got these FBI guys believing them. They get into Blairsville, and the dogs take off for this convenience store—and the agents let them go inside, where they start barking. To make matters even worse, apparently someone this morning had already reported there was a man who looked like Eric in the store who had been driving a car with Tennessee plates, so now the FBI is inside, they've got a videotape, and they won't let anyone look at it because it might be evidence.

While Stone was taking all this in, he also noticed the local sheriff pulling up. Naturally, none of the Feds had bothered to call him, so Stone had to go head off exactly what he feared was going to happen, which was the second federally sponsored clusterfuck in as many days. He had Mefford soft-soap the sheriff while he tried to get to the bottom of the videotape by asking the FBI agent to see it. Can't do that, said the agent, who was a recent Academy graduate, and immediately started in with the same line about how it's evidence.

Stone was by now not a happy man, which took a lot of doing, since normally he can roll with just about anything, so he said you are on my turf and we are looking at the damn tape. When the guy still put him off, he called down to the Task Force in Atlanta and got his FBI guys on the phone, and they proceeded to chew the agent out. By now the agent got the point that Stone was going to watch the tape, so they headed inside to put it in the machine. Only the guy didn't want the store owner to watch and asked her to leave, but he couldn't operate the machine without her. After all this go-round, they finally brought her in, she popped the tape in the machine, and of course the guy looked nothing like Rudolph. Stone tried to explain to the young FBI agent that the reason the bloodhounds got so excited when they came into the store was they smelled hot dogs cooking on a rotisserie.

Would that it ended there. But the saga of the Superdogs (as the Task Force would soon dub them) wasn't over yet. Stone and Mefford finally got out of the store and realized there was nobody left, all the dogs and unmarked cars had disappeared. Down the street at the Burger King, where they went for dinner, the TV people were doing live shots about the hunt for Eric Rudolph coming to Blairsville, but the hunters seemed to have gone.

That's when Stone got another message on his pager, asking if he knew where the dog team was. He returned the page, told his communication center he assumed they'd gone back to Murphy, then learned the reason he got the call was because the folks in Murphy were also looking for them. He told them to page Dave Bartlett, and the reply came quickly this time. They were even farther into Georgia, now in a town called Helen. Helen is a small tourist area near the beginning of the Appalachian Trail in north Georgia, whose claim to fame is that everything in the town, down to the local gas station, is done up Swiss style. You are driving along expecting *Deliverance* and all of the sudden you've entered the world of *Heidi*.

Now, the Superdogs had invaded Helen. When Stone got Bartlett on the phone, he learned the dogs ran the same routine, intersection by intersection, all the way down to Helen, and the SWAT team was fixing to bust down the door of someone's motel room. Of course, no one had told the local sheriff, which meant he could end up on the scene with his guys and get into a shoot-out with the Feds, not realizing they were there on a manhunt. Stone had seen that type of miscommunication lead to tragedy during a drug bust, and he was trying to limit the damage here.

Stone told Bartlett he'd personally call the sheriff, but that Dave should get the hell out of Helen; if the Superdogs and their handlers didn't want to leave, then they'd have to deal with the consequences. By this time, they're too deep into it, and they pulled someone (Bartlett thinks it is the male half of a honeymooning couple) out of the motel room at gunpoint before realizing, once again, this guy wasn't Eric Rudolph. About the only breaks they caught out of the Helen fiasco were that no shots are fired and the only TV truck that followed them down from Blairsville got there too late to hear about the screw-up at the motel.

It was one of those "when you look back on it now, it makes a great story" episodes, but at the time, Stone and his guys felt like north Georgia had been invaded by a bunch of bumbling Feds. Not that the FBI field office in Atlanta was happy either. Word around the Task Force was that the man who ran the Atlanta office told his counterpart in North Carolina that if any more of his agents crossed the state line, they would be arrested on sight. The Superdogs and their handlers, who actually seemed like nice and smart guys except for that unfortunate episode, were sent back to Texas a few days later. The next time the searchers were going to do some tracking of Rudolph, Stone would make sure they brought in the dogs and their handlers from the Georgia Department of Corrections, the ones that were used all the time to go after escaped prisoners. But right now, this wasn't so much a manhunt as a traveling disaster. They didn't seem any closer to finding Eric Rudolph, and they were already starting to annoy the people they wanted and needed the most to help them out, the locals. If this went on much longer, it could really start to get ugly.

While the Superdogs were causing such fits and starts, Garrett the Bomb Dog was helping lead the search of Rudolph's truck. He smelled explosive residue in a couple of places—on the steering wheel and in the back, on a paper bag from the BI-LO grocery store. There was also a receipt from the store, which had one of Eric's fingerprints on it (his were the only fingerprints they found in the truck). Reading the receipt, the agents saw the list of things he bought and the date and time stamp, their first clue about Rudolph's actions right before he disappeared. They found another receipt inside a Burger King bag, which added to their time line.[13] Based on the times, they figured he must have gone to the Burger King, bought his Whopper, fries, and a Coke, then gone to the BI-LO to get his supplies, tossing them in the back. What they still didn't know, but seemed likely, was whether he abandoned the truck that very same night. If so, it would have been about the same time agents were showing up at his door. It also meant he wasn't likely to be that far away, not unless he had another vehicle stashed somewhere.

In all, the agents searching Rudolph's truck took 129 items. Probably the most important were the receipts from BI-LO and Burger King. But they also found a green military-style shovel and its cover, one of those entrenching tools, and they wondered if it could have been the one that the Hooded Man was seen carrying by that witness at the Sandy Springs clinic. They took away lots of swabs and vacuumed up samples from all over the truck. There were rosary beads tied to the rearview mirror and a medallion with a swastika, both also destined for the crime lab. The only cash they found here was some loose change: a quarter, two nickels, and thirteen pennies.[14] There were walkie-talkies, a scanner, and a variety of wires and adapters. Some of the agents wondered whether this meant Rudolph had other communications devices with him; others wondered if these might have somehow been tied up with the remote detonator that was used in the Birmingham bombing.

It would take some time before agents could go through all of the items they had taken not only from the truck, but also from Eric's trailer and storage unit (they would go back to Cal's at least two more times and make some other significant finds). There were lots of promising leads, they thought, that might give them a strong forensic trail back to Birmingham and Atlanta. Already, they had done one test for a particular type of explosive called ethylene glycol dinitrate (EGDN) the ATF described as the primary explosive ingredient in nitroglycerine-based dynamite. If you found EGDN at a bomb site, you could be pretty certain that it meant this particular type of dynamite was being used. And if you found it other places, like in a truck or a trailer, then the forensic argument was someone had either been using those places to store the explosive or more likely they got some residue on their hands and transferred it there. The ATF had found EGDN all over the bomb site at the New Woman clinic in Birmingham. They also found it in his trailer—on the towel taped to the bottom of the master bedroom door, on the baseball cap on top of the dresser in the same bedroom, and on a cushion from the rocking chair. And now they said it was on the steering wheel cover in the truck, as well as on a paper grocery bag from BI-LO.[15]

This was evidence enough for Doug Jones to get his warrant changed. A week after his truck was found, Rudolph's status went from material witness to suspect. Doug Jones announced that there was now a warrant for the arrest of Eric Robert Rudolph on suspicion of bombing the New Woman, All Women clinic in Birmingham, causing the death of Officer Robert Sanderson and the injuries to Emily Lyons. Now they could say they were going after an accused cop killer.

The only problem was one that was pretty obvious to everyone involved. There were now well more than a hundred agents running around western North Carolina looking for Eric Rudolph, but no one could find him. He was on the run, and the trail seemed to have gone cold. Had he disappeared into the woods or found another way out of Cherokee County? At this point, the people chasing him didn't really know. If this was hide-and-seek, they had no idea where they should be looking—or even what sort of adversary they were up against. Having already lost the battle of Martins Creek, maybe it was time for a different approach. Maybe if they learned more about Eric Rudolph's life, even got inside his head, they might be able to figure out where he had gone.

6.
THE STRANGEST THANKSGIVING EVER

WHEN THE FBI sets its mind to doing something, it can often achieve impressive results. From the very day of the clinic bombing, once Eric Rudolph's name popped up in the search of the license plate on the Nissan truck, the Bureau set out to learn what it could about him. Agents had tracked down Eric's sister, Maura Rhodes, and her husband, Keith Rhodes, within hours of the Birmingham bombing and discovered they didn't know that much about his current situation. The next day, before they had run down the Caney Creek address, they also talked to Joel Rudolph, one of Eric's brothers, who lived in the same town of Hendersonville, North Carolina, as Maura and Keith. Joel said he wasn't trying to be unhelpful, but he didn't know where Eric lived![1]

Joel said he had last seen Eric five days before the Birmingham bombing, on a Saturday afternoon, when Eric came by his place in Hendersonville, North Carolina (Hendersonville is south of Asheville). Eric was driving his gray Nissan truck with the camper shell. Eric usually showed up like this once or twice a month in Hendersonville.[2] As far as Joel knew, Eric didn't have a regular job, though he had worked in the past doing carpentry and hanging drywall. Joel said that Eric had told him when he was about to leave that he was returning to his place over in Tennessee and had a six-hour drive ahead of him. Joel had some more information that might be useful; he advised the agents that their mother was very protective of Eric and, by the way, his brother had been in the military and might know something about explosives.[3] As if that wasn't enough, Joel said that Eric would frequently go camping for weeks and didn't use a tent; he was also an experienced hunter.

Maura, Keith, and Joel were first, but other family and friends, including Joel's ex-wife (and still close friend) Deborah were identified and interviewed during the next few days. Eric Rudolph's life story was put into a time line. Once they learned about his possible military service, agents pulled his army records, then spoke with his fellow soldiers, instructors, and commanders. The day that Rudolph officially became a suspect, February 14, 1998, the FBI published its own forty-four-page biographical dossier of him.[4] It was part chronology, part profile, and still quite raw in terms of information (there were leads, particularly about Eric's travels, that later would turn out to be incorrect because he apparently misled his own family). The profile didn't include a list of the books agents had taken away from his trailer or storage unit, but it was a pretty impressive document done on such short notice.

The table of contents hints at what made this suspect so unusual and why it was put together not only by the Charlotte Field Office, but also by the Domestic Terrorism Analysis Unit. Under a chapter titled "Family History, Development and Education" were some intriguing headings: "Move to Topton, North Carolina," and "Schell City, Missouri," and the "Church of Israel." There was the section on "Military Service," which interestingly showed a time period of only seventeen months. That ended in 1989, but the next section skipped to 1996 and mentioned his relationship with a woman, a declining relationship with a neighbor, and travels to the western United States. Then, before ending with "Personal Traits" (and a bibliography), there was an intriguing section, entitled "Possible Exposure to Christian Identity Extremists."[5] Anyone suspected in an abortion clinic bombing (and already being strongly considered for the Atlanta bombings by that Task Force) would certainly have some interesting associations in his past, but even a quick scan of this table of contents, which was in its way a first glance at the life and times of Eric Rudolph, suggested a biography—including military service and then possible exposure to the extremist views—that bore some resemblance to that of Oklahoma City bomber Timothy McVeigh. Clearly, this was a life that bore examining.

The biography began with the basics, including two photographs. Eric Robert Rudolph, who also used the aliases of Eric Randolph and Bob Randolph, was a white male, five feet eleven inches, weighing 150 pounds. He had blue eyes and brown hair. Date of birth was September 19, 1966, in Merritt Island, Florida. His FBI number was listed, as was that of his North Carolina driver's license. Rudolph's passport, expired on August 9, 2000 (although it had already been seized in the search at Cal's).[6] And Eric Robert Rudolph had a Social Security number, which one can hardly avoid having in modern America, but would certainly prove to be at odds with what was later discovered about his beliefs. Conveniently for investigators, they had a set of Rudolph's fingerprints, which were listed here, thanks to his military service (which was how they were able to make the ID on the BI-LO receipt so quickly).

In abbreviated fashion, the dossier then laid bare the outlines of a life, although it would take Charles Stone and others considerable time to fill in the blanks. It said that Eric Robert Rudolph was the fifth of six children born to Robert Thomas Rudolph and Patricia Ann Rudolph, née Murphy. That his siblings were Damian Thomas Rudolph, Joel Christian Rudolph, Daniel Kerney Rudolph, Maura Jane Rhodes, and Jamie Michael Rudolph. Robert Rudolph was a veteran of both the army and navy who then went to work at McDonnell Douglas. His work took him to Cape Canaveral and the space program; the family lived in nearby Merritt Island when Eric was born. Later, Robert got a job with TWA at Miami International Airport, and the family moved to south Florida. Interestingly, the report noted that although the children were raised in a devoutly religious environment and that both parents were at one time active Catholics, Eric and Jamie were not baptized as Catholics. By 1969, it says, the family left the Catholic Church. Robert and Patricia became active Baptists in Fort Lauderdale, Florida, even serving as youth ministers.[7]

Then this outlined life takes a sharp rightward turn, hinting at an exodus and a period of wandering. In Fort Lauderdale, the family met a man named Thomas Wayne Branham who became a close family friend. Branham moved to a place called Topton, North Carolina, and soon let the Rudolphs know there was a piece of property available next to his. They purchased the land, and Joel and Daniel were sent there to begin building a house. But the patriarch, Robert Rudolph, never made the journey; he died of cancer in 1981.[8]

The family made the move to Topton the next year, and here is where the fissures with normal society, already hinted at, become apparent. After briefly attending Nantahala High School, Eric wrote a term paper questioning whether the Holocaust took place. There were allegations he was drawing swastikas and Nazi symbols on his body. He dropped out of Nantahala after the ninth grade and was home-schooled by his mother. Their neighbor and friend, Tom Branham, who had been close to Eric, allegedly fell out with the family after he was arrested by the ATF, when he says the Rudolphs failed to come to his defense.[9]

Then, in the mid-'80s, the report outlined a further journey into the extreme, as Patricia took Eric and his younger brother Jamie on another journey, this time to Schell City, Missouri, where they were involved with a Christian Identity preacher named Dan Gayman, and his Church of Israel. In defining CI, the report shows just how far Patricia Rudolph had taken her family from the mainstream. Here, Christian Identity is described accurately as a belief system which maintains that white Europeans or Aryans represent the true chosen people of Yahweh, that they are the real Israelites. Jews are not considered the people of the Bible, but rather the spawn of Satan. CI minions, it says, believe the world is on the verge of a final, apocalyptic struggle between these good Aryans and Satan's evil minions, who include Jews, the federal government, mass media, U.S. banks, and homosexuals.

This character, this Dan Gayman, who they visit, is someone well-known to the FBI, the report notes. He would be named in a federal indictment in 1987 as having received $10,000 in illegally seized funds from members of a group called The Order, an extreme right-wing paramilitary group that had its heyday in the '80s. Gayman was eventually a prosecution witness when members of The Order were tried on sedition charges, according to the biographical material. How long Patricia and Eric were exposed to Gayman's world was unclear, because this dossier said other members of the Rudolph clan couldn't agree whether they spent six months or two and a half years in Schell City.[10]

Eric and Patricia returned to North Carolina, where he spent two semesters at Western Carolina University in Sylva, studying history, political science, math, philosophy, and writing. Eric had already gotten his GED (general equivalency diploma) after being home-schooled. His mother joined him in Sylva and transferred ownership of the Topton house to her son Daniel, along with Eric. The report said she did this so she was eligible to live in government-subsidized housing.[11]

Then, another strange turn in this outlined life. After this exposure to a movement which clearly hated everything associated with the federal government, Eric Rudolph enlisted in the U.S. Army on August 4, 1987, as a recruit. He did basic training at Fort Benning, Georgia, and got assigned to Army Airborne. Then, after eighteen days of leave, he reported in December 1987 to Fort Campbell, Kentucky. Early the next year, Eric completed Air Assault School. He also took an army-sponsored course in American history at Hopkinsville Community College, which was located near Fort Campbell. After that, according to the FBI's dossier, things appeared to go bad. Eric was counseled four separate times over the next few months for his attitude and insubordination. Three times he was written up on what the army calls Article 15 charges: once for disrespectful language toward an NCO (noncommissioned officer) and for failing to log in a female visitor to the base, then for not showing up for duty, and finally for marijuana use. By the end of 1988, the army decided it had had enough of Eric Rudolph and began discharge proceedings. The next month, in January 1989, he had been given a general discharge.[12]

Life after the army was then briefly recounted: Eric began a romantic relationship with a woman from Tennessee that is on and off for three years, before ending sometime in 1992. That is also the year he started to travel overseas. He took a brief trip that began in the Netherlands and lasted two weeks. The report said Eric was now back living at the Topton house and stayed there until it was sold in 1996. He did odd jobs in carpentry and construction, but had few expenses because the house was fully paid off.

But there was trouble in Topton. His neighbor, Tom Branham, claimed his relationship with Eric Rudolph soured and not just because of Branham's troubles with the law a few years earlier. Branham told federal agents that he believed Eric had become heavily involved in the marijuana trade, that Eric always seemed to have lots of money but no steady work. Branham said Forest Service vehicles in the area were taking away plenty of confiscated marijuana out of the Nantahala National Forest (another acquaintance of Rudolph backed this up, claiming Eric was not only growing and selling marijuana, but also planting bear and booby traps around his marijuana patches out in the woods). Branham also claimed Eric was threatening him and his family, that he killed Branham's cat because it was killing wild rabbits that Eric might need for food. Buried further in the report, however, was an important caveat—that Branham's story of his falling-out with Eric may have been just that, because allegedly the two men were seen together, acting in a friendly fashion, after this falling-out.[13]

Eric's life in Topton came to an end in early 1996, according to the report, when his mother decided to sell the house (remember it was located next to Branham's land). The report suggested at least one neighbor believed Patricia Rudolph had run into problems by this time with the Internal Revenue Service for failing to pay taxes, and there might have been a lien on the house. For whatever reason, the report said Eric collected the $40,000 in proceeds from the sale and neither Eric's mother nor his siblings say they got any money from the house.

This sketch of a life concluded with a list of personal traits and characteristics provided by Eric's family and associates (this is FBI-speak, but it did point out that even Eric's friends felt he kept them at a distance). He was a loner, according to others, who kept to himself and avoided close contact with all but a few family members and associates. Another word used to describe him was "transient"—even his siblings, including Maura, said he was secretive about where he lived and rarely gave them addresses or even phone numbers. His brother Jamie, who lived in New York's Greenwich Village, told agents that when he wanted to get in touch with Eric, he did it through their mother. Eric was intelligent and well-read and appeared to be a history buff, with a particular bent toward the Civil War, said his brother Daniel. He was a skilled outdoorsman and survivalist, and they said he used his truck as his base; he was also extremely skilled at reading topographical maps and navigating by compass. Eric was a handyman with extensive carpentry skills, but Daniel said he also knew his way around explosives and that he had seen his brother with bomb-making manuals. His family and associates confirmed what the Feds found in their searches, that Eric also owned several firearms, including rifles, a shotgun, and pistols.[14]

What remains unclear from this dossier is what Eric actually believed in. By all accounts, he was at least a political conservative, but this circle of family and associates disagreed on whether he was a right-wing radical. Jamie said sometimes Eric's political and economic opinions made him so uncomfortable that he tried to find ways to end the conversation, but for all that, his brother wasn't antigovernment, anti–law enforcement, or even antigay. But others used different words to the agents preparing this dossier: revolutionary, radical, anti-Semitic; and prone to violence. He made no secret, these people said, of his hatred for the ATF and the IRS. One acquaintance said Eric didn't believe in putting money in banks; another said he sounded like Hitler. There was some question about how much further contact he might have had with Christian Identity groups and supporters. Strikingly, for a man now accused in at least one abortion clinic bombing, there was no mention at all of his attitude toward abortion in the five-page synopsis of Eric's life, except to say he didn't seem to have any.[15]

There was a wealth of detail in the dossier about Eric Rudolph's life, which hinted at possible motives and background. But it was all done in a hurry, and the Atlanta Task Force, for its part, still wanted to know more, to fill in the significant gaps that would help them understand the man who might also be their suspect. Reinterviewing family members and friends meant you could get more and richer detail. As well as trying to expand the investigation, this could help them on two counts. They thought it might lead them to Eric, which was their primary focus right now. It could also round out whatever case they were going to make against him for all the bombings, not just Birmingham.

Which was how Charles Stone came to be knocking on the door of Eric's former sister-in-law Deborah Givens (she actually still used Rudolph as her surname to most people) in a Nashville suburb at the end of February 1998. She had been forthcoming in the initial round of interviews, and Stone thought she might have a lot more to say. Stone got permission to do the interview because his boss thought that given what seemed to be the family ideology, having a nonfederal agent in on these chats with family members might make things go easier. There was another reason, which had to do with the territorial nature of the FBI. Now they were on the home turf of the FBI's Nashville Field Office, it was probably easier for the FBI in Nashville to deal with a non-Fed as well, rather than someone from a different FBI field office!

Stone was teamed up with Dave Jordan of the Nashville FBI office (under FBI regulations, interviews were always done by two people or more). The two hit it off instantly; both were target shooters in their off time, and they could chat for hours about guns, ammo, and life. Jordan was also a good listener, especially in interviews, and didn't give off strong FBI vibes, which was about to prove very useful. He and Stone had just finished off a hamburger dinner and headed over to Deborah's, figuring they had their best shot at catching her when she got home from work. But now a man was answering her door, saying Deborah isn't here, try back in an hour.

They thanked him, head back to Stone's Ford, and started driving away. That's when it hit both of them. The guy looks familiar, a lot like Eric. They're pretty sure it isn't him, but they have been studying the photos and realize it is probably his brother Joel. He's answering the door at his ex-wife's house. Should they go back or not? He seemed pleasant enough. They were a couple of blocks away when they decided to give it a try. Stone and Jordan turned around and headed back to Deborah's house.

When they knocked on the door again, and Joel came back to answer, they started the whole conversation over again. This time they asked, "aren't you Joel Rudolph?" Yes, he said, so they introduced themselves properly this time as Agents Stone and Jordan and explained they'd like to talk to him for a few minutes about his brother. He invited them in, and a few minutes soon become a couple of hours as they got into the conversation. Stone, like many investigators, has a philosophy about these sorts of discussions, especially after dealing with so many people with strong political beliefs, from Klan members to folks from the Communist Workers Party. Don't talk politics, don't get into arguments. You won't win, and they won't end up being helpful. Just know for your own peace of mind that just because you aren't challenging them, doesn't mean you agree. The aim is to walk away knowing more than when you got there.

So that's how it played out. They let the conversation be about them for a bit. Joel was interested in how they got into law enforcement, why they did it, and their approach to people, even their ideas about right and wrong. That gave them an opening; Jordan and Stone made it clear they saw themselves as honorable people doing the right thing. This wasn't about any sort of grudge against Eric. Stone explained some of the facts of the case, why they were looking for Joel's brother, and how they wanted to arrest Eric, not kill him. Stone had put four people on death row, and he figured that if you are straight with their families, they will be straight right on back.

Joel accepted this and seemed to appreciate the respect. At which point he said, I don't think it is Eric who did the clinic bombings. We've talked about abortion before. Eric didn't have a strong stance about abortion. He said abortion had been going on since women first started getting pregnant, and it would continue to go on no matter what happens. Then Joel started talking about the bombing at the Otherside Lounge and dropped another revelation on Stone and Jordan. He said about the gay bar bombing, that he and Eric had a gay brother, Jamie, and that Eric knew his brother was gay and loved him. This was news to the agents, but that was the way investigating went. The more you learned, sometimes the more confused it got. There were contradictions, paradoxes, nuances, and many different perspectives on the same life or event.

Joel was quiet, but also a very personable guy. Stone and he talked easily, even joked about being divorced and staying on good terms with your ex-wife, something they had in common (Stone was still getting over the surprise of finding Joel was staying at his ex-wife's house; his own first marriage had ended amicably, but this seemed way friendlier). They talked about refinishing hardwood floors, something Joel had done in Deborah's house and that Stone was fixing to do at his house.

There was more talk about Eric. Joel recounted how he and Eric used to hike the mountains near their home in Topton together back in the 1980s and would sometimes come across abandoned cabins and sheds. Joel thought his brother might have taken advantage of these in the past, during his long trips into the Nantahala National Forest, which bordered their home, and that he could be doing that right now. He told Stone and Jordan of a time about ten years before when Eric and he had buried some food and other provisions out in the woods. It was all important information, and it gave them more of a personal feel for Eric, just where he stood and how important the woods were to him. And it was all an unexpected bonus. They hadn't even spoken to Deborah yet!

When Deborah returned that night to her house, she was shocked to learn that Joel had spent hours with Stone and Jordan, let alone talked to them at all. She figured this only could have happened because he was away from the mountains, away from the pressure of his family, and away from the federal agents who seemed to be keeping tabs on family members (a short time later, Joel and Deborah would leave Nashville, drive across America, something she had dreamed of doing for a long time; like Joel, she would admit they had an unusual relationship—at least that's what her friends in Nashville called it—for a divorced couple. And it wasn't just Deborah. Her daughter asked Joel, rather than her own father, to give her away when she got married).[16]

The first time Deborah talked to Jordan and his local FBI partner, right after Eric had been identified, she had been the one to tell agents that Eric was a radical and revolutionary. She thought Eric's antigovernment attitudes, especially his anti-IRS rhetoric, stemmed from his mother's tax problems. She also said that Eric had talked about the Aryan Nations, a prominent extremist group, and about Christian Identity. She had mentioned Eric and Patricia's trip (along with Jamie) to Schell City and Dan Gayman's Church of Israel compound—and although she wasn't completely sure about this, she thought there might have been a group called CSA involved. CSA stood for a radical group that was called the Covenant, Sword and Arm of the Lord, which had been the subject of a three-year FBI investigation in the late '80s (this lead was something the Task Force was never able to pin down).[17] Interestingly, of all the interviews that the FBI did in those first few days, Deborah was the only one to request her identity be protected.

This time, there was even less reticence when Jordan showed up with Stone. She might have taken her cue from Joel, and the way he was impressed by the two investigators. Deborah talked to them a bit that night, more the next day, and several times over the next few months. As Stone and the others were discovering, in many ways, this wasn't just about Eric. He had been nurtured in a peculiar and particular environment, and it seemed like you weren't going to understand him unless you understood his family.

More than anyone, Deborah was able to shed light on this Rudolph netherworld. In an America which seemed to appreciate normal families but glorify dysfunctional ones (President Carter's family, for example, with his colorful mother and his wayward, alcoholic buffoon of a brother may have best typified the Southern variant; but there were countless others in fact and fiction), the Rudolphs took the cake. A Southern-born screenwriter like Alan Ball came up with the family that populated *Six Feet Under*, but Patricia Rudolph and her clan would have stretched even his fertile imagination. So far, there was one son who was an accused bomber, another who was gay, hints of a protective and dominant mother, a trek into the wilderness, and exposure to extremist views. And they were just getting started exploring the Rudolphs.

For Deborah, the real introduction began during what she remembered as the strangest Thanksgiving ever. The drive from Nashville to Topton, North Carolina, is a pretty one, even in late November, when the leaves have long since dropped from most of the trees. There's still a surprising amount of green amongst the hardwoods, from spruce, short-needle pine, and mountain laurel. Deborah Givens was excited and nervous as she made the six-hour trip, trying to take in the scenery, preparing herself for her upcoming visit. It was Thanksgiving 1984, and she was about to meet her boyfriend's family, who were all gathering at the family home in Topton. She didn't know much about them, only that the mother ruled the roost and there were lots of brothers and a sister.

Deborah had only been going out with Joel Rudolph for a couple of months, but it looked serious. They had met at a restaurant in Nashville. Deborah was eating lunch, and this cute guy a few tables over was sort of flirting with her. She sent her phone number over with a waitress in the hopes that he might call and ask her out. Now, she was headed with Joel to meet the Rudolph clan up in the hills of North Carolina, to an area known as the Nantahala. As they got off the main roads and closed in on Topton, Deborah could understand why this terrain of mountains and forest was called Nantahala. It was a Cherokee word for land of the noonday sun, because it seemed that only when the sun was directly overhead would its rays penetrate some of these valleys.

Deborah and Joel drove past the Nantahala River and a series of mountain streams and creeks that fed into it. The road names gave some clue of their progress into the Nantahala National Forest, where the Rudolph house was located: from Old River Road, on to Wayah Bald, and Winding Stairs Road, right on Briartown Church Road, then finally up the steep, gravel-covered Partridge Creek Road. But the family she was about to meet bore little resemblance to the Partridge family, except that both were headed by women. Truth was about to be a lot stranger than Hollywood fiction.

Deborah had some forewarning of what she was about to face during that Thanksgiving in the hills. Joel let her know pretty much from the start that he and his family believed that the Bible, their Bible at least, was the history of the white race. He laid it out for her; there were other races (they were called the mud people and included Jews) but as far as what the Rudolphs believed, Adam and Eve were white Anglo-Saxons. He told her that what she heard preached in a regular church was only about 17 percent of the real Bible. It seemed, in its crazy logic, to make sense to her at the time.[18] Although Deborah didn't realize it, this was her first exposure to the world and beliefs of Christian Identity.

Joel gave her another glimpse into the Rudolph family closet of beliefs. When they were talking about his father, Joel became extremely emotional. Deborah learned the family legend: when Robert Rudolph had been diagnosed with cancer in the early '80s (the family was living in south Florida at the time), the doctors told them his condition was terminal. But they had heard of a miracle cure, something called laetrile, which was made from apricot pits. You could get your hands on it if you went to Mexico. Patricia and the boys were ready to make this happen, yet the doctors wouldn't agree to this course of treatment. They thought laetrile was a fraud and a cruel hoax, and the Food and Drug Administration agreed.[19] It said laetrile was worthless and should be banned; the doctors treating Robert Rudolph were adamant, Joel told her; they wouldn't let it be given to him. Robert Rudolph died in 1982, and it became clear to Deborah that Joel and others in the family (she would later include Eric among this number) believed that the government was in some way responsible for his death.[20] To Charles Stone, this was crucial to understanding Eric. He would later say, after being convinced the evidence showed Eric was the bomber, that the laetrile legend was perhaps the first signpost pointing him on the road to Centennial Park, the Otherside Lounge, and the abortion clinics in Atlanta and Birmingham.

The trip to Topton and the house on Partridge Creek Road would be Deborah's total immersion into Rudolph-land. She had only ever spoken with Joel's mother before on the phone. Deborah had heard from Joel how Patricia Rudolph came from a strong Catholic family in the Philadelphia area, the Murphys, and at one time that she entered a convent, preparing to become a nun, before changing her mind. Instead, she married Robert, also a devout Catholic, and later both became estranged from the Church. Not really knowing what to expect, she was overwhelmed in person by Patricia's warmth and hospitality. Pat also had a sense of humor, and it was her wit that put Deborah at ease that Thanksgiving. For Deborah, it would be a wonderful holiday, one that she still cherished as a memory years later, even as she pondered the profound oddity of the Rudolph clan's beliefs.

She remembered being surrounded by a family full of strong opinions. These opinions would soon reveal themselves, but she was struck first by what she saw on the family's bookshelves. There were a number of books about evolution and why it wasn't true; there were also underground newspapers, including one she noticed called *The Thunderbolt*, which was an avowedly racist and anti-Semitic publication.[21] *The Thunderbolt* was notorious for publishing articles that included canards such as how blacks (that's not what they would call them) as a race had inferior intelligence because the slopes of the foreheads meant they had smaller brains.

Deborah had already heard some of the story of the Topton house. Joel told her how the family bought the property, which contained a half-built house, at the urging of family friend Tom Branham (Branham had met the Rudolphs in south Florida, becoming a close family friend who helped them build an addition to their Fort Lauderdale house. He had gone on a back-to-nature kick, and that was how he came to move to Topton in the first place). It may have originally been bought as a future retirement home, but that was before Robert died from cancer. Pat's vision for Topton changed. She was determined to move her children out of a south Florida environment she was increasingly uncomfortable with, to get them away from drugs, crime, and race-mixing, and to God's country, where they were surrounded by their own and could fend for themselves.[22] Joel and Daniel had moved up there first to help Branham finish out the interior (Eric would do his share when he came north with Pat and Jamie). Along the way, Daniel, Joel, and Eric also picked up a trade, learning their way not just around carpentry, but also how to hang drywall.

The family was in many ways self-sufficient at Topton, growing and canning organic vegetables, for example, and having their own water supply, which they distilled to remove any impurities. Deborah noticed some ingenious touches, like how you could flip a switch so the wood-burning stove heated the water for your shower. All of that made plenty of sense if you lived up a dirt and gravel road in the mountains, especially during the winter. The house may have been within shouting distance of the Georgia border, in the Deep South, but you could still find yourself snowed in and cut off from civilization for days or weeks at a time. This was definitely four-wheel drive country.

It was the way that Joel and the rest of the Rudolphs referred to the Topton house that made Deborah realize how differently they viewed it and the outside world. Either on that trip or the next time she visited, Joel mentioned if anything ever happened in the United States, they didn't have to worry because they had a place to go in the mountains. What sort of thing? she asked. A revolution or martial law. What if the country was invaded or if there was World War Three? Topton was their safe haven, Joel said. Deborah realized how far-fetched this was, that it was not the sort of thing that ordinary people spent their lives thinking about.[23] At the Rudolph house, this was what passed for dinner conversation.

Sometime during the Thanksgiving holiday, Deborah went next door and met the man who convinced the Rudolphs to move to the mountains. Tom Branham's house was just a bit down the hill from the Rudolphs and couldn't have been more different. Theirs was tidy inside and out, an off-white one-story structure with a basement and well-tended siding. The front yard was kept trimmed, and you didn't see the usual sort of local yard art consisting of rusted-out cars or trailers propped up on cinder blocks. A family lived here, and you knew it from the minute you drove up.

Branham's house looked like some sort of overdone parody, Ode to the Cinder Block. The house, which some in the media would later charitably and unaccountably refer to as a compound, was an elongated unfinished concrete block structure, set back from the road. Instead of the tidy garage and outbuilding that the Rudolphs erected, there were some shantylike structures. As far as Deborah could figure after going over to his house, he had never thrown away anything in his life. There was a collection of scrap metal that rivaled a junkyard, and it somehow seemed to have been integrated into his crazy-quilt master plan along with the cinder block. He took the Rudolphs one step further in the self-sufficiency department. Tom Branham made sure she knew he wasn't going to be caught short come the war or apocalypse; he had plenty of food on hand and enough kerosene and gasoline to power his generator for a long, long time.

Deborah wasn't sure if Branham had become some sort of father figure to the Rudolph boys. She knew it was at his urging they had made their way to Topton and that he had taken the boys under his wing, guiding them through the completion of the house. Her Thanksgiving visit took place only three years after Robert Rudolph had died, two years since they had moved north, so if anybody fit that role of surrogate father, it would be Tom Branham. Not that she thought he was qualified. She didn't know anything about his history, but he wasn't shy about expressing his own antigovernment views. And if she had to use one word to describe Branham, it would be paranoid. How else would you explain that concrete bunker of a house he lived in?[24]

There was another piece of Topton lore that someone shared with Deborah during the holiday, something that made it clear just how deep the Rudolph family's ties had already become to North Carolina. Deborah thought it was Pat who brought it up in conversation, although it could have been Joel. Robert had been cremated after he died, and Pat brought his ashes with her from Florida to Topton. He was there with them, in spirit and in what remained of his physical presence, buried on the property.

All this was background, in a sense, the culture in the petri dish that nourished Eric. It gave the investigators a lot to chew on. But what ultimately mattered to Stone and Jordan, and the rest of the Task Force for that matter, was Eric. It was during that Thanksgiving that Deborah first laid eyes on Eric. He had actually already been in Nashville, working alongside Joel, both of them realizing that being self-sufficient up in Topton was not going to pay the bills, at least not then. Joel stayed, picking up odd jobs doing construction and ultimately meeting Deborah, but Eric had already decided to go back home.

She remembered the contrast between the brothers. Nobody was shy about expressing themselves in Topton, but Joel would do it in a gentle and, to her mind, spiritual fashion. Not Eric. From the first, she noticed he would get in there and let fly. He may have only been eighteen at the time, but he spoke with a certainty that was either a sign of maturity or the arrogance of youth. Even then, she had the sense that although he might be influenced by the opinion of a father figure like Tom Branham, he was too much of a loner, too much his own man, to accept anyone's authority for long. For all the time she knew him, this would remain Deborah's take on Eric—strong-willed, independent, full of harsh and extreme opinions. Deborah would say you never got into a discussion with Eric; it was always him going off on this or that and God help you if you tried to get a word in. Yet, he seemed to have his mother's sense of humor and even a bit of her warmth. She felt that it was an uneasy relationship, never one where a bond of trust emerged.

Deborah would always use Joel as a yardstick against which she measured Eric. Joel wasn't overwhelmed by the family mythology, and while he absorbed much of the Rudolph belief system, he had a spiritual quality which she admired and that seemed to let him be at peace with the world (she always thought her ex-husband would have been at his happiest being Mr. Mom, raising four children while his spouse went off to work). Joel was capable of having a soul mate—which was her—and even if it ultimately didn't work out between them, the mountain man and city girl, she thought that was more down to her and her ways.

Eric was just a different sort altogether. He was the sort of person, she said, that would be famous or infamous. That's why she would tell the investigators and others she wasn't surprised that morning after the Birmingham bombing to hear him being named as a material witness. The story of that Thanksgiving was just part of it. During the course of several interviews, Deborah would describe the arc of Eric's life over the next dozen years as she knew it, as he moved in and out of her and Joel's orbit, even as she was moving in and out of the Rudolph universe. There would be Deborah's take on Eric's military career, why he joined up, what happened while he was in, and why he left. She would tell investigators in great detail about his marijuana growing, and his dope dealing. How he broke off one long-term relationship and took up another, to a woman she introduced him to in Nashville. How that didn't work out either, for sort of the same reasons that she and Joel ultimately split up. And she would try to sketch in a picture of those final years, when Joel had moved for a time back to Topton to share the house with Eric as they tried to refine the Topton experiment in self-sufficiency.

In turn, investigators would have questions for her. Sometimes she thought they were testing her to see if she was telling the truth, asking more about the marijuana, wanting to know why one of Eric's listed addresses was a house she lived in just outside of Nashville. They asked her if he dealt cocaine, if he ever robbed banks, what his favorite holiday was, and who was his favorite relative. If he were in a room and agents were trying to negotiate, they wanted to know who in the family he might talk with.

Much of this continuing conversation between Deborah and the agents was about Eric's beliefs, how they were nurtured, and whether he might be part of a conspiracy or operating on his own. In many ways, Thanksgiving with the Rudolphs was the place to start, although the sessions were never that chronological. Deborah and Joel headed back to Nashville once that holiday was over; a few months later they would be married. Eric was about to embark on a different sort of journey as Pat took him and Jamie out to Schell City, Missouri, for that visit to Dan Gayman's Church of Israel compound. Deborah would learn of the visit in a peculiar way. Patricia began sending Joel and her audiotapes of Gayman's sermons on Christian Identity and his teachings about the Bible and the white race.[25] They could listen or not to the tapes—and Deborah would usually toss them—but Eric's exposure to this ideology of hate was far more direct (so was Jamie's, but in his case, it certainly didn't take). For the Task Force, there was no way to overstate how important a source Deborah was becoming, just in helping them understand Eric.

While Deborah and Joel were willing to talk to Stone and Jordan, one member of the Rudolph family wasn't feeling so inclined. Since his initial interview, when he told agents about his brother's familiarity with explosives, Daniel Rudolph had been in emotional turmoil. A couple of weeks after his interview, a lawyer hired by the family publicly complained about the FBI surveillance on Daniel's house in Ladson, South Carolina, a little town near Charleston. James Bell called a news conference to say not only that he doubted the evidence against Eric, but that his brother and other members of the family were suffering harassment by the federal government as part of a plan to provoke Eric.[26] Daniel's wife, Christine, and her parents then paid a visit to the Task Force headquarters in Atlanta, privately asking agents to back off. Christine's parents said they were concerned about the emotional well-being of their daughter and son-in-law.

Daniel was certainly sending signals that something was wrong, that the pressure was too great. But no one—neither his family nor his neighbors in Ladson, South Carolina—could imagine what would happen next. Daniel's neighbors on Beverly Drive, like his neighbors in his previous house in Miami Springs, Florida, and his neighbors in Topton, remembered him as a quiet, caring, and stable person.[27] His role in the family seemed part big brother, part semidad (Damian was the oldest, but he moved away before the family trek to North Carolina). Daniel had met his wife Christine in Miami, where they lived while she was getting a master's degree in music. Once she graduated, they moved to South Carolina and set down roots in Ladson.

Daniel had worked with his hands since moving to Topton from Florida in the '80s. Remember that he had been one of the original ones to go north, to help finish the Partridge Creek house alongside Tom Branham, before Patricia had brought the younger boys there. He had moved back down to south Florida in the early '90s, after Hurricane Andrew devastated Maura's house in Homestead. These days, in Ladson, Daniel still worked as a carpenter, and the sound of his power tools was a familiar one on Beverly Drive.[28]

Daniel had the house to himself on the afternoon of March 10. When he came into his workroom, there was already a video camera set up and rolling to capture what would happen next. Those who would later watch the videotape have the horror of it imprinted on them. Daniel was dressed in coat and tie, more like he was headed to a job interview or church than his own garage. He looked at the camera and said, "My name is Daniel Kerney Rudolph, and this is for the FBI and the media." On the video, the room is dark, and it's not always easy to see what's happening. The first sign of anything unusual came next after Daniel took off his coat and began setting a tourniquet. Even then, you don't expect what is coming next.

Daniel didn't wait much longer after that, less than a minute. He squatted down and laid his left arm on a worktable. With his right hand, he turned on the power to a compound miter saw, one of those big electric saws with a serrated circular blade. Then, with what can only be called a carpenter's touch, he brought down the handle, and made a straight cut through his left forearm, just below the wrist. On the tape, which was poorly lit, you heard as much as you saw. The whir of the saw, the grinding through the bone. There was a low sort of groaning before Daniel held up his left arm, which no longer had the hand attached. He picked up either a towel or rag and put it over what was now his stump before leaving the garage.

Remarkably, Daniel drove himself to the emergency room at the local hospital. When the staff at the Summerville Medical Center began treating him in the emergency room, they asked Daniel what happened to his hand. Once he told them, an emergency medical vehicle was sent to the house and a call made to the Dorchester County Sheriff's Office. A deputy went out to his house to meet up with the EMS folks, and after knocking a couple of times, he broke a pane of glass and made his way into the garage.[29] The deputy found Daniel's hand and the video camera, which was still set up on its tripod. The hand was put on ice and rushed to a different hospital, where Daniel had been transferred. Ironically, Daniel's carpentry skills may have made a difference. It was a clean cut and perpendicular, making it easier, if that word can be used, for the surgeons to reattach it to his left arm.

Why would you get up one day and think that was a good idea, wondered one police officer who had seen the tape.[30] Charles Stone watched it with his boss and one of the other senior Task Force members. They all thought it was the most damned bizarre thing they had ever seen. Stone used to joke with some of the FBI guys that there were days he felt like cutting off their heads, but he could never imagine doing that to himself. He had his own theory about Daniel and his hand, that Daniel regretted telling the Feds about Eric's interest in explosives when they first interviewed him. Maybe he thought what he told the agents would be used against Eric, and that he might have to testify against his brother (there is privilege between husbands and wives, but not between siblings). That the pressure of the surveillance magnified this remorse, made it combustible. There was another angle to this, thought Stone. Even though Eric had no way of knowing what his brother had said about him, perhaps Daniel was trying to send a message. That he would never talk again, never reveal anything else about Eric, that he would cut off even his own hand before that came to pass.

His boss at the Task Force thought the video was something Stone needed to see, because by now it had been decided that Stone would be the one to interview Eric if he was captured (or negotiate with him if they got into a hostage or barricade situation). This all dated back to Park Dietz and his profiling; even before Eric had been identified, Dietz had been recommending that whenever the bomber was captured, his interrogation should be done by someone who wasn't a federal officer. Which was another reason, aside from a way of avoiding federal turf wars, why Stone was becoming the designated expert on the Rudolph family. First Joel, and his revelation about Jamie being gay. Then Deborah and her portrait of the family. Now this videotape. To the outside world, Daniel's actions seemed just one more manifestation of some demented hillbilly family, but up close it was even more bizarre. There was a strain of paranoia here, something that perhaps Daniel and Eric had in common. But for all the investigating and all the psychologizing, the real question still had to be asked: Was any of this helping get them closer to finding Eric?

7.
UP IN SMOKE

THE FIRST COUPLE of times the FBI searched Eric's trailer and storage unit, the Atlanta folks hadn't been in on the action. They wanted a look, just in case they might spot something that could help with their cases. Tom Mohnal, the FBI explosives guy who had built the mock-up of the Olympic park bomb, was going to be part of this foray. Charles Stone decided to tag along. At the trailer, Mohnal and the techs spent much of their time getting things like paint chips and fiber samples, the forensic nitty-gritty that could often make a case. But they also took away a copy of Clausewitz's *On War*, a nineteenth-century master-work of political and military strategy, not your ordinary bedside reading (it was a present from Eric's mother, who inscribed it). And they found a military-style ammunition can, an important discovery.[1] You could find those cans at just about any military surplus store—a lot of folks used them as portable tool chests, but to the Task Force, ammo cans were components in the Sandy Springs clinic bombs.

Cal's Mini-Storage seemed to offer more of the same. There were lots of work tools and an assortment of clothes, so very carefully, the group started to make an inventory and collect items including bolt cutters, a sledgehammer, and pieces of gray and black duct tape.[2] Both sorts of tape were used in the bombs, but duct tape was a lot more common than ammo cans, so making a match in the lab would be even more of a challenge. They bagged up a pair of hedge clippers and sections of a garden hose; they eyeballed but left behind what was clearly a whole bunch of equipment for growing marijuana, including indoor growing lights, potting soil, and more hoses and tubing. This would be collected another time, a couple of months later, when agents would also find some high-grade pot seeds.[3] But this search was about bombs and bomb-making equipment. They were hoping to find links to Atlanta and Birmingham that would supplement the material taken away in the initial searches.

That's when Charles Stone had his turn at what he would refer to as forensic glory. Inside Unit # 91 at Cal's, where Eric Rudolph stored his gear, Stone saw a rectangular metal piece. It wasn't that long, maybe eight inches by three inches with a rounded flange in the middle, the sort of thing you would fit a wooden handle in. It looked a lot like one of those metal brackets that fit at the end of a mop pole and connect the sponge from the mop to the handle. The place had already been searched twice and nobody had noticed it before—or if they did, they didn't understand its potential significance. But to Stone it was a "holy shit" moment. As in holy shit, that is the sort of plate that fits on the end of a drywall sanding pole, something he'd been looking for since the Centennial Park bombing.

It turns out one of the few parts of that bomb that was recovered was a piece of wood with a metal cap on it. The lab guys had figured out fairly quickly that this piece of wood might have been used as a handle for the pack—and later, agents would discover this was the sort of thing you learned in the military; how to find a wooden pole (they called them dowels), lop off a piece of it, and make a handle for your ALICE pack. When Tom Mohnal made his model of the Centennial Park bomb, one of those wooden handles was part of it.

But that was only the half of it. Stone had been looking for things to do in the early days of the Task Force, and one of them was how to identify that piece of wood. It bugged him, because he knew he'd seen something like that before. So he got an FBI photo of the pole piece and started showing it around. When he took it to one commercial supplier, the guy said this wasn't the sort of thing he sold, but he thought it looked like it came from a pole sander, the sort of thing used for smoothing out Sheetrock. That's when Stone realized where he had seen that type of pole before; the man who was removing a skylight from his house had one in his truck! Stone went to his local Ace Hardware and got one and then sent it off to the FBI lab to see if the brand matched. It did, and after that, the Task Force quickly figured out this particular brand was something you could get at Ace Hardware, which had thousands of stores nationwide, including one in Andrews, North Carolina.

So here Stone was, looking at a pole sander head, exactly like one he had purchased at his local Ace Hardware. The one in Cal's still had the Ace Hardware price tag on it. He didn't find a half-cut piece of pole with a threaded end on it, which might have been a forensic coup de grace, but just as importantly, he didn't find any pole at all. Which meant the lower part of that particular (but still missing) pole, the end that didn't fit into the metal plate, could have been the one that was found in Centennial Park—and he would always wonder where rest of it was.

After running the sander head through testing and comparing it to the remnants of the wooden handle recovered from the Atlanta bomb scene, the lab folks would say the metal pole sander head was made by the Marshalltown Trowel Company and that the piece of wood used as the handle for the ALICE pack was "consistent" with the top end of a drywall sanding pole made by Marshalltown Trowel Company.[4] And they would get another piece of the puzzle when the owners of the Topton house, the people who bought it from the Rudolphs, gave the FBI a videotape they made when they were thinking of buying the house. On it, as the camera pans across the inside of the garage, hanging up on a Peg-Board is what looks like the drywall sander with the pole and head bracket all put together.[5] Holy shit, indeed.

The Task Force team made another stop on its Eric Rudolph tour aside from the Caney Creek trailer and Cal's. They went out to the Topton house and got a look-see courtesy of Frank and Sandy Sauer, the folks who would later give them that video. The house had been redone, new furniture and fresh paint, so they weren't expecting a forensic bonanza. At the least, though, they might get a sense of atmosphere (one look at Tom Branham's property next door would certainly fill the bill on that score) and see the sort of job that Eric and his brothers had done on the place. They walked the property, noticing the little trout pond that Eric had created by damming up part of the creek that flowed through the property. The agents poked their heads into the little goat shed out back. While the rest of the group was getting ready to go, Stone was inside visiting with Frank Sauer. That's when Sauer said to him, do you want to see Eric's secret room? Two holy shit moments in the same day might have been tempting the investigative gods, but Stone said yes, of course.

Sauer led him down some stairs to the garage. At the foot of the stairs, there was a landing that was a couple of feet higher than the rest of the garage. Underneath it was a piece of wood, sort of a door that led you into what looked from the outside to be a crawl space. Stone, by his own admission, wasn't the most agile person, but he got down and stuck his head into the room before calling the evidence techs back into the house. On that videotape that Sauer and his family shot when they got the initial house tour, you can see what it looks like inside the room. In fact, Eric was the one who showed it to one of the Sauer children while the camera was rolling, calling it his root cellar. The room was a small, unfinished area. The walls were covered with Cellofoam Super-Sheath insulation, and there were brackets hanging from the rafters to hold fluorescent lights. It was wired for electricity, and Eric explained there was also a sump pump that would keep it dry, just in case.

The evidence guys didn't find anything when they searched the room, at least no traces of explosives or anything like that. It had been cleaned out, along with the rest of the house, before the Rudolphs moved out (it was already that way when Eric was showing the house to the Sauers). But to Stone, the very idea that Eric had something like a secret room in his house was telling. If he had a room like this here, what other hiding places did he have beyond his back door, out there in the woods? After seeing what was at Cal's, Stone also had a good idea how Eric had been using the room. He had worked on enough drug task forces to make the connection between all the marijuana growing equipment, including the lights and hoses and gardening supplies, and a sealed-off basement room with electricity and a sump pump. This had clearly been used for some serious indoor marijuana growing, no matter how cleaned up it was now.

And that was the thing that didn't seem to fit about Eric—the marijuana. Almost as soon as agents began to interview his family and associates, they kept running across this notion. Eric as a doper, growing and selling pot. And Eric as a stoner, smoking his own product. Not what you would expect from someone who was also being portrayed as a right-wing extremist. You thought pot and tie-dye, maybe some leftover hippie values (and there were a few folks like that up in the Nantahala); but marijuana and Christian Identity, that was an unlikely combination. It just didn't seem to make sense.

Remember, too, that the Task Force's go-to shrink, Dr. Park Dietz, had put together an uncannily accurate profile well before Rudolph was ever identified. One of the things he specifically mentioned was the Atlanta bomber was so paranoid about losing control that he would avoid illegal drugs.[6] Still, it was out there on the table, this Eric and marijuana thing, and even though it seemed out of keeping with the rest of the profile, maybe it was also an important way of understanding him. Especially since growers—and there were a lot of them—who illegally used national forests and parks to raise their crops could be masters of camouflage.

Getting folks to talk about Eric and marijuana was tricky. Not many were eager to tell tales on themselves, especially about drugs and particularly to the FBI. The agents had to make it clear they were interested in Eric (and of course anyone who might have helped him or be hiding him right now); and that this was about a bombing and a cop killing, not about popping anyone for smoking a joint.

The approach seemed to work with most. Deborah spent a portion of that first meeting with Stone and Dave Jordan outlining Eric's involvement with marijuana. But they had already begun to get some of the picture from Tom Branham and another acquaintance of Eric's. Branham's account of his growing estrangement from Eric after Rudolph returned to Topton in 1992 was centered around his suspicion that Eric had become involved in drug dealing.

Branham himself had experience on that score, having been busted at least once in the 1980s for possession, after being stopped by the police in North Carolina.[7] He claimed Eric told him that he smoked pot so he would get thrown out of the army after he failed to make the cut for Special Forces, an account seemingly confirmed by the circumstances of Rudolph's discharge.[8] Branham also said that later on, after Eric left the army, most of the people who visited him in Topton came late at night and had Tennessee plates, which made him suspicious. Then there was the bit about seeing the Forest Service trucks hauling away marijuana plants from the area during their periodic eradication patrols and the fact that Eric didn't seem to have a steady job but always had cash.

You could explain all that away given that pot growing in the Nantahala was popular; that Joel lived at the house as well, and he had lots of friends from his time in Nashville; and that while Eric might have been working some odd jobs, there were few living expenses when it came to Topton. Plus Branham didn't have strong credibility with the law, given his past escapades. But another person who said he was a friend of Eric's dating back to 1990 told the FBI that Eric and Joel made their living off marijuana they grew near the house. This person claimed that he had visited some of Eric's pot patches out in the woods with him and that Eric always brought along his shotgun. He said Eric planted booby traps around his plants, including bear traps and even set up where a trip wire was supposed to set off a shotgun. He thought the Rudolphs could have been making $100,000 a year growing and dealing marijuana, but if that was the case, he didn't have a clue what happened to the money.[9]

A friend of Eric's from high school, perhaps being more circumspect, said that he thought Eric and Joel were growing pot out in the forest but claimed they never showed him where. All he said he really knew was that if he wanted marijuana, all he had to do was ask Eric for some. This was all when Joel was living in Nashville, married to Deborah, and he was suspicious that Eric's frequent trips to Tennessee were more about selling dope than paying social calls. Interestingly, this friend's grandfather, himself an old bootlegger (making moonshine predated growing pot as an illegal pastime in the hills of North Carolina, but the two had much in common), used to share a drink or two with the Rudolph boys and told investigators that although he had no hard proof, he thought they were growing dope out in the woods and selling it in town.

The most complete account of Eric's career in dope came from Deborah, beginning with that interview she did with Stone and Jordan. Deborah laid out a history of marijuana growing and selling by Eric that dated back well into the 1980s, from the time that she and Joel were married. Her account would be verified in part by several others from Nashville as well as Rudolph's army buddies and his girlfriends.[10] The U.S. Forest Service even turned over a tape to the Task Force it thought was of Eric visiting a pot patch out in the forest. The tape had been taken in the 1990s during a routine surveillance operation. The Task Force was never able to confirm that it was Rudolph in the video. But the FBI compiled its own summary of witnesses describing Eric's involvement with pot. The conclusion from reading that report: before, during, and after his time in the military, Eric Rudolph was not only raising and selling high-grade marijuana, but he may have been his own best customer.

Eric never did anything by half measure, and marijuana was another example. Mission-driven was the way Charles Stone described it. Not for Eric to get a few seeds, plant them, and sell the product with no regard for quality. Deborah said that Eric would study *High Times*, the magazine devoted to marijuana, like a businessman doing product research. He was in it for the money, and he was determined to grow the best pot around. That meant starting with the best possible seeds, and in *High Times*, there were ads that hinted how you could get them. At least once he went to Amsterdam, where marijuana use was legal, to buy seeds he then smuggled back into the States.[11] Eric became something of an amateur geneticist, trying to breed the most powerful plants, even offering to buy back seeds that he might have inadvertently sold to customers.[12] And apparently he succeeded in his efforts, earning two hundred dollars an ounce or more.

Investigators ran across some indication that Eric was dealing during the short period of time when he went to Western Carolina University in 1985–86. But Nashville was where he brought most of his crop, and because he often stayed with Joel and Deborah for weeks on end, she saw it firsthand. Eric was a grower, but he was also a loner, so he found one or two other people to do the real selling job for him. One acquaintance liked the pot so much that he began to buy it on behalf of his friends, sometimes getting a pound or more. He said Eric's marijuana, which fetched top dollar on the Nashville market, was distinctive and that for the eight years he smoked it, he could always tell whose it was. And he said you could always tell when Eric would show up in Nashville, just after growing season was over in the mountains. About this time, on one of her trips back to Topton, Deborah told how Eric took her out into the woods and showed off some of his plants; as evidence of his devotion to his enterprise, he would even haul jugs of water to his pot patch to make sure the plants were getting their proper share.

The business seemed to have slacked off during Rudolph's brief stint in the military, but his marijuana use certainly didn't. A barracks mate at Fort Campbell, Kentucky, told the FBI Rudolph always seemed to have a couple of ounces of pot on hand and that he made it clear this was homegrown from North Carolina—and that he grew it in the mountains four to five miles from his home. This army friend said that Rudolph wouldn't go out with the other soldiers; instead, he would hang back in his room and get high, reading military manuals and a book called *The Little Black Book of Explosives*.[13] When he was off duty, Eric would make the hour drive from Fort Campbell to Nashville, where he would crash at Joel and Deborah's place. Deborah would say that it was all about pot, pizza, and sleep. Eric would get high, sometimes with a buddy that he might bring along, they would call Domino's for a couple of pies, then crash until well into the next day.[14] His girlfriend at the time and one of her friends said they spent a lot of time getting high with Eric, but his girlfriend and an army buddy said Eric was also drinking heavily.

Marijuana offered Eric an escape route from the army, as well. His ex-girlfriend echoed what Branham told investigators, that he let it be known he was smoking pot, hoping to get caught. When he tested positive after a urinalysis, Rudolph was busted in rank, and his unit commander soon decided that the army could do without him.[15] By January 1989, he was gone.

Eric's career in the marijuana trade seemed to accelerate after that. He started moving some serious weight, as they call it, four pounds at a time. And he was doing crazy-ass stuff. Sometimes he would send army duffel bags full of marijuana to Nashville via the Greyhound bus, mixing it with coffee so the scent would be hidden. One time he brought it himself, on the bus, wearing his army uniform as cover, even though he had been out for a while. He got someone to remove the side panels from their car doors so he could send marijuana to Nashville that way.[16] Eric had broken up with his previous girlfriend, and his new one disapproved of his dope dealing. She told Stone and Jordan how one day, she found a large duffel bag of his pot in her apartment and told him to get it out of there because she was afraid of the consequences. He said he did, but she still suspected that Eric was keeping a personal stash there and smoking when she was out.

Then there was the time Daniel sent some film to a local pharmacy to be processed. Apparently there were some shots of Eric's plants on there, and someone might have sent a copy of the pictures to the police or Forest Service, because some similar-looking photos ended up on the wall of the local post office. One person claimed that when Eric's mother found out about this, she hit the roof, made him pull down his plants and get rid of his crop. Instead, he brought it to Nashville, dried the leaves there in someone's house, and still managed to sell it. Patricia Rudolph wasn't keen on losing the Topton house because of her son's shenanigans, said this person, and she wasn't thrilled about Eric's career choice either.[17]

After Pat moved out and Daniel followed, Eric was pretty much running the show in Topton (until Joel moved back up there from Nashville when he split up with Deborah). It was about this time, in the early '90s, that Eric started talking about growing some of his plants using hydroponics. That's a way of growing the plants indoors with little soil, using lights and lots of water instead. It had become popular beginning in the 1970s. All that reading of *High Times* seemed to be paying off for Eric. He was going around talking about making sure he kept the rest of his power usage in Topton to a minimum, since the Feds were known to track marijuana growers by monitoring their electric bills, looking for unusual increases.

This seems to have been what the secret room was used for. Deborah heard about it via Joel, and knew where it was in the house, but was never invited to take a look. From what she and others understood, Eric would nurture his baby plants in the secret room, then take them out to the forest and replant them. One clue that the investigators picked up on was that he sometimes put them near the power lines which crossed through parts of the Nantahala area. By the time that the Topton house was sold, all of the growing equipment had been pulled out of the basement, put in storage at Cal's. What wasn't clear is what Eric had done with his various marijuana patches out in the woods.

Even though the Task Force decided it wasn't going to pursue possible drug charges, running down the story of Eric's excursion into marijuana was more than an academic exercise. Stone and the others were getting more glimpses at a complex personality. And they were learning some useful information. For a start, Rudolph had access to cash and possibly lots of it. The numbers weren't completely clear (everyone seemed to be quoting different prices, between $140 and $240 an ounce) but if Eric was able to sell twenty pounds of his high-grade pot a year, he could be making anywhere from $45,000 to $75,000 a year, although his friends put the figure at $100,000. All the agents found when they searched his trailer at Caney Creek was $1,600. He was paying his bills in cash, to be sure, but he wasn't exactly living an extravagant lifestyle, leaving tens of thousands of dollars unaccounted for.

Which fit into another part of Eric's ethos. If you are a grower, you have two ways you can deal with that sort of money. The Cali Cartel, to choose an example, spent a fair portion of its effort not just into bringing drugs into the United States but also into laundering the proceeds. You want to clean up the money, so you can spend it. On the other hand, if you are someone who doesn't trust banks, doesn't trust the government, and your mother has already tussled with the IRS over taxes, then growing and selling marijuana was a good way to stick it into their eye. You were earning money off the grid, and you were probably going to damn well keep that money to yourself, maybe even bury some of it. Paying cash, not too much so that you attracted attention, was a good way of keeping the government out of your business, making sure you left as few tracks as possible along the way. Eric liked to pay cash, as the Feds had already found out, whether it was for food or rent, or even his other bills.

Then there was the p-word, which Park Dietz had used in his initial profile. Paranoia. Eric didn't just grow and sell his pot, he used it in a big way. He liked to get stoned and think, said Deborah, but he also loved to smoke a joint and watch Cheech and Chong videos. The comedy duo's act was totally about being high, and Eric could watch their movies endlessly. He did a wicked impression of Cheech Marin's stoned Chicano accent and convulsed with laughter watching their movies. *Up in Smoke*, their first and most popular movie, was a hapless, stoned odyssey across Los Angeles in search of the primo marijuana bud, a plot sure to appeal to a connoisseur like Eric.

Cheech and Chong, in their own particular way, were endlessly paranoid, in this case about a police sergeant named Stedenko, who was their nemesis in the movie. That was the point about marijuana, whether you smoked just a little bit or, like Cheech and Chong and Eric, an enormous amount. It made you high, sure, but it also made you paranoid. The better the pot, the greater the paranoia.

Eric struck many of those who knew him as mellow when he was stoned, but he was already steeped in the paranoid culture of the far Right, where the prevailing worldview seemed to be that black helicopters from the United Nations were a heartbeat away from jumping ugly on America's heartland. His adventures in the marijuana trade seem to have begun around the same time in the mid-'80s that his mother had taken him out to the Church of Israel compound in Missouri, and it must have made for an interesting contrast. But what if these two different influences fed on each other, especially when he was getting high almost constantly? If instead of staying away from illegal drugs, as Park Dietz had hypothesized, he went in the other direction, just how much of his paranoia came from the marijuana—and how much from the militia-type madness Eric was imbibing from other quarters?

There was another part of the Rudolph back-story, that like the marijuana, didn't seem to fit. How in the world did someone so antiauthority and whose family believed much of this extremist credo end up in the army? It wasn't quite as bad as the ATF and IRS, but it was still part of the federal government. Deborah said everyone in the family was shocked by Eric's decision to enlist.[18] It hit them, if you will pardon the pun, like a thunderbolt. But he claimed he wanted to see if he could make the cut and become an Army Ranger. If you were his mother, it wasn't exactly a career path you might approve of; then again, maybe it would be better than growing dope.

Which Eric continued to do, even after he joined up. But it turns out Eric learned some interesting skills when he was in the army. He signed up on August 4, 1987, for a four-year stint, after passing a battery of tests where he scored slightly above average. The army noted that its new nineteen-year-old enlistee was five foot ten inches tall and weighed 140 pounds. He was assigned to Company A, 2nd Battalion, 58th Infantry Regiment, 2nd Infantry Training Brigade at Fort Benning, Georgia, for his basic training. Basic went well, and Eric earned expert badges in hand grenade and M-16 use as well as his Army Service Ribbon.[19] After that, Private (E-1) Eric Rudolph did Airborne basic, still at Fort Benning, and earned his jump wings, what you get when you successfully do a parachute course. But he had apparently already failed in his attempt to make Ranger, his ostensible reason for getting in the military. The exact reason is unclear, but it appears that an injury prevented him from getting very far in the training. Which wasn't unusual. Ranger School was incredibly tough to get into and even tougher to pass.

Despite that, Rudolph's military career seemed to be going well. He was promoted to E-2, a higher level of private, after being sent to Fort Campbell, Kentucky, and he earned his Air Assault Qualification Badge. Rudolph was now part of the 101st Airborne Division, a storied part of the army. Eric's new company commander had served in the Rangers and liked to give his soldiers the benefit of his training. That, he told the FBI, included teaching them about improvised demolitions and how to make improvised antipersonnel devices that used C-4 or dynamite with nails or other metal as shrapnel. Part of the training was how to direct the force of the blast from these improvised devices, which could include a coffee can, a gasoline jug, or even an ammunition can, by planting them in a particular way. He also trained his soldiers in using primary and secondary explosive devices in battlefield attacks. Everybody, said the company commander, down to the lowest-ranking soldier, got this training.[20]

Eric's enthusiasm about explosives, if that's what it can be called, led him to smuggle some twenty-five pounds of C-4 plastic explosive out of Fort Campbell in an ammunition can. One of Eric's roommates, the one who talked to the Feds about his marijuana use, says Eric took the C-4 and detonating cords back to North Carolina, which was where Rudolph said he was going to live like a hermit after the army.

This same buddy called Rudolph a great soldier who wanted to get everything he could out of the training in weapons, demolition, and survival. Rudolph always had a pen and paper handy, taking notes on every subject, whether it be communications or nuclear, biological, and chemical training. He was even a bit of a know-it-all, according to his buddy, who learned well beyond his rank and was unafraid to criticize instructors if he felt they were giving out the wrong information. One thing you did learn at Fort Campbell, he said, was how to use a wooden dowel as a handle for their packs when you used it without a frame.

The 101st also trained its soldiers in Survival, Evasion, Resistance, Escape (SERE). Eric told his buddy he would not be a POW, that there was no way he was going to be taken alive. On one SERE exercise, Eric even got into a fight with the soldier who had taken him prisoner. That wasn't acceptable to Eric, who kept demanding to be shot and killed!

If Private (E-2) Eric Rudolph sounded gung ho, then it was a misleading impression. Having already failed to make Ranger, he was beginning to figure out he wasn't cut out for the army, and the army was learning the same thing. Eric was still outspoken in the barracks about his antigovernment views, not something one normally expects from an enlisted man. He also chafed at the army way, complaining to his girlfriend at the time about the menial jobs he got as a junior enlisted man. She said he became a bit psycho about it, and was particularly obsessed with one drill sergeant he hated. Eric was also still smoking pot, which was perhaps made easier by the fact he could escape from the base and be at Joel and Deborah's in under an hour.

It was pretty clear where all this was headed. Eric wasn't army material, and there was no way that was going to change. His company commander thought part of the problem was heavy drinking by Eric, and the rest was due to authority and discipline issues. He recalled that Eric also hung out with some of the other Chapter 14 soldiers (the ones about to be kicked out for disciplinary reasons), and he remembered there was a skinhead in the unit but wasn't sure if Eric was associated with him. There seemed to be a bad undercurrent in the barracks as well. Routine inspections turned up copies of books like *The Anarchist Cookbook* and *Revenge: Getting Even*, and the company commander suspected they were making the rounds of his troops.[21]

There was never anything violent about what Eric did. Instead it appeared that he made up his mind it was time to leave, and once again worked single-mindedly toward achieving this particular goal. There had been one incident for attitude, back on New Year's Day at the beginning of 1988, on the same day he was promoted. But now it appeared that Eric was determined to be "chaptered," kicked out of the army, and he was counseled three times in the same month. He threw equipment, refused to fall into position, used disrespectful language, and generally mocked authority. One of the NCOs who tried to work with Eric on attitude adjustment got the clear message that Rudolph no longer felt the army had anything left to teach him. Finally, after testing positive for marijuana, which even the army felt was deliberate, Eric Robert Rudolph and the United States Army parted company. He had lasted one year, five months, and twenty-two days.[22]

So what was he doing there in the first place? Was this just some wild idea on Eric's part, some romantic version of Eric as a Ranger? Did he know himself so little as to think that the army could change him, turn him into something he clearly wasn't? Or was it some sort of personal test to see how he matched up against the best of the best, his discipline against theirs? Clearly there were things that he wanted to learn while he was in, hence the ever-present paper and pen. But to what end? Even more than the marijuana, the military didn't seem to fit who Eric was.

Deborah would have her suspicions, in retrospect, and they would be shared by the investigators who studied both Eric and his short-lived military career. Maybe Eric really did think he could become a Special Forces warrior, but whether or not he made the grade, he was there to gain some useful skills. The demolition courses, even though they didn't include pipe bombs, went into even more detail than he could have expected. SERE school was where he learned all about escape and evasion, how to handle himself in the woods. Charles Stone was particularly fond of that phrase, mission-driven, and he kept seeing the pattern in Eric's actions. If you are going to grow marijuana, read up and experiment, buy your seeds in Amsterdam, then come up with a killer crop. If you are going into the army, learn what you are interested in: explosives, guns, and survival skills. Then either make Ranger (if you really meant it) or find a way to get out. But did this mean he had some sort of master plan? Only Eric would know the answer to that.

One thing was clear. Eric's survival skills had clearly jumped a notch. He used to go camping in the woods with his friend Randy Cochran. This was something they had been doing for years, since the Rudolphs had moved to Topton. They would hunt turkey and deer, doing overnights in the Nantahala Gorge. Randy remembered one trip they took after Eric left the army. It must have been cold because Randy had a sleeping bag, but all Eric used was his poncho liner (they did have a campfire). That was hard-core, Cochran thought.

When you combined the marijuana and the military, there were a lot of conclusions you could reach as an investigator/fugitive tracker—and at this point it was definitely a fugitive hunt. Eric knew his way around these woods, and he also knew how to survive in them. If he could hide his pot plants from the Forest Service, he was going to be able to hide himself as well (growers often had elaborate lairs out in the woods). And if they found him or his hiding place, it could get tricky. If he set booby traps to protect his plants, then he was pretty damn likely going to have something more in mind to protect himself.

Why did the Task Force even think he was still in these parts, and why did they think he was on his own? Part of what you learn in SERE school is deception, so the whole thing with his truck and the shopping spree at BI-LO could have been an elaborate ruse. But they didn't think so, not with that particular shopping list, which seemed geared toward long-term, or at least six months of, survival. Eric's experiences in the army, not to mention when he was selling his dope, suggested he wasn't the trusting sort, not even with members of his own family. Besides, they kept hearing stories of how he would just pick up and leave the Topton house, returning days or weeks later without explanation.[23] Most importantly, the bombs seemed to be the work of one person, so if they thought he was the bomber, why would they think he would trust his fate to someone else?

Park Dietz weighed in with his opinion. Now that Eric had been identified, he was brought back in to review the case files and to visit Andrews (it was the next town up the valley from Murphy and the closest real community to Topton and the Nantahala) along with Birmingham and Atlanta. He thought Rudolph was their man for all the bombings and that he would stay close to home, trying to hide and survive on the familiar terrain of western North Carolina.

Which was why there was now a command post in Andrews, for the combined fugitive hunt and investigation. Everything had been rolled into one, which meant it was a bit of a bureaucratic nightmare. The chain of command included FBI offices in Birmingham, Charlotte, and Atlanta, not to mention Washington, and there were all the other agencies, which not only included the ATF and GBI, but also the Birmingham Police Department, the U.S. Forest Service, the local sheriffs and police chiefs in Macon and Cherokee Counties, and the North Carolina State Bureau of Investigation, until it had a falling-out with the Feds over turf.

Perhaps the most telling thing about this new setup was who was running it. Terry Turchie was an FBI inspector whose previous claim to fame was running the Unabomber investigation when Ted Kaczynski was finally caught after an eighteen-year run. Nabbing the Unabomber was one of the rare FBI high-profile success stories during the Waco–Ruby Ridge–Richard Jewell era. Having Turchie run the show up in Andrews meant the FBI was bringing in its ace (and also someone who knew just how long such an investigation could take place). There was some bloodshed on the bureaucratic floor because of the reorganization. After FBI Director Louis Freeh ordered the consolidation, some in the ATF cried foul and kept up the pressure until they got one of their own put in alongside Turchie.[24] When the ATF finally got cut in, it went for home-field advantage, bringing in North Carolina native Don Bell to supervise its end of the hunt. Bell and Turchie were both easygoing by nature and managed to keep the frictions between their agencies to a minimum on the ground.

At this point, there were really not many agents up in western North Carolina, certainly not for the ground they had to cover. Right after Rudolph was identified and the truck was found, there had been more than a hundred agents, perhaps as many as two hundred, that were part of the manhunt. But that was scaled back in less than three weeks' time when they couldn't find him. The new plan, which envisioned a more long-term presence, called for twenty investigators (who doubled as a SWAT team) and fourteen support staff, along with four supervisors, and access to a helicopter. The Nantahala National Forest was a half million acres, and now that it was springtime, there was little you could even see from the air, because it was double canopied, with hardwoods and pines growing over the ever-present mountain laurel.

The big question was where to look. Sheriff Jack Thompson, who may have known the woods as well as anyone from his days at the Forest Service, was among those telling the Task Force that Rudolph could be holed up in someone's unoccupied summer cabin—or that he could have built one of his own. On virtually every one of the roads that snaked through the area, you could see at least one tumbledown shack, which meant even more potential hiding places.

Just how comfortable was Eric in the woods? They were hearing all sorts of stories. When Rudolph was showing the Topton house to Frank and Sandy Sauer, he told Frank that he loved the Nantahala and often went on two- or three-week camping trips. Even before he joined the army, it seemed that Eric and his brothers, along with Randy Cochran, liked to play war games in the forest. Especially one called fox and hounds, where they dressed up in camouflage and tried to hunt each other down. Eric was particularly hard to catch. His favorite hiding spots were down in caves or up in the trees. He'd think nothing of shinnying up a tree, even if the lowest set of branches was fifteen feet up.

Another self-described friend, who claimed he had played this game with Rudolph as a teenager, said that Eric talked about building a bomb shelter in the woods and stocking it with food. This echoed what Joel Rudolph told Stone and Jordan about how he and Eric had once buried food and provisions out in the forest. This particular friend was one of those who raised the possibility Eric was hiding out in a cabin, but couldn't offer any specifics.

His fellow soldiers also talked about Eric's love affair with the woods, as did his former girlfriend and another female friend. One ex-soldier said Rudolph spent his vacation time hiking the trails near his home and that he boasted about being able to drink pure springwater from the mountains. Eric even showed him one location near his house where he drove pipes into the rock to tap a water source. With another, he talked about using the Appalachian Trail, a network of hiking trails that ran from Georgia to Maine and through the Nantahala, as a way of moving easily and anonymously. They discussed living off the land, using this hiker's highway to move from one prestocked cabin to another. This soldier told investigators that all Eric had to do was grow a beard and not cut his hair and that he would be virtually unrecognizable, especially out on the trail.

His former girlfriend from his army days said Eric took her to some of the more secluded spots out in the woods, where she would later take members of the Task Force. Both she and a mutual friend told the FBI in separate interviews they thought Rudolph would be most likely to hole up in the Nantahala.

Still, they were checking out other places, particularly the nearby area of eastern Tennessee. Remember what Eric had told Joel the weekend before the Birmingham bombing, when he dropped in on him in Hendersonville—that he had a six-hour drive home to his place in Tennessee. Also remember that Eric and Joel had both lived in Nashville. His sister, Maura, thought Eric was renting a place somewhere along the Tennessee–North Carolina border. Rudolph told a woman he briefly dated in 1997 that he lived over in Tennessee with his uncle. His gray Nissan truck was bought from someone over in Mount Juliet, Tennessee, in 1994—and the man who sold it to him said he had only advertised it locally.

There were also a whole lot of reports coming in to the Task Force, which later proved to be false, of folks spotting Eric or giving him rides. One in particular had them also scurrying toward Tennessee. It was an elaborate story by an Andrews local of how he picked up Eric at a Big D convenience store, where he spotted Eric using the phone. The man described Eric's clothing down to a camouflage baseball cap and said he had a few days of beard growth. Eric said he wanted a ride over to Copper Basin, Tennessee, and the man said he would be happy to help him out (he knew who Eric was), but that the man first had to stop and make a truck payment. Eric said he didn't mind waiting! All this was supposed to have taken place in early May, months after Eric disappeared. The story was too good to check, as they say in the news business, but when investigators looked into it, they discovered it was an elaborate hoax. Eric was becoming the local version of Bigfoot. There were sightings, but so far they had all been in the category of local legend. Nevertheless, the Task Force had to check out each and every one of them. Who knew which one might turn out to be true.

The woods and hills of western North Carolina weren't just full of cabins and shacks offering Eric possible haven. There were caves—not as many as eastern Tennessee, but certainly a few—and there were dozens, if not hundreds, of old mines. Randy Cochran had described a particular trip to one of them around Christmastime a few years earlier to investigators. The trip was already family folklore because Eric had allegedly gotten up from the table and left the house without saying a word, heading off into a snowstorm (his sister would say that Eric was away for three weeks).[25]

The way Randy Cochran told it, Eric had gone caving, alone, for several days, and there were several inches of snow on the ground. Cochran was able to offer a specific location, called Blowing Springs Cave, in the nearby Nantahala Gorge. A mutual friend, who said he met Rudolph through Cochran, also told agents about a trip to the same cave he took with both men in the spring or fall of 1995. It was the first time he met Rudolph, and they had an easy conversation, mostly about guy stuff, hunting and fishing and even caving. They drove over to Blowing Springs Cave and spent about four hours exploring inside.

Charles Stone didn't know the first thing about caving, but this was enough to get him interested. A cave might be a natural hideout, even more secluded than a cabin, not to mention a place where someone could set up their own bomb factory. He called back down to Atlanta and spoke to someone at the Georgia Department of Natural Resources, asking for help. You've got a world-renowned caver right up there in North Carolina, he was told, actually two of them—a husband and wife named Cato and Susan Holler in Old Fort. Stone made a cold call to the Hollers, then went over to see them at their place near Asheville. They lived out on a lake, on a small island, and it turns out they were tickled to be asked for help.

Cato Holler was a practicing dentist, but he and his wife were avid cavers, spelunkers as they are called, and both were fellows of the National Speleological Society. Stone proceeded to fill them in on Eric, how the Task Force thought he might be looking for a dry cave, a water source, and a place to cache supplies. Cato Holler explained there were more mines than caves in western North Carolina, something to do with the amount of limestone (there were far more caves in eastern Tennessee), but there were certainly a number worth exploring. At one point, Stone asked if they had any books on caving, because he was looking for some sort of primer for his own personal interest. The Hollers laughed and took him up to their library, which had hundreds of books and journals about spelunking.

They left it that the Hollers were willing to come over to Andrews and help out, having more than a passing knowledge of the caves in the Nantahala area. After a few weeks of getting nowhere on other leads, Stone called them and asked if they could help the Task Force check out the Blowing Springs Cave. They set up a rendezvous, meeting on the side of the road that led from Andrews out toward the gorge. Both the Hollers were in good shape, maybe better than the agents, despite being in their fifties. All that caving toned your muscles.

They met up with an ad hoc tactical team of GBI, FBI, and ATF agents—and a bomb dog. Cato Holler took the lead, while Susan stayed back at what was now their temporary roadside base with Terry Turchie and Don Bell. Stone joined them; if he wasn't going to crawl into Eric's basement room, there was no way he was going into a cave. The team climbed up a steep slope, more like the side of a mountain, to the cave. The agents went in and looked but didn't find any evidence that Eric had been there. No trash, no scent of explosives. Once they cleared the chamber, they brought Cato in, not wanting to put him in the possibility of harm's way.

Then it got interesting. The agents weren't sure the right way to go, so they asked Cato to come up to the front. Space had gotten pretty tight, and he crawled over the others. He found the next section of the cave, but instead of having him hold back while they went in, someone handed him a pistol and said, after you! Fortunately for Cato, no one was lying in wait. Pretty soon, they brought in the bomb dog to sniff for explosives and searched this chamber thoroughly, again coming up empty.

Instead of going back the way they came, Cato took them out a different way. The only problem being a drop from the mouth of the cave to the ground, maybe a few feet, and now the bomb dog wouldn't leave. After a few minutes of cursing and cajoling, they finally got the dog out. They didn't realize it at the time, but the Cave and Mine Team had just made the first of what would be many forays in the months to come. And it would be years before Stone found out that on this first expedition, the agents got Cato to take point and sent him in with a pistol.

It had been three months since Rudolph's truck had been found by the coon hunters. In that time, agents had talked to just about anyone who might know him (with the glaring exception of his mother). They had investigated his links to marijuana and the military, searched cabins and their first cave. Like Park Dietz, they were pretty sure, although not certain, that Eric was still in the neighborhood, if 500,000 acres can be called that. Sheriff Thompson was sure of it, and he was sure Eric was on his own, using the woods that had been his backyard since he moved to North Carolina as his hiding place. The Task Force already knew this wasn't going to be easy or necessarily quick.

But the rest of the country was moving on. Eric Rudolph was becoming old news, sort of like the Unabomber had, except when he surfaced with another one of his devices. If you're the FBI, you have a couple of options, short of sending in an invasion force, when you want to bring new life to a fugitive investigation. You can increase the reward money—and you can put someone on your Ten Most Wanted Fugitives list. That's what the Justice Department did with Eric Rudolph in early

May, putting on a news conference with all the bells and whistles to drum up some publicity for its fugitive hunt.

FBI Director Louis Freeh admitted this was being done to put more attention on Rudolph; and from now on, Eric's picture would adorn the wall of every post office in the country as part of a wanted poster, along with the FBI's Web site. And for the first time publicly, Freeh said that Rudolph was not only wanted for the Birmingham bombing, but was the only person they were interested in questioning about the Atlanta bombings. The forensic reports on the material recovered from Rudolph's trailer, truck, and storage unit, including that pole sander, were beginning to come in, and they were matching up with the various bomb components. The FBI was making it clear there were a million reasons for anyone who knew where Eric Robert Rudolph might be hiding to give him up. The only question was an obvious one: Did anyone know? Eric had once told one of his friends that he was going to vanish into these woods one day. Now, to borrow the title of one of his favorite movies, it seemed that Eric Rudolph had gone up in smoke.

8.
NORDMANN

HE WAS PROBABLY in the danger zone. When the FBI calculated how long the food Eric Rudolph had bought on that last-minute shopping trip at BI-LO would last him—the seventy-two pounds, 8.3 ounces of tuna, nuts, green beans, oatmeal, and raisins—they came up with a figure of four to six months. That's if he counted his calories carefully, went down to a minimum of 500 or so. Not easy, especially during the cold winter months when a body needed fuel. They assumed, especially after their interviews, that he had more than adequate supplies of fresh water. Finding a mountain spring to drink from was something Eric could probably do in a matter of minutes, if not hours. Maybe he could last longer if he had other food supplies—if he had some other cache or if he was breaking into summer cabins. But all things being equal, it was about time for Eric to surface.

Surface he did, right under the noses of the Task Force, only to vanish again. It was another demonstration of just how difficult this all-too-real game of hide-and-seek was for the seekers. And up in the hills and hollers of North Carolina, the legend of Eric Rudolph began to grow.

The news came in a phone call. "It's bad, Kenny, it's really bad." Macon County Deputy Sheriff Kenny Cope wasn't expecting a call from

George Nordmann on Saturday morning, July 11. He knew Nordmann; they were by way of being neighbors in Topton, living only a couple of miles away. Both of them knew the Rudolphs, Eric and Kenny being around the same age. Now Nordmann was trying to explain how Eric had just been to see him and taken his truck. All he could do was keep repeating that line—"It's bad Kenny, it's really bad."

The hills of western North Carolina seemed to attract more than their share of odd and colorful characters, and George Nordmann certainly fell into that category. In his early seventies, Nordmann ran the Better Way Health Food Store in Andrews, just a few blocks over from the Task Force command post. If you wanted an amiable lecture on the virtues of echinacea or a coffee enema or needed some special herbal recipe that he promised was safer and more effective than something from a doctor's office, then you stopped in at Nordmann's. After a few minutes walking around his cluttered store and talking with him, you realized a few things: George was soft-spoken, as friendly as they come, and really seemed to care about what he was prescribing for you; he was highly educated—even if you didn't buy into all of his explanations for his various herbs, you could still respect his scientific background—and George was a Right-wing extremist of the ultra-Catholic variety who would bend your ear about conspiracies.

George had lived in the area for some twenty years, these days by himself, though with a gaggle of children (George and his wife had ten), someone was always looking in on him. Like the Rudolphs and Tom Branham, he chose Topton as a refuge from Florida's citrus belt. He'd gotten an engineering degree from the University of Florida, returned home to grow oranges, but began to feel in much the same way as Patricia, that Florida schools were becoming too integrated for his taste. He tried to make a go of it in the Pacific Northwest, where his brother lived, but that didn't work out. Someone had handed him a brochure written by a man named Nord Davis, extolling the virtues of the Nantahala, so he decided to give that a try, and pretty soon the Nordmann brood moved north to Topton.[1]

When he first moved up there in the late seventies, he worked as a part-time teacher at the Nantahala School, the same one that Eric would later attend for a year. Nordmann was also a devout, old-school Catholic (though his wife had divorced him years before) who didn't have much time for all the changes the Church had gone through since Vatican Two. He was down the line when it came to matters such as birth control and abortion and made sure everyone who visited either his house or his store knew it. Word around town was that when one of his unmarried daughters got pregnant, he had her stay around the house until she gave birth. When things started to go awry with her delivery, they finally had to call an ambulance and get her to a hospital.[2]

So, here was Nordmann calling Cope, and when Kenny heard what Nordmann had to say, he called his boss, Sheriff Homer Holbrooks, saying Homer, you are not going to believe this. Cope couldn't quite believe it himself. I got a gentleman here who has been contacted by Eric Rudolph.[3] Cope and Holbrooks called the Task Force, and pretty soon the whole tale started to unfold and another shit storm hit the area.

Here's how it played out, the gospel according to George, how Eric Rudolph came and went.

It began with Bobo, George's dog. Bobo was about four years old, a mixture of chow and collie. George said he was a good watchdog and kept a careful eye on the property, warning him of intruders. Sometime around late May, maybe early June, Nordmann noticed that Bobo wasn't feeling well. The dog was refusing to eat. Then one day he simply disappeared. A couple of weeks later, when George was walking his property, he found Bobo dead. The dog must have died several days earlier, at the least, because he was already decomposing. In retrospect, Nordmann told the Task Force, he realized Eric poisoned his dog.

But he didn't understand it at the time. That was just part of it. There were other strange things going on around the Nordmann residence. Like the cast-iron skillet that was left out in the kitchen. He never used that particular skillet and neither did his daughters. And some of the health supplements he kept around the house were missing, including a case of E'mergen-C super energy booster six-gram powdered drink packets (just add water and you get a fizzy, fruity energy drink). There were some other items, vitamins especially but also protein supplements, that Nordmann had already opened and started to use, which had also disappeared, that he was able to list:

- a 150-tablet bottle of NOW brand predigested amino acid 1500

- a 120-capsule bottle of NOW brand amino acid 1000

- a 60-tablet bottle of Nature's Plus mega B-150

- a 90-tablet bottle of Nature's Plus amino acid chelated Ultra-Mins

- a 30-tablet bottle of Nature's Plus sustained-release Ultra-Two

- a 16-ounce bottle of NOW brand whey protein

Around the same time that Nordmann noticed these items were missing, he said he found a $100 bill sitting on his stove, but he thought maybe one of his daughters had left that out.

What you have to understand about Nordmann is that he was a pack rat, that the man made Tom Branham look wasteful, and his house up on Long Branch Road was a reflection of the man. It was a junkman's dream. You drove up the proverbial winding mountain lane to his house, and the first thing you saw were a dozen or more cars, mostly beat-up old pieces of metal, lining his driveway. Then you noticed the chickens wandering around in the yard.

The house was a cross between an elongated shanty and a tumble-down shack that seemed to meander back on his property, even sort of running on to the chicken coop. On the main floor, you saw plenty of religious pictures and something that looked like an elaborate Catholic shrine. There was a basement, lined on the outside with corrugated metal, where he kept his health food supplies—a bewildering inventory of protein supplements, herbal remedies, dried foods, and other natural products, like honey. The first time Charles Stone was in there, he wondered how anyone could keep track of what was in there, but Nordmann was the sort who swore he knew where every last jar or can or packet or pill was, in spite of the disorder, and he was pretty specific about what he said was taken.

Why Nordmann waited until after Eric's visit to tell anybody about these odd goings-on is something only he can answer. And there would be many more questions about why he waited so long after Eric showed up to call Kenny Cope. It would be the subject of intense debate within the Task Force and the local law enforcement community for years to come. Many of the locals and not a few on the Task Force viewed Nordmann as someone who went out of his way to help Eric and questioned the true nature of his involvement. The head of the Task Force was inclined to believe George and had a good rapport with him, although some of the agents felt this was a case of bending over backward to placate local feelings. But on one point, the evidence does seem to be consistent with Nordmann's story, even if you can come up with an alternate explanation. If he was beginning to get the feeling he was being stalked, he was right.

Nordmann said it was around 7:00 P.M. on Tuesday night, July 7, when he returned home after a day at his store in Andrews. He just pulled up the short driveway from Long Branch Road to his house when he noticed Eric standing there, waiting for him, about twenty-five to thirty feet away. He told agents that he said get out of here to Eric, who he certainly knew, but then somehow they ended up talking for a half hour. He said right off Eric told him that he wasn't guilty of what he had been accused of, but there was no way the Feds were going to be able to catch him.[4]

"I look like a hippy," Rudolph told Nordmann. His hair had grown out and was pulled back in a ponytail. He also had a beard that was about two inches long (the long hair and beard reminded investigators what Rudolph had told one of his army mates about how he could change his appearance if he ever needed to hide out).

He'd been watching George and his house for quite a while, Eric explained, which began to account for some of those strange occurrences that had been happening. Rudolph mentioned that he'd seen Nordmann's daughter Mary from a distance when she visited the house and noticed she was pregnant (in fact her due date was about two weeks away). If that wasn't enough to convince Nordmann that Eric had been watching him, Rudolph also talked about how Nordmann had installed a new lock on one of his exterior doors a couple of weeks earlier. Eric said he had been eating the cherries off of Nordmann's trees, thank you very much.

Rudolph was wearing a camouflage field jacket and pants, a matching set in military style. Nordmann couldn't tell what sort of shirt Eric was wearing because the field jacket was fastened all the way up to his neck. Nor could he say what sort of shoes or boots Eric was wearing. He said he didn't notice. But the fact that Eric was wearing a pair of olive drab knit gloves in early July caught his attention. When George asked, Eric just said, I wear gloves, and Nordmann understood this as meaning Rudolph was trying not to leave any fingerprints. Eric wasn't wearing a hat or glasses, but he did have a small pair of black binoculars attached by a strap around his neck.

The pants were baggy, and as Eric tugged at the waist, he said he had been living on five hundred calories a day. That's one of the reasons he was here. He needed Nordmann's help. He had a map and a place where the law could never find him, but he wanted to get enough food and other supplies to last him a year—and he was willing to pay George for his trouble.

What he really wanted was for Nordmann to get the supplies and drop them alongside a road, he didn't say which one, and then Rudolph would pack them in to his hiding place. That's the way he had done it before, Eric said, and he mentioned that he had a way of eluding tracking dogs. Rudolph wouldn't tell him where his hiding place was, only that it was some distance away from Nordmann's house. Eric said they, which George took to mean the authorities, had found some of his food before he could hide it all, so he had to restock, lay in enough supplies to last him until the following summer.

Rudolph must have been making a list in his head for a long time. Now, as Nordmann watched, he wrote it on a piece of paper. It included batteries for his radio, the old ones were running low said Eric; a camouflage tarp that he thought George could get at Wal-Mart; and some screen material he could use to grow sprouts in a jar. Most of all, he needed to get some fat in his diet and listed a whole mess of canned goods he wanted. Nordmann said Rudolph reached toward his jacket pocket as if he were about to get out some money, but didn't pull any out.

Nordmann told investigators he was nervous about helping Eric and figured the best thing he could do was to play along with him, pretend to be cooperating. He acted as if he would get the supplies but told Eric that he would not drop them off anywhere for him. He wasn't getting in that deep. Let me take your car, Eric said. No, Nordmann told him, that's not going to happen either. How about this, Rudolph said, I will tie you up. That way no one will think you helped me. I don't want to do that either, Nordmann told him.

One of the first things you are trying to figure out as you hear this story—and Nordmann says he was trying to understand it himself—is why had Eric chosen him. What made George so special? Part of the answer may be the natural food supplies that Nordmann had and that everyone in Topton, all of Macon County for that matter, knew that he kept at his house. Part of it may be that Eric thought he could trust George, thought he was a kindred soul.

It turned out they had some history, Eric and George. Not a lot, but some, if you bought George's version of events (interestingly, Nordmann had never been interviewed before this by the Task Force, not when they were chasing down leads nor when the initial profile of Eric was being written). George couldn't remember when exactly, but a few years back the two of them had gotten into a spiritual discussion. Again, part of what George couldn't remember is if this took place at his house or his store, or how they got started on the subject or even many of the specifics.

But he remembered the gist of it, that it was one of your basic what's right and wrong discussions, what the Ten Commandments say, that sort of thing. George said he remembers Eric complained that his mother was into crystals and New Age stuff, not what George would call functioning Christianity. They talked about abortion, and George quickly figured out that Eric was strongly against it. Eric was dead-set against anything that smacked of liberalism, and George thought he was even somewhat radical. George said Eric was both headstrong and set in his ways, a young man who definitely had his own ideas about things.

Remember that Nordmann was a Catholic, and he knew that Eric's family had started out Catholic. Eric made it clear he was interested in Catholicism, that whatever brand of religion his mother was currently into was clearly not his thing, so Nordmann invited him to come to Mass at his church. Which was a very traditional one called the Holy Trinity

Chapel over in Benton, Tennessee, run by Dr. John Grady and the Order of St. John of Jerusalem.⁵ This was unrepentant old-style Catholicism, with the Latin Tridentine Mass, and the Order of St. John claimed a history dating back to 1048 A.D. It was proud of the fact that its priests had all been ordained before Vatican Two, when the Church began to reform itself and move away from Latin as the basis of its service. Eric took up Nordmann's offer and attended one Mass at Holy Trinity, but that was the only time George says he saw him at his church.

That had been a while back, but Nordmann remembered, and before Eric disappeared that July night back into the woods, Nordmann gave him something: rosary beads. They were blue plastic beads on a white nylon cord, with a plastic cross. They were made by George's children. Since the Feds had found rosary beads in Eric's truck back in February, they were curious. Had George ever given Eric rosary beads before? No, was the answer.

So Eric and George had this previous spiritual connection, and George certainly had access to food, but what about Eric's friends, the ones he grew up with and played war games with out in the woods? They were still in Topton, especially Randy Cochran, in places just as isolated as Nordmann's. Why George and not one of them? Nordmann couldn't remember how they got on the subject, but Eric started telling him about Randy—Nordmann had certainly heard of Cochran, Topton not being a booming metropolis, but didn't think he had ever met him—and how the two of them used to talk about hiding food and supplies in the woods. But now, Eric said, he thought Randy was trying to rat him out, passing along information to Kenny Cope, who Eric also clearly knew in his capacity as both a Topton resident and sheriff's deputy. It might have been bullshit, some sort of head fake or disinformation plot aimed at the authorities, but Eric told George that he had lied to Randy Cochran in some of those conversations about hiding in the woods.

There was something else in this conversation between Eric and George, something that investigators kept quiet but worried the hell out of some of them. After Eric wrote out his shopping list, he asked George whether he knew where the Feds who were looking for him had set themselves up. Nordmann said yes, it wasn't far from his store. Eric drew a map of Andrews with some guidance from George on the same piece of paper that held the shopping list. He got Nordmann to pinpoint the location of the Task Force office and seemed to fix it in his mind. Nordmann actually kept the paper with the shopping list and map, so he was able to show it to investigators later. They realized now that not only were they looking for Eric, but he might also be looking for them. Or of course, he could have just been making sure to avoid them.

About thirty minutes after Nordmann first spotted Rudolph in his driveway and told him to get the hell out of there, Nordmann said Eric left. Vanished. It would have been about 7:30 P.M. ET on Tuesday night, July 7, 1988, a summer's night when there was still plenty of light left. The only trace of Eric was the paper that had the shopping list and the map. Which raised the obvious question to Kenny Cope and Sheriff Holbrooks and the Task Force. Why didn't George Nordmann simply walk inside, pick up the phone, and call Kenny Cope or 911 or anyone, including one of his children, right then and there? Or even get in his car and drive into town? If that was too obvious, why not say something the next morning when he went into Andrews and opened up his store?

Nordmann said he was too scared. That if Eric had been watching him before, then he was probably still watching him. So if he called anybody, Eric might be watching that. And if the sheriff or the Feds starting showing up in a big way, then Eric would know he ratted him out. So he said he would just play along, pretend to cooperate, but make it clear to Rudolph that he had his limits, that he wasn't going to be his wheel man. Maybe, if he was lucky, Eric would just go away. Then it might be the right time to call in the cops.

Nordmann said over the next two days, he got some of the items on Eric's list: corned beef, pork and beans, sardines, fruit cocktail, coconut butter, a huge tub of honey. Thursday morning, before leaving for his store, George laid out these supplies inside his house. He left them in clear view of anyone who came inside, along with a note addressed to Eric. It said something along the lines of: God says no on the use of the car. Here are a few things. *Don't ever* contact me again. (Which raises another question, did Nordmann tell his daughter to stay away from the house and, if so, what was his reason?) That night, Nordmann said he spent the night at his store in Andrews, perhaps knowing full well that he was leaving the coast clear for Eric. If Rudolph was watching the house, this was the time to go in and take what he wanted.

The next morning, Friday the 10th, George drove home at about 8:00 A.M. He said the first thing he noticed was that his pickup truck, a blue 1977 Datsun, was gone. When he went inside, the bundle of supplies for Eric was gone, too. So was a bag of apples that Nordmann said he had bought for himself the day before. In their place were five $100 bills and a note from Rudolph (the handwriting was the same as that on the list Eric had made for Nordmann Tuesday night). The note was in pencil, on a piece of gray cardboard. Nordmann said he got rid of it but told investigators it said, "SORRY YOU WERE FEARFUL IN HELPING ME. THE FEDS AND DOGS WILL NEVER FIND ME. A CALL WILL TELL YOU WHERE YOUR CAR IS LOCATED."

That was Friday morning. For reasons that only George Nordmann knows, he waited yet another full day before calling Kenny Cope. Even if he had not meant to give Eric a head start, that's exactly what he did.

Nordmann's call Saturday morning triggered a chain reaction. Once Terry Turchie found out that Rudolph had surfaced and then vanished, along with Nordmann's truck, he made sure there was a lookout on the pickup. But it wasn't nationwide this time. It was going to be a quiet search and local for now. Nobody thought Eric was going very far, not with all the supplies. The betting was he would be heading somewhere close by, in Macon or Cherokee Counties, as if finding him in either place was going to be all that easy.

The Task Force started grilling Nordmann and also searching his house and property. Opinions were immediately split about George and his version of events. A lot of folks took a look at his story and said they just didn't buy it (to this day, there are some, including local law enforcement, who think, even though the evidence isn't there, that Eric continued to use Nordmann's as a base). They certainly couldn't figure out why he waited the first time or the second time to report his contact with Eric. Or why he simply didn't drive into town to tell either the sheriff or the Task Force folks, since he obviously knew where they were. Nordmann had never been shy about his political opinions, so there was some talk that maybe he helped Eric because both were so antiabortion. Nordmann said the answer was simple: he was afraid. That was his story and, as the saying goes, he was sticking to it. Agents questioned him several times. They even gave him a lie detector test. Nordmann passed.

George apparently didn't give a damn what anyone thought. The day after he called Cope, agents searched his house, working their way through his mess of a basement/storeroom, poking around his chicken coop, and trying to find any clues they could. While they were doing that, Charles Stone was passing the time with Nordmann, not exactly questioning him, more like visiting, hoping that maybe he'd get the same sort of revelation like he got from Frank Sauer about Eric's secret room. No such luck. They had a pleasant chat, and Stone learned all about Nordmann's five daughters, plus got an earful about herbal remedies, but no special tips about Eric. But there was something Nordmann wanted from Stone and the Task Force. He wanted that $500 that Eric had left for him! That was his money.[6] And he wanted his truck back. It was their job to find it for him.

The next day, they found some evidence to back up Nordmann's story. The agents going through George's house had widened their search to include his property and found three campsites behind his house. None of them showed any evidence of store-bought food, which is what you'd expect if these were casual, overnight campers. Instead, they found some brown eggshells, which fit with what George had been saying about those odd goings-on around his house a few weeks back, around the time that his dog first started getting sick. One of the things that had gone missing around that time (which was when he also claimed to have found the $100 bill) was a bunch of eggs. Some investigators from the Forest Service went through the campsites and said the best they could figure, looking at the age of the eggshells, the way the ground had been tramped on, and everything else, someone had used these about six weeks earlier.

There were some kids across the street from the Nordmann house, riding around on an all-terrain vehicle, just watching all the searching.

They were spectating, country-style. The kids rode their ATV up a hill to get a better view, and when they did, they ran over some trash. They thought the folks over at Nordmann's might be interested. When the agents got up there (you just crossed the road and climbed a couple of hundred feet up a ridge), they found another campsite.

This one looked really interesting—and fresh. There was some beaten-down foliage and from it, you had a clear view of Nordmann's house and especially his driveway, a classic concealed observation point. The way some branches were messed up and some bark skinned on a poplar tree, it was apparent that someone had been climbing it, twenty feet at least, to have a look around. There was a campsite with a fire pit that had some slivers of cooked onion. There was buried trash, including a sardine can that had been opened somewhat recently. There were remnants of a wrapper from one of those Emergen-C powdered drinks, the sort that George had said were missing from his house. There was an empty plastic fruit bag with a fingerprint. When the ATF lifted that off, the print matched with Eric's. He must have forgotten to wear one of those gloves Nordmann saw him with.

It sure looked like significant parts of Nordmann's story—and the story he said Eric told him about watching the house—were checking out. First the campsites on the property, as Eric began pilfering things from George's house and likely poisoned his dog to cover his tracks. Then the more close-in stakeout from up on the ridge across the street, until he made his direct approach to George.

A few days later, tracking dogs found some other evidence that seemed to tie in with the idea that Eric had been casing the area, taking his time before approaching Nordmann. The dogs and their searchers were about a mile down Long Branch Road, passing by the house belonging to a family named Solensbee. There were actually two types of dogs in the search team: hounds that were trying to follow Eric's scent and the bomb dogs, trained to sniff explosive traces. Both of them started barking, doing that alerting action, to let their handlers know they found something curious around the property.

No one was home, so they talked to one of Solensbee's neighbors. He told them the family was out in Montana on vacation, but he had heard something strange over from the house and he could remember about when it happened, because it was a day or two before the Fourth of July. He heard noises, like a board dropping and a metal scraping sound, something like tin being pulled across concrete. His dogs started barking like crazy, but after a while, they settled down. The Task Force finally reached Henry Solensbee and got permission to search his house. There was evidence someone had been inside recently, some saltines left out by the kitchen sink, and the searchers were convinced Eric had been there, but they didn't turn up any fingerprints.

In one sense, and not a good one, history was repeating itself. Back in January, they missed Eric at his trailer by a matter of hours, if not minutes. Now they were in the same position—another damned truck hunt. This time they were looking for a 1977 blue Datsun pickup, not a 1989 gray Nissan with a camper shell. But aside from that, it sure felt the same.

For several reasons, though, they were sure that Eric wasn't going far. First off, Nordmann's truck was a beater, the sort of vehicle that could get you from here to there, but not any great distance. The headlights didn't work, and it had a leaky head gasket (although Nordmann said it had a full tank of gas). You weren't going to make any cross-country dash in that truck. From everything that Eric allegedly told Nordmann, even if you discounted the possible deceptions, which you had to because he said he had lied to Randy Cochran, it was apparent that he was somewhere in the area. Which was just what Park Dietz said, just what Sheriff Jack Thompson had said, and just what Kenny Cope was telling reporters who asked. Why go anywhere else when you know these woods so well? Eric could have done that in January, but he didn't. Besides, it's not as if the Task Force had any luck finding him.

Then there was the matter of what Eric had taken from Nordmann's house. He told George that he wanted to get together enough food to last a year and stash it in his hiding place. From the way he had tried to convince Nordmann to leave the food at the side of the road, so Eric could pack it in, it sounded like searching in and around the Nantahala was more than ever the right way to go. Besides, once they figured what

Eric had taken, they realized this wasn't a guy who was going to run far. Or necessarily even walk that far, because when you added everything up, it was too damn heavy.

Just as it did with the haul that Eric had taken away from BI-LO back in January, the Task Force made a list. This time they had to rely on Nordmann and the list he said Eric made for him; there was no store receipt. Aside from the vitamins and supplements, which Nordmann said that Eric had already pilfered from his house, here's what they came up with:

- corned beef—2 cans

- sardines—2 cans

- fruit cocktail—1 can

- pork and beans—unknown quantity

- canned beets—unknown quantity

- canned peas—unknown quantity

- other vegetables—unknown quantity

- honey—1 five-gallon bucket

- tallow—3 or 4 quart jars

- raisins—1 or 2 gallons

- apples—2 bags

- carrots—about 6

- bananas—a few

- wheat bread—2 homemade loaves

- oranges—1

- bulgur wheat—1 or 2 gallons

- dried black beans—about 2 gallons

- dried lentils—2 one-pound packages

- dried mixed pinto and great northern beans—2 one-pound packages

- cayenne pepper—2 or 3 one-pound packages

- Now brand vitamins and minerals—2 sandwich-size baggies full

- AA batteries—several

- Rubbing alcohol—1 bottle

- Peroxide—1 bottle

- Butcher knife

- Disposable lighters—two (with beer logos on them)

- Food Lion brand paper matches—3 books

- Maroon covered pencil

- Small blue covered spiral notebook

- Plastic bucket

- 2-liter plastic soda bottles with tops removed for sprouting seeds—1 or 2

- Package of 33-gallon black trash bags, brand unknown

- Hardbound book of sermons on the New Testament with greenish gray cover

The last item in particular must have pleased the devout Nordmann. When you added everything up, it came to more than two hundred pounds (the honey alone weighed sixty pounds). Rudolph was going to have to cache all of that somewhere, and it was going to take more than one trip, maybe several, from wherever he dumped the stuff to wherever his hiding place was. Even if they found the truck, it could be like last time, meaning where he left it may not have been close to his hideout, and they'd have to try and chase down the trail between the two. Assuming of course they found the truck.

Which they did, two days after Nordmann called Kenny Cope. It was noon on Monday, the 13th, the same day that the folks working Nordmann's house found Rudolph's campsite. Forest Service and Task Force agents spotted the truck just off the side of a Forest Service road that ran through the Nantahala a few yards up from an area called the Bob Allison Campground, a place sometimes used by hikers and overnighters in the National Forest. The campground was 14.6 miles southwest of Nordmann's house by the most direct roads. To get there, you had to drive down toward and then around Nantahala Lake, then cross over from Macon into Cherokee County.

There was a handwritten note in the truck that said, "TRUCK BROKE" and requested that persons finding the note should call George Nordmann at the Better Way Health Food Store in Andrews, North Carolina. The ATF lab compared the writing of that note and the shopping list/map that Nordmann said Eric wrote out for him and decided they matched. The ATF bomb dogs also sniffed explosive residue in the driver's seat, and it later tested as being consistent with the main ingredient in commercial dynamite.[7] The Task Force didn't think Rudolph was carrying dynamite with him when he was making his run with the truck; instead, they guessed his clothes might have already been impregnated with explosive residue and that some came off in the truck.

As interesting as the note and explosive residue were, what the Task Force really wanted to learn from the truck was where it had been. They didn't get any fancy soil samples or anything like that, and they didn't know what the odometer had been set at before Eric took off with it. The only real clue they had came from the gas tank. Nordmann had said he had filled it up recently. Based on that statement and its own tests of the truck's mileage per gallon, the ATF lab figured that Rudolph had driven the Datsun somewhere between fifty and seventy-five miles. Now, if they could find out where he had taken the truck before the Bob Allison Campground, then maybe that would lead them to Eric.

All of which meant going public and asking for help. So far, between the Task Force, the sheriff's department, and the Forest Service, they had kept a lid on this, trying to move quickly and bag Rudolph without having to do it under the eye of the media. That was about to change. They had the truck. They were about to bring in a small army of trackers and hunters to go after Eric, and they were getting ready to alert the media. The circus was getting ready to come to town.

Before that, there was one more thing they wanted to do: make a new sketch of Eric Rudolph, based on Nordmann's description. At Charles Stone's urging, they called in Marla Lawson, the GBI sketch artist who had done the original drawing of the goateed man in Centennial Park. There was only one catch. She was on vacation, it being the dead of summer and all that. No problem said Stone, we're sending a helicopter for you. Forget that, she replied, I don't do helicopters. Eventually, after many hours driving from the Georgia coast to the mountains of western North Carolina, Marla (that's how she signed her sketches) got to Andrews, and they sat her down with Nordmann.

The sketch she produced was about to become ubiquitous, offering as it did an ostensible new glimpse of Rudolph. It showed a handsome young man, who looked to be in his twenties with darkish hair and piercing blue eyes. The hair is slightly disheveled, what might be casual preppy, until you realize it is pulled back behind his head into a ponytail. The cheeks are prominent and a little flushed, maybe an artistic flight of fancy, but also a way of showing how the Eric Rudolph who appeared a little fleshy in some earlier photos, now looked a bit gaunter and weathered. Jeremiah Johnson–ish, for those who remembered the handsome mountain man character played by Robert Redford in his younger days. Someone more likely to be staring back at you from the face of an outfitter's catalog rather than a wanted poster.

Terry Turchie and Don Bell, who were running the Task Force operation in Andrews, and Woody Enderson, their titular boss from the Task Force in Atlanta, went public with the news about Eric's brief reappearance on Tuesday the 14th, taking the opportunity to show off the new sketch and asking for anyone who might have seen the blue Datsun truck sometime beginning the Thursday before, either down along Nantahala Lake or around Bob Allison Campground or along one of the roads in between, including Old River Road or Junaluska Road.

They never mentioned Nordmann by name, although his identity would leak out within the next couple of days. The Feds also tried to make nice with their local counterparts, tossing them kudos, noting that the person who reported the contact with Eric had called a sheriff's deputy, not the Task Force. Enderson vowed they would catch their man and reminded the public about the million dollar reward, but he also reminded everyone that Rudolph was to be considered armed and dangerous. Just in case anyone was wondering, he also said the number of people on the ground was about to grow, perhaps double, from the thirty-five to forty agents and support staff who were already there.

That would be the understatement of the summer. The Feds were about to throw some serious money and manpower into the search, which was going to do wonders for the economies of Andrews and Murphy. After all, it wouldn't look good if the searchers were outnumbered by the media, which had once again shown up in full force from Atlanta, Birmingham, and even New York. The Atlanta TV stations once again brought up their own helicopters along with their satellite trucks, just like they did when Eric's truck was discovered. Before the week was out, the Task Force got tired enough of sharing the airspace that they had part of the area declared a no-fly zone.

The word went out to FBI field offices all over the country to send members of their local SWAT teams; eventually the Bureau's elite Hostage Rescue Team (HRT) would get tapped as well. The ATF was also being hit up—it had its own version of SWAT and HRT called Special Response Teams (SRT)—so pretty soon, the whole federal alphabet soup was there. Since much of the search was being done in the National Forest, the U.S. Forest Service had to throw in its enforcement agents (the Park Service would also get involved). Unlike SWAT, HRT, and SRT, the Forest Service agents actually knew their way around the woods, since that was their beat, and they had been chasing pot growers and moonshiners in the Nantahala for decades.

Where to put them all? The day that the bosses were making the announcement about Eric and the truck, Charles Stone was driving the area along the Macon and Cherokee County border, along with John Behnke, who was the FBI case agent on the Centennial Park bombing. Rudolph still hadn't been indicted for that yet, just the Birmingham bombing, but he was the only real suspect, and the forensics seemed to be confirming enough of the evidence against Rudolph that charges in the Atlanta bombings were likely to be filed soon. So Behnke was there and certainly wanted in on the capture, but first Stone and he had to find a location for Camp Fed, the new command post for the army of searchers that was about to hit the area.

They thought it made sense to find someplace on federal land, thinking that would make their lives much easier. Federal land in these parts meant the Nantahala National Forest, and with all those folks, it made sense to pick one of the campgrounds, which would give them room enough to set up a helicopter landing zone, as well as a tent city. They wanted someplace close enough to Nordmann's house and the whole Topton area, but not too far from the Bob Allison site. As they were cruising along, they noticed a place called Appletree Group Campground, which seemed to not only fit the bill, but actually have a back road shortcut up to Topton, the sort of route that Eric might have taken.

The only problem with Appletree was a Forest Service employee who kept saying—in the way of so many bureaucrats around the world—no, it just can't be done, this is a campground. He didn't get it, that he was standing at the epicenter of what was about to a world-class-size manhunt, and these guys didn't care if some Boy Scouts were going to have to find a new campsite. After a few calls up the food chain and some bureaucratic big-footing by folks in the Forest Service who understood the urgency of the request, they got the OK. Then Behnke made a call to the FBI's Critical Incident Response Group (CIRG) in Quantico, Virginia, and the trucks started rolling.

Stone was amazed. He was used to seeing the Feds screw up a one-car funeral, but this was a lesson in what can be done the right way when you have the resources. The CIRG trucks made it to Appletree from Northern Virginia several hours later. Even though it was closing in on midnight, these guys pulled out some portable generators and floodlights and started building a command post. By the next morning, they had the site up and running, with tents and secure phone lines, even a row of portable toilets. Just in time, too, for the invasion. The alphabet soup, which also included the GBI and BPD (Birmingham Police Department), began arriving in full force. A few folks had never left, including some of the investigators who had been chasing down leads up in the Andrews area since Eric disappeared the first time.

The manhunt was actually already under way. Ever since the Superdogs fiasco back in early February, when the FBI had brought in the bloodhounds from Texas and they had gone on that wild-ass chase down into north Georgia, the Task Force had switched to plan B. Which Stone had thought should have been plan A all along. For years, whenever he had gotten involved in one of these fugitive manhunts down in Georgia, he'd call in the prison folks, the Department of Corrections (DOC), and their dog teams, who were led by a tough customer named Duke Blackburn. Duke and he went way back and were even neighbors of sorts in Coweta County, south of Atlanta.

When Duke heard about the Superdogs screwup, especially how it happened on his turf, he reminded Stone that he'd made a career and a damned good one bagging prison escapees and other fugitives during manhunts, and if the situation called for it, he and his team were ready to go, even if that meant North Carolina. Stone and the Task Force actually brought Duke's folks up in April, after getting a tip that a witness had seen a camouflage-clad figure crossing the highway that runs between Andrews and Murphy. One of the DOC teams spent the day trying to pick up a scent without any luck, but it was a good dry run in case something big broke.

Which is how it came to be that the first searchers for Rudolph this go-round in western North Carolina were the bloodhounds from the Georgia DOC along with their handlers (their North Carolina counterparts somehow never got involved). The trackers wore black combat-style uniforms and sunglasses and may have looked scarier than any of the federal agents working alongside them, although unlike many of the Feds, the DOC teams would actually talk to the locals and in accents they understood. The DOC folks had another important assignment handed to them. After the Task Force learned Eric was pumping Nordmann for details about their location, they asked the DOC to take over perimeter security. Duke's crew started running patrols to guard the Appletree site and even set up a microwave security system aimed at detecting intruders (there was also an alarm system set up at the Andrews office Eric was so interested in).

The DOC trackers, along with some ATF bomb dogs and their handlers, started the search at Nordmann's property, where the campsites near the house and across the street seemed to offer them their best leads. While some folks had actually called in after the news conference and reported seeing the truck, there wasn't much going on there. One woman thought she passed it late night on Thursday, near midnight, as she was driving down Long Branch Road, which would have fit in with what Nordmann was saying, since that is the night he stayed over in town at his store. Some other folks saw it either near or parked at the Bob Allison Campground over the weekend, which was after Nordmann called Kenny Cope but before the Feds found the truck and went public with the whole story. That helped, but they were hoping someone might have spotted the truck somewhere else and given them a way of overcoming Eric's head start.

One person did say he thought he might have seen the truck sometime before the news conference, he couldn't remember exactly when, heading both east and west on Otter Creek Road the same day. Otter Creek was in the other direction from Nordmann's house, northeast, where Bob Allison was southwest. The trackers did work their way up there over the next few days, but they started from Nordmann's property and tried to see if the dogs could pick up Rudolph's scent.

The day after they found the campsites, one of the search teams found a sardine can and a boot print in an area northwest of the house, not more than a couple miles away, at a place called Poplar Cove (remember that one of the things they found at that campsite across the street from Nordmann's, where they recovered one of Rudolph's fingerprints, was a sardine can). The can and the boot print were found along an aqueduct, one of a series of aboveground pipes that snaked through the national forest, carrying water to hydroelectric plants. Walking along or even on top of the aqueduct was a way of cutting through the woods in quick fashion, since the area around it was cleared, as opposed to taking one of the trails or bushwhacking, so they had to consider that Rudolph might be using this route.

The next day, the search team found several broken shrubs nearby and more boot prints. If these were from the same person, and that person was Rudolph; he had been there a week earlier, as near as they could tell from working the site. They followed the trail for a quarter mile as it took them from the Old River Road, down Wayah Road, to an old barn along Otter Creek Road, before it ran cold. The Old River Road was interesting because it was the shortcut, which could get you from the area around Eric's old house in Partridge Creek all the way over to Appletree and even the Bob Allison Campground, without ever going out on the highway. The searchers were already aware that it used to be one of Eric's favorite routes.

That was about as far west as the initial searching went or at least as far west as the trackers were turning up possible leads. Most of the early work was done around Nordmann's house. One search team followed footprints that led south from one of the campsites on George's property. The trail went up and over a small peak called Camel Mountain, before the prints petered out. Three days later was when the dogs picked up Rudolph's scent and took their handlers to the Solensbee house, just down Long Branch Road from Nordmann's. A couple of days after that, the dogs thought they picked up Rudolph's scent again, and the tracking team went up a nearby dirt road before ending up at an old shed.

Then they started working an area that was a little farther from Nordmann's house. If you plotted it on a map—and the Task Force did—the searchers had already hit two areas, right around the house and campsites, plus that area over to the west. Now they moved north and to the east, where they came across something that really got their attention: dead dogs.

One of the search teams was working the area north of Otter Creek on July 19, just across the water from where the trail had run cold at the old shed, when a resident told agents that his dog had been poisoned, and he'd buried it just that day. Since Nordmann had already told them what happened to Bobo, this definitely sounded like it could have been Eric's handiwork. As they started asking around the neighborhood, the Task Force discovered that two other dogs had been poisoned the day before! Agents dug up one of the dogs and took it away for an autopsy, where they discovered it had been poisoned by antifreeze (ethylene glycol, the toxic part of antifreeze, is a sweet-tasting and odorless liquid, so it isn't hard to get a thirsty dog to drink it). If Eric was the culprit, and they were pretty sure he was, after what happened to Bobo, then he must have moved in this direction and might even still be around, trying to disguise his presence.

The search was moving east. One team was checking out the Appalachian Trail, which cuts through the Nantahala. They were hiking south, down from a peak called Wesser Bald, when one of the dogs took off and started toward a cabin. The dog acted as if it had picked up Eric's scent and began digging, until it finally came up with a gum wrapper. The trackers noted how close the cabin was to some power lines (walking along the power lines was another way of getting through parts of the forest, just like going along the aqueduct route, since the area underneath was usually cleared). When they went over to the power lines, they spotted boot prints.

There were other indications that they were on Eric's trail. That same day, not too far north of there as the crow flies, maybe a few hundred yards away, on the other side of the power line, another dog picked up a positive scent. The trackers thought it was relatively fresh, might only be two or three days old from the way the dog was acting. Another dog picked up a scent nearby and even followed it across one of the small creeks in the area where the agents noticed a partial footprint. The dog lost the scent about a hundred yards after crossing the creek.

It kept going like this over the next few days—the search parties coming across evidence of someone, maybe but not necessarily always Eric, out in the woods. A partially filled stove can here, the smell of smoke there, but that was it. They were losing Eric's scent. It felt like they were close to him, might have even had him if Nordmann had called Kenny Cope sooner. But just as some two hundred agents of all sorts were pouring into North Carolina and hitting the woods, trying to flush him out, Rudolph had disappeared once again.

They had no way of knowing it at the time, but the visit to George Nordmann's house would be the last known sighting of Eric Rudolph for five years.

9.

MOTHER PATRICIA AND THE ELECTRIC JEW

CHARLES STONE WASN'T sure who came up with the idea. Probably his boss, Woody Enderson, but it didn't really matter. What mattered was the assignment. It had already been decided that if Eric Rudolph were ever caught, Stone would do the questioning since he wasn't a federal agent. That part had been Park Dietz's suggestion, based on his profile, that the bomber would be mistrustful of the Feds, if not paranoid about them. Stone had also done pretty well in his initial contacts with the Rudolph family, talking to Joel and Deborah. Now the assignment was to reach out to Eric's mother. She might be the key to solving this mess, especially if Eric ever got in touch with her. If Stone could convince Patricia Rudolph that her son needed to surrender, and if Patricia had some way of communicating that to Eric, then maybe this could all be resolved peacefully. At least, that was the theory.

Stone was finally about to sit down with Patricia, and as far as he was concerned, this ought to be pretty damn interesting. Every conversation about Eric, be it with family or associates, seemed to involve his mother and the whole Rudolph psychodrama. All that stuff: the Catholic upbringing, rejecting the Church, moving to North Carolina, the Christian Identity odyssey, the whole antigovernment fervor. And that was just her.

Then there was Eric and how it all affected him. There was a lot to talk about, to be sure.

It was now almost two weeks after Eric's escapades at Nordmann's house, which only added to the urgency of the meeting, but Stone had been trying to arrange this sit-down for a couple of months before that. It hadn't been easy. Remember this was a woman who loathed the federal government with every fiber of her being and had weaned her children on this belief, years before her son ever got into trouble. So imagine how she felt when FBI agents showed up at her trailer in Bradenton, Florida, and started searching the place, looking for Eric. Then some FBI agents from Birmingham apparently contacted her again, and she thought they were trying to give her the runaround, get her to rat out her own son. Patricia was in no mood to cooperate, and she made that quite clear (she had also made a point of glowering anytime there was a TV camera pointed in her direction, which had not won her any sympathy from the public). For almost five months, Patricia hadn't talked.

Like any good American, the former novice and would-be nun had decided it was time to lawyer up. Given her ideology, that's about the last thing you would expect her to do. Lawyers ranked somewhere down near government agents as Satan's minions in the Rudolph view of the world. But then again, Patricia was full of contradictions. She didn't want her kids to have Social Security numbers, but she made sure to claim her own benefits and qualify for government-subsidized housing programs. Patricia found a kindred spirit, at least for the moment, in David Payne, a lawyer from Asheville, North Carolina. The family had started with James Bell. He was the lawyer from Charleston who complained early on about the harassment of Daniel Rudolph. But that didn't take, partly because it seemed Patricia didn't have a hand in hiring him, so pretty soon she moved on to Payne. It's not clear how the two hooked up, but when Stone got in touch with him, Payne made it pretty clear that he shared some of Patricia's political beliefs.

Stone didn't particularly care. He didn't care who he talked to or what their agenda was, provided he could achieve his own agenda, which was bringing Eric in. If that meant talking to Patricia or her lawyer, then he'd go back to his dealing-with-the-devil strategy. But first he had to soothe both Patricia and Payne. The lawyer was furious because the head of the FBI's Birmingham Field Office had just tried to contact Patricia again, this time writing a letter directly to her, ignoring the fact that Payne was her lawyer and that any communication should now come through him.

So the FBI had succeeded in angering off both Patricia and her lawyer. Stone decided on some common courtesy and a little Southern charm to resolve the situation. Instead of doing the "I'm with the government and I'm going to pound you and your client over the head" routine, he got to talking with Payne and discovered the lawyer was a fellow hunter and he tried to ease the way by talking about that. That seemed to loosen Payne up a little and give Stone a chance to make his pitch. It also helped that Stone wasn't a Fed; that would make talking to him go down much easier with Patricia and her sense of pride.

The pitch was pretty straightforward. Stone wanted to talk with Patricia. It wasn't going to be an interview, and Stone certainly didn't expect Mrs. Rudolph to help him try to catch her son, especially knowing what he did about the family history. But he did want to lay out the facts of the case against Eric, and he wanted to let Patricia know that if Eric contacted her, how she could facilitate a peaceful surrender. The message was: this is about capturing Eric, not harming him. Stone wanted her to understand that, because he wanted to correct a misimpression flying around the militia community; that the Feds were hunting down Eric, and when they found him, they were going to kill him. Payne had already made it clear Patricia believed this was the case, that the manhunt for her son was literally that.

There was already an irony at play here, and it had to do with the Rudolph paranoia about the government. The Task Force had started out by surveilling various members of the Rudolph family, which was what seemed to set Daniel off. But they weren't actually tapping the Rudolphs' phones and weren't sure if Eric had called any of them. Wiretaps were way too expensive in terms of money and man-hours, even if they could get a warrant. For that you needed probable cause (remember that this was well before 9/11), and the Task Force didn't have that. For a time, they were getting running reports on what calls were coming in and going out from some of the family phones, but they weren't actually listening in. That was one of the reasons Stone wanted to talk to Patricia. He had no real way of knowing if Eric had already contacted his mother. The funny thing was that it didn't matter! Some of the Rudolphs were so paranoid about the federal government, they believed it was always listening in.

Stone was trying to get past that mind-set. He wanted to let Patricia know that if Eric actually got in touch with her, whether by phone or letter, then there were ways to talk with him that could help all the concerned parties. Patricia and her lawyer finally agreed to the meeting. Maybe Payne was trying to spin him a line, but when he agreed to the meeting, he said that Stone was the first person from the government side who kept his word, and that counted for something. Neither Payne nor Stone realized it at the time, but the day after they finally agreed on the meeting, George Nordmann reported Eric's visit to his house. The fact that Patricia didn't back out after the news surfaced about Eric's reappearance and subsequent disappearance was an even better sign, as far as Stone was concerned. Maybe she understood the urgency of hearing him out.

So here they were, at a Holiday Inn conference room in Bradenton, Florida. Since the FBI still had that rule about more than one agent being there when it came to doing interviews, even though Stone was adamant this wasn't an interview, he had brought along a partner. Not a Fed, of course, but Captain Pat Curry from the Birmingham Police Department. Curry's presence—he ran homicide at the BPD— would help reinforce one of the basic facts that Stone intended to lay out: this was about the murder of Robert Sanderson, a police officer. He wasn't going to get into a political debate with Patricia, he knew better than that. Even if Curry never uttered a word, he would be making a strong statement.

The meeting started with a double dose of Rudolph weirdness. The night before, Payne had called Stone to say that Daniel Rudolph might be joining them. Sure, said Stone, who would have loved to get the entire Rudolph clan in one room and have a conversation with them. But here he was, and of course the first thing Stone and Curry noticed was the brace on his left arm. How could you not? Here they were, looking at Daniel, looking at the brace, trying to see if his hand was working and thinking to themselves, what sort of fucked-up person cuts off his own arm?

That was part one of the weirdness. Fortunately, neither Stone nor Curry made a faux pas about the arm. They didn't ask, and Daniel didn't volunteer. Part two came when Stone, trying to be a gracious host, offered them a choice of juice, soda, or bottled water to drink. The meeting was originally supposed to be at Pat's house, but Payne had switched it to the hotel where Stone and Curry were staying. Anticipating, even hoping, that the meeting would run long, Stone had laid in some beverages and was now making the offer. No thanks, was the reply, and both Rudolphs brought out their own water bottles. Not plastic water bottles, but glass ones. And not a commercial brand. These were more like syrup bottles, which had been washed, then refilled with some sort of springwater. Stone had a flashback to his conversations with Deborah about how the Rudolphs distilled their own mountain water when they lived in Topton and realized to himself, yes, these folks truly are different. He also wondered, a little sarcastically, whether Patricia had found some natural spring at her trailer park so she could avoid the dangers of fluoridation. Of course, he kept this all to himself, not wanting the meeting to get sidetracked by a lecture on the dangers of government-treated water.

After everyone introduced themselves, Stone went into his spiel. He talked about the Atlanta cases, outlining what had happened each time, who had been killed and injured, and what the Task Force knew about the bombs. He laid out the forensic evidence, not all of it but enough to make the point there were definite links. Then Curry ran through the bombing in Birmingham, and how one of his fellow officers was murdered. Curry told how there had been eyewitnesses in Birmingham who had identified Eric and his truck. Stone picked up the story from there. He wanted to make it clear, albeit in a nonthreatening fashion, that everyone concerned with the investigation felt that her son was behind all of these bombings, and they were determined to bring him to justice.

If Eric got in touch with her—and he deliberately didn't ask her if

Eric had already been in touch—then he wanted her to know and he wanted her to let Eric know, that no one wanted this to end in violence. This was about Eric surrendering or being captured peacefully. No bloodshed. She could play an important role by publicly acknowledging this. Stone wasn't asking her to make a public plea for Eric to surrender, although he would have loved for her to make the offer (she didn't). He just wanted her to know that this wasn't WANTED DEAD OR ALIVE, even though it seemed to be getting portrayed that way in some quarters. Patricia was particularly concerned about this. She seemed to have an image that trigger-happy Feds were going to find her son and then reenact Waco or Ruby Ridge, taking him down in a hail of gunfire.

Stone also told Patricia and Daniel that if all this with Eric somehow ended up in a barricade or hostage situation, that he would be the chief negotiator with Eric. That was true, but it also made for a smart psychological ploy, because now they thought to some degree Eric's fate rested in his hands. He wanted each of them to give him a piece of personal information he could relay to Eric, something that might convince him if the situation demanded it that Stone had gotten this from his closest relatives and they were cooperating in his surrender. Both agreed. Patricia's item had to do with a particular incident at a family meal. As for Daniel, Stone wasn't sure what to do with his tidbit. One of the things you learn as a negotiator is to keep family and friends away because you never know when one of them might say something that would set your suspect off. Daniel was a wild card, and if he really cut off his arm as a gesture of solidarity with his brother, then there was no telling whether his message to Eric might be aimed at lighting his brother's fuse rather than getting him to surrender peacefully.

Stone had given his word that this wasn't going to be an interview, and he wouldn't ask any questions, but he was hoping that once he made his case, that the Rudolphs wouldn't be able to resist talking. They weren't. Patricia had a few things to say, and most seemed to be aimed at convincing Stone and Curry that her son was innocent. But first she wanted to talk about George Nordmann, which was natural enough since Eric's visit to his house was fresh on everyone's mind. She called him a

Centennial Park shortly before the bombing. The "Speedo boys" are sitting on the bench at the base of the NBC sound tower where the bomb has been left. *(Southeast Bomb Task Force)*

Enhanced shot of "Speedo boys" sitting on bench at the base of the NBC sound tower shortly before their confrontation with security guard Richard Jewell. *(Southeast Bomb Task Force)*

Centennial Park bombing caught on videotape
by Robert and Nancy Gee.
(Robert Gee)

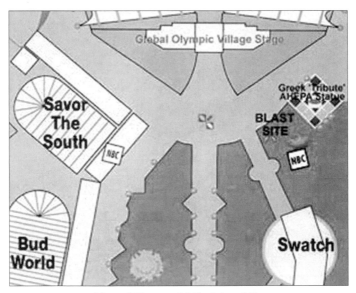

Map of Centennial Park bombing.
(Southeast Bomb Task Force)

"Blobman" photo of man sitting on bench in Centennial Park;
investigators believe this was the bomber.
(Southeast Bomb Task Force)

Enhanced photo of "Blobman" done by NASA.
(Southeast Bomb Task Force)

Bomb components from Centennial Park.
(Southeast Bomb Task Force)

"Goatee man" sketch from Centennial Park bombing.
(Southeast Bomb Task Force)

Sandy Springs Professional Building
275 Carpenter Drive, N.E.
Sandy Springs, Georgia

ABOVE: Map of Sandy Springs Clinic bombing.
(Southeast Bomb Task Force)

BELOW: Map of Otherside Lounge bombing.
(Southeast Bomb Task Force)

The Otherside Lounge
1924 Piedmont Road, N.E.
Atlanta, Georgia

THE BOMBINGS IN SANDY SPRINGS
AND MIDTOWN WERE CARRIED-OUT
BY UNITS OF THE ARMY OF GOD.
    YOU MAY CONFIRM THE FOLLOWING
WITH THE F.B.I. THE SANDY SPRINGS
DEVICE'S GELATIN-DYNAMITE —
POWER SOURCE 6 VOLT D BATTERY
BOX DURACELL BRAND, CLOCK
TIMERS. THE MIDTOWN DEVICE'S
ARE SIMILAR EXCEPT NO AMMO
CANS, TUPPERWARE CONTAINERS
INSTEAD - POWER SOURCE SINGLE
6 VOLT LANTERN BATTERIES
DIFFERENT SHRAPNEL, REGULAR
NAILS INSTEAD OF CUT NAILS.
    THE ABORTION WAS THE TARGET
OF THE FIRST DEVICE. THE MURDER
F 3.5 MILLION CHILDREN EVERY YEAR
WILL NOT BE "TOLERATED". THOSE
WHO PARTICIPATE IN ANYWAY IN
THE MURDER OF CHILDREN MAY
BE TARGETED FOR ATTACK. THE
ATTACK THEREFORE SERVES AS
A WARNING: ANYONE IN OR AROUND
FACILITIES THAT MURDER CHILDREN
MAY BECOME VICTIMS OF
RETRIBUTION. THE NEXT

First page of letter claiming
responsibility for Atlanta bombings.
(Southeast Bomb Task Force)

WHERE INNOCENT PEOPLE MAY
BECOME THE PRIMARY CAUSALTIES,
A WARNING PHONE CALL WILL
BE PLACED TO ONE OF THE
NEWS BUREAU'S OR 911. GENERALLY
A 40 MINUTE WARNING WILL BE
GIVEN. TO CONFIRM THE AUTHENTICITY
OF THE WARNING A CODE WILL
BE GIVEN WITH THE WARNING
AND STATEMENT. THE CODE
FOR OUR UNIT IS 4-1-9-9-3.

" DEATH TO THE NEW WORLD ORDER"

Final page of letter claiming
responsibility for Atlanta bombings,
including secret code.
(Southeast Bomb Task Force)

Emily Lyons being evacuated by paramedics after Birmingham Clinic bombing.
(Larry Kasperek—Birmingham Post Herald)

Alice Hawthorne and her daughter Fallon Stubbs. Alice was killed by the Centennial Park bomb.
(John Hawthorne)

Officer Robert "Sande" Sanderson, killed in Birmingham Clinic Bombing.
(Birmingham Police Department)

FBI TEN MOST WANTED FUGITIVE

MALICIOUSLY DAMAGED, BY MEANS OF AN EXPLOSIVE DEVICE, BUILDINGS AND PROPERTY AFFECTING INTERSTATE COMMERCE WHICH RESULTED IN DEATH AND INJURY

ERIC ROBERT RUDOLPH

Date of photograph unknown

Date of photograph unknown

Aliases:
Bob Randolph, Robert Randolph, Bob Rudolph, Eric Rudolph and Eric R. Rudolph.

DESCRIPTION

Date of Birth:
September 19, 1966
Hair:
Brown

Eric Rudolph wanted poster.
(FBI)

Map of Alabama, Georgia, and North Carolina.
(Sheri Debellotte)

Rudolph's truck after it was discovered
by hunters (Charles Stone in GBI windbreaker).
(Tommy Mefferd)

Pole sander head discovered by Charles Stone
in Eric Rudolph's storage unit.
(Charles Stone)

Inside Eric Rudolph's storage unit.
(Charles Stone)

Eric Rudolph sketch
based on George Normann's description.
(Marla Lawson—Southeast Bomb Task Force)

Eric Rudolph while visiting
his brother in New York.
(Southeast Bomb Task Force)

George Nordmann at his health food store, 2004.
(Charles Stone)

Eric Rudolph's Caney Creek trailer.
(Charles Stone)

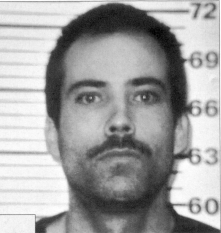

Eric Rudolph's mug shot taken shortly
after his capture in 2003.
(Cherokee County Sheriff's Department)

Eric Rudolph as a teenager.
(Deborah Rudolph)

Eric Rudolph rappelling
in North Carolina.
(FBI)

Eric Rudolph U.S. Army
induction photo.
(Department of Defense)

Eric Rudolph in hiking clothes.
(Southeast Bomb Task Force)

Rudolph family house in Topton, North Carolina.
(Charles Stone)

Daniel Rudolph, Patricia Rudolph, Jamie Rudolph, and Joel Rudolph (l–r)
outside Topton home during the 1980s.
(Deborah Rudolph)

Rudolph family in the living room of their Topton home.
Eric is on the far right with his arms around his mother, Patricia.
(Deborah Rudolph)

Patricia Rudolph at her Topton home.
(Deborah Rudolph)

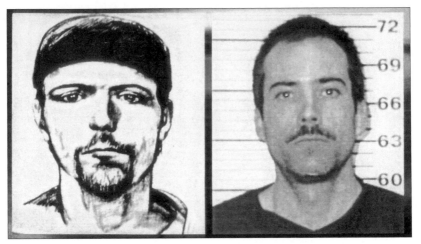

"Goatee man" sketch side by side with Rudolph mug shot.
(Southeast Bomb Task Force and Cherokee County Sheriff's Department)

Eric Rudolph being escorted from Cherokee County jail
by Police Chief Mark Thigpen and Sheriff Keith Lovin.
(Louis Ledford)

"fanatical Catholic." The way she told it, she was the one who had taken Eric and Daniel to his church, whose name she said she couldn't remember, some fifteen years ago.[1] Patricia did have one good thing to say about Nordmann—that he made good homemade bread!

She kept going on about this whole idea of Catholicism and abortion. She said Eric was not active in the Church. After being told about the rosary beads found in his truck back in February, she said those were from her aunt. She also went into a convoluted explanation about how when she lived in an apartment in North Carolina, there was a doctor who had lived two doors down from her and he was connected to abortion clinics in Birmingham and Atlanta, as well as Asheville. Eric had parked his truck there sometimes. It was just a coincidence, she seemed to be saying. It isn't clear what triggered all this, except there had been a newspaper article back in February talking about how the Allen Avenue address in Asheville that was on Eric's driver's license was in the same complex where an abortion doctor had also lived.[2]

Patricia gave her take on Eric's beliefs.[3] After abortion, she turned to homosexuality, since the bombing of the gay nightclub had already been mentioned by Stone. "Homosexuality is not an issue with Eric," she said. She had gone with him to New York the year before, and they had visited with Jamie. Eric knew his brother was out of the closet, but he didn't reject him. Far from it. Eric had broken bread not only with Jamie, but also his boyfriend. She was a bit more cryptic when it came to his views on race, saying that when he was in the military, the whole black-white issue was forced on him, but that most blacks were assimilated into society and not totally black. But that wasn't why he left the military, according to Pat, who made no mention of the fact her son was given the boot for smoking marijuana.

You wouldn't expect a mother to talk badly of her son. Stone didn't, so he was neither surprised nor disappointed when Patricia had an explanation for everything, like the rosary beads. Why did Eric leave the army? With her mother's eyes, she saw her son as a natural leader who was upset about not making Ranger. Then he was in a training exercise when another helicopter crashed and some of his buddies were killed, she said. He didn't want that to happen to him.[4] Eric showed up at Nordmann's wearing binoculars? That must be a mistake; he had lost his pair during that trip with her on the way up to New York. Tom Branham? She hadn't seen him in years. Yes, they had become friends in south Florida and they would go up to visit him in Topton during the summers and they did move up there after her husband's death because of him. But she was annoyed with Branham because she thought he had talked Eric out of going to college. As far as she could remember, Branham never talked about abortion. And she didn't think he was involved with Nordmann, either.

Patricia said the last time she saw Eric was when she had moved into the trailer in Bradenton. Eric had come down, along with her daughter Maura's husband, and they had helped her with the move.

All the while, Daniel would chime in with his own explanations. At one point, he appeared to backtrack from what he told agents back in February, when he had talked about Eric's knowledge of bomb-making. This didn't surprise Stone, who was convinced Daniel was still feeling guilty about that and that it played into the whole self-mutilation episode. This time around, Daniel said his brother didn't have the technical ability to build bombs. But then in the next breath, he was bragging on Eric, saying he could read instructions in a book and do just about anything. Why, he had rebuilt a car engine on the dining room table, using only the owner's manual as a guide!

Daniel's information seemed to come at random. He said it was Branham who introduced the Rudolphs to Dan Gayman, the Christian Identity preacher out in Missouri. That Robert Rudolph had worked as an aircraft mechanic and in baggage (it is unclear if he meant as a baggage handler). That after his father died, Daniel made wooden crafts to support the family, while his mother made quilts. That Eric was proficient at rough framing, painting, and hanging drywall. That Eric was a rock and roll buff.

Daniel said he was far more opposed to abortion than Eric was and much more likely to blow up a clinic! Eric was actually ambivalent about abortion, and used to say it had been around since women started getting pregnant and that wasn't likely to change. Daniel also claimed his brother didn't believe in the idea of born-again Christianity. Nor was he

anti-Semitic, in his brother's telling, since Eric thought Judaism was a religion, although not a heritage. Stone wasn't clear what Daniel meant by
this, but it sounded like he was trying to explain away some inconvenient
attitudes and statements that Eric had made.

One thing Daniel mentioned was an interesting possible connection
between his brother and George Nordmann. Daniel thought Eric might
have dated one of Nordmann's daughters, in fact the one who had the il-
legitimate baby, although that would have been years before she got
pregnant. Daniel, like his mother, knew the last woman Eric had been
with in a long-term relationship, and both were aware it had broken off
some time before. The last time Daniel said he saw his brother was at his
own wedding in Atlanta in May 1996.

All in all, thought Stone, the meeting went well. He never really
asked any questions, which was the agreement with Payne. But that
wasn't the purpose of the get-together. Mostly, as he laid out the case, he
and Pat Curry just listened and collected all the nuggets they got from
mother and son. Patricia and Daniel asked a lot of questions about the
evidence, then would respond to some of the specifics. Okay, most of
their statements were self-serving, but there might still be some useful
leads. Stone thought they might have established some sort of understanding. Patricia was as warm and cordial as one could expect, and Stone
thought she handled herself pretty well, considering the weight the federal government was putting behind trying to find her son. Especially in
the last two weeks, with the whole Nordmann incident, when the newly
energized manhunt was one of the stories dominating the news. He knew
that if he had been in her position, he would have been a lot more in-
timidated than she was acting.

The two investigators stayed behind to compare notes. Even though
they weren't going to write this up as an official document, since they
promised it wouldn't be treated as an interview, they wanted to make
sure they had an accurate account of the meeting.[5] When they went
down to the hotel dining room a little while later to get some lunch,
they noticed Patricia and Daniel were also eating there (they didn't
check to see if the Rudolphs were still drinking their own water!). Join
us, said Patricia. We'd love to, replied Stone, but we better not. "Your

attorney isn't here, and I just think it might be inappropriate if we talked to you without him being here." Stone wasn't being disingenuous; although he would have loved nothing more than getting another crack at Patricia, he remembered full well how Payne had gotten bent out of shape when the Birmingham FBI had written her the letter without including him.

Having turned down the offer regretfully, but in the hope this might be the first of many conversations, Stone and Curry went over to the other side of the dining room and had their lunch. But not before Patricia actually thanked them for being honest with her. She even asked Stone to keep her informed if there were any developments in the case. Then, as Stone and Curry were getting ready to go to their own table, Patricia said she wouldn't ask her son to surrender. You see, she couldn't do that. She had already placed Eric in God's hands. But if he did get in touch with her, she promised she would urge him to explore all his options.

They had left it that David Payne would work on some sort of press release where he would emphasize that Patricia's primary concern was for the safety of her son and those involved in the search effort. It wouldn't call on Eric to surrender, but instead make it clear that there was a promise by Stone and the Task Force that deadly force would only be used if one of the searchers felt his or her life was in danger. Payne kept his side of the bargain, and the release went out the next day, on Saturday June 25. The headline for much of the media was that Patricia feared her son would be shot by searchers. They also picked up on another line, which was clearly aimed at Eric: Mrs. Rudolph wants her son to know many believe he is innocent of the charged offense.[6]

There was one strange footnote to the meeting. Stone got a call from David Payne several days later. I don't normally do this, he said, but you need to have somebody on top of Daniel, because he thinks you are the Antichrist! Payne was Patricia's lawyer, but not Daniel's, so he could say this without compromising his professional ethics. Payne said he thought the meeting in Bradenton had gone well, but recently he had phoned Patricia to follow up on some details. Daniel answered, and he started ranting and raving about both Payne and Stone. Whatever caused that outburst, it had an impact. Stone wouldn't have another meaningful conversation with Patricia ever again.[7]

Which meant there would be so many questions unanswered. How did Patricia get to be the way she was? Just what exactly had she exposed Eric and his brothers to, first through Tom Branham, then with Dan Gayman? What other connections did the family have on the extreme Right? How was it that Eric turned out so differently from Jamie, who made the same visit to Schell City, or even from Joel and Daniel, who appeared to share many of the same beliefs? For that matter, how much did Patricia know about Eric's marijuana growing? There were probably just as many questions that Patricia Rudolph couldn't answer about her son, since by now it was clear to Stone and the others that Eric lied or misled even his own family about such basic questions as where he lived and where he was going. But all these were really ways of getting to the most basic question, the why of it. If Eric was indeed the bomber, why did he do it?

The truth was, the Task Force wasn't so much interested in the why of it anymore. Not now that they thought they had most of the rest of it figured out. Particularly the who, as in Eric, and much of the how, what, where, and when. The whole question of motive was important if it gave them some sort of clue about how to catch him. They were also making a big assumption by now, which made motive less important. It was partly based on Nordmann and partly based on their profile of Eric. Did Eric act alone—and even if he did, was anyone helping him now? The Task Force at least was convinced by this point that the answer on both counts was a definite NO (there were a lot of local law enforcement folks up in North Carolina who felt quite differently). There was a picture in the media, which had discovered enough about Eric's past to know of the Gayman connection and Branham and some of the wackos that inhabited the Nantahala, to allow some to come up with a pretty convincing conspiracy theory. But from pretty early on, well before Rudolph was identified, Park Dietz had pegged the bomber as a lone operator. Everything they had discovered about Eric since then made it appear to the case agents that he was a loner, that he wasn't really close to either his friends or family, and that he had real issues about working with anyone else.

The whole Nordmann episode seemed to confirm that to investigators. If Eric had been working with anyone else or getting any support afterward, then why did he have to show up at George's house and try to get food from him? Even if Nordmann had effectively helped Eric by getting him some supplies and giving him a head start, the fact that he got in touch with the authorities was a good sign. It had to get Rudolph thinking that if he couldn't trust George, then who could he trust? As tempting as it was to believe in conspiracies, as far as the Task Force was concerned, there just wasn't any evidence of one.

Even if the Task Force had all but put aside the question of why, it was still important. Not the least of which was because America cared, in its way, about the answer. Ever since the end of the Cold War, this was supposed to be a time of unprecedented peace and prosperity, a Pax Americana that replaced the Berlin Wall. It was President George H. W. Bush who boasted of a New World Order, where America would be the only superpower. He seemed true to his word, building a coalition that was able to throw Saddam Hussein and the Iraqis out of Kuwait in short order.

If the rest of the world was convinced about this New World Order, it wasn't playing so well at home. The end of the Gulf War didn't bring prosperity and a peace dividend, but instead there was economic decline. On this newly emerging thing called the Internet, there was dark talk of conspiracy from quarters that hadn't been heard from in many years. Murmurings that this New World Order was really a plot by Zionists (it was always the Jews and always had been for these people) to use the American government and its agents to enslave the American people, put it under the tyranny of the United Nations and its black helicopters. It was a crazy fantasy, but then so was the idea that the Berlin Wall would ever fall—and now here was a president who seemed to be embracing their darkest fears.

Not that most Americans believed this crazy shit, but something was going on out there. In a way it was akin to what was happening everywhere else, even in places like the Balkans. The Cold War had kept the lid on for both sides, put everything into a simple us versus them situation. Now the lid was off, and it was time to settle old scores, and all the hatreds were bubbling up again. Croats were killing Serbs who were killing Muslims; Hutus were killing Tutsis.

In America, strange things were happening. We had met the enemy and he was us, to borrow the old phrase. There was the whole bizarre incident at the Branch Davidian compound in Waco, when the ATF tried to go in and take away weapons from a religious cult. It had turned into something more than a hostage situation, becoming a cause célèbre for the extreme right, proof that the government and its jackbooted thugs (that phrase again) would stop at nothing to crush religious freedom. Most Americans were disquieted by the government's heavy-handed tactics but even more appalled by the bizarre antics of David Koresh and his cultlike ways. When the whole compound went up in flames a few weeks later, after an armed siege ended in dozens of deaths, it seemed that America was at war with itself.

It didn't matter if you believed the FBI's version of events that this was a perverted combination of mass suicide—which was later borne out by an independent government commission—or the supporters of the Davidians, there was something seriously wrong going on. Already there had been a fiasco in a place called Ruby Ridge, Idaho, where the government had killed a woman and child while trying to serve a warrant on a white supremacist named Randy Weaver, who was wanted on weapons charges. Never mind that a U.S. marshal had been killed, too; for the extreme right, Ruby Ridge and Waco were clarion calls to the ramparts.

Then came the bombing of the Murrah Federal Office Building in Oklahoma City, two years to the day after the flames at Waco. One hundred seventy-eight people died. Despite some initial claims that Middle Eastern terrorists were behind the bombing, the horrible truth became clear in a matter of days. Timothy McVeigh, a former U.S. soldier who had fought for his country in the Persian Gulf, had carried out the attack with the aid of his friend Terry Nichols. He would later cite Ruby Ridge and Waco as the reasons for his anger at the federal government.

America was at war with itself. Every state seemed to have one or more militia groups, as they called themselves, filled with putative citizen-soldiers who claimed their rights under the Constitution to keep and bear arms as a well-regulated milita (hence the name). The militia groups were part of an extremist galaxy, which was more commonly known as the Patriot movement. Patriots, sometimes calling themselves Christian Patriots, could include not only militia members, but tax protestors, survivalists, Christian Identity followers, and those who claimed they were sovereign citizens. It was a sometimes bewildering array of extremists where groups with seemingly incompatible aims jostled for followers and supremacy.[8] There were dozens of programs on shortwave radio aimed at these true believers, whose beliefs sometimes veered between an extremist view of the Constitution and something far worse: hatred of any other—be they black, Jew, Asian, or feminist. Andrews, North Carolina, seemed to have more than its fair share of these people. One of them had been stopped in 1996, carrying a deactivated rocket launcher in his car.[9] There was also this compound just outside Andrews, run by a former IBM systems analyst named Nord Davis, that was home to something called the Northpoint Tactical Teams. By the mid-'90s, both the ATF and groups monitoring the far right said that western North Carolina had become one of several areas around the country militia and Christian Identity hate groups were using as a haven.[10]

So when Eric Rudolph was finally identified and accused of being the bomber, the why of it did matter. This was the man, if the government could be believed, who had attacked the Olympics, bombed two abortion clinics and a gay nightclub, killing two people and aiming for so many more. The similarities to McVeigh were especially chilling: former soldier, an angry and dedicated young white man with a set of very dangerous skills and a deep immersion into the world of the extreme Right. They might be lone wolves, but it seemed they knew where the pack was and had spent some time there. God knows how many more of them were out there. America did care. If Eric Rudolph was the bomber, why did he do it? And what, or who, might have nurtured his hate to such a boiling point?

It was possible to build a genealogy of hate, starting with the roots and the soil that nourished Eric and following the branches of the family tree until you got to him. There were two phrases that Deborah Rudolph had used that resonated, gave you a place to start your investi-

gation. She said that Patricia, the former novice, was always in search of
the true Church and dragged her children along on her spiritual odyssey.
And that Eric, who so loved to flop around her apartment getting high
and watching Cheech and Chong movies, could not watch TV news
without talking back to the box, angrily calling it "the electric Jew."[11] So
you had these two starting places—Mother Patricia and "the electric
Jew"—to try and understand what drove Eric Rudolph, what might have
led him into a world of hate.

Jamie Rudolph would say his brother learned to hate the government
when Patricia took her two youngest sons on a pilgrimage to Dan Gayman's Church of Israel compound in Schell City, Missouri, in 1984, part
of that quest for the true church.[12] But Eric Rudolph began learning to
hate well before his family ever left south Florida. This was long after the
Rudolphs had left the Catholic Church and moved on to the South Dade
Alliance Church, which was evangelical, and long after they had met
Tom Branham. Branham says they met in 1971, and two years later he
had moved to Topton, where the Rudolphs would frequently visit him.
After Robert Rudolph's death, Patricia realized it was time to get out of
Florida, because Homestead was changing and becoming more black and
Hispanic. The way she remembered it, a black kid knocked down Eric at
school, and the principal didn't do anything about it. Jamie was having
troubles, too, so they left.[13] But Jamie remembered it differently, that
Eric referred to blacks as niggers even before they left Florida and got
into fights with them. He thought Eric's views were closer to the folks in
Nantahala than Miami by the time he got there—and that once he got
there, he did his best to fit in.[14]

The move was in 1982. By the time Deborah Rudolph paid that first
visit to Topton to meet her future in-laws, at Thanksgiving of 1984, the
family (or at least Patricia, Daniel, Joel, and Eric) already seemed to have
been living the survivalist dream, raising their own goats, chickens, and
ducks, growing food in the garden, and distilling their own water. Along
with their homegrown food, racism and Christian Identity were also on
the family table by then. Eric had already written that ninth-grade paper
at the Nantahala School where he denied the very existence of the Holocaust.[15] Deborah's visit took place before Patricia took Eric and Jamie to

Schell City and Dan Gayman, not after, which begs the question: Where did this hate come from?

Not, it seemed, from their church in Florida. The South Dade Alliance Church was evangelical but mainstream. Its pastor, who would later move to a suburban church in Atlanta and make headlines by embracing the minister of a rural, historically black church,[16] described South Dade Alliance as full of born-again Christians. Reverend Fred Hartley remembered the Rudolphs and conducted Robert's funeral. He did say Patricia had her own, unconventional set of beliefs without going into specifics.[17] Patricia said she was angry at God after her husband died of cancer, but clearly the spiritual and ideological journey started well before his death when both rejected Catholicism.[18] Patricia's journey started even earlier. She had been a follower of Dorothy Day, the lay activist and radical pacifist who founded the Catholic Worker Movement. Day herself had many battles with her Church and its leaders and became a beacon for those in the sixties who wanted to combine social activism with somewhat traditional religious beliefs. Patricia was inspired enough to start on the path toward becoming a nun. When Patricia broke with the Church (Deborah said she would rail against its corruption, spiritual and financial), she also rejected the liberal, if not radical, beliefs of Dorothy Day. But she remained religious, and when Tom Branham first met the Rudolphs, they were holding prayer meetings at their house in Fort Lauderdale.[19]

In Branham, the Rudolphs had chosen a friend who would take them to a new place in their spiritual search. Branham would reject the notion that he became a surrogate father figure to the younger Rudolph boys after Bob Rudolph's death, but they spent great amounts of time around him, first during summers when they visited from south Florida, then when they became neighbors on Partridge Creek Road. They even attended some of his home-based prayer meetings. Branham said he never had Patricia's permission to discipline the boys, but it is clear he did have a great deal of influence over them—and they had the run of his place. He supervised the Rudolph boys (except Damian, who didn't move to Topton) as they learned to target shoot with a .22 caliber rifle. Although he said he never saw Eric experimenting with explosives, all the boys would have seen him make homemade explosives, using black powder and special fuses he ordered through a magazine. Eric learned other things from Branham, including some carpentry skills, how to use a chain saw, and even how to use an arc welder to cut metal, which was of particular interest to investigators trying to figure out about the steel plates in some of the bombs. Branham told Patricia that Eric would make a good welder after watching him practice.

By the time the Lord led him out of Florida to the mountains of North Carolina—Tom Branham's own words—and helped him find a lot with southern exposure, water and surrounding Forest Service land, Branham was already headed to the fringes. Damian Rudolph, the oldest son, the one who didn't make the move to North Carolina, told investigators that Branham had started out by being a hippie relic, and when he first moved to Topton, his excuse of a house was open to all, including blacks. But Branham began moving to the Right and kept on going, well past conventional conservatism (there was never anything conventional about Branham).

One of the extremist ideologies spreading in the late '70s and early '80s was about being a freeman, literally a free man. Those who studied the movement say it in turn sprang from another group, called Posse Comitatus, that had emerged in 1969. Posse Comitatus, which was founded by a former Nazi sympathizer, held that the only legitimate government was local government, and the highest official was the county sheriff. Any other government was to be resisted, by any means necessary. For a few Posse members, those means were violent, and one died in a shoot-out with federal authorities, after he had earlier been involved in a gun battle that killed two U.S. marshals.[20] Most of the loosely organized Posse members pursued a nonviolent course. They took to creating their own putative courts, which they called common law courts, issuing their own liens against various government officials (although they would still use the real courts to further their aims, filing the liens and other legal papers there as well). Some took this a step further, declaring themselves freemen, and refusing to recognize any legitimate governmental authority, becoming active tax resisters.

Tom Branham declared himself a free man, and soon the Rudolphs were involved in his struggle.[21] It began with the HJ Heinz Company and some coupons. According to the head of security for Heinz, Branham was showing up at swap meets and trading counterfeit Heinz coupons for real ones.[22] Even before the Rudolphs moved to Topton, Branham was using Eric and the other boys to help him sort his coupons during their summer visits to his place. The company sued. In his own defense, Branham replied that he was an unemployed laborer, but more importantly that he was a Sovereign American Freeman, and he denied the court had any jurisdiction over his person.[23]

This declaration of independence was only the beginning of Branham's legal troubles. Even though Heinz would later drop the charges, when a U.S. marshal went to serve the order, he spotted what he thought were illegal firearms at Branham's house, and a search of the property began, despite the fact they didn't have a search warrant. Branham wasn't there, but two of his nephews were, along with Eric. The nephews said that Eric was particularly incensed by the search and began telling the marshals that they didn't have a proper search warrant and that this wasn't the Soviet Union, before they eventually kicked him out of the house. Patricia would later say she was also outraged by what the marshals did, and she helped guarantee Branham's bail when he was arrested and charged with possession of three unregistered firearms.[24] Eventually the charges were overturned on appeal, and Branham got off, despite representing himself again, this time as a "free and natural person." But not before the brush with the law seemed to confirm everything bad that the Rudolphs, mother and son in particular, believed about the federal government acting beyond its powers.

There would be another branch on Eric Rudolph's ideological family tree. Although Branham never used a lawyer, he did have a mentor of sorts to guide him through his legal troubles. Nord Davis had been an IBM employee in New York State back in 1966 when he quit the company in protest over its decision to sell computers to Communist-bloc countries.[25] At the time, Davis was a member of the right-wing John Birch Society, but even that seemed too tame for him. After stops in New Hampshire and Massachusetts, Davis moved to a 200-acre compound outside of Andrews and founded his Northpoint group. It was never quite clear just how many members Davis attracted to his movement, which he considered to be both Christian Identity and part of the patriot movement. Like others who subscribed to Christian Identity, he believed that Caucasians were the true lost tribe of Israel (they had ended up in Britain, according to CI theology) and that the Bible was the history of this white race, not the story of the Jews.[26] Interestingly, one of Davis's writings did talk about the "diadem of the Army of God" although it was unclear if this bore any relation to abortion or those carrying out bomb-ings of clinics using the name Army of God.

Davis's newsletters and pamphlets (he proudly claimed to have been the largest customer at the Andrews post office) were a bizarre blend of conspiracy and fantasy. One issue claimed his self-dubbed Northpoint Tactical Teams mined Haiphong Harbor in 1972, then gave an ultima-tum to the U.S. military that forced President Nixon to follow suit, thus speeding up the end of the Vietnam War. Other conspiracies involved the CIA smuggling drugs from Central America into the United States and of course one that involved the killing of JFK (you couldn't be a bona fide conspiracy nut without having your own theory on JFK). He also claimed to have led a secret mission to Jordan that somehow averted large numbers of casualties during Operation Desert Storm, which he dubbed the First New World Order War.[27] Indeed, Davis wrote exten-sively about the New World Order, even claiming to know its leaders (Henry Kissinger and David Rockefeller, if you are interested). Newspa-per reporters who interviewed Davis after Waco wrote that he became emotional at the mention of Attorney General Janet Reno's name and angrily said her blood needed to be spilled to atone for what happened at the Branch Davidian compound.[28] Davis did run weapons training courses on his property, but for all his hate rhetoric, the group that most closely monitored him, North Carolinians Against Racist and Religious Violence, said there was no evidence that any Northpoint member ever actually committed an act of violence.[29]

An FBI report on Davis noted that in addition to spending the last twenty years of his life preaching the gospel of the white race, he was also an antitax protestor, which led him into conflict with the IRS. Davis also made the rounds on the extremist circuit. He was one of the speakers at a memorial service for a militia leader in Montana in 1996. The FBI said he was also linked with the militant wing of the racist Aryan Nations movement. When a group of self-proclaimed Montana Freemen got in a standoff with the FBI, Davis went out and offered his services as a mediator, which were rejected by the FBI.[30] Davis's connections in the Christian Identity movement also brought him in contact with Dan Gayman and the Church of Israel.

Branham admired Davis, particularly his speaking abilities, and asked him to serve as his counsel during the civil hearing with Heinz, even though Davis was not a lawyer. That was in 1984, but Branham said they had only sporadic contact after that. Tom Branham was finally arrested on the weapons charges in October 1986, more than two years after the search of his property and months after a bench warrant had been issued for his arrest. An ATF report about the incident said Branham was an alleged associate of Nord Davis, whom it called "a Christian Patriot." The report went on to say that Branham was allegedly taking "Free Man's Law Classes" in the Andrews area and that those may have been sponsored by Davis. Branham claimed that he only had sporadic contact with Davis after 1984, that when Nord Davis died in September 1997 of prostate cancer, he only found out after the funeral had been held. But it was in 1984 that the name of Nord Davis would become linked, through Tom Branham, to the Rudolph family.

Everybody involved—at least those who have talked about it—has a different version of the trip that Patricia Rudolph took Eric and Jamie on to the Church of Israel in Schell City, Missouri. Remember that the trip came soon after Deborah's Thanksgiving visit and not that many months after federal agents had raided her neighbor's house. Patricia said she made the visit to Dan Gayman's compound at Branham's suggestion.[31] Branham, for his part, told the FBI he didn't know Gayman, had never been to Missouri, and really didn't know much about why they went; his impression, or so he later said, was that it was some sort of summer camp visit to a church group.

The most curious account came from Dan Gayman himself. Gayman said the Rudolphs, he described them as a woman with two young boys (Eric would have been eighteen at this point, Jamie fifteen) arrived at the compound about one o'clock in the afternoon sometime in late November.[32] Patricia Rudolph introduced herself and said that a man by the name of Nord Davis had recommended she stop there for help; that she was on her way to Florida to see her daughter and had run into serious car trouble and was out of money. Gayman didn't have any money to give her but could offer her a place to stay. At that point, Patricia offered to show her husband's death certificate to prove she really was a widow. He said he wouldn't turn anyone away who had been recommended by Nord Davis, since he knew Nord casually.

What is odd about Gayman's account is why Patricia would say she was on her way from North Carolina to Florida and somehow end up a thousand miles out of the way in Missouri (Patricia did have some relatives near Saint Louis, but that never entered into Gayman's account). It is also unclear how Gayman would remember the scene so clearly, except for the date, while still insisting the Rudolph visit was so inconsequential. Gayman's version of the Rudolph visit was also at odds with the story told by his son, Tim, and daughter-in-law, Sarah. They later became estranged from Dan and broke away from the Church of Israel in 1991, branding it as a cult. In Tim and Sarah's version, Patricia was there because she had met Nord Davis and through him had read some of Dan Gayman's literature.[33] What she read convinced her it was worth coming to the Ozarks, where the Church of Israel was located, with Eric and Jamie (Tim and Sarah said that Daniel visited once during the Rudolphs' stay).

Tim and Sarah described what life was like at the Church of Israel, circa 1984. Sarah arrived there with her parents from South Carolina, in something of the same fashion as the Rudolphs, when she was sixteen. She would eventually stay behind when her parents left, and soon married Tim over their objections. Tim grew up there, home-birthed and home-schooled. It was very rural out in their part of the Ozarks, and he was surprised, when as a teenager visiting Kansas City, he saw his first black person. They worked hard, dawn to dusk, doing farm chores. Life centered around the Church, and many of the followers who lived in the vicinity would be there every day, doing their tasks and praying, even if they worked other jobs. Three times a year they had feast days and those would attract believers and visitors from all over the country. In the 1970s and early 1980s, Tim said that included folks from the Ku Klux Klan and Posse Comitatus people (he described them as being very anti-Semitic) along with tax protesters. Leading figures in the extremist movement, including Richard Butler of the Aryan Nations visited Schell City, along with what he called hard-line Christian Identity preachers.[34] Dan Gayman, in turn, was a guest at the Aryan Nations compound in Hayden Lake, Idaho. In the '70s, Gayman had linked up with a Louisiana-based Christian Identity group called the National Emancipation of Our White Seed and gone on a West Coast speaking tour with the group's founder.[35]

The year the Rudolphs showed up was an interesting one in Dan Gayman's life. That summer, in July 1984, members of a paramilitary group called The Order showed up at Schell City. They said they supported Gayman and what he was trying to do and gave him $10,000 in cash. Gayman took the money but later turned it over to the FBI when he said he learned that The Order—which was trying to finance white revolution—had gotten the money through a series of bank and armored car robberies. Dan Gayman would say that all along he rejected violence; that's why he had resisted an attempt by the Aryan Nations in 1980 to join up Christian Identity with the Aryan Nations. Ultimately, there was a grand jury investigation and members of The Order were indicted on sedition charges. Dan Gayman wasn't indicted and testified as a prosecution witness.[36] The federal government lost that case, but members of The Order (those who didn't die in shoot-outs with the police) ended up in federal prison, some after being convicted of murdering a liberal radio talk-show host in Denver and others for carrying out the bank robberies.

Dan Gayman would later give himself and his church an ideological makeover. Tim Gayman said his father wanted to appear more like Jerry Falwell to convince people that he was just another fundamentalist concerned about America's moral direction rather than a white supremacist.[37] If Gayman believed in white pride, he would now argue, then he was a separatist, not a supremacist. He and his church didn't believe they were better, just different. This was the line used by many in the extremist movement in the '90s to present a more acceptable face. Even if that's what they really believed, that wasn't what the Rudolphs walked into back in 1984.

One of Gayman's writings gives a flavor of his Christian Identity beliefs, which were the sort also shared by Nord Davis back in North Carolina. Called *Fables vs Truths*, it listed what it says are Jewish fables, then the Bible Truth. In many ways, it is a Christian Identity version of a catechism. The first Jewish fable, Gayman wrote, is that the Jews are God's chosen people. But the Bible Truth—the Christian Identity Bible, of course—is that the Jews are the Devil's seed and the children of the Antichrist. The second Jewish fable is that Jesus was a Jew; instead, Gayman's Bible Truth is that Jesus is God, and neither of his earthly parents were Jewish. All races are not descended from Adam, he wrote of another "Jewish fable." Rather, Adam is the father of the white race only. Finally, the Twelfth Fable and Truth: "That all races are equal in ability is fable," wrote Gayman; the truth being that "the white Adamic man was formed by God to be the superior race, and that all races belong in a divinely ordained station under the rule and leadership of white Christian people."[38]

How much of that message Eric Rudolph actually heard out of the mouth of Dan Gayman is unclear. Gayman said that the Rudolphs kept to themselves, lived off in a trailer, and only sporadically attended services; that only one family had much contact with them. Patricia refused to enroll her sons in the church school, insisting on continuing her home-schooling. But Tim and Sarah remembered things differently. Eric was definitely a believer in Christian Identity, even before he got to Schell City. They said he had been influenced in that direction by his neighbor back in Topton, whom they described as a violent man.[39]

The younger Gaymans said that Dan was eager to mold Eric and that he was especially happy when Eric began to date his daughter Julie. Although Eric believed in the tenets of Christian Identity, Tim and Sarah say he began to see through Dan Gayman the man. If Eric was accepting the message, he was rejecting the man, not allowing him to become an authority figure or surrogate father. Tim and Sarah spent a fair amount of time with Eric (they had even gone on double dates with him and Julie) and said the Eric they knew was very funny, but also a very troubled young man. What appeared to have complicated matters even more was that Eric stopped dating Julie Gayman and instead took up with a young woman named Joy, who was the daughter of another Christian Identity preacher. In Tim and Sarah's telling, Eric and Joy were actually engaged for a short time but never got married.[40]

Perhaps that's why it all ended quickly and badly. Patricia said of the time spent at Church of Israel that everyone makes mistakes, and she wanted to leave it at that. He does his thing, we do ours, she said, referring to Dan Gayman.[41] But what she meant isn't as clear, because even after she returned to Topton with Eric and Jamie, she apparently continued to spread Gayman's message. Deborah and Joel would get audiocassettes of Dan's sermons from Patricia that Deborah would first toss in the closet and then later in the trash.[42] As for Eric, as his brother Jamie pointed out, he left Schell City apparently confirmed in his beliefs about Christian Identity. It isn't clear whether he completely cut his actual ties with the Gaymans either, despite Dan's insistence that was the case. When the federal agents found Eric's address book at Cal's Mini-Storage, it had an entry for Tim Gayman.[43]

The Rudolph family connection to Nord Davis, which Patricia used to get her to Schell City, didn't end there. Deborah Rudolph remembered Davis's name frequently being invoked during her visits to Topton. It was Nord said this or Nord was telling me, she said, as if he was almost a member of the family. Deborah never met the man, but as a family newcomer she was interested in who he was and what he was writing. It was obvious to her that everyone in the family, Eric included, seemed to know Davis quite well. They were always interested in what he was writing or saying and who he might be bringing to speak to his group.[44] The Southern Poverty Law Center, which exists to monitor such groups as Nord Davis and his Northpoint Tactical Teams, also highlighted the connection specifically between Eric and Nord Davis, calling Eric a follower of Davis (something that Davis's followers would later deny).[45] Deborah thought that Patricia Rudolph was attracted to men with strong beliefs, and she put Nord Davis in that category, along with Tom Branham and Dan Gayman. Just how those beliefs rubbed off on Eric would be the big question.

Patricia Rudolph took pride in home-schooling her youngest children (perhaps the trip to the Ozarks was an extended field trip in her eyes) and said she raised Eric to be a creative thinker.[46] He was also an inveterate reader, according to just about everyone who knew him, be it army buddies, girlfriends, or his own family. It is in the library of Eric Rudolph, confiscated and catalogued courtesy of the FBI, that you can get a sense of how he completed his own education after Schell City by examining what he chose to read and to keep. There were some of the classics, including *The Canterbury Tales, A Christmas Carol, Crime and Punishment*, and a series entitled Harvard Classics. Some books were clearly assigned readings from his brief time at Western Carolina University. There were, for the military man, several manuals from his time in the army, including manuals on machine guns and automatic weapons, alongside a series on famous battles in the Civil War. There was a book about General George Patton, another about Lord Nelson, yet another about Napoleon. His passion for military history even extended to Thucydides on the Peloponnesian War and two copies of the *Iliad*. Eric also tackled the big thinkers, including Nietzsche, Berkley, Hume, and Kant, not to mention Aristotle. Lest he be completely humorless, Rudolph also had a copy of comedian Jeff Foxworthy's, *You Might Be a Redneck If . . . .* These books, including the large number on military history, seemed to speak to an intellectual curiosity and a passion for reading that was noted by those who knew Eric.

There were other books that, in retrospect, would be the sort that gave investigators pause, including several manuals on radio scanners, a how-to book on using night-vision goggles, a volume on general chemistry belonging to Jamie, books on burglary and auto theft and one on methods of disguise. One was called *Guerilla Capitalism: How to Practice Free Enterprise in an Unfree Economy*, which had an underlined portion on page 79 about how the reader was totally responsible for reporting and paying taxes on personal income, and included advice on how to avoid leaving a paper trail when paying bills. Perhaps most troubling of all, there was even a publication entitled *Basement Nukes*, which purported to be a how-to book on building cheap weapons of mass destruction.[47]

Other books amply testified to Eric Rudolph's education in hate, the one he continued with his own self-guided course long after that brief visit to Missouri. Some of the books, on their own, might be seen as part of a legitimate Great Books course—including Oswald Spengler's *Decline of the West*. Spengler was a German historian often seen as paving the way for the Nazis with his savage critique of Western values in the 1920s and '30s. But although he was held by many to be anti-Semitic, Spengler favored assimilation not annihilation of the Jews. Paired with Will and Ariel Durant's series on Western history and philosophy, which Eric also had, that might seem innocuous enough. Durant and Spengler were often taught side by side since they had contrasting views of history. You might even make the case with the copy of Adolf Hitler's *Mein Kampf*, given Eric's clear interest in the military history of the Second World War, that he was trying to understand the mind of the individual and not merely imbibing the message of hate and anti-Semitism.

That is, until you saw the other books and magazines. Some were published by the Institute for Historical Review, a group that had long been associated with the supporters of Holocaust denial. The deniers insisted they were historical revisionists, that they were trying to set the record straight, although a number of courts in Europe and Canada have found otherwise.[48] Their argument, which varied from book to book, was roughly this: there were no gas chambers at the concentration camps; and although a number of Jews died in Europe during the Second World War, it was nowhere near six million, and most succumbed to disease. These deniers invariably talked about the "myth of the Holocaust" and how it was wielded by Jews as a way of achieving political ends, including the creation of Israel and the control of the U.S. government. IHR, which was founded by a notorious figure named Willis Carto (who also founded the ultra-right Liberty Lobby), achieved dubious fame in the 1980s when it challenged all comers to prove that at least one Jew had been gassed in Hitler's concentration camps, offering a $50,000 reward. When an Auschwitz survivor stepped forward and offered proof, IHR tried to back out, until a California court ordered it to pay the award.[49] The books from the Institute for Historical Review included such gems as *Anne Frank's Diary—A Hoax*. There was also *Confessions of a Holocaust Revisionist* by Bradley R. Smith, who was the media director for IHR. His book claimed to be devoted to critiquing some of more "ludicrous Holocaust tales." Rudolph had two other IHR-published books, both written by F.J.P. Veale, a British lawyer who was lauded by his comrades as a stalwart member of the British Union of Fascists.[50]

Rudolph seemed to be a fan of *The Barnes Review*, a magazine founded by Willis Carto after he left IHR, where he had been accused of embezzling large sums.[51] The Barnes Review publications on Rudolph's shelf included such titles as *Shakespeare Was Wrong About Othello*, *Ancient Egypt: Were the Pharoahs Blond*, and *Pearl Harbor-FDR's Treason Exposed*. Eric's bookshelf also included other works, including *The International Jew* by Henry Ford, Sr., which was actually a series of articles first published in the industrialist's own newspaper, *The Dearborn Independent*, from 1920 to 1922. Ford, who also published the rancid forgery known as *The Protocols of the Learned Elders of Zion*, basically sketched out his twisted vision that the world's problems, from Bolshevism to booze, and jazz to Zionism, could all be laid at the feet of the Jews.[52]

As if that wasn't enough, Eric also had a copy of *Imperium*, a tract written in 1948 by Francis Parker Yockey, that was something of a manifesto for a white European/American empire that would rise above the culture-distorters—Yockey's term for Jews.[53] Yockey's message had a following among the hard core; a white supremacist convicted of murdering a black man in Texas by dragging him behind a pickup would quote from Yockey's book after getting the death penalty.[54] Eric tried to spread the message. He gave a copy to one of his army buddies, telling him to take care of it because to Eric it was akin to the Bible. He also mentioned the book favorably to George Nordmann.[55]

So this was the education of Eric Rudolph, a syllabus of hate, partly self-guided and partly influenced by his mother, Tom Branham, Dan Gayman, Nord Davis, and the Church of Israel. Many of the virulent strains that were part of the extremist Right—from Christian Identity to the Freemen movement—went into his intellectual makeup and helped him shape his worldview (being a lover of many things Teutonic and Nazi, he might prefer the German term, *Weltanschauung*). That worldview was expressed often and vigorously to those who knew him, whether they wanted to hear it or not. Deborah said there was no arguing with Eric when he got started talking politics. Jamie would try to avoid the issue altogether. When Frank and Sandy Sauer first came to Topton, looking to buy the Rudolph house, Eric began to go off on one of his tirades before his mother reminded him the Sauers were there to buy a house, not hear his political views.[56]

What usually set Eric off was the television. It wasn't just Deborah who noticed his ranting about the "electric Jew." Randy Cochran thought the best free entertainment to be had in Topton during the early '90s was to go over to Eric's house and watch the nightly news with him. There was no telling what Eric would say, but usually he would rail against the Jews he said controlled the media, as well as blacks or other minorities. Randy got the Christian Identity message from Eric, who called Jews the serpent's seed. If it was up to him, said Eric, he would kill Jews and piss all over them. Randy was just one of many who heard Eric go on about the Holocaust and how it never happened. The Jews were running—and ruining—the country, he said. Frank Sauer got a dose of that when he came to buy the house. Deborah heard it, too. So did a former girlfriend and another woman he knew.

Eric left visible reminders of his anti-Semitism. Months after the Sauers bought the Topton house from the Rudolphs, Frank's son would notice there was a Nazi swastika carved into one of the pieces of furniture. On another, there was a Star of David, with the words *No Juden* (no Jews) carved next to it. Another piece of Eric's handiwork showed up in the house of his girlfriend's father. Eric did some work on the man's house after he got out of the military. Rudolph painted the stairway hall and worked in an elaborate but hidden pattern of swastikas. When his girlfriend's dad noticed it, he was angry and threw Eric out of the house. This woman said Eric's obsession went even further. He admired his SIG Sauer pistol because it was German. He admired the girlfriend because she, too, had Aryan traits (Eric's girlfriends were always the blond-hair, blue-eyed type). Rudy, that's what she called him, wanted to get her pregnant so they could have Aryan babies. After the swastika-painting incident, that didn't happen. Instead, she broke up with him, and Eric moved back to North Carolina.

You got other parts of the package with Eric as well. Along with the hatred of Jews and the love of racial purity, came the racism. Jamie was surprised, during Eric's visit to New York, when Eric didn't make a racial remark one night after dinner, especially since Eric had been making his feelings about blacks clear to him for fifteen years.[57] Patricia said that part of Eric's problem with the army was black drill sergeants.[58] But others heard the racist remarks in more unadulterated fashion (remember that Christian Identity taught that all nonwhites, including Jews, were "mud people" and that the white race was superior). Eric, they said, hated blacks. No secret to that. This wasn't merely an affirmative action gripe. Blacks were the beasts of the field, according to his reading of the Scriptures.[59] He warned about a coming race war and the need for segregation. Eric liked to quote a Bible story about a man and woman from different tribes who were killed for marrying. Look, he said, that's what happens when the races mix. Once again, it was the television that could set him off. If he was watching a sitcom or a movie and Eric saw an interracial couple, he would go off on a tear.

The wild card in all this seemed to be homosexuality, certainly a red flag to someone with Eric's worldview. His mother and siblings all held up his relationship with Jamie as proof that Eric held no grudge against gays. To the contrary, his love and embrace of his brother seemed to stand in direct contradiction to that (their implicit point was clear: if Eric loved Jamie, he could never have bombed the Otherside Lounge). Even his brother's lover, Cameron Ferguson, found Eric to be a pretty nice guy.[60] No one will say when Eric actually learned of his brother's homosexuality and if he did indeed become a convert to tolerance; at least in this particular case, it was either newly found or he managed to keep everyone else who knew him in the dark. One of his army buddies remembered Eric's enthusiastic approval when he told Rudolph that he had beaten up a gay man.[61] Deborah was struck by the word SODOMITES in the Atlanta bomber's letters because it was a word that Eric had used to describe gays to her.

Perhaps the most telling information comes from a woman who knew Eric through one of his girlfriends, the same one who broke up with him after the swastika incident. Janet* said she saw Eric perhaps

---

*A pseudonym

three hundred times over a period of eighteen months, that they hung out together as a trio often. Like others, she got Eric unplugged, especially in front of the television, where she said he ranted and raved about the Holocaust. Janet said Eric referred to gays as Satan's children, saying they should die or be killed. He would like to teach all gays and Jews a lesson, particularly by using bombs, he said. What makes Janet's account so interesting is that she was struggling with her own sexual identity at the time. But she said she was careful to hide this from Eric because she was scared how he would react, especially after his statements about homosexuals. Janet would break off contact with Eric and their mutual friend for this reason (eventually, after getting married and divorced, she decided she was a lesbian). Her experience, which took place years before Jamie's coming out, stands in stark contrast to his. Even Jamie wondered if his brother could have been thinking one thing, yet doing another, when he opened his arms to him.[62]

If Eric's opinions on homosexuality were seemingly contradictory, his feelings about abortion seemed more confusing. Patricia started life as a Catholic, and her first role model, Dorothy Day, was strongly antiabortion despite her otherwise liberal opinions. But Patricia said she never talked about abortion with Eric.[63] The family ethos was clearly antiabortion, according to Daniel, which he emphasized when he told Charles Stone he was more likely to bomb a clinic than Eric. Daniel made it seem that Eric's feelings on the matter were practical—that he thought abortion was something that had always taken place and always would. But the issue of abortion seems to have been little discussed, never coming up, for example, when Eric visited Jamie.[64] Deborah said that Eric's calculus about abortion was based more on race than anything else. He felt that if white women continued to get abortions, then pretty soon demographics would take over, and the white race would find itself in the minority. He didn't oppose abortion, only abortion for whites. And fertility mattered to Eric. Not just his own Aryan babies, either. Deborah Rudolph had a daughter by a previous marriage before she hooked up with Joel; but at that point, she was unable to have more children. It was always her impression that Eric saw her as inferior because she couldn't bear more children and increase not only the Rudolph line, but also the white race.[65]

Eric's views on abortion, at least the way he expressed them to Deborah, seem to contradict what we traditionally understand to be the antiabortion position. That stand is based on respect for life and taken to its extreme, as some did, it meant murdering a doctor or a clinic worker to prevent countless other murders in the form of abortion. Eric's view seemed at odds with that, since it didn't sound as if he cared one whit whether nonwhites had abortions. In fact, it sounded as if he preferred that.

Which was actually consistent with Christian Identity (CI) belief, according to a man named Kerry Noble. Noble was himself a member of a CI-based group called The Cross, The Shield and the Arm of the Lord that during the 1980s became committed to the violent overthrow of the federal government and was loosely tied to The Order. Noble was deeply immersed in the CI belief system and was well acquainted with the teachings of both Dan Gayman and Nord Davis. Noble, who spent several years in federal prison on weapons charges, said that Gayman was adamantly against the use of violence, and he called Davis one of the intellects of the CI movement.

He was able to untangle the CI teachings about abortion, which he said were well-reflected in Eric's statement to Deborah about abortion and the white race. Remember that it is all about a race-based view of Christianity, said Noble, that there was the white (Christian) race who represented the true Israelites, and then there was everyone else. The everyone else was often referred to by CI followers as mud people. What mattered was the preservation of these true Israelites. Abortion or homosexuality (or even infertility) was all about Jews, who were definitely Satan's spawn, and mud people who are rolled into one, plotting to get rid of the white race. What happened to others didn't matter; if any of the mud people wanted abortions or to be gay, more power to them. If Eric spent any time around Dan Gayman, said Noble, that's the message he would have gotten loud and clear because it was fundamental to Christian Identity at that time.[66]

What about right-to-lifers or even the most extreme antiabortion followers? For them, Eric Rudolph had become something of a poster child. The extremist antiabortion movement—the real Army of God folks—held an annual dinner called the White Rose Banquet, where money was raised to support the cause and those who went to jail for the cause were celebrated. Jessica Stern, who wrote *Terror in the Name of God*, attended the 1999 banquet and said that when Eric Rudolph's name was mentioned during the fund-raising auction, a "frisson" of excitement went through the room.[67] On a Web site that billed itself as the Christian Gallery and carried what it said were Army of God pictures, there was a graphic that was headlined "The Army of God: Atlanta Bomb Squad Division" that appeared after the Sandy Springs bombing. But Kerry Noble said while there could be common cause between the right-to-lifers (Stern calls it the save-the-babies movement) and Christian Identity followers, at an ideological level it extended only as far as white fetuses. You would use the same lingo, abortion was murder, and you certainly didn't want to alienate them. The Army of God contingent may talk about martyrdom and killing in the name of the Lord, but they would be surprised, said Noble, to realize that in the eyes of true Christian Identity followers, they were considered secularists. It was all about the white race, he stressed.[68] For a CI believer, right-to-life was only a way station to true beliefs.

It said something about Rudolph that even when he was in the army he was antigovernment, not surprising given the way he had been raised. After Waco and Ruby Ridge, his feelings grew more intense and bitter. He certainly wasn't alone in this, as the comments of Nord Davis and so many others attested to. When the Oklahoma City bombing took place, he told Randy Cochran more stuff like that was going to happen. Do you think Tim McVeigh is a hero Randy asked. He would be to a lot of people, Eric replied. Randy thought Eric included himself in that group. Then Eric said, McVeigh got what he deserved. Not from God, but from the government. Rudolph was interested enough in the case to have bought a book about McVeigh called *All-American Monster*.[69] Eric also told Randy that the Olympics would be the next target for terrorists to make a statement, but the conversation didn't go any further.

Eric was fond of quoting (more likely misquoting) Thomas Jefferson about the need for revolution every twenty years when he got on to the subject of a race war or revolution.[70] Joel Rudolph said his brother believed in what he called "justifiable revenge"—that change could frequently occur by violence or force. But when Eric talked about taking up arms, he mentioned robbery not revolution. He never mentioned anything like The Order to Randy (or the Phineas Priesthood, another radical gang of bank robbers). Eric told Randy he wanted to rob an Ingles supermarket (a regional chain which had a store in Murphy) because the owner was Jewish. Rudolph claimed he had already robbed a convenience store and gotten an incredible rush from it. The Task Force never turned up any evidence that Rudolph actually committed armed robbery. But there was confirmation that Eric was talking about it. Someone who bought marijuana from Eric over in Tennessee told the FBI of similar conversations with Eric. This person remembered a time when Eric crashed at his house; he noticed that as Eric was undressing, he was wearing a bulletproof vest under his shirt.

You could even tie in the marijuana growing to all this. It was antigovernment by its very nature, you got paid in cash, and there damn sure weren't any tax stamps to be paid. Eric did talk about the New World Order and the banking system, which were always favorites of the conspiracy theorists on the far Right. They weren't content with getting rid of the IRS and the income tax; they thought the Federal Reserve was part of a plot by international (read Jewish) bankers to take over the country and the world. Eric was taking this free man thing in his own direction. With the exception of his time in the army, he was pretty careful to make sure he lived off the grid. No credit cards, no bank accounts. If he had to pay the rent, after he moved out of Topton, he used cash or a money order. The idea of not leaving a trace wasn't just a matter of personal preference. It was another tip of the hat to his ideological ancestors in the tax protestorfree man family tree.

No matter how carefully you constructed this genealogy of hate, and got to its final flower, it still didn't tell you why. Why the Olympics? Why Atlanta? Why Eric and not Daniel, who by his own admission would be more likely to bomb an abortion clinic? Why did Jamie, who went to Schell City with Patricia and Eric, end up gay in Greenwich Village while Eric was hiding out in the woods, a fugitive and accused bomber? Even if you believed, as Charles Stone did, that Eric began to hate the government from the time his father died; or, if like Jamie, who wondered if his brother was capable of doing such acts, you believed he learned his antigovernment and antiabortion beliefs from the Church of Israel, none of that still told you why Eric Rudolph might have started acting out on his beliefs. There were those who tried to get at a more proximate cause, a trigger. Park Dietz had believed, well before Eric was ever identified, that the bomber could have been set on his course by the arrests of the Georgia militia members in the months before the Olympics. The militia Web sites and newsletters were full of warnings at the time that the federal government was going to use the Olympics as an excuse to make that final crackdown, usher out America as we knew it and bring in the New World Order and United Nations troops. To anyone who was paying attention and truly believed this, it must have seemed like the American apocalypse had finally arrived.

Now look at Eric Rudolph's final two years before he disappeared. It was clear he resented what he thought was happening in western North Carolina. When Frank Sauer came to buy the Topton house, Eric talked about the Floridians and Atlantans who were leveling the tops of mountains in his Nantahala and building chalets there. He had no use for them or from whence they came. He didn't like Atlanta, and it was pretty clear he didn't like the sort of people who lived there.[71] He loved the woods outside his back window, and Frank Sauer knew this wasn't salesmanship, trying to get him to feel the same love and buy his house. Sauer wondered, even as he was spending time with Eric and getting his dose of Eric's Holocaust-denying, why Eric was thinking of leaving a place he cared for so much. Eric talked of going out West, something he also told his family. Maybe he meant it, they certainly believed him, even if they knew in the backs of their minds that he had never been straight with them about his whereabouts before.

Deborah Rudolph thought she knew the answer. If—and she was adamant about the if—Eric was the bomber, then maybe what finally set him off was selling the Topton house. This was Eric's safe haven, the place in the mountains where the Rudolphs could retreat to when the worst happened in urban America. He kept coming back, be it from Nashville or the army. He had broken up with his last girlfriend because she wanted to live in Nashville, and he couldn't bear to live anywhere else than the Nantahala. Patricia no longer lived in Topton. She had left years ago, moving first around North Carolina to be close to various children, including Jamie and Maura, before finally heading back to Florida (this time she chose the west coast, the Sarasota-Bradenton area, which presumably was more ethnically congenial than south Florida). In the meantime, it was never quite clear what was going on with the ownership of the house. Patricia had deeded it over to Daniel and Eric; then it apparently went solely into Eric's hands. Whether this was to avoid further problems with the IRS or not and whether Eric paid his mother are matters still somewhat unclear, as motives changed in the retelling by various family members.

What was clear was that by late 1995, the house in Topton was on the market. This was after Eric had moved back and Joel had joined him. Eric went into a self-sufficiency, almost survivalist, mode (and a pot-selling mode, if you believed Branham), trying to see if he and his brother could make a go living on what they produced. Joel would still talk to Deborah, despite their marital breakup, and he would complain that all Eric wanted was for them to eat trout, trout, and more trout from the family pond. There was still drinking and pot-smoking and carrying on. Eric would still hang out occasionally with Randy Cochran and even tried to get a relationship going with a woman who lived up around Murphy. Randy did say that Eric grew incredibly paranoid around this time; convinced the Feds were bugging his house, he covered the windows with blankets and told Randy he was throwing Joel out. Joel left, moving to Hendersonville. Deborah said he had grown tired of Eric's lifestyle and views, and much as he loved his brother, he wanted and needed to get out of Topton. Daniel had also moved on and was trying to make a new life, first in south Florida, then in South Carolina.

It wasn't clear whether it was Patricia's idea to sell the house or Eric's. Technically, she didn't own the house anymore, but when Frank and Sandy Sauer brought their two children up to look, Patricia was on hand, ready to bring Eric to heel when he tried to bend Frank Sauer's ear about politics. It didn't take the Sauers and Rudolphs long to cut a deal, and a few weeks later, after fourteen years, the Rudolphs were gone from Partridge Creek Road (not before Eric and his brothers came back to get the Jacuzzi, something that annoyed Sandy Sauer, who thought it was included in the purchase price). The house sold for about $40,000. According to the deed, the money was paid to Eric Robert Rudolph, who promptly went out and got a cashier's check with the proceeds.[72]

Which brings us back to Deborah's theory, about how Topton was Eric's safe haven. It was the place where his father's ashes were buried beneath a tree; the place where Eric could disappear from, out into the woods, but always return. The place where he had carved the swastika, built the secret room, and come of age. Losing that, whether it was his idea or his mother's, could have unmoored him, thought Deborah. He didn't leave and head out West, although he became increasingly evasive with his family about where he was living. Perhaps he was embarrassed by his circumstance, as he moved from Topton to Marble to Caney Creek, but if so, he hid it well, just as he was hiding lots of things. For many in the family, including Daniel and Damian, the last time they saw him was at Daniel's wedding in Atlanta in May 1996. Jamie of course saw him in October 1997, when he took that trip with Patricia up the East Coast, going to Civil War battle sites, stopping in on family in Philadelphia, then coming to New York. And he made that trip to Florida, shortly afterward, to help his mother move into her new digs.

Perhaps Deborah was right, that selling the Topton house may have lit the fuse. Even if Eric was around to provide the answer to that final question of why, he may not have understood himself well enough to do so. The genealogy of hate, the one that led from Sister Patricia to Mother Patricia to Eric and the electric Jew was important, to be sure. But at this point Rudolph was still a fugitive, so the real issue for his pursuers was not why, but where. The fact that he had not left the area after selling the house only underscored for them what the Nordmann episode showed: that he was tied to the area in ways both practical and emotional. Although the genealogy took them along some interesting routes—from Branham to Nord Davis to Dan Gayman—they felt there was still no evidence that Eric respected or trusted anyone, including his own family, enough to rely on them for help. It was down to them against Eric. It just wasn't clear whether that meant the odds were in their favor or his.

10.
RUN, ERIC, RUN

IT WAS TWO hundred against one, and it wasn't even a fair fight. The Feds had that many agents, along with dogs, helicopters, infrared radar, thermal imaging cameras, listening devices, and all the latest technology. Eric Rudolph had the cayenne pepper he got from George Nordmann. Lay some of that down behind you, and no tracking dog in the world is going to be able to follow your scent. One of the searchers said it was like living an episode of that TV show *MacGyver*, where the Richard Dean Anderson character was a secret agent and improvisational genius, who seemingly escaped from any situation with a mixture of low- and high-tech knowledge. When you factored in that most of the agents were urban cowboys, more used to taking down a suspect in a barricade situation than tromping through the woods, while Eric had spent more than fifteen years in the Nantahala, then maybe the odds changed a bit. Add in that other number—500,000—as in acres of forest for Eric to hide in—not to mention the caves and mines in the area—and you could excuse yourself for thinking that perhaps the odds were actually in Eric's favor.

That didn't stop Eric from becoming the underdog in local eyes. Not just a fugitive, but maybe a bit of a folk hero, though certainly not to everybody in the area. The first T-shirts began appearing in Murphy less than three weeks into the manhunt—a leading indicator of both public sentiment and the American desire to make a buck off the whole situation.[1] They showed Eric's face on the body of a deer and read RUN, RUDOLPH, RUN. There was another style with just his face and the caption HIDE RUDY HIDE. Not like the Rudolphs ever really felt like they fit in when they moved to Topton. One of Jamie's earliest memories of Topton was being bullied in school, while Eric stood his ground.[2] In a place like that, you would always be those folks from Florida, no matter how long you lived there. You had to be satisfied with being left alone, maybe the grudging acceptance of a nod at the video store. Your friends and acquaintances, more often than not, were other outsiders, Tom Branham or George Nordmann or Nord Davis. Which of course was another important point that often got overlooked—most of the Christian Identity/Freemen/Patriot/milita folks in western North Carolina were actually outsiders who moved to the area, lured by cheap land and a tradition of live and let live, not to mention the lack of minorities.

But this was different. When the army of Feds invaded—and hadn't that happened once before, about 140 years ago—there was something of an us versus them feeling. History counted in these parts. Cherokee County raised more than a thousand men for the Confederate Army, and it was a point of pride that the last battle of the Civil War, at least east of the Mississippi River, was fought here at Hanging Dog Creek between the Yankees and remnants of the Confederate Home Guard.[3] Why, they even burned down the Murphy courthouse in 1865, though this appears to have been the work of some local deserters who had joined up with the Yankees at the last minute and were trying to destroy some existing court records.[4] This wasn't the Civil War, and most folks didn't have time for someone accused of murdering a police officer. There was a minority, however, who, even if they hadn't given Eric the time of day before, did have sympathy for someone charged with bombing an abortion clinic.

Andrews, North Carolina, had a town slogan you couldn't miss: THE LITTLE TOWN WITH THE BIG HEART. Winning those big hearts and minds of the little town was not an easy task, even though it could be of crucial value in a fugitive case. From the start, the Feds hadn't done a particularly good job. Back in February, when they first arrived on the scene, they screwed the pooch with the Superdogs and the initial manhunt. What also didn't help then was they were searching for Eric for almost two weeks as a material witness before he was named as a suspect and they actually issued an arrest warrant. That confused matters with some of the local folks, who kept wanting to know what he was charged with. Even now, after Eric had been put on the Ten Most Wanted list, he still hadn't been charged with the Atlanta bombings. In the minds of many, this was about abortion. Eric, not the government, seemed to many to be on the right side of the issue.

The leaders of the Task Force knew they had a problem, and they knew it was getting worse, not better. This latest invasion of Murphy and Andrews, after Eric's brief reappearance in early July, was the obvious trigger. Terry Turchie was running the operation up in Andrews, and his memos to Washington were frank about the challenges of winning over residents of the area. The local population, he wrote, should be continuously reminded that Rudolph has been charged with the murder of a police officer. Rudolph is not a "folk hero," and the crime he has been accused of makes him inherently dangerous. But that would be a tough sell. Many, he continued, are mistrustful of the U.S. government, and he went on to talk about the need to treat the people living in the area with fairness, kindness, and respect.

It would have been so easy to do the small things right, but many of the new agents just didn't get it. Charles Stone had grown up in rural Georgia, and he tried to explain it to them this way: if you go through someone's field and you come to a gate, leave it the way you found it. If it's open, leave it open; if it's shut, leave it shut. That's country courtesy. No one wants to be chasing their cows or sheep all afternoon because you didn't understand the basics. And on the subject of courtesy, try saying hello for a change. That's what folks do around here. Some of the agents looked cross-eyed at a blade of grass, let alone people. Even the simplest greeting often got the thousand-yard stare in return. But in these parts, if you were out on a country road and someone said hi, all you had to do was return the greeting, and maybe even ask about the weather. The locals weren't trying to turn this into some scene from *Deliverance*. But some of the agents drafted in for Rudolph duty sure thought they were. To Stone, it boiled down to good manners and common sense.

Not that the agents had a corner on the paranoia market (Eric, of course, was in his own league when it came to paranoia). No matter how often Turchie and others said we are only here to find Rudolph, there was a minority who just didn't believe them. One letter making the rounds in Cherokee County at the time talked darkly of a plan to create some sort of extreme chaos, aimed at flushing out the Resistance, which was anyone resisting the government. This missive ended with a post-script: We have just learned from a close friend that her brother was of-fered a job as a welder. He was sent to a city where they put him to work welding shackles down the side of train interiors. He said the trains were black and double-decked. Shackles were placed on both levels.[5] The scary part about this letter was that it came out before Nordmann, before the Feds brought in all the new agents and the helicopter and the base camp at Appletree, which was surrounded by the black-clad guards from the Georgia Department of Corrections. Talk about wish fulfillment, al-beit of the negative sort. The great summer invasion was a confirmation of every militia fantasy that existed. One local surgeon, no fan of the militia, nevertheless thought the scenes of base camps and helicopter missions were more reminiscent of the Soviets in Afghanistan than the America he knew.[6]

When it came to blunders, probably the biggest one took place on a Sunday morning, and it involved the helicopters. You don't mess with Sunday morning anywhere in America, particularly not in the South and certainly not in a small town. But sure enough, one Sunday morning, just as church was getting going, one of the Task Force helicopters came swooping overhead. Charles Stone was a few blocks away, at his rented place, when he heard the sound. His reaction was a decidedly unsacred one. *Oh Jesus*, he thought, *we are going to catch shit for this and rightly so.* The pilot wasn't intentionally buzzing the churches, but he might as well have been. And it wasn't just Sunday mornings. Wednesday nights were when the Baptists and Methodists had church suppers and Bible study. The overflights those evenings also caused a lot of angry mutters and not a little bit of disgust about the damned Feds. Turchie finally caught on, even though the damage had been done. When night flights were expanded in early August, he made sure to get the word out early and often.[7]

Winning over the clergy mattered. You weren't going to find any pastor or priest stand before his flock and talk about abortion rights, not in these parts. But if the Task Force could convince the preachers that this was about a cop killer and not abortion, then that message might get spread on a Sunday morning. A Presbyterian minister in Andrews went on the record saying some in his congregation were scared of reprisals if they turned in Rudolph, but he urged them not to let that keep them from doing the right thing.[8]

It certainly didn't help matters when Reverend Conrad Kimbrough, a retired Catholic priest and antiabortion activist filling in at the St. William's parish church in Murphy, told the Associated Press that "if a person's intention is to prevent [Rudolph] from being killed they may be right" and that he doubted that Rudolph would be found "to be an unprincipled killer."[9] He also said that Emily Lyons, the nurse maimed in the Birmingham bombing, didn't deserve support because "she was instrumental in killing babies." Kimbrough's remarks might have reflected the sentiments of his congregants, but they certainly angered his bishop, who issued a statement that he made Kimbrough hand out to anyone who visited St. William's. It said that while the Catholic Church abhorred the violence of abortion, it had no truck with anyone who used violence against abortion providers.[10]

T-shirt sales were picking back up, though it was unclear how many of the two hundred or so buyers were bemused lawmen. In a perhaps unwitting homage to Chuck Berry, who was himself taking a bow to Rudolph the Red-Nosed Reindeer, there was a new ballad called "Run Rudolph, Run." It never quite made it to the Top 40 or *Billboard*, but if you were in these parts you could hear it played around town. To a couple of Appalachianologists, the lyrics about a "baby killing factory" and Eric and the lawmen were emblematic of a long Scotch-Irish tradition in the hills, the same sort that had produced the ballads about Tom Dooley and John Henry in the past 150 years.[11] That mountain tradition, which was helping to shape this into an us versus them, locals versus outsiders mind-set, also included a history of moonshiners, who brewed their own good old mountain dew in illegal stills and were always trying to stay one step ahead of the "revenoors" (the tax men, who were the forefathers of the ATF).[12] They didn't realize that Eric had already been imitating their game of hide-and-seek with the Feds while growing pot in the Nantahala. In any event, Rudolph was on his way to being a folk legend in the making, one declared.[13] The longer he was on the run, the more the legend would grow.

For the moment, Rudolph wasn't a legend, he was a hamburger. The Rudolph Burger was part of a special at the Cherokee Café. You also got the FBI curly fries (they were going in circles, the burger disappeared before you were looking, get it?) and in a bow to the media, a Skycam Coke. The irony being that many of the consumers of those hamburgers were the lawmen themselves. Which was another part of this equation. As annoying as it was to have all these guys underfoot and overhead, they were paying the bills and paying handsomely. A local boot shop, which had also sold Eric a pair, lucked out, filling orders for upward of two hundred pairs from the Task Force. If you had a motel room, a trailer, or anything else with a roof over it you could rent, then you were in luck. All those agents needed someplace to stay. The tab for the Task Force was probably well past $20 million at this point, and while a lot of it went toward overtime and lab work, a good chunk of change was being spread around the towns of Murphy and Andrews, and folks were eager to cash in.

Perhaps no one prospered like Peggy Ellison at the Lake's End Grill, which was out of town over by Nantahala Lake. She was the first one to admit you couldn't buy the sort of publicity she was getting for putting Rudolph Eats Here on the sign outside her restaurant or from selling bumper stickers and T-shirts that read "Eric Rudolph: 1998 Hide and Seek Champion." The real twist was that these days most of her customers were federal agents. Peggy had scored the contract to cater meals for them, and she was cleaning up. She told a reporter that her next stop was Disney World.[14]

The manhunt wasn't hurting another important business either—tourism. Campers were still hiking the Appalachian Trail, which was a good thing, because it was easier to find a campsite than a motel room in the area. The hikers and the searchers had to get used to each other's presence, since the Task Force remained mindful of Rudolph's statement that he would use the Appalachian Trial as a way of getting around. The trail was under regular surveillance. Rafters were still making their way to the Nantahala River where the whitewater had been an increasingly big business for a quarter century. The Nantahala Outdoor Center, the biggest company in the area, ran thousands of people down the river every summer. This year was no different, but the Task Force was keeping an eye on NOC. No one thought Eric was really trying to leave the area, but if he did, then blending in with the rafters would be one way of getting out.

The Task Force was throwing everything it could into the actual search. There were several teams out on patrol on a daily basis. They were working something of a grid system, trying to go methodically through the forest, looking for any possible sign that Eric had been there. The first areas to be searched were around Nordmann's house, then progressively outward as they picked up possible clues. It was tough going, even with air support. There were long hikes through dense brush. Part of the problem was you couldn't see much on either side of you. A person could be just a few yards away, and you could be looking for them all day without finding them, particularly if they didn't want to be found. You couldn't see them, but they sure could hear you. Stone said sometimes the teams sounded like Sherman's army when they were coming through, a comparison that cut a little close to the bone.

It could be a bit like hand-to-hand combat when you were in a patch of mountain laurel. As well-trained as the SWAT teams were, this wasn't what they trained for. If you wanted them to take down a building, end a hostage crisis, they'd be ready. But this was different. It was tough work—hot, sweaty, and sometimes dangerous. There was no doubt it could be dispiriting, too; despite the natural beauty, this could wear you out. One local resident witnessed a federal agent from up North having a near-meltdown at a gas station. I don't care if we ever find him, the man was saying in a rather agitated way, I don't care what he has done. I'm getting out of here and never coming back. These damned yellow flies are killing me![15]

There were some folks used to doing this sort of hunting; the Forest Service had its own agents spread out all over the United States. In their job, you had to be a combination of tracker, hunter, watcher, and lawman. There were agents who had the Nantahala as their beat. They spent time doing surveillance on marijuana growers like Eric (in fact, they thought they might have videotaped him once during an operation earlier in the '90s), running after arsonists, and chasing other lawbreakers who used the national forests.

Les Burril ran the Forest Service agents in a six-state area that included the Nantahala. His agents were quickly drafted into the Rudolph hunt, mainly to be trackers and guides for the FBI and ATF tactical teams. The problem was, he only had so many agents for all six states. Rudolph was priority number one, he had gotten that message loud and clear from Washington, but even though his folks spent a lot of time looking at trees, they didn't grow on trees.

The Forest Service trackers and the tactical teams spent a lot of time chasing water. The mountains and valleys were full of springs, rills, creeks, streams, and rivers; just about every type of running water someone on the run could want (including that big aqueduct). Most of it, especially above a certain altitude, was drinkable. The calculation was that his base camp or camps was going to be near running water. Instead of following the money, the searchers were following the water, sometimes working their way upstream. Water served another very important purpose for Rudolph, which they'd already run across. Every time he crossed water, it made it harder for the dogs to follow his scent. Even if he were sneaking in and out of town, he could work his way through the streams and rivers that snaked through Andrews and Murphy.

The Task Force tried to shrink the terrain using technology. The helicopters had thermal imaging, which wasn't much use during the summer. Searchers used GPS (Global Positioning System devices) to give them accurate readings on their positions as they worked their zones. They tried to get the U.S. government to make satellite passes over the forest, but that didn't yield much. The view from space was just as difficult as the view from the helicopters; the forest was too dense to show one man on the run. If Rudolph had been trying to build a missile base, maybe it would have shown up on the satellite photos.

Along the Appalachian Trail and in other places closer to town, listening posts were set up. Agents hid out in the forest with the assignment literally to keep their ears (and eyes) open. The listening posts would more likely be useful at night, when the chatter of the forest quieted down. The agents weren't just listening for a man who might be muttering to himself about the New World Order and sodomites. They knew that wasn't very realistic. But they were hoping to hear if someone who wasn't a deer or bear was moving around at night on a regular basis. And they were listening for one sound in particular.

From the start, when they searched Eric's trailer and storage shed, they realized he probably had a portable generator at his disposal. They had heard about it during interviews and found a set of instructions for a $1,000 generator (they also couldn't account for some carpentry tools and at least one more ALICE pack along with rappelling gear). And George Nordmann said that when he got his truck back, there was something missing—a couple of cans' worth of gas. The red cans were there, but not the gas. Add that to an eyewitness report that had Eric filling up a gas can a few days before he went on the run, and the thinking, according to a task force memo, was he had the generator and was probably operating it at his base camp. So the listening posts were there in part to catch the sound of a gas-powered generator, which was fairly distinctive and something that would carry out in the woods. If agents happened to pick up radio noise, from someone listening in on a transistor, then they'd check that out as well.

It was time-consuming and part of a larger effort. The Task Force was using remote cameras as well. These devices weren't necessarily designed for being left outside around the clock. Plus you always had the risk that someone would be out on a hike and trip over a wire, then start following it. The next thing you know, you had someone show up at the command post with a camera.[16] Or worse, they would let everyone know there was a camera in the area. That's what happened with George Nordmann. Just in case lightning struck twice, the Task Force had put in some cameras at Nordmann's house. Go figure that the first thing George did was tell everyone he could about the cameras!

The search was being run out of the Appletree command post, at least for as long as the weather permitted. If you could get past the black-uniformed guards from the Georgia Department of Corrections, it was an impressive sight. There was an LZ, landing zone, where helicopters took off and ran missions over the forest. You had twenty phone lines running to the various tents where tactical operations were being coordinated. There was a special microwave relay so the agents could use their radios and phones. You even had a satellite dish to monitor the news on CNN (and watch movies at night). Not to mention a row of twenty Porta Potties. Charles Stone was proud of how the operation was set up, and he was looking forward to showing it off to his boss, the head of the Georgia Bureau of Investigation. When GBI director Milton "Buddy" Nix showed up, he took one look around the Appletree compound—the tent city, the communications gear, the helicopters taking off—and just shook his head. Nix was a former FBI agent, and he'd seen this before. "You know, Charles," he said in soft Southern drawl, "Waco started out looking just like this."

No one actually lived at Appletree, but operations were being run around the clock. Which was a bit of a sticking point, not just for church-goers. It seems the FBI liked night operations, as long as someone else was doing them. The Bureau just didn't want its own agents out in the woods after dark. Not safe enough, you see. That didn't do much to impress the other members of the Task Force, especially when they saw just how nicely equipped the HRT was. The ATF ended up drawing the short straw and got most of the night duty in the woods.

Yes, Appletree was a pretty impressive sight—if you could get in. The guards, who were supposed to be on the lookout for Eric in case he decided to surprise the agents with an explosive present, regularly turned away gawkers. In some cases, these were militia members driving by to confirm their worst fears. Other times, it was locals or tourists. But one time in particular, the guards turned away a bunch of North Carolina state troopers, in full uniform no less, who were there for a meeting. Turns out they didn't have the proper picture ID.

The Highway Patrol officer, who was a local, and his men had come over to meet with the various agents in charge to make a suggestion. After being turned away, they rode off hot under the collar, getting a ways down the road before someone at the command post realized the mistake. Finally, the meeting took place, and the state guy offered his solution to the Feds. Get rid of this elaborate spread. Give us five of your agents to work with five of our troopers. We'll send them out in the community, plus do license checks. Sooner or later, we'll get the sort of lead that will turn up Eric. Not necessarily the most well-thought-out proposal, and he didn't really expect the FBI was just going to pack up. But he didn't expect to be told that giving him five agents was too expensive! Imagine the OT, he was told. All the state trooper could think was: you have two helicopters and twenty gleaming shitters—and you are worried about overtime?[17]

The Task Force was doing slightly better with the local sheriffs. Jack Thompson and Homer Holbrooks were invited to all the major events, so the Feds could be seen to be cooperating with the people who knew the area best. But there was more show than go. Jack Thompson had covered the woods as a Forest Service employee, and he had some particular ideas about where Eric might be, but he also quickly got the impression that no one in the Task Force gave a damn what he thought. He suspected Eric was using one trail—the Fires Creek Rim Trail—in particular because it was a good shortcut for anyone spending a lot of time in the woods.

The Task Force did work its way through the Fires Creek Wilderness Area in its post-Nordmann search, after it went through three other areas: Piercy Creek, Partridge Creek, near Eric's old house, and Otter Creek, where there were some of those post-Nordmann signs that Eric had moved in that direction. The idea was you went through an area and moved on. But that didn't really account for what would happen if Eric waited out a search and moved back into a particular area, which was what Sheriff Thompson suspected he might be doing.

Sheriff Thompson had no illusion about finding someone in the forest. He would tell you about a five-year-old who wandered out into the woods. They had two hundred people out there looking for the boy in a pretty small space, just a handful of acres, shouting out his name. They might have been within ten feet of the child, but didn't find him until the next day, and that was only because a dog sniffed him out. Fortunately, the boy was unharmed. But there was no doubt, this was tough terrain.[18] The way to get Eric was with that reward, said the sheriff, I'd turn my brother in for a million dollars, wouldn't you?[19]

Normally, a million-dollar reward would bring out the bounty hunters. But the days of Steve McQueen as Randall in *Wanted: Dead or Alive* were long past, if they ever existed beyond a TV show. These days, the bounty hunters tended to be city folk with sleeveless sweatshirts that were good at showing off their tattoos. A few showed up in North Carolina and came around asking Charles Stone for maps and some advice where to look. Westerners used to call guys like this dudes, and Stone suspected they wouldn't last long. They didn't. Just for good measure, Woody Enderson warned them off during a news conference in early August, reminding them of the rough terrain, poisonous snakes, and stinging insects. If they needed any more incentive to stay away, all they had to do was hear a quote from Andrews Police Chief Clay Hardin. The thickets are so dense you sometimes can't see someone two or three feet from you at night, and from twenty feet away in the day. There's rattlers big enough up there to puke up a buck deer![20]

The Task Force wanted to find Eric, no doubt. And in the minds of most agents, he was Eric, not Eric Robert Rudolph or even Rudolph. They were definitely on a first-name basis with their nemesis. But they didn't just want to find him, they wanted to mess with him. Part of this was natural enough because they were getting frustrated. It was also a strategy that their shrinks had been recommending (there was a tent full of behavioral folks at Appletree). Keep up the pressure, make him hear footsteps. Park Dietz advised that the constant pressure might lead to exhaustion, and exhaustion might be in the end what would make Rudolph surrender. Turchie laid it out in one memo: "Rudolph will only feel pressure maintained if he sees or hears vehicles driving the forest roads with blue lights and searchlights. The challenge is to appear to be everywhere. . . ."

That was part of the idea behind the night ops. If he is out there and he hears us, he won't get sleep. He'll start making mistakes. They tried to get even more devious. They put what they called bait trucks out there, leaving certain material out that Eric might want to pick up and take with him to his campsite. If he took it, then they could track him back using GPS and catch him. But Eric never bit. Then they tried more mind games. North Carolina was full of military bases, especially over toward the eastern side of the state. The Nantahala had traditionally been a place where the Green Berets would hold exercises. This was no time to invite them in, that would probably send local sensibilities over the edge. But they did suggest to some folks at Cherry Point, the air base near Camp Lejeune, that if they were out flying training missions anyway, it might be a good idea to practice doing their lazy eights over the Nantahala National Forest. Maybe that would get Eric's attention, feed his paranoia.

Some memos should never see the light of day. They are cooked up by someone in a basement or a back room who might have a bit too much time on his or her hands and a bit too little contact with the real world. By that measure, the one entitled "BEHAVIORAL CONSIDER-ATIONS REGARDING FUGITIVE ERIC RUDOLPH" was a classic. Dated July 26, 1998, it was the work of two agents residing in the Appletree head shed, where the behavioral folks hung out, in consultation with the FBI's, Violent Crimes unit back at Quantico. When Charles Stone read it, he went for the faint praise route—they meant well. He'd watch these agents in a meeting, one always deferring to the other, diffident about actually expressing an opinion. But he wondered if they had ever talked to a murderer or negotiated a hostage release or even left their offices.

If it was mind games the Task Force wanted, this memo had some suggestions. It was fortunate that one in particular never leaked to the media, given how strained relations already were between the Task Force and certain segments of the local community:

The current composite of the long-haired and bearded RUDOLPH makes him appear handsome and sympathetic. His picture resembles a common likeness of Jesus. Since the accuracy of a composite is of no great evidentiary or investigative concern now, as we already know who he is and his photo has been published, we suggest making subtle changes to the sketch, emphasizing a degree of gauntness, stress, intensity, and with those, malevolence. A few subtle strokes of the artist's pen could accomplish this, and the updated sketch could be re-released.[21]

Maybe he should contact Marla Lawson, the GBI sketch artist, Stone thought, and show her the memo. Once he scraped her off the ceiling, maybe he could get her to not only make those "subtle strokes" but also add a couple of devil horns while she was at it. Yeah, that would work. Malevolence 101.

The behaviorists didn't stop there. They thought surrender wasn't out of the question, but suicide unlikely, while "suicide by cop" was a distinct possibility. They thought while the game of hide-and-seek was empowering to Rudolph, over time he would get increasingly paranoid and stressed as his adrenaline faded. They were actually less worried than most of their colleagues that Rudolph would attempt to strike at the Task Force; in fact they thought it would be a point of pride on his part that he could one day tell his pursuers that he had the chance to shoot them but didn't pull the trigger.

All this was by way of setting the table. In the event that Rudolph confronted searchers, the profilers (they weren't real shrinks after all) had some suggestions. Most of them were actually good common sense and standard practice: allow him to talk; be nonjudgmental; find some common ground and build rapport, perhaps by talking about hiking, camping, fishing, the latest videos, or history. Rudolph will be hypervigilant, even paranoid. But be vigilant yourself. If he offers you food, don't eat it. He might try to poison you.

There was also a bit of what they called geographic profiling. That is to say that Rudolph was most comfortable on his home ground and would stay within those bounds. The best way to find him would be to analyze what he had said to Nordmann and others, using that to lead to possible hiding places. If you were someone else on the Task Force, you might find this advice a bit condescending and redundant, since this is what the searchers had been doing all along. They had been bringing one of his former girlfriends and a few other acquaintances up to the area to point out where they had been with Eric.

The profilers did zero in on a couple of points that were worth follow-ups. What did Eric mean when he told George Nordmann that he had a map and neither the Feds nor the dogs could follow him? The profilers thought it could have meant something special like an old mining map, since Rudolph didn't mention that it was a topographical map (then again, it could have meant nothing at all). And why did he bring up Randy Cochran, then insist he had lied to him in the past? Perhaps he had said something to Randy that might give the Task Force a clue where he was hiding, and it kept gnawing on him when he was out in the woods.

Interestingly, they didn't talk much about Eric's need for human interaction. He was an introvert, who could mostly do without people, but sometimes needed an audience. That was most likely the case, but Park Dietz had made a more interesting point to Charles Stone—perhaps the way Rudolph satisfied himself in the interaction department was by watching. He spent a long time keeping Nordmann under observation before approaching him. Maybe he passed the time in part by watching others, living the voyeur's life.

There was a long section written about the possibility of negotiating with Rudolph. It had already been decided Charles Stone would take the lead, precisely because he was Southern and not a Fed, but the profilers chose to repeat the obvious (perhaps they were confusing Southern with dumb, which sometimes seemed to be the attitude). Even though he had plenty of real-world experience negotiating with murderers and hostage takers, they wanted him to remember they were the experts, so they suggested using a neurolinguistic programming technique called mirroring. In other words, if Eric spoke slow and deep, so should he. Play to that primordial instinct that humans have to feel kinship with others like us, were their words. Oh, and if he asked what your name was, or you wanted to introduce yourself, use a German-sounding name like Peter Schmidt or John Hess, since the only people he seems to have admired are the Nazis.

They had another piece of advice, which is worth quoting in full, just for sheer entertainment value. There may have been a kernel of truth in it, but taken as a whole it was breathtaking in its kookiness:

> Rudolph is an avid viewer of films. He has likely seen the Rambo series and other movies whose themes are of heroes, causes and survival. Revisit his folk hero status, and liken him to Rambo or Billy Jack (both of whom surrendered). If he surrenders peacefully, he can use whatever trial there is as a forum for his beliefs. We know that he has been fantasizing about and preparing to be on the run for a number of years. It is unclear, however, what options or plans, if any he has considered beyond merely hiding. Consider asking him how he sees or wants the script of this drama to end. Remind him that Rambo surrendered. He will probably remember that Rambo was later released from prison to perform missions for the Government. The tired, hungry and frightened Rudolph may be looking for some type of miraculous ending to this drama. Based on the above suggestions, he may project such a favorable ending to a scenario.

If talking about *Rambo* wasn't going to work, maybe talking to the man who fancied himself the real-life Rambo might. When he first heard the name of Bo Gritz, Charles Stone didn't know much about the man except perhaps that he was a highly decorated Green Beret from Vietnam who had something to do with POW missions. But when Stone interviewed Eric's friend Randy Cochran, he learned something interesting. Cochran said the only time he ever saw Eric ever get emotional was when he was talking about some tapes he had from Bo Gritz. Eric actually broke down and cried listening to the tapes. It was called something like SPIKE, he said, a self-defense course. After a little research, Stone learned that SPIKE stood for Specially Prepared Individuals for Key Events, and it was a course Gritz ran that he claimed was self-preparedness training designed to bring Special Forces skills to your very own home. It turned out that Gritz had become a looming figure on the far right both as an icon and an entrepreneur and that he had a regular shortwave radio program that he broadcast from his home in Idaho.

What's more, there was a strong link between Bo Gritz and Nord Davis. Gritz had conducted some of his SPIKE training in Andrews for the Northpoint Tactical Teams and other folks so inclined.[22] This definitely called for further investigation.

Gritz was going to be in Atlanta soon for a Preparedness Expo—a merchandising road show for the extremists designed to pick up supporters and more importantly part survivalist-oriented customers from their cash for such wares as water filters, blowguns, fruit dehydrators, and in those days, Y2K survival kits (you could also get anti-Semitic and racist tracts, and often buy weapons). This was back in June when Stone was still trying to arrange a meeting with Patricia Rudolph. He had the idea that if Gritz was someone Eric admired, and knowing that Eric likely had a radio with him, that maybe he could get Gritz to broadcast a message to Eric asking him to surrender peacefully. Gritz had played a role in ending the Ruby Ridge standoff, eventually coaxing Randy Weaver out of his cabin, and maybe he could do something of the sort here. The head of the Task Force agreed that it was worth a shot, so Stone went out to the Expo and, after paying his admission, didn't have a bit of trouble finding Gritz. There was a line of folks waiting to talk to the man, who was after all a genuine hero, and to bask in his glory. The guy standing in front of Stone gave Gritz an expensive looking pocket-knife when it was his turn.

Stone badged Gritz, pulling out his GBI credentials and explaining who he was. They talked for a few minutes, and Gritz agreed to broadcast an appeal to Eric. He also had his folks check their records, which showed that Rudolph had never paid to take any of his SPIKE training, at Nord Davis's place or elsewhere (Nord Davis was dead by this point, but his son Ben also claimed there was no record of Eric ever being a part of their group).[23] Stone thanked him, handed Gritz his business card, and that was the end of that. Or so he thought. He got out of the Expo before Gritz did his shtick for the audience, complete with his trademark closing act burning a United Nations flag. Stone didn't hear the Gritz appeal when it was broadcast, but someone later told him that the message had gone out over the shortwave radio.

Bo Gritz was not the sort to go gently into the night. Especially not with the prospect of national media coverage by getting himself involved. Sending out an appeal to Eric on the shortwave was just a first step. By this time Patricia Rudolph had met with Stone and had also issued the press release that mentioned she was worried about the safety of her son. Bo Gritz had just the solution. He was coming to North Carolina, and he would lead Eric out of the woods. Safe passage, he called it, and if Eric came out, he would turn over the million dollar reward money to Patricia Rudolph. Even though bounty hunters weren't really an issue, Gritz tried to make them one by saying it was time to thwart those with blood money in their eye and save Eric Rudolph.[24] Gritz had a name for his upcoming action—Operation Cross—and now he was putting out the word for volunteers. He had already lined up Randy Weaver to join him on his latest adventure.

That was another thing about Bo. When he injected himself into the Ruby Ridge standoff as a mediator (God's vision, he said) and achieved a degree of success, he also angered more than his share of Feds. No matter how badly the Feds had handled Ruby Ridge, in their minds Weaver was a criminal and murderer, and Gritz had helped get him off. As if there weren't enough complications, the FBI Hostage Rescue Team now on the scene in North Carolina was the same HRT involved in Ruby Ridge. Lon Horiuchi, the HRT sharpshooter who had shot and killed Randy Weaver's wife, was going to be in Andrews when Weaver and Gritz showed up![25] Stone got his share of cross-eyed looks from some of his federal brethren when word got out that Gritz was coming to North Carolina, especially after Gritz incorrectly claimed he was coming at Stone's invitation. Stone had a response to that; just in case the worst ever happened and they did end up killing Rudolph in some sort of shoot-out, at least after Gritz's visit they could say that Rudolph had the chance to surrender to his own ilk. By now, after Eric's conversation with Nordmann about needing new radio batteries, they knew there was no way Rudolph couldn't know that Gritz was on the way.

This had all the makings of a screwup that would dwarf the Superdog incident. It might even rank up there with Richard Jewell. The media couldn't get enough of Gritz, who was as colorful as they came and never at a loss for a sound bite, so the satellite trucks were back up in Andrews in force, just at a time when it seemed like the search was beginning to wind down. Naturally enough, because he was the one who got Gritz involved in the first place—even though the last thing he wanted to do was to have Gritz show up—Charles Stone got handed the job of being Task Force liaison with the Gritz brigade. By now, he had done even more research on Gritz and thought he had a bit more of the man's measure. Bo was charismatic, you got that just from talking with him, but to Stone's mind, he was probably more politician than true believer.

Gritz had come a long way from his days in Vietnam when he seemed the epitome of the Special Forces hero. His series of escapades attempting to go after POWs and MIAs after the war had first made him something of a hero, but nothing ever came of them, and soon a number of folks began to denounce him for preying on the hopes of POW families. After the movie *Rambo* came out, that nickname seemed to stick to Gritz, and it only added to his cachet, even though the man who created the character said he had never heard of Gritz.[26] These days he billed himself as a Christian Patriot and was also a real estate developer, fronting a development for like-minded folks in Idaho called Almost Heaven. Bo had briefly been David Duke's running mate when the former Klansman ran for president in 1988 (Nord Davis was apparently the choice of this same Populist Party to be secretary of defense in the extraordinarily unlikely event the Duke ticket was elected), but then withdrew his name from the ticket.[27] Four years later, Gritz ran for president as the Populist Party candidate and actually got 107,014 votes, which was .10 percent of the popular vote, and more than twice the ballots Duke had received.

When he was talking to Stone, Gritz seemed to skip most of the extremist rhetoric, which was why Stone suspected some of it might be an act aimed at playing to his fans and electorate, such as they were. In any event, after Gritz had flown his plane into Andrews, accompanied by Randy Weaver, and had his first news conference, he sat down with Stone, and they worked out some rules of engagement. As far as Stone was concerned, the idea was to keep Gritz's self-proclaimed band of Patriots well away from the Feds and vice versa. However angry some of the Feds were about Gritz and Weaver being there—and some made their feelings quite clear—the last thing they needed was some run-in where they once again came across as the heavy-handed bad guys. Thankfully, the HRT and Lon Horiuchi were off doing their own thing. None of the Gritz brigade had any clue their least favorite government sharpshooter was within a thousand miles of them. But hell, if they could find Eric, more power to them. After visiting their campsite at Bob Allison—where Nordmann's truck had been left by Eric—Stone wasn't counting on it. Most of the men wearing their baseball caps with the Cross of St. Andrew (the Confederate emblem) and carrying tricolor bandanas struck him as pretty sorry looking, and he thought they had less business hiking through these woods than he did. Even Bo was getting beefy these days, not quite the svelte young Green Beret he remained in his own mind.

And so it went. When they weren't trying to stay out of the rain, Gritz and his teams spent the August days pushing through the undergrowth, getting a feel for just how tough the search was, yelling out into the woods such phrases as "Eric Rudolph! We are volunteers with Bo Gritz. . . . We are here to provide you safe passage!"[28] If they actually made contact with Rudolph, the Gritzies were planning on turning him over to the local sheriff, since according to their ideology, he was the most legitimate law enforcement authority. It never came to that. Gritz caused a brief flurry when he claimed that his folks staked out a cabin and that Eric had gotten past them, but that came to naught.[29] Stone thought what really happened was the man who was supposed to be doing the stakeout had fallen asleep and was just trying to cover his own ass. By the time the week had ended, Gritz was claiming he had information that there were a handful of people helping Rudolph, but he never provided anything to back that up, and the Task Force thought that information was about as valid as his claims of POW sightings years before.

With that, Gritz did something that his country was never able to do in Vietnam; he declared victory and came home. He and Weaver flew out of North Carolina, heading back to Idaho, and the circus left town. Only in his case, there was a bizarre epilogue. Just a few weeks later, after his wife of twenty-four years (they were also business partners) filed for divorce, Gritz put on his uniform, medals and all, and tried to go see her. When she gave him the brush-off, he drove out of town, got out of his truck, and pulled out a pistol. He didn't put the gun in his mouth or try shooting himself in the head, as most would-be suicides did. Instead, he pointed the gun at his chest. He would later say it was divine intervention that the bullet damaged a few medals and only wounded him, but the police report would suggest it was less a miraculously averted suicide attempt than a cry for attention from his estranged wife.[30] Whatever the truth, Gritz ended up divorced. Months later, Charles Stone was at a gun show south of Atlanta when he heard someone hailing him. He turned around to discover it was Bo Gritz, who with a smile on his face and in apparent good health, introduced Stone to his new wife.

Even before the arrival and departure of Colonel Gritz and his merry band, there was a tectonic shift in the world of terrorism, and the aftershocks were already being felt in the Nantahala. The enemy within had been the obsession for these last few years, but thousands of miles away, at a dusty training camp for terrorists in Afghanistan, America's priorities were being changed. In late May, in that interregnum between Eric's first disappearance and his visit to George Nordmann, a bearded Saudi named Osama bin Laden was holding forth to a group of mostly Pakistani journalists. In case anyone had missed it three months earlier—and most had—he was declaring war on America. His group, al Qaeda (the Base), was allying itself with other Moslem terror groups and declaring jihad against the Crusaders and Jews, which really meant the United States and Israel. There was ironically much common ground between these Islamic terrorists and the extremists back home. Like most haters, they blamed the Jews for so many of their own problems, always seeing them behind every conspiracy. And although the Islamists didn't jump on the phrase New World Order, they meant much the same thing when they talked about the Crusaders. It was always a plot, whether you were in Idaho or western North Carolina or Afghanistan. Washington–New York–the Zionists, they were going to steal your land and take away your freedom and by God, they wouldn't let you worship your own God, whether you called him Allah or Jesus or Yahweh.

On an August morning just weeks later, bin Laden and al Qaeda made good on their threat, launching simultaneous suicide bomb attacks on the U.S. embassies in Kenya and Tanzania. That was August 7. A few days later, while on part of the Task Force's charm offensive with the local citizenry, Terry Turchie announced that the Rudolph search was being scaled back from about two hundred agents to eighty. He told teachers and students at Eric's old school, the Nantahala School, that the agents weren't actually going from North Carolina to Nairobi or Dar es Salaam. Instead they were going to be sent home, to cover others who were being sent overseas.[31] Turchie's remarks were quickly dressed up in a more politically correct version: this was a restructuring that had nothing to do with the bombings in East Africa; the Task Force had accomplished its immediate goals and was moving into a new phase, which needed fewer people. But more agents would be brought back in as warranted.[32] The truth was somewhere in between—Turchie had indeed proposed the restructuring before the East Africa bombings, but the attacks by al Qaeda caused the cutbacks to be sped up.

Turchie and several of his colleagues were about to make another politically incorrect move, although this one would not be made public. Stone, Don Bell from the ATF, and Duke Blackburn joined Turchie and Enderson in writing an extraordinary letter to Attorney General Janet Reno asking her to allow Rudolph to be charged in the Atlanta bombings. The forensic work was done, the grand jury testimony had been given, and in the minds of just about everyone on the Task Force and in the U.S. Attorney's Office, it was time to file a criminal complaint and indict Eric.[33] Atlanta was ready go, they wrote. But Reno hadn't signed off yet, and they were suspicious her caution tied back to the original debacle with Richard Jewell. Their argument to that was simple: not only was the evidence clear, but it would help them do their jobs. As long as this was about winning hearts and minds, with the ultimate aim of finding Rudolph, then an indictment would give them important ammunition.

Abortion mattered as an issue, they wrote, and strongly held religious beliefs may have prevented many people in the western North Carolina area from fully cooperating with the Task Force. Many of these same people would feel differently if Eric Rudolph was charged in the Olympic park bombing, but until and unless he is, Turchie et al. wrote, they will choose to view him only in terms of the abortion issue. Everyone they had discussed this with, from the local sheriff and civic leaders to the Forest Service employees who worked the area, agreed. They held up George Nordmann as a case in point. He was reluctant to come forward in a timely fashion in part because of his beliefs about abortion. Now that he had been exposed to the Task Force and seen how it worked, he told them he regretted having waited so long before coming forward.[34]

Whatever the reason for the restructuring, be it bin Laden or not, the fugitive hunt was moving into a new phase. The mission now was to do more with less. Instead of several daily patrols out in the forest, there was manpower to send out two a day. The search was also headed underground, into the caves and mines that honeycombed the area around the Nantahala. There had been the one-off trip into a cave with Cato and Susan Holler earlier in the year, but now the Task Force realized it needed a more systematic approach. The prospect that Rudolph could be chilling out underground while their patrols were out beating the bush was beginning to dawn on them. One of the things agents had discovered when they searched Eric's old home in Topton, the one he sold to the Sauers, was some rappelling gear (they also had a photo of Rudolph rappelling into a cave). The Hollers had explained why geologically there weren't that many caves in the area—a relative term, since they compared it to eastern Tennessee, which was filled with them. But mines were different. Just about every local they met would tell them about an old mine they used to know about or play in when they were kids. The farther you got from town, the more likely you were to hear such a story.

There was history behind this. Even before the white settlers arrived, the Native Americans mined the area. In the late 1700s, western North Carolina was the scene of America's first gold rush after a large nugget was found in Cabarras County. Mica, quartz, and feldspar were more commonly mined in the years after the Civil War, and talc was another big favorite, though there was some gemstone work going on.[35] Part of the problem, the Task Force discovered, was that mines would go in and out of business. There weren't that many small mines in operation these days, but mom-and-pop mines had been common for more than a hundred years. Finding accurate records was a challenge. You might find a map from the 1960s, but that would only show you the mines open and operating at that point. If you wanted to make sure you had a complete record, the best start you could make was by literally getting maps of the area done about every ten years dating back to the 1870s and 1880s and trying to make a master document! Even then there was no guarantee you had a complete list. Sometimes the best leads came from residents who knew about this mine where an uncle used to work or that shaft where they used to play when they were kids.

Help arrived in an unlikely form. Back in July there had been a call for volunteers, and Darren Free had heard it. Darren lived over Asheville way and ran a glass company, but his true passion was a mixture of archaeology, mines, and cave exploration. Any excuse to get underground worked for Darren. He liked to say he was part Cherokee, part Indiana Jones, and it was true he was interested in adventure. Plus, he took exception to what Eric Rudolph was accused of doing. There was no need to win Darren's heart or mind over, he was already sold. Besides, about a year earlier, he had gotten interested in the old gold mines in the area and had begun doing his own exploration. So when that call went out, Darren went in and volunteered, just sort of leaving his glass business to fend for itself (which was a bit of a problem, since he was the company). He started as an unpaid volunteer and soon got on the payroll as a consultant. Before you knew it, Darren was a media star, taking Leslie Stahl from *60 Minutes* and Brian Cabell from CNN down into the Nantahala's underworld, giving them a stark demonstration of what searchers were up against.

Here's how Darren Free laid out the numbers. As near as they could tell, there were about forty to fifty mines in the immediate search radius of fifteen miles. If you widened the search area by a few more miles, which seemed a real possibility the way Eric was moving around, then you had four hundred-plus mines.[36] There was no way they could look in all of them. There was no way they could find all of them. Darren liked to make that point by dragging folks out to a particular area and get them to play "try and spot the mine entrance." Inevitably, you lost. An old mine entrance might be, in fact often was, hidden in rhododendron bushes (apparently they grew well in the acidic soil that was a by-product of some of the mining).

The Task Force did try to find some of the mines from the air. You looked for tailings, the slag that had come out of the mines years before, and also how vegetation looked in an area. If you knew what you were looking for, there were supposed to be some telltale clues. But it was an expensive and tedious process. In the end, with the aid of the ERDAS Company in Atlanta, the Task Force was able to use computer imaging and graphics to build a database of mines in the area, but there was no way it could be all inclusive.

High tech could only get you so far. At some point, you actually had to go down into the mines and caves. This was a grueling process, even worse than searching the forest itself. You never knew what was down there. Shafts would run on for a while, into dead ends. Or there would be signs of a cave-in. Or a mine that had simply been abandoned, with some of the equipment intact. Poison gas was always a concern (the canary in the mine was a cliché, but it also had real meaning) so the Task Force brought in some fancy electronic gizmos that would let you know what you might be breathing. They even got some experts on mine safety from OSHA and the Department of Energy, to make sure no one was going to get gassed.

Fortunately, unless you happened to be on the squad, the FBI got most of the assignments underground. The HRT was trained in rappelling, so it did the jobs that required serious rope work getting in or out. Usually it was the regular SWAT teams, and they ended up doing a lot of climbing, crawling, and caving through what were sometimes rather slimy conditions. This wasn't the sort of job for anyone who was scared of bats and mice. Not to mention the potential for nasty critters like snakes. The good thing about doing this during the summer and fall, aside from it being cooler underground, was that you weren't likely to run up against a hibernating bear.

But you might find some bees. During one particular search, the SWAT guys were down in a mine, while some distance away there was a security team and a nearby resident who had pointed them in the right direction. Suddenly the security team and the local guy heard someone crashing through the underbrush, and the search team leader yelling, "BOYS, YOU BETTER RUN." You could understand why this didn't sound very good. As the security team grabbed for its guns, the agent burst into the clearing, surrounded by a swarm of bees. Somehow, coming out of the mine, he had stepped on a nest of yellow jackets underfoot. His body armor kept him from being stung on most of his torso, but he was taking a beating on his neck and face.

There were risks for Eric, too, in going underground. He could have easily gotten trapped in a mine shaft, whether from a cave-in or flooding. He might have run across a bear. Or been overcome by poison gas (some of the caves had sulfates, and if water from a rainstorm came in, the hydrogen sulfate by-product could be lethal). They might never know what happened to Eric; it could be he was down some mine and had fallen off a ledge, breaking his neck. After weeks of looking underground, however, the Task Force had the same results as it did elsewhere, which was to say no Rudolph.

Darren, for one, was convinced Eric was down there. It all made sense, from what he knew of Eric's past and the way he liked to go out into the woods as a teenager. The way he saw it, Eric had found at least one mine or cave, maybe more. These underground facilities had a steady, year-round temperature, usually in the high fifties or low sixties, where a person could settle in. Why, he bet that Eric's main hiding place was a comfortable place—had a bed, decent flooring, his generator, and lots of the food he had taken from Nordmann's. Maybe there was another one where he kept the explosives and bomb-making equipment he was supposed to have. Darren would tell you how other fugitives had been found in caves or mines with such amenities as wall-to-wall carpeting and running water. And don't forget, he said, there were places in China and elsewhere where folks chose to live in caves, whole communities.

Eric was still alive. The Task Force knew it even if the last physical proof it had came from Nordmann's house and truck. While the searchers were aggressively trying to find him, both above and belowground, they realized their next lead might come from another Nordmann-type situation, waiting for Eric to surface again. That had been part of the point of the letter to Attorney General Reno. If he showed up and if someone called in quickly enough this time, then maybe they would have a shot at him. Such a strategy would work best if Eric chose to rely on a person, just as he did with Nordmann.

He didn't. The Task Force got a call over Labor Day weekend from a man visiting his family's summer cabin up in Tellico with his wife (Tellico was to the north and east of all the area where they had been looking for Eric over the summer). The family didn't use the cabin all that much, even during the summer, not since his father had died; his mother didn't come up very often on her own anymore. But the cabin was well stocked, at least it had been, until they arrived and discovered it had been burglarized.

This was one sort of scenario the Task Force had been anticipating. Even though they had been hoping Rudolph would make contact with someone, they thought he must have felt burned when Nordmann went to the police. So it made sense that he would try and knock over a vacationer's cabin—or even camp out there for a while—but they thought it more likely to happen once the season turned and more of the cabins were abandoned for the winter. Labor Day, or whenever the break-in actually occurred, was a little earlier than they expected. Still, if he had staked out this cabin for any length of time, he would have realized it was a target of opportunity.

They worked the crime scene, hoping to turn up some prints, just to prove it really was Eric. No such luck. Once that was done, they got the couple to make a list of what was missing. What they came up with helped convince the Task Force that Eric indeed had paid a visit. Gone were:

- A nonworking compass

- Collapsible camping cups

- A tube of Pepsodent toothpaste

- Two yellow and white washcloths

- Several romance novels

- Kleenex

- Toilet paper

- Paper towels

- Three bars of Ivory soap (other brands were left)

- One snakebite kit

- One bottle of Top Job cleaner

- Plastic grocery bags

- One pair of rubber rain boots

- A green hammock

- Two sets of packaged sheets

- Three blankets

- Volumes 1, 2, and 4 of *Foxfire* (a series of books on Appalachian living and folk remedies)

- Topographical maps of the area

- A variety of ammunition, including .22, .12, and .20 gauge

- One pair of men's hiking boots

- Size 34 men's underwear, T-shirts and socks

- Wrapping paper

- A porcelain bowl

- One bottle of antifreeze

This wasn't exactly the sort of loot your average burglar would take, even up in the mountains. He might be more inclined to take the portable record player or the vacuum cleaner or the books about guns. Although, interestingly, if it was Eric and he needed gas for his generator, there were two metal gas cans that were full, which were left behind. Those would have been the heaviest items to carry. Whoever hit the place didn't take some of the other books, including *Foxfire 3* and some gun manuals. The burglar also left behind other men's clothing as well as non-Ivory soap.

The missing antifreeze certainly got the attention of investigators. Winter was coming, to be sure, and the prudent burglar could never stock up too early. But they remembered back to the dog poisonings around Nordmann's house. Those were done with antifreeze. A little more ethylene glycol might come in useful down the road if you were planning on doing some more moving around. The boots and socks would always come in handy, not to mention the underwear, which would have certainly fit Eric, maybe been a tad big, depending on how his diet was going. You couldn't exactly be choosy about your reading material either. If bodice-rippers were the only thing on offer, then it was that or nothing. And the sheets meant perhaps Darren was right, that Eric had a nice setup somewhere underground by now, and this was the easiest way to change the linens.

On a more practical level, the *Foxfire* books were invaluable as survival guides.[37] They were chockablock with herbal remedies and tips on mountain living. Volume 1 even included instructions on how to dress a hog. As for why the burglar left behind Volume 3, even though it had a section on wild plants, it might have been because most of the book was about making dulcimers and raising animals, not particularly useful skills for a man on the run. As for the choice of soaps, Ivory was the only brand that was odorless, which made a difference if you thought you might be tracked by dogs, and it floated, if you dropped it into the water (Ivory also didn't make suds, so you didn't have to be worried of leaving any traces downstream). When they put it all together, they were convinced this was Eric's handiwork.

Then came the great trout hunt. One of the search teams had begun working in the Tellico area after the burglary. When a prowler said to fit the general description of Rudolph was reported nearby several days later, the searchers thought they might be hot on Eric's trail. As they worked their way through the area, they came upon the Tellico Trout Farm. It wasn't unusual to find fish scattered near the ponds; there were bears and other critters that liked to raid the farm for a snack. But from the look of it, this trout head appeared to have been cut off by a knife, not by a bear's claws or teeth. What with the other seeming evidence of Eric in the neighborhood, this fish story took on a life of its own. Especially when you added in the memory of Eric living in Topton on nothing but trout for a time in the mid-'90s.

The FBI moved in with its high-tech gear. Thermal imaging cameras, designed to catch body heat, were set up around the perimeter of the Tellico Trout Farm and some other fish farms nearby. To the bemused manager at Tellico, the whole process was explained as being like the movie *Predator*, where Arnold Schwarzenegger was able to spot an alien by the heat traces he left (only in real life, the cameras were black-and-white). With bated, or would that be baited, breath, the Task Force awaited the results of its surveillance, hoping that the fish thief would reappear. The camera caught some blue herons. They got an otter. There was a family of mink. Charles Stone was hugely entertained by video of a bear trying to shake loose a metal container that he thought had fish inside. It would have made a good episode of *Animals Gone Wild* or some such show. But nothing for *America's Most Wanted*. Not one shot of Eric.

There was another would-be sighting that had the searchers going in the opposite direction. The Task Force got word from the Nantahala Outdoor Center, which ran most of the whitewater activities in the area, that a bearded man in fatigues had been spotted sneaking around their headquarters. What was even more intriguing was that NOC reported food missing, including some dressed pork and canned goods. It all seemed to fit. If you wanted to get in and out of the area, the easiest place to blend in was around NOC. Another bearded guy amongst all the rafters, canoers, and kayakers—who would be paying attention to him?

The Task Force had to respond. They went out and set up another surveillance camera, leaving it there for a year and periodically checking it. Once again, a dead end. It was only years afterward that a NOC executive would admit his folks never really suspected Eric Rudolph was in the area. Instead, they were plagued by thefts, and they suspected it was employees who were stealing food and holding barbecues on the sly. Bringing the FBI in, whatever the pretext, was a good way to send the river guides a message. And it worked. The thefts trailed off dramatically. But again, no Rudolph.

Maybe, if all else failed, Operation Full Moon would work. The Task Force didn't expect Eric Rudolph to turn into a werewolf. But Turchie noted that Rudolph had stolen Nordmann's truck on the night of a full moon, most likely because it was a lot easier to find his way around in the woods with all that ambient night light. It was early October, and they were coming up on another full moon on the 5th. He wanted his folks out in force just in case. But the night passed without incident. No werewolves, no Eric.

Turchie did get something on his wish list. On October 14, 1998, twenty-seven months after the Centennial Park bombing, Eric Robert Rudolph was indicted for that crime and the bombings at the Northside Family Planning Clinic and the Otherside Lounge. In Washington, FBI director Louis Freeh, echoing Turchie's memo to headquarters written at the beginning of August, said he hoped nobody saw Rudolph as a folk hero. Back on the ground in Murphy, Sheriff Jack Thompson said the message should be that Eric was a crook and a dangerous man; he hoped news of the indictment would change some minds in his neck of the woods.[38] The FBI also released a photo of Rudolph wearing a T-shirt and khaki shorts, the outfit it thought he was wearing, along with a hooded sweatshirt, of course, the night of the Centennial Park bombing. Whether the photo or the news of the indictment would have any practical value was another matter altogether.

The leaves were changing and falling off the trees. Autumn was coming to the Nantahala. While the search had been scaled back since mid-August, the Task Force leaders had planned all along to rev it back up, bringing in more agents once it started getting cold. They also had an idea to multiply the number of searchers by enlisting the help of a group of folks that would soon be invading the forests for quite a different reason. Here's what they were thinking: with the leaves off the trees, it would be a lot easier to spot anyone moving in the forest. One of the things that was so frustrating during the summer was that damned double-canopy forest. From the air, if you could see through the trees, then you still had to contend with the ground cover, the mountain laurel, which was also a few feet high. When you were in it, you were lucky if you could see five feet on either side of you. And flying above it wasn't much better.

It would also be cooler, which meant the high-tech gear might be more useful. The Task Force had something called FLIRR at its disposal, which was an acronym for Forward Looking Infrared Radar. Basically, it was a variation of the thermal imaging cameras they were using at the fish farms and Nantahala Outdoor Center. Only it didn't work so well during the summer because the ground retained so much heat that it was hard to spot warm bodies. The colder the air temperature, the more a person (or a bear) might stand out.

Then there were the hunters. Western North Carolina was prime black bear country, and the season coincided with the Task Force's planned fall offensive. Not that it was called that, they weren't that tone-deaf. In fact, Turchie and his troops kept trying to emphasize their mantra to anyone who would listen: we're only here to find Eric Rudolph and when we do, we will leave. Once they found out that their season wouldn't be screwed up by the manhunt, the hunters seemed to be enthusiastic about helping, and they had some pretty impressive resources. Charles Stone and some of the other agents went to visit the Macon County Coon Hunters Association at the invitation of Sheriff Holbrooks. This wasn't a ragtag bunch of good old boys with shotguns. There were doctors and lawyers along with blue-collar folks. But more importantly, the dogs were top-notch, some of them worth in the thousands because of their tracking abilities. These people and their dogs were going to be out in the woods anyway, so if you could get them on your side, then you had hundreds, if not thousands, more eyes and ears and noses at your disposal. The one drawback was that quite a few hunters relied too much on modern technology and would send their dogs out into the woods alone, monitoring their progress using tracking beacons, instead of going in there themselves.

Stone and a state game warden also met with bear hunters in Andrews, telling them what to look for. First off, of course, was what the search teams looked like and how to make sure they weren't in the same area. You didn't want the hunters taking a shot at an FBI guy clad in body armor who was out beating the bush. Nor for that matter did you want one of the Feds winging a hunter (not that you already didn't have the usual potential problem of hunters firing on each other accidentally). But there were some other clues out there. Look for those Emergen-C power bar labels, Stone told them. We know Eric took some of those, so if you see something like that, it could tell us he's been around. Look for other signs that are unusual, as if someone has been around recently, might be storing food. Just don't try to play hero, because what we know about Rudolph tells us that he's armed and dangerous. There were a few grumblers, of course. One woman said her husband went to a meeting between the Task Force and some bear hunters and came away thinking that the agents wanted them to pick up every empty can of Beanee-Weenees they saw and put it in a baggie to bring back for possible evidence. More importantly, a lot of the locals, not just the hunters, thought it was more likely that Eric had found someplace to hole up in town, that he was in someone's basement, rather than out in the woods.[39] Still, a million dollars was incentive enough to keep your eyes open.

It would be tempting to say that all of this worked. The plans were smart and also had the virtue of deputizing an important segment of the local populace. Just think of how badly it could have gone if someone in the Task Force had tried to interfere with the hunters instead of winning them over. But while it was a good season for the bear hunters, it wasn't a good one for finding Eric. The searchers tried. They went back over the areas they had covered during the summer. They even went into a bear sanctuary where the hunters weren't allowed, just in case Eric decided to do a Grizzly Adams and hide out there (which certainly made for an interesting selection process when they were deciding who should go into the bear haven).

Even the FLIRR could only get them so far. One evening, the helicopter patrol thought it spotted something. They had gone over an area earlier in the day. Now, after nightfall, they were doing another scan, looking for body heat. There was a reading, clear as you could get. It looked like a campfire and a camper. Everyone piled into the command center and plotted the next moves. Come dawn, they would take down the site, capture whoever was there, and if luck was going their way, why, they might be able to announce Eric's capture by lunchtime. After an all-nighter, they launched. What they came back with was one surprised young camper who thought he was getting away for the night. No glory on this one, although it was a useful exercise just in case there was a next time.

The hearts-and-minds campaign on the other hand seemed to be working. Stone for one thought they were making real headway. Most of the locals seemed to accept the Task Force was here to stay, at least until Eric was caught, and that the agents might be learning some manners. There was the Atlanta indictment and playing to the bear hunters. Turchie was making the rounds, speaking to whoever would listen, trying his hardest to keep the locals in the loop. Whenever the Task Force made a move these days, it wouldn't keep it a secret. If there were going to be more night ops, especially helicopters swooping over houses, then the agents learned it was better to announce that in advance. It wasn't like there were any secrets anyway in that small of a community, except for the big one—which was Eric's whereabouts.

But on the evening of November 11, everything seemed to go south in a hurry. There were about fifteen to twenty folks working in the Task Force command post in Andrews (they had moved back from Appletree when the weather turned cold). The building was really just an extremely large, thin-skinned metal shed, an old warehouse-type structure, with some plywood on the inside. There were a couple of what sounded like rifle shots and just about that time, an FBI agent from Birmingham named Bob Rolen felt something graze his head.[40] Someone was out there, firing on the command post! That got everyone going. The helicopters were launched, as much to keep them out of harm's way as anything else. While one was flying over Andrews, a laser was pointed at it, and the crew thought it was being targeted, maybe by a sniper or even worse, by a missile. The situation was going to hell in a hurry. Try and imagine the confusion.

When the helicopter radioed in, a whole convoy of law started heading toward the location where the laser seemed to be coming from. Philip Rogers would later admit that it wasn't the brightest idea to go out in his backyard and point his son's new toy laser at the helicopter.[41] He said he didn't know there had been a shooting at the time. Rogers and a local militia guy named Ramon Sparks said they were getting ready to head to police headquarters (it was that militia thing again, where you only recognized the sheriff as being legit, not the Feds); when the convoy met up with Rogers and Sparks at the police station parking lot, it got kind of ugly. There were a lot of angry agents, and they weren't in the mood for any niceties. It got a little rough, and neither side was willing to back down. Rogers would be released, perhaps a little chastened by the whole affair, but Sparks and his supporters, including one who billed himself as citizen joe 6-pack, kept going after the Task Force, firing off a letter of complaint to the local paper and telling everyone who would listen that Sparks and Rogers had been beaten and that this just fit with the rest of it.

The rest of it, as far as the militia types were concerned, included a State of Emergency, the New World Order, and of course just plain bad manners by the Feds. On the last count, there was no doubt that they had some cause for complaint. But there was more than a tinge of self-importance or paranoia (or both) to their gripes. Those helicopters swooping over their houses? Sure they were aimed just at Eric Rudolph. Citizen joe knew better. He would tell you as he did in e-mails and Web postings, about Russian troops directing traffic in another North Carolina town if you gave him half a chance. To him, the FBI was the IFBI (International Federal Bureau of Investigation) and the ATF was either Actuating Toddlers Funerals or Abortions The Fad.[42]

They were sure, in fact positive, that western North Carolina was under a State of Emergency but that no one would admit it. In early December, a couple of these folks showed up at the gates of the compound, which was something of a regular occurrence. What are you looking for, asked Charles Stone, who was curious enough to have gone out to talk with them. The tanks, they replied. It seemed that word had gone out on some of the militia radio programs that there were tanks in Andrews. Stone had to work hard to keep from laughing. Tanks? Do you see any? What would we do with tanks up in the mountains? He thought logic might actually work with them, but as they drove away, he wasn't so sure. He just couldn't believe the idiocy of some of these people.

In a sense, Stone was partially responsible for feeding their paranoia. He thought it would be a good idea to have a medevac helicopter on hand supporting all those agents out in their search parties. Back home, he would have just picked up the phone and called the adjutant of the Georgia National Guard, who then sent out some of his folks. They'd worry about the paperwork later. He did that here, and the Georgia National Guard was only too willing to send up a company from the 171st Battalion Aviation Unit. You would have thought he had violated some national defense policy, which he might have, since there were all sorts of rules and regulations. The Pentagon got involved, and so did FBI headquarters, and eventually the paperwork was cleared up. But once the militia guys like joe 6-pack saw those green helicopters, they were just sure the black UN helicopters were about to follow.[43] Lord knows what these guys thought when they saw the C-130s flying overhead during the summer!

It turned out the men eventually arrested for the shooting had nothing to do with the militia. One of them might have been angry because he had made a complaint about police brutality by some local cops; when the Feds investigated and didn't find any evidence to uphold his claim, he turned his anger at them. Eddie Dewayne Carringer and Wayne Henry Burchfield pleaded guilty to firearms charges (Carringer also pleaded out on two assault charges). A third man admitted making false statements to investigators.[44]

When federal agents had shown up in Murphy on the night of January 30, 1998, the last thing they expected was that they would be there on January 30, 1999. By the time that first anniversary rolled around, they had a much different perspective. Eric Rudolph just couldn't be found. Not that they had looked everywhere. You couldn't do that when you were searching a half million acres of woods or hundreds of mines and caves. When the anniversary stories were being written, the story lines were usually the same: frustrated but resolute searchers, annoyed and in some cases resentful locals, and a missing man. Sometimes the details varied: one story might mention the T-shirts; another might mention the Rudolph burger; most would have at least one local opining that Eric was in someone's basement. We're going to catch him, vowed the Feds. But after a year, not everyone was so sure.

11.

"I THINK HE'S DEAD"

WHEN CHARLES STONE first met them, the two young women were laughing. Lisa* was Eric's former girlfriend —the one who went out with him during his stint in the military and the one who broke up with him in part because he had painted a swastika in the front hallway of her father's house. Janet** was the sidekick, the friend to both Lisa and Eric, the one who was confused about her sexual identity but afraid to say anything to Eric because of his virulent statements about gays.

Here the women were, at Atlanta's airport, being introduced for the first time to Stone and his partner by Dave Jordan, the FBI agent from Nashville. They were here to meet with members of the Task Force and then head up to North Carolina to show the places Eric had taken them in the Nantahala. Next month, they would be back down here again to testify before a grand jury. But right now, as the introductions were being made, Stone was curious. "What was so funny?" he asked. "Oh, on the

---
* A pseudonym
**Also a pseudoym

way down we were just doing one of those Top Ten lists," Lisa said with a grin and maybe a bit of a smirk. "The Top Ten ways to figure out if your boyfriend was a terrorist!" And with that, the young women lost it again (this was the spring of 1998, back when you could maybe talk like that on an airplane without bringing down a load of trouble on yourself, even if you were being self-deprecating).

"Just when you thought this case couldn't keep surprising you," Charles said to his partner Chris Olivie. This being the first time he met Lisa, Stone was struck by her resemblance to his partner—both were blond-haired, blue-eyed, and might have been mistaken for sisters by people in the airport. A few days later, when he met Eric's other girlfriend, Nancy,* the one who came after Lisa and was introduced to Eric by Deborah Rudolph, he began to notice a pattern. Again, they could have been sisters. When Nancy stood next to Lisa, you understood just how seriously Eric took this blue-eyed, blonde-haired Aryan-look thing. But today's assignment was Lisa and Janet—Nancy would come later— and as Stone soon found out, the surprises were by no means over.

The party of five (Lisa, Janet, Jordan, Olivie, and Stone) decided to grab lunch at a steak house before heading into Task Force headquarters. Stone was sitting next to Janet, and they got to talking about Eric. How she met him, that sort of thing. Then as an aside, Janet mentioned that Eric had talked about bombs. For Stone, it was as if all the noise around them in the restaurant had ceased. He was taken aback, but he didn't want to show it to Janet. This was the first time anyone had heard something like this. He just nodded a bit and she started going into great detail, even drawing a crude sketch of the bomb she said Eric had drawn for her. *Wait a minute*, he thought, and leaned forward to ask her a question. "Have you told the FBI any of this?"

"No," she said. "They never asked."

In a way it was understandable. Everyone was now so focused on the fugitive part of the case, where do you think he is and all that, that asking about anything else might seem off point. So he wasn't going to point

_____
* A pseudonym

fingers. But he sure as hell was going to learn everything he could about Eric and this bomb talk. Stone got Jordan's and Olivie's attention and said, "You need to listen to this." When they were ready, Janet ran through it once more, and they, too, got the holy shit look in their eyes.

After lunch, they went to Task Force headquarters and did this more formally. Then they brought in one of the ATF agents, who had the requisite knowledge about bombs, and did it again. Janet laid it out each time. Some of the back-story they already had from reading up on her previous interviews with the FBI—that she knew Eric for a period of about eighteen months between 1989 and 1991 in Nashville, when he was going out with Lisa, who was her close friend. How during that time, she probably hung out with them separately or together three hundred times, getting stoned, shooting the shit, almost always at Lisa's house. She was by her own admission the third wheel, the one quietly coming to grips with her own sexual issues. Janet reviewed all the stuff about Eric and his political opinions, how he hated blacks, Jews, and gays. He would even get on a milk crate at Lisa's house and commence to preaching, which was something he said he wanted to do, and his message was usually something about how a racial war was imminent. Nancy said Eric told her he wanted to injure the people he hated, particularly gays and Jews.

Janet thought all of the talk about bombs started because Eric knew her family had a business that included a processing plant. He was curious when he heard about the big storage area there and all the tools that were kept there for routine maintenance. Janet thought he wanted to get his hands not just on the tools and wire that were kept there, but any leftover explosives that might still be around from the time the plant was built. In any event, he kept asking, but she kept putting him off, because she didn't want to be party to anything that might turn talk into reality.

And talk Eric did about bombs. There were two types he was interested in, he explained. One was a pipe bomb. Janet thought he talked about using metal plumbing pipes. Eric said he would use gunpowder and that getting that was easy; if necessary, just pour it out of loaded shotgun shells. He wanted to use lots of metal to boost the shrapnel. The other type of bomb he went on about involved dynamite inside a military ammunition box. You can pack everything in nice and tight, add screws and nails for extra shrapnel (the ammo can would also do its part), and you had your bomb. You could even control the direction of the blast by the way you packed the ammo can and where you placed the bomb. But where would you get dynamite? she asked. From construction sites was the answer; it was easy if you knew where to look.

How to set off the bomb, that was Eric's dilemma. He told her he had two choices. There were timers, to be sure, windup clocks, but what if one went off accidentally while you were working on the bomb or even planting it? And surely the ticking noise might give it away. Better to use some sort of remote control. She thought he talked about walkie-talkies. That was much safer and besides, he said, it would be cool to see the blast and how people reacted. All you had to do to carry the bomb in to wherever you wanted to plant it was put it in a knapsack or duffel bag. He had a backpack at Lisa's house and showed that to Janet. Something like that would work just fine and no one notices it or you. Or you hid it inside a tool or tackle box. No one looked in those either.

That's when Janet drew her sketch, which she said was a rough copy of the one Eric had made for her. It was crude, a pipe bomb, with both ends sealed off either by soldering or welding. What stuck in her mind was that Eric was very specific that the ends would be sealed with red plastic. A wire ran out one end of the pipe, but it wasn't a lit fuse, it was an antenna for electronic detonation. Eric wasn't clear how the bomb was wired to the timing device.

What Janet could never quite figure out was why Eric was talking about all this with her. She thought a lot of it was boasting and sometimes he seemed to ask her advice, especially about remote control devices. All I know about bombs, she answered, was what you've told me. Maybe it was because she was his "listening post" and didn't challenge him when he got on one of his rants. It might have also been because she admitted she was a bit fascinated by bombs herself and may have even initiated one of the discussions. Eric told her he was trying to learn more about bomb-making but didn't want to buy any of the books that might tell him more, at least not through the gun magazines, which advertised them. The government might be keeping tabs on those mail orders, he said. When Stone showed her copies of various manuals, she picked out *The Anarchist Cookbook* as the one Eric was interested in buying.[1] When it came down to it, Janet was surprised that Eric was actually suspected of carrying out any bombings. For all his vitriol, she thought it was all talk and no action.

After laying all this out, Janet was shown the mock-ups that the Task Force had made of the various Atlanta bombs. She immediately homed in on a bag of 4d flooring nails, which were used in the Sandy Springs bombing. Eric had shown her the same type of nails, she said, in his brother Joel's pickup truck. She said Eric had picked up a handful of the 4d nails and said they were perfect "little projectiles" when used in a bomb. She said Eric had all sorts of other nails, including the 6d wire nails that were the type used in the Otherside Lounge bombing, but he never talked about those in a bomb. The windup clocks he mentioned as timers were similar to the Westclox on display at the Task Force head-quarters. And he had also talked about using flashlight batteries in his bombs, including the distinctive six-volt shaped ones that were found at the Sandy Springs bomb site. Janet had also seen a green backpack like the one used in the Otherside Lounge; that was the one Eric showed her at Lisa's house when he was talking about hiding a bomb.

When Janet finished laying out her story to the agents, they realized she'd be coming back to Atlanta soon, this time to testify before the grand jury hearing the bombing cases. For now, the task was to take Lisa off to North Carolina, which she had visited twenty to thirty times with Eric. Lisa had gotten to know Eric's brothers on these visits, and she even grew comfortable enough with Pat to help her out with her hair. She had favorite spots to go hiking with Eric, and she took agents there, as well as along the back roads he drove down. Eric bragged that he knew the woods around his house like the back of his hand—and how he grew marijuana under the power lines that cut through the forest near there (he never actually showed her his plants growing in the wild; he took her to places where he said he had been growing pot). She often got the feel-ing when she was in the woods with Eric that he was testing her, seeing how much hiking and heavy lifting she could stand. She thought that probably got back to this whole bit about Eric saying he wanted to make

Aryan babies with her. What stood out in her mind was one particular occasion, when they were visiting one of their favorite spots. Eric would often get all secretive when they were in the woods, she said, but this time he asked her if she would ever betray him. Lisa didn't understand what Eric meant at the time, but now she thought he meant to hide out in the area if he ever was in trouble.

The next month, Lisa and Janet were indeed back in Atlanta to testify before the grand jury. That's when the ex-wives' club, or to put it more accurately the Eric Rudolph ex-girlfriend's club, had its first meeting. Charles Stone wasn't sure whether he was in a soap opera or if any of his law enforcement skills were going to be called upon when Lisa met Nancy, who went out with Eric after Lisa broke up with him, but they seemed fine. No Top Ten lists but no catfights either! Of course, when they looked at each other and it seemed as if they could have been looking in the mirror, it wasn't hard for either of them to figure out that Eric favored a certain type (that Aryan look).

What struck Stone as sad, but not particularly surprising, was that Nancy blamed herself for Eric's problems. Some people were like that, taking on other people's blame. Eric never talked to her about bombs, and when she told him not to use her place to store his marijuana, he didn't—or at least said he didn't. She knew she always brought out Eric's soft side, that he wanted to protect her. But that was his voice on the 911 tape from Centennial Park. She was 100 percent sure of that. If only she hadn't broken up with him, maybe he wouldn't be out in the woods right now! When Nancy and Stone last spoke, she still held out hope for Eric. Through her tears, she told Stone she was keeping her old phone number, just in case Eric might find a way to call her while he was on the run.

The prosecutors in Atlanta (Birmingham's indictment was fairly straightforward, involving the two eyewitnesses) were relying on more than the testimony of Rudolph's former girlfriends—or Janet. As FBI Director Freeh admitted, they didn't appear to have any eyewitnesses, at least for Centennial Park. In large part, this was going to be a forensic case, which could also be tricky since the famed FBI lab had its share of troubles in the 1990s.[2] They had to link items from Eric to the bombs. And they had to prove Eric had the knowledge. Some of that came from

Janet, some from fellow soldiers and commanders. From Bill,* who knew Eric from their marijuana days in Nashville, they got more testimony about Eric's interest in remote control mechanisms. Bill was the one who said Eric went around with a Kevlar vest underneath his shirt, and now he had more to say. Eric never talked bomb-making with him, though he thought once that Eric had mentioned he could steal dynamite from construction sites. Bill had a hobby—remote control toy helicopters and planes—and he said this really got Eric going. He wanted to know everything he could about the transmitters and how it all worked. Eric said it would be cool to attach an explosive device to one of these airplanes and drop it from midair. All this could have been idle talk, but Bill gave Eric a bunch of catalogs.

There were some other things that Bill remembered. Eric had used a different name, once introducing himself as Bob. Randolph? the agents asked. That's it, Bob Randolph. When he asked Eric about that, Eric just said he didn't like people to know who he was or where he was from. *Oh well, that's the pot business*, Bill thought, *you do get paranoid*. Since Eric had also talked to him about taser guns, walkie-talkies, and setting up surveillance cameras at his house, he wasn't particularly surprised about the fake name.[3] The fake name was important. Although investigators had run into the Bob Randolph issue early on, right after the Birmingham bombing, when they were trying to find Eric's address, it hadn't seemed a crucial issue. Now they had someone in Nashville from the early '90s saying Eric used the Bob Randolph name there. More importantly, they turned up another witness who could connect Bob Randolph, gunpowder, and Eric Rudolph's voice.

Dave Jordan had taken to visiting gun shows in Tennessee looking for leads about Rudolph. At one of those, he saw a man who was selling large quantities of Accurate Arms gunpowder. David's Reloading Supplies was the name of the business. Nothing illegal about it, but about three pounds' worth of Accurate Arms #7 and #9 smokeless gunpowder was in the Centennial Park bomb. Jordan realized that being an FBI

---

* A pseudonym

agent wasn't the best way to get someone at a gun show to open up, so he called Stone, a gun buff, and asked him to come back up to Nashville to meet with the guy. At the end of April, Stone and Jordan interviewed the man, whose name was David Mosley. For most of each month, Mosley was a sales rep for a sign company. But at monthly gun shows around Nashville, he sold powder. One of his best customers was a thin, youngish white male who over the years purchased lots of smokeless gunpowder, including Accurate Arms #5, #7, and #9, maybe three hundred pounds' worth in all. He always paid in cash, and he never quibbled, just the sort of customer any salesman would want.

You bought gunpowder if you were intending to pack your own bullets or shells, and the different numbers were for different sorts of guns. Mosley remembered recommending #7 as better for a 9 mm handgun, #5 was more of an all-purpose powder for handgun ammunition, while #9 was good for .45 Magnums or some shotgun shells. The man mostly bought Accurate Arms #7 smokeless powder, which he said was for his 9 mm, but he also talked to Mosley about how #7 had the most energy, which Mosley took to mean explosive uses. Mosley said he could see where the conversation was headed and changed the subject.

Mosley couldn't pick the man out of a photo lineup, although he did say the man looked a lot like picture number two (that was Eric's picture). You have to understand, Mosley told agents, I'm a sales rep, and in between that and my gun shows, I see a couple of thousand people a week. So I'm not the best with faces, but I do remember if there's something else unusual, like a name. And he had no trouble remembering the guy's name. That one was easy. Bob Randolph. Hard to forget, since there was a famous target shooter named Eric Randolph. When he asked the man if he was related to Eric Randolph, it was kind of odd, because Bob Randolph got all agitated with him and disappeared on him for a year.

Another peculiar thing about the man, this Bob Randolph, was his voice. He sounded like he was talking through clenched teeth, very precise. Stone and Jordan gave Mosley a toll-free number to call, which had been set up so people could listen to the 911 caller warning about the bomb in Centennial Park. The agents waited while Mosley called and listened. No doubt about that either. Mosley said it was him, you could tell by the first few words—"There is a bomb in Centennial Park"—even though he thought the 911 caller then tried to deepen his voice and disguise it. David Mosley had earned his ticket to Atlanta, to testify to the grand jury.

The investigators kept trying to pan for forensic gold. Randy Cochran described reloading ammunition with Eric and even visiting gun shows with him, but not the ones in Nashville where he allegedly bought the gunpowder from David Mosley. Randy said he would remember the brand if he heard the name. Accurate? That's it, he said, Eric used that for reloading his 9 mm and .223 caliber. He also recalled the time when they were cleaning up after reloading, and Eric said something to the effect of, I have plenty of extra for reloading or making bombs. But no, Cochran hastened to add, they never talked about making bombs.

Cochran presented some problems as a witness. One of the first times the FBI talked with him back in February, he said that if he had to rate the voice on the 911 tape as being similar to Eric's, he could only give it a 2 out of 10. By the time June had rolled around and he was getting ready to testify before the grand jury, Cochran sang a different tune. Now, he was certain the voice was Eric's. Why the change? Back in February, said Randy, he was worried that if others were involved with Eric, he might be putting himself in danger with a positive ID. And Cochran admitted that once, after a conversation with Eric about bomb-making books, he went out and bought a couple himself, one at a motorcycle rally and one at a gun show. In between the time Eric's name first appeared in the news and agents came to interview him, Randy destroyed the books, afraid they might cast some suspicion on him.

On one subject of particular importance, Randy Cochran's account remained consistent between February and June. After all the painstaking early work, including the testing at the Oak Ridge National Lab, scientists were able to tie the steel plates from the Centennial Park and Sandy Springs bombings not only to each other but also to what they said was a unique batch made at Gallatin Steel in Ghent, Kentucky. Later, they were able to determine that batch had been distributed by Franklin Machine Company in Franklin, North Carolina, which just happened to be where Randy Cochran had been working since 1994. Which certainly made Randy's role of interest. Cochran explained that Eric and Joel Rudolph had indeed once come with him to Franklin. It was about six months after he started there back in 1994. Randy needed to go over to work to repair his then-girlfriend's Bronco. It was the weekend, and he invited Eric and Joel to join him.

When they finally reached Franklin and Randy got to work underneath the SUV, Eric and Joel wandered off, neither bothering to help him. They were on their own for at least a half hour, he said. Neither of them took any scrap away, said Randy, but they didn't need to. Just hanging out on the premises would have given anyone the idea how little security there was and how easy it might be to come back and take what you want. It was another link in the forensic chain for the investigators and prosecutors. To an astute defense attorney, it might look a lot different, but the Task Force and U.S. Attorney's Offices in Atlanta and Birmingham were working with what they had.

This was like an episode of *CSI*, only this was real life, and the stakes were a lot higher. The aim was simple: tie the bombs to each other and tie Rudolph to the bombs. Sometimes it was witnesses, like Cochran, who said that Eric had two or three ALICE packs, similar to the one in Centennial Park. Or his military buddies, who testified how they learned to cut poles and use them as handles for ALICE packs when they were at Fort Campbell. The pole sander head and the handle from the Centennial Park bomb were another step; however, even though they could match brands, Marshalltown, and had a videotape showing an assembled unit in the Topton house, there was no way to show an exact match between that pole sander head and the pole used as the handle on the backpack in Centennial Park. Likewise with all the plastic containers recovered from Eric's house. They seemed to be the same brand as the ones used in the bombs, and there were eyewitnesses to testify how Eric used to carry his marijuana in them; there was even that database search, which showed how rare it was to use plastic containers in bombs, but you still couldn't make an exact 100 percent match. It was a matter of building up the odds. Piling the steel on top of the containers on top of the pole sander and asking, Who else could it have been?

Which is why there was a container expert, not to mention a battery expert and an expert on just about every possible forensic link at the Task Force. In that sense, Charles Stone thought, all the time and money was well spent. There was even a 4d nail expert, which was of particular importance. Here, it seemed that it was possible to establish a direct tie. But it didn't come without hundreds of hours of legwork and lab work. The nails in the second of the two Atlanta clinic bombs were identified as 4d cut flooring nails, information that had even been made public back toward the end of 1997, when a frustrated Task Force laid out the components of the Atlanta bombs. These weren't your average nails, you used them mainly when restoring old floors, so the Feds were able to trace them back to the Tremont Company. Not only did Janet identify 4d nails as something Eric carried around and thought would make little projectiles in a pipe bomb, the Task Force recovered what it said were eighty-six of the 4d nails made by Tremont from Eric's storage unit at Cal's.[4]

Here's where it got really *CSI*-ish. Agents went to Tremont and observed a production run in June 1998, which showed them how each batch of some 60,000 or so nails got a unique set of toolmarks. Several hundred of the 4d nails were recovered from the Sandy Springs bomb site and 119 of those had close enough toolmarks to have come from a single production run. Of the 86 4d nails found at Cal's, the ATF lab said 7 had the same toolmarks as the 119 nails from the bomb. The rest had insufficient marks for comparison.[5] Again, a defense attorney would go at those numbers from all sorts of angles, but if you were a Task Force agent or a scientist or an assistant U.S. attorney, you were going to consider taking this evidence to a grand jury in a heartbeat.

There was more, some of it circumstantial. After the agents had tried to trace the twelve-volt battery from the Centennial Park bombing, the next bomb had the identifying numbers scratched off. So did two AA batteries found in Rudolph's truck. Then there was a certain type of electric wire, Tandy brand 278-567 was used in bombs at all three Atlanta sites (Rudolph had easy access to a Radio Shack, but so did millions of other Americans); there was gray two-inch wide duct tape, Shurtape PC-618, in both the textured and untextured styles, that showed up at each bombing; and there was the black electrical tape, as well, although sometimes that was 3-M brand and sometimes not.[6]

There were brown fuzzy fibers all over the place that the scientists thought came from work gloves. Some had shown up at the Centennial Park bomb. More of these fibers shown up at the Otherside Lounge bombing; some brown fibers were snagged by the adhesive on the stamps and envelope flaps on the Atlanta Army of God letters, as if someone tried to send them off wearing work gloves. Two tufts of brown fiber were also found under the driver's seat in Rudolph's pickup. When the FBI lab examined them, it said one of the tufts of brown cotton fiber in Eric's truck had the same microscopic and optical properties as the brown fibers found at the Otherside Lounge bomb and on the envelopes. The phrase from the scientists, which was very carefully stated, was that these fibers were consistent with originating from the same source.[7]

The Birmingham eyewitnesses were what prosecutors were planning on using to place Eric there. The license plate and visual identification were enough to make the Atlanta prosecutors jealous. Especially when to their mind, the best they could do in Centennial Park was Blobman—or the sketch of the goateed man, which didn't seem to resemble any picture of Eric they had seen. This was a guy who lived off the grid, paying cash whenever he could. That meant there were no credit card receipts, for example, that might show him buying gas here or there. In the Task Force headquarters in Atlanta, there was a time line to show Eric's whereabouts, based in part on financial transactions like rent payments. It was mostly white space.

The Task Force could place Eric in Atlanta in 1996 during Daniel's wedding, but that was in May, not July. The family, Eric included, stayed the weekend of May 17–19 at a Days Inn motel on the northeast outskirts of Atlanta. It was a big month for the Rudolphs; one week earlier the Topton house had been sold. Eric told his family that after the wedding, he was headed out west to Idaho, Montana, and Colorado, but there was no indication he actually went then or any other time. In fact, at the beginning of June, Eric was in Asheville, exchanging the cashier's check he got for selling the house for at least three checks in smaller amounts. He bought insurance for his truck the next day and registered it at the North Carolina DMV. On June 13, 1996, he rented the first of his post-Topton residences, a trailer in Murphy. Four days later, he visited three different banks—in Franklin, Bryson City, and Sylva—cashing in some money. Then, on July 12, he paid his landlord, Esther Sneed, and left for two to three weeks. Eric told Sneed he was going to look at property in Georgia.[8]

The Centennial Park bombing took place on July 27, 1996.

Esther Sneed said it was either August 2 or 3 when she saw Eric for the first time since he paid his rent in mid-July. Later that month, on August 13, Eric paid his rent again. It is curious that sometime in August, Eric's sister said she got a call from him, saying he was in Coeur d'Alene, Idaho.[9] If he actually took the trip, it would certainly have raised eyebrows, since that would have placed Eric just a few miles from the location of several white supremacist groups, including the Aryan Nations, which was located at nearby Hayden Lake. But it is impossible to tell—and Eric's sister had no idea he had even rented a place in Murphy, less than two hours from where she lived. Eric was certainly around in mid-September, when his mother and sister took off for a trip to Ireland (he was at his sister's house while she was gone). He kept paying his rent on time, the middle of each month.

Eric paid his January 1997 rent on the 13th. A day later, according to his landlord, he also bought propane gas to heat his trailer.[10] Two days after that, on January 16, 1997, the Sandy Springs office building was bombed.

Eric was getting ready to make another move. In early February, he switched addresses, moving to Vengeance Creek in nearby Marble. He bought some miniblinds from Wal-Mart, according to a receipt, applied to turn on the electricity, and filled out a change-of-address form at the post office. By February 8, according to his new landlord, he had moved in. On February 21, the Otherside Lounge was bombed.

Eric's paper trail remained skimpy through much of 1997. The best indication he was still living in and around the Murphy and Andrews area was a steady pattern of video rentals at Plaza Video in Murphy and Party Time Video in Andrews. He did buy a new TV/VCR at Wal-Mart, over in Franklin, according to a store receipt that was found on his property.

In early October, Eric was once again ready to make a move. That's when he rented the storage unit at Cal's, moving out of Vengeance Creek three days later. Eric hit the road with his mother for that trip up north. They went to Virginia to visit Civil War battle sites, then visited some of Patricia's family, the Murphy clan, in Philadelphia. They stayed a short time at James Murphy's summer house in Cape May, New Jersey, then in early November, they came into New York City to visit Jamie. When Eric returned to North Carolina, he rented the trailer at Caney Creek Road, using the name Bob Rudolph or Bob Randolph. He used his real name to open an electricity account at Murphy Power, rented a post office box, and on November 20, 1997, moved into Caney Creek.[11]

Eric couldn't completely evade the New World Order, even paying with cash and money orders, but he was doing his best. Once again, he left tracks at Plaza Video, his movie addiction providing the most complete paper trail of his whereabouts. There was some information from a woman he had begun seeing, but she was under the impression once he left Topton, that he was living in Tennessee. Even his brother Joel had no idea where Eric really was. There were a few more clues from December and January—he was in Bradenton, Florida, on December 12 to help his mother move into her new digs at the trailer park there. On the 20th, he paid $275 in rent. And on the afternoon of Christmas Eve, Eric was at the Wal-Mart in Murphy, buying dead bolts, gloves, and hose clamps. The day after New Year's, Eric bought kerosene for his trailer; a few days later, he paid his power bill, then on the 20th, he paid his rent. There were more video rentals. The 24th of January was when he came over to Hendersonville to visit his sister and brother-in-law, who still had no clue where he was living.

It would be five days later that Eric's truck—and a man who resembled him—was spotted in Birmingham on January 29, 1998. Which still left all those maddening empty white spaces on the wall, especially on the days of the bombings, when the Task Force and prosecutors were hoping to place Eric in Atlanta. They couldn't prove he was in North Carolina those days, and they couldn't prove he wasn't, either. That left just the forensic evidence—or so it seemed.

It turned out the Task Force might actually have one eyewitness in

Atlanta, at least to the Sandy Springs bombing. Remember Adam Scott?*
He was the tree guy who had seen the hooded man in the parking lot of
the Sandy Springs building when he went inside to get his methadone
treatment. Agents revisited Scott shortly after Rudolph was identified.
This time, he told them the sketch that had been made of the hooded
man was only about 70 percent accurate as far as he was concerned! He
said he hadn't been watching news coverage of the Birmingham bombing or subsequent manhunt. When they showed Scott some pictures of
Rudolph taken over various years, he identified one of them as the man
he had seen outside the clinic that morning in January 1997.[12] Getting his
identification to stand up in court might not be so easy, since the agents
who reinterviewed him only showed him pictures of Rudolph, which
didn't constitute a proper photo lineup. As for that entrenching tool he
thought the man was carrying, it turned out that there was one in Eric
Rudolph's truck when it was discovered several days after the Birmingham bombing. There was no way, of course, to prove it was the same
shovel, but the idea was to keep piling up the potential connections so
that if it came to it, no jury would be able to write all these links off as
coincidence.

One of the things the Task Force could never nail down was the
source of the detonators. Nor could the agents trace the dynamite used
in all but the Centennial Park bombs. Different batches of dynamite
didn't really have their own DNA. Sure, you could tell it was dynamite
by taking some swabbings after a blast, but telling the particular brand
was another matter. The markings such as the date stamp would have to
survive the blast, in which case it wasn't good dynamite. That didn't happen with any of these bombs, so it was almost if not impossible to tell
whether what was in the Sandy Springs bombings came from the same
batch as either the Otherside Lounge or New Woman bombs—or if they
all could be matched against some particular supply.

The Task Force had a theory about that; it could just never be
proven. Agents researched theft records on high explosives, especially in

---

* A pseudonym

the North Carolina area near Rudolph's home. What turned up was the theft of 350 pounds of dynamite (the bombs only used a tiny fraction of that) from the Austin Powder Company, a construction business in the Asheville area. Asheville was about two hours from Murphy and Andrews. What was particularly interesting was the date the theft was discovered, December 20, 1996, which would have been just about four weeks before the Sandy Springs bombing. When they discovered that the lock on the magazine door at Austin Powder had been drilled out, the agents theorized that it was done with Eric's cordless electric drill. The Task Force never found the drill, but they did find a box for it when they searched Eric's storage unit. It was one of those loose ends they hoped to clear up if they ever found Eric's lair. The fact that Nordmann's truck had tested positive for explosive traces kept them believing that there was a cache of explosives and that Eric was still in contact with it.

Although the Birmingham case would be more centered on the eyewitnesses, there were some forensics that might play a role. They were hoping to prove the Birmingham letters, which contained the same secret code as Atlanta, were a handwriting match to not only Atlanta but Rudolph. There were similar black plastic battery holders used in the Sandy Springs and Birmingham bombs. When an autopsy was done on Officer Sanderson, the coroner found a hose clamp in his body. The search of Rudolph's trailer turned up that receipt from Wal-Mart for the two hose clamps bought on Christmas Eve, and the lab said these clamps would have been identical to the one found in Sanderson. But the Feds never found another hose clamp.

Those were the criminal cases. Each of them, in Birmingham and Atlanta, would be known simply as *The United States v. Eric Robert Rudolph*. But neither could ever get beyond the indictment stage without a defendant. The United States was ready. The only problem—Eric Rudolph was still missing.

That left the manhunt, which was beginning to resemble one of those movie images of the calendar pages flying off into the wind. The first anniversary would soon be giving way to the second and to the third. Each day, each season, the chances of finding Eric Rudolph seemed to diminish as the searchers themselves slowly emptied out of Andrews and Murphy. The number would fall to about fifty by the summer of 1999; two years after that, there were just a couple of agents left in the area and maybe a dozen working the case from Task Force headquarters in Atlanta.

Charles Stone was one of the first big names to go. He had been on the case from that July night in Atlanta. But as 1998 drew to an end, so did his twenty-five-year career with the Georgia Bureau of Investigation. Stone had been successfully dealing with type 1 diabetes for most of his time in law enforcement. Recently, however, he started having some eye problems related to the diabetes. When he had complications following laser surgery, his endocrinologist delivered a message: his job, especially all this running around North Carolina, was killing him. Retire or the consequences could be fatal.

Woody Enderson was the next to leave. His departure came in the summer of 1999, after a spate of stories marking the one-year anniversary since the last time Rudolph was seen (by George Nordmann). Enderson said he thought Rudolph would be caught, eventually, and his replacement, Steve McCraw, made all the right noises about continuing the dogged pursuit for Rudolph.[13] There had been a series of cabin break-ins over the winter—in at least one instance investigators thought the only reason had been for a shower and shave—and while the Task Force couldn't say for sure it was Eric, Enderson said they suspected he was still out there.[14] In March, there had even been an abortion clinic bombing in Asheville, which was two hours' drive away from the Nantahala. No one was hurt, and investigators there were quick to rule out Rudolph as a suspect. The bomb simply wasn't what they thought was his style.[15]

The manhunt had taken its toll on the searchers. Some, like Stone and Enderson, retired from their agencies without ever seeing a resolution. Terry Turchie moved quickly up the FBI food chain, leapfrogging from assistant special agent in charge to deputy assistant director, where his job covered counterterrorism. He later retired and took a job at the Lawrence Livermore National Lab. One agent assigned to the Task Force wasn't quite so fortunate. He simply didn't wake up one morning, a casualty of the hunt. The father of another agent, who was flying his own plane down to see his son and deliver a birthday cake baked by the agent's mother, crashed. His plane was never found, and even though it could have been lost anywhere along its flight path, more than a few agents were convinced it went down in the Nantahala or nearby Blue Ridge National Park—a striking testimony to the impenetrability of the woods where Eric was hiding.

For many of those assigned to the Task Force, it would take just a beer or two in the succeeding years for the stories to start flowing. The time spent in North Carolina was like a break to some agents; a summer camp in the woods where you got paid to attend. The Nantahala had some of the prettiest country in the Southeast, and if you weren't crawling through the mountain laurel or dealing with all the bureaucratic nonsense and agency egos, if you just kicked back and enjoyed yourself on occasion—and there was certainly no shortage of partying—then it was a damn fine place. One couple in particular did its share to break down interagency rivalries. That ultimately ended nine months later with an unanticipated addition to the law enforcement community and a paternity suit!

By the spring of 2001, there was only a token federal presence in Andrews. But out in Utah, there were the beginnings of a massive contingent as security preparations were well under way for America's next Olympics, the 2002 Winter Games in Salt Lake City. Part-time actors wearing fake blood writhed in fake agony in a suburban parking lot as local EMTs wandered around waving Geiger counters, practicing their response to a dirty bomb full of radioactive material. If some of the exercises resembled Atlanta's, it was no accident. Dave Tubbs, a former FBI agent who helped run the Centennial Park investigation in its early days and had briefly gotten caught up in the Jewell fiasco, had retired and was overseeing Salt Lake's security operation. Jim Bernazzani, who was also involved early in CENTBOMB, had become one of the Bureau's leading experts in counterterrorism, and was playing an advisory role.[16] Bill Forsyth, the FBI bomb tech who had been one of the agents to crawl up to that suspicious green pack in the park, was training his state and local counterparts in Salt Lake City.

There had also been at least one major change because of Atlanta.

Much to the FBI's bureaucratic chagrin, the Secret Service was brought in to handle venue security. There was confidence that this time, it would be different. The Games were smaller than Atlanta, more controlled. Salt Lake was a pretty homogeneous place, and the sorts of crowds and countries that came to a Winter Olympics tended to reduce fears, at least in early 2001, of Middle Eastern terrorism being imported to the ski slopes of the Wasatch Mountains. There was hope that the cold weather and the venues, especially the ski slopes, would somehow discourage the use of chemical or biological weapons. The major domestic concern was no longer seen as being from the extreme Right, even though there were pockets of antigovernment behavior in Utah, and there were militia, Freemen, and white supremacists not too far away in Idaho and Montana. This time around, the worry was from fringe radical environmentalists, a seemingly leaderless group called the Earth Liberation Front, which had already struck at least one ski slope in Colorado.

Eric Rudolph was there. Not in body—and no one seriously expected him to show up. But he was there as a metaphor, the skunk at the garden party, the reminder that no matter how much you planned, no matter how many tabletop scenarios you ran, or how many hostage-taking exercises you practiced, it could all be undone by one man. Publicly, no one wanted to mention his name; if you looked close enough, you would see the involuntary flinching when you brought him up. It was easier to walk you through the command center or show off the latest high-tech gear. We are prepared for everything was the official line, even the lone wolf, yet privately that remained the most vexing concern.

The next Olympic Games (Sydney didn't really count, since it was so far away), even the preparations for the next Olympics in America, was another of those occasions, like the anniversaries of the bombings, the anniversaries of Rudolph's first disappearance, and the last confirmed sighting, that became a painful benchmark of a fugitive investigation that had all but disappeared itself. There had been Rudolph sightings as far afield as Moscow and the San Fernando Valley; one time, early on, agents thought they had a lead and were ready to pick up a man off a flight, only this Rudolph turned out to be African-American.

Up in North Carolina, the question, "Where is he?" replaced the bitching about the Feds running around Macon and Cherokee County. If anything, the complaining about the Feds being there had been replaced by the complaining about them being gone. It was a lot quieter around Andrews these days. George Nordmann may have been quietly plugging along at his health food store, still talking about the salutary effects of herbs and resolute in his belief that the Holocaust never happened, but for others, the end of the large-scale manhunt meant financial trouble.[17] Peggy Ellison didn't have the Lake's End Grill anymore—her landlord had decided business was too good and decided to take over the space for himself—and once the Feds pulled out, there were no big catering contracts. She managed to bounce back, opening a café in Andrews that became the local breakfast and lunch place, but the town itself missed the federal money dearly, especially after one of the largest local employers, Lee Jeans, closed down its plant there.

The Feds were all but gone, but the question remained: Where was Eric Robert Rudolph?

"I think he's dead!" said Steve Cochran. As he tromped through one of his family's fields in the spring of 2001 after having a beer, Randy's brother was angry. He was one of those folks in Topton who hated it when the Feds were there in force, especially since the Cochrans got so much attention, and he hated it now when the Feds were all but gone. All but gone wasn't entirely gone, and the Cochrans still got their share of visits from agents, and Steve felt his family, especially his brother, was under suspicion. Just keeping tabs, reminding you that there is a million dollar reward if you hear from Eric, but legal trouble if it turns out you are helping him. That was the way the Feds worked, even if there were only two agents in town instead of two hundred. The Task Force was into outsourcing these days. They were still working with hunters, and they also had a new program, they called it the Scout Program, where they put retired federal employees, including former Forest Service guys and ex–park rangers, on a small retainer, just to keep their eyes and ears open. One man's outsourcing is another man's Big Brother, and as Steve Cochran had another sip of beer, he made it clear that to his mind, the new Task Force policy just plain sucked, by trying to convince folks that it was all right to spy on their neighbors.[18]

Getting back to Eric, Steve thought he had died and died alone, some-where out in the woods. Maybe he had fallen off a ledge or gotten an in-fection or just gotten too cold. Eric was dead, and all the rest was a smoke screen, as far as Steve Cochran was concerned. Cochran wasn't the only one thinking that way. By the end of 1999, almost two years into the man-hunt, the retiring head of the ATF was also ready to write Eric's obituary. "He's in a cave and he's dead," said John Magaw, who could only offer gut instinct. Magaw said it had been a long time since there was proof of life, even a cabin break-in, and that it just wasn't possible for Rudolph to sur-vive out there on his own.[19] But if Eric was dead, no one had found a body, which only compounded the frustration. There were plans in place to do DNA testing, should it ever come to that, but so far it hadn't.

Deborah Rudolph had a different take. She thought her former brother-in-law took the money and ran. He's been overseas before, she argued, and who is to say he doesn't have a fake passport. If he really had been planning to run for a long time, then maybe he'd figured out a way to take his marijuana money and get the hell out of the United States. Mexico was unlikely, though Canada was a possibility. But he'd been to Europe before, and he'd be a lot more comfortable where people looked like him. Maybe not Germany, where he might actually stand out as an admirer of Hitler, she thought. Austria or Holland. He'd been to Am-sterdam before, why not again?[20]

Emily Lyons had yet another theory. She thought Rudolph was alive, he was in North Carolina, and he was getting help.[21] She wasn't alone in thinking Eric was alive. Two-thirds of North Carolinians surveyed in 1999 thought Rudolph was still out there somewhere. Only 5 percent agreed with Steve Cochran and John Magaw.[22] Lyons may not have real-ized she was echoing the suspicions of many local residents when she thought Eric was getting help. But she pointed to a recent case which she thought proved her point. James Kopp, who at the time was accused (he was later convicted) of murdering an abortion doctor in Buffalo, had been discovered hiding out in France. Kopp had been getting help from a couple back in the U.S., who were wiring money. If someone was help-ing Kopp, Emily said, then someone else in the antiabortion under-ground is helping hide Eric Rudolph.

Perhaps the most elaborate theory came from the ATF's Jim Cavanaugh, who had been involved in the Birmingham investigation. Forget this business about caves and mines and campsites. Rudolph was alive, and he was living within a three hundred-mile radius of Murphy, somewhere in a small Appalachian community, somewhere in his own perceived comfort zone. He had a trailer, cable TV, and a VCR, but no phone. After all, who was he going to call? He worked drywall, maybe some construction, places where he could get paid in cash, no questions asked. You might even see him on a Friday night, sitting by himself in the corner of the local bar. Maybe he even had a girlfriend, but she had no idea who he really was. Where it would all end, and perhaps end badly, was the day that Rudolph was stopped in his pickup truck (he would have one of those, too) and he couldn't produce a driver's license. Then there might be a shoot-out, and Rudolph would at last be unmasked.[23]

Todd Letcher wasn't having any of that. Letcher was the keeper of the flame, the latest head of the Southeast Bomb Task Force. His was the unenviable job of presiding over an investigative force that had shrunk nearly to nothing, especially in North Carolina. The remnants of the Task Force had a couple of floors of a small office building in northeast Atlanta, a few miles up the road from the FBI and ATF field offices. Mostly, the Task Force responded to leads and kept track of evidence, which was a big deal that was getting bigger when Tim McVeigh's execution was delayed after some questions about the FBI handling of evidence in that case. They were still working at the time line for Centennial Park and still trying to fill in those white spaces in Eric's life.

The youthful-looking Letcher, who once headed FBI Director Louis Freeh's security detail (Freeh was another soon to leave), was an optimist. Eric Rudolph was still alive, absent any evidence to the contrary, and there was nothing to suggest he was anywhere else but near his former home in North Carolina. Yes, the Task Force was much smaller than it had been, but no, neither the FBI nor any other law enforcement agency had closed its books on Eric Rudolph. They were going to find him one day, hopefully sooner rather than later, and they were going to find him near where they thought he was. That's what every indication from the investigation and the manhunt told them.[24] Charles Stone, who still kept tabs on the case, agreed with Letcher. So did Darren Free, who would occasionally set off on his own into the Nantahala, hoping to find Eric. In the meantime, Letcher was looking for any publicity he could get for the case, be it CNN or *America's Most Wanted*. These days, most of the calls the Task Force got came after a story about Rudolph aired on television.

The adage was justice delayed is justice denied. The victims' families in Birmingham and Atlanta prayed that wasn't the case. So, too, did Doug Jones. The U.S. attorney in Birmingham knew the clock was ticking on his own chance to bring Rudolph to court. There had just been a presidential election, and there was no place for a Democrat like Jones in the new Republican administration. But Jones had just finished prosecuting a case that could have parallels with Rudolph. He'd brought two men to court close to thirty years after that notorious church bombing that gave his hometown the unflattering nickname of Bombingham, and he'd gotten convictions. He had another man in his sights, hoping to prosecute him as well. It took a long time, but it could be done. Would that be the way of the Rudolph case? He hoped not, but he wondered.[25]

Felecia Sanderson was doing her damnedest to keep the case alive. She visited members of the Task Force in North Carolina on several occasions, bringing them cookies, making them coffee, encouraging them in their hunt for Eric Rudolph. She was there so often that regardless of her reason for being there, she developed a certain fondness for the natural beauty that surrounded her.[26] For members of the Task Force, Felecia Sanderson was a constant reminder—this was why they were here; this was the human face of tragedy and that it was her husband Robert (Sande) who was killed in the Birmingham bombing. Felecia didn't revel in victimhood, far from it. She used the platform she had unfortunately earned and tried to keep the focus on what was at stake: capturing an accused murderer, her husband's accused murderer.

Don't tell her Eric Rudolph was a folk hero. Don't insult her like that. You were thinking of buying one of those T-shirts that said Run Rudolph, Run because it might make a cute or clever souvenir? Felecia Sanderson had an answer to that. She printed up her own batch of T-shirts that also had Rudolph's picture. Only these said, FBI Most

Wanted Fugitive and Million Dollar Garbage on them. If that wasn't clear enough, they also said Serial Bomber. She took her message to *America's Most Wanted* and to Katie Couric on *The Today Show*.[27] Each member of the Task Force also got one of Felecia Sanderson's pins, the ones that showed they were members of the Sandbomb Task Force, that they were doing something worthy for a law enforcement colleague.

Privately, there was suffering that no memorial service or television appearance could completely ease. Felecia missed the homemade gravy her husband made at Thanksgiving but wouldn't make her own version for her two sons; hers was always too lumpy, she said. And there was no Christmas tree at the Sanderson house; that was another thing that Sande did because he was just a big kid at the holidays.[28] Felecia was from a cop family—her father and grandfather were police officers—and that helped, especially when it came to raising the couple's two children.[29] So did the moral support she got back from the Task Force she so strongly supported. But it could get ugly and disheartening at times. Felecia sued the police chief and City of Birmingham in a disagreement over the amount of Sande's back pay. She eventually got the amount she felt was owed, with interest, but a jury refused to award her anything for the mental anguish she might have suffered while getting the whole mess sorted out.[30]

Anger. Suffering. Those were two words John Hawthorne had been on intimate terms with since the Centennial Park bomb killed his wife and injured his stepdaughter. It was tough on Fallon Stubbs. She missed her mom something fierce, and when she walked up on the stage to get her high school diploma without Alice Hawthorne in the audience to see how her baby was growing up, it cut Fallon to the core. But she was resilient, she had her mother's ability to smile even through adversity, and Fallon was getting there. Her teenage energy helped. And she would always walk in her mother's footsteps, by choice. Fallon's choice for college was where her mother went—Albany State.

It was rougher on John. He bottled up a lot of the anger and mixed it in with the anguish. John had gotten remarried, but he wanted his hometown and his home state to remember Alice for who she was and what she tried to do. It was hard to ride over the slights, which began the day his wife died. However Atlanta Olympics chief Billy Payne may have meant it, trying to reassure an international audience, John Hawthorne heard the phrase "there's only one person who died" and filed it away.[31] Damnit, that one person was his wife and Fallon's mom. You could walk through Centennial Park these days and never see the memorial to the victims from that night. John and Fallon had trouble finding it; the memorial was just a tiny inlay on the ground in a corner of the park. Would it have been too much to let Fallon carry the Olympic Torch maybe just a few yards when it was on its way back through Georgia before the Salt Lake Games?[32]

The anger masked the private grief. There wasn't a part of Alice that John didn't miss: her smile, her fearlessness, her smell. It had gotten so bad a couple of months after the bombing, he said, that he thought about ending it all, just jumping off the balcony at the hotel where he was staying. John was a military man by training, not given over to introspection, but this was as bad as it got. He was driving back to Albany one night, coming down from Charlotte, when his car hit a patch of water and hydroplaned. He should have been a goner. His car certainly was. It was totaled, but he walked away without a scratch. John realized he'd been thinking about Alice as everything slowed down the way it can when you're in the middle of something really scary and life-threatening. Alice had pulled him through.[33]

There was a way to get John's eyes to light up. Ask to see what was inside those rolled-up sheets of heavy paper he was carrying under his arms. This was going to be his memorial to Alice, a community center named after her, in her hometown of Albany where she had done so much. The plans were brilliant and daring, but when you got to the reality part of it, John's eyes darkened again. Getting the money, and this would cost millions, was tied up in city and state politics. Instead of a community center, it seemed the only way Albany was honoring Alice was with a Chamber of Commerce award for excellence in her name.

John had visited North Carolina, seen the command post, and talked to the agents. He wasn't the sort to make T-shirts. That wasn't his way. The truth was, when he saw the terrain, he was discouraged. You could be at this for years. He knew the bomber hadn't targeted his wife, that he was all about making a larger statement and killing more people. But John Hawthorne wanted justice. Were they ever going to catch Eric Rudolph? He wasn't so sure.

Emily Lyons wondered the same thing. She daydreamed about looking across a courtroom at Eric Rudolph and asking him why. A daydream it was, not just because he was still out there on the run. Emily had lost one eye in the blast and most of the vision in her other one. So she probably couldn't read his face that well or look deep into his eyes. But she hoped he'd be looking at her, see the scars on her face that the countless operations couldn't completely repair. Would that matter to him? she wondered. Maybe she could demonstrate for the court how the bomb still lived on inside of her. The X rays were frightening enough, so were the scars on her arms and legs. But she could really make her point with a little magnet. Just run it up and down her leg and watch the skin pull out. That was the nails inside her, the ones the doctors still couldn't get out, the ones that stood up at attention every time she got out the magnet.[34]

This was a hell of a way to become a hero, by surviving this. The woman who had been wheeled out of the hospital by her husband in the spring of 1998 looking like she was headed straight to the cemetery had survived the bomb, survived the operations that ran her medical bills easily past a million dollars, and survived the indignities which visited her daily. Thank goodness for workmen's compensation! Emily's on-the-job injury had made her an icon for the abortion movement, a survivor who could reduce a roomful of activists to tears with her presence and rouse them to cheers with her words. As she got healthier, she traveled the country to spread her own message about abortion and its enemies. What she really wanted was just one answer that she said could only come from Eric Rudolph. All he had to do was tell her why. It was a fantasy, and Emily had despaired of it ever becoming reality. What would she do if it ever did, if she ever had the chance to see Eric Rudolph in a court of law? "You better hold me back," she said.[35]

All that was before 9/11. To those who had suffered from the Atlanta and Birmingham bombs, the attacks on New York and Washington were a painful reminder of the sudden, swift impact of terrorism. It was hard to watch and hard not to feel kinship for their fellow victims. In one way, though, the outpouring of aid and comfort for the 9/11 victims might have actually been galling. No one had offered to pay any compensation to the Atlanta or Birmingham families (or the families of Oklahoma City or the first World Trade Center bombing, either) beyond what insurance or, in Emily Lyons's case, workmen's comp covered. But there were some practical side effects as well. Todd Letcher and the Task Force were immediately put to work running the 9/11 tip line for the FBI, fielding tens of thousands of calls from around the country.

It was only natural and fitting that the 9/11 investigation took priority. Something bigger was going on here. The enemy, the number one priority, was international terrorism, specifically Osama bin Laden. That meant the FBI's order of battle changed. Its primary responsibility now was to prevent the next attack, and its focus was on the threat from militant Islam. Investigations came second. And of those, international terrorism investigations took precedence. Of course, the FBI was still committed to catching Eric Rudolph, even if Todd Letcher had to go out and do it on his own (once he was freed up from the tip line). But the attention and the money were now pointed toward a new enemy.

There had been among some of the searchers and some of the profilers a belief that Eric Rudolph was empowered by the game of hide-and-seek that had been going on for three and a half years. If this had been in its own perverted way a game, a contest between the hunters and the hunted, where Rudolph gained power by his every evasion, then that game was coming to an end. In the world of terrorism, Eric Rudolph was becoming irrelevant, old news.

Did he understand that, if he was still alive and listening? After 9/11, Eric Rudolph was no longer America's Most Wanted Terrorist. He hadn't really been for a couple of years, ever since Osama bin Laden joined him on the FBI's Ten Most Wanted list, and he certainly wasn't now, not after the attacks on New York and Washington. Eric Rudolph, and by extension domestic terrorism as a whole, had been reduced to a subordinate role, in fact a subordinate clause, to the World's Most Wanted Man. Now, when Eric got mentioned at all, it was in the following way: if you can't catch Eric Rudolph, then how do you hope to catch Osama bin Laden?[36]

12.
DUMPSTER DIVING

THIS IS THE way the story ends. Not with a bang, but a Dumpster.

Jeff Postell had been a police officer for less than a year. The rookie. Low man on the duty roster at the Murphy Police Department. The guy working the night shift on the weekends. No complaints from him, though. Jeff couldn't wait to be a cop, had wanted to be one since he was a kid. When he was a teenager, he'd been a member of an Explorer post, which was an extension of Boy Scouts, and his post specialized in law enforcement. That was about the time Eric Rudolph had vanished, and the really cool thing for Jeff was that he got to meet a few FBI and ATF agents. When he was twenty, Jeff did his time at the police academy while still holding down a full-time job at Wal-Mart doing security. He actually had to wait until he reached his next birthday until he could be sworn in at the Murphy PD. So here he was, working weekend nights, fifth of five on the seniority list. One thing he knew: everyone was a rookie sometime, everyone did the night shift. Police work was egalitarian that way, whether you were in Murphy, North Carolina, or Los Angeles, California.

If you worked nights, you did a lot of cruising around town. See and be seen. Murphy wasn't exactly Mayberry. Methamphetamine—aka crank—was no stranger to this part of western North Carolina, and most nights recently the jail was full up because the sheriff and the police chief were trying to run that problem out of Cherokee County. But this Friday night had been pretty quiet, a couple of traffic stops, and as it bled over into Saturday morning, Postell was now the only patrol officer on duty. He was doing something called business checks. That was another night shift duty. Pretty simple, actually, you drove through downtown or by the empty parking lots at the series of small shopping centers out on the edge of town, just looking for some unusual activity. A light on, perhaps, or someone inside. Then you doubled back, drove down the alleys back behind the shopping centers or stores, where the delivery trucks came. Basically, you were the night watchman for the town.

Most of the deputies had been doing this for years, almost on automatic pilot. You knew they were coming before they got there. You heard the car, and most importantly you saw the headlights. If you wanted to hide or, better yet, get the hell out of there, then you did. But Jeff Postell was a rookie and eager. He had paid attention to the man he called his training mentor, and he made it a point to vary his routine. There was never a set pattern or set time when Postell did his business checks. Sometimes he came around a back alley really slow, sometimes a lot faster. Always looking for the tactical advantage. And he had one trick that was about to pay off big time. He always cut the headlights on his patrol car. He had side alley lights he could shine if he needed to, but even those he'd pop on at the last second. No, you wouldn't be expecting it if Jeff Postell showed up when you were in an alley.[1]

By now it was past 3:00 A.M., well into Saturday morning, and Postell's shift was more than half over. He pulled his patrol car into the parking lot of the Valley Village shopping center out on the road toward Andrews. Crept past the stores. The Family Dollar, Advance Auto Parts, Skyway Computer Solution, the Save-A-Lot grocery store, and the little Sears Roebuck storefront operation. Nothing doing there. He came around past the Sears to the alley running around the back, cutting the headlights first. Always expecting to see something or someone, even if 99.99 percent of the time he didn't.

This was that .01 percent of the time. He cut on the alley light that stuck out from the right front door of his car, the one that gave him visibility on that side of the cruiser and let him see the loading dock of the Save-A-Lot. There was someone back here, he looked like a man, and he looked odd. Maybe a prowler, maybe a B and E (breaking and entering). Whoever he was, he was squatting in the middle of the road, and he had something in his hand, it could have been a pistol or a long gun. The man took off when he saw the police car. If you were going to run in this alley, you didn't have many choices. You could keep going down the alley, in which case a car was going to catch you real quick. You could try to go over the far side on the left, which went into a little grassy field, then dropped down toward the Valley River. Or you could dive back behind all the stuff by the grocery store loading dock, where there were a couple of Dumpsters and some milk crates. This guy chose the milk crates.[2]

It all happened real fast in clock speed, but for Postell, time seemed to slow down as the training kicked in. He stopped the car, called for backup, then got himself out and, while drawing his weapon, crouched behind the driver's door, using it as a shield. Postell looked over toward the right, where his alley light was pointing, and he started using that command voice, just like you're supposed to, making sure that the guy out there knew who was in charge. "DROP ANYTHING IN YOUR HANDS. COME OUT WITH YOUR HANDS UP. GET ON THE GROUND. FACEDOWN. PUT YOUR HANDS BEHIND YOU."[3]

And it worked. The man came out from behind the milk crates, did a face plant right in the middle of the alley, and Officer Jeff Postell of the Murphy Police Department cuffed him. It was 3:27 A.M. on the morning of May 31, 2003.

Backup arrived just then. First was Charles Kilby from the Murphy PD, who was actually off shift but still completing some paperwork before heading home. Then a deputy from the Cherokee County department, Sean Matthews, and finally Jody Bandy, an officer from the TVA (Tennessee Valley Authority) police. It was getting crowded back there behind the Save-A-Lot, the radio chatter and idling police cars overriding the more prosaic sounds of the crickets and the slight rushing of the nearby river.[4]

Officer Postell commenced doing a field interview, now that he had a second to breathe. First, a few observations. The guy was about five feet eleven inches (taller than him) and slight. He was wearing a dark work shirt and work pants, a pair of jogging shoes. He had on a camouflage jacket. He looked pretty dirty. Unshaven, a few days of stubble on his face. He didn't smell, not that you noticed, which was interesting since way more often than not you were going to get a strong whiff of alcohol and/or body odor when you made a stop like this. Booze and crime just seemed to go together, a great American combo like a burger and fries, but this man seemed to be sober as a judge. The man's pants legs were darkened, as if he might have come out of the nearby river. A quick check over by the milk crates revealed that the item he had been carrying was a long flashlight on a sling. Another look, this time over in the grassy field, turned up a backpack, which was empty except for a few plastic grocery bags.[5]

What's your name? Postell asked. Jerry Wilson. Where are you from? Ohio. Have any ID? No. What are you doing back here? The man explained that he was homeless and looking for food. What's your date of birth? The man gave Postell that information, and he radioed it back to headquarters, asking the dispatcher to run it through NCIC, the National Crime Information Center, a computerized database for law enforcement. If the man had any priors, some sort of record, it would kick back pretty quickly. No Jerry Wilson showed up, not with that date of birth. Either the guy didn't have any priors or he was lying. Jeff Postell may have been twenty-one and a police rookie, but the idea that a possible suspect might be trying to take advantage of him wasn't exactly unheard of.

While Officer Postell was running all this down, someone else was taking a good look at the man. Deputy Sean Matthews—known as Turtle to one and all in the local law enforcement community—was the third man on the scene. The prowler or whoever he was lay on his stomach; Turtle had him roll over so he could take a better look. There was something about the guy, something about his eyes and that stare, which seemed pretty damn familiar. Of course! That stare was on the wanted poster in the sheriff's office. Cherokee and Macon County's most famous, make that infamous, would-be resident. Mr. Eric Robert Rudolph himself. Wow. Matthews couldn't swear to it, but he had met Rudolph once before, many years ago back in Macon County. He was about ten years younger than Rudolph, but the guy was hard to forget. Matthews told one of the other officers, then took Postell aside and told him about his suspicions.

They were going to have to take the guy back to the jail anyway, while they sorted all this out. It had started out looking like a felony stop—a suspicious man possibly armed, maybe in the process of committing a burglary. But it didn't look like he had actually broken into anything, so it wasn't even clear he was going to be arrested, especially if all the guy planned to do was forage through the Dumpster for food, which made sense if he had a backpack full of plastic bags. Jerry Wilson or whoever the hell he was may have been playing them by saying he was homeless, but under North Carolina's Safekeeping Law, that meant they had to do something. Get him to a shelter was what it said in the regulations, though the truth was come morning they were just as likely to take him to the county line and tell him to beat it.

That's how it could have ended. Homeless man given a couple hours of time at the county jail, maybe even a meal and a shower, then pushed out, nobody the wiser. That's no doubt how Jerry-or-whoever-the-hell-he-really-was-Wilson must have hoped it was going to work out. He hadn't counted on being spotted in the first place by Postell's trick with the headlights. Now, he wasn't counting on being ID'ed, either. Who cared about a homeless guy anyway?

To the jail they all went. At the very least this was going to kill the rest of the shift, writing up whatever paper needed to be written. And if Turtle was right . . . Well, at this point, that just seemed crazy, but they could check it out easy enough. The Cherokee County jail is a redbrick building right behind the more formal stone-fronted courthouse, just off the square in downtown Murphy. The Murphy PD is a block away, and the Sheriff's Department is a couple of converted trailers a few steps across the parking lot from the jail. Law enforcement central. Postell, Matthews, and company parked their vehicles and walked Mr. Probably-Not-Jerry-Wilson up the gray wooden steps leading into the jail building.

It was getting close to 4 A.M. by now. Outside the weather was mild, promising another beautiful day in the mountains. Inside, Sean Matthews was getting amped up with the idea that this might really be Eric Rudolph. There were wanted posters over at the sheriff's office and police station, but it turned out they didn't already have one at the jail. They sat the man down, still cuffed, and Postell went to find a computer terminal. He and the TVA officer, Jody Bandy, got on the Internet and did a quick search, printing out one of the FBI wanted posters for Rudolph. Whoa! Maybe Turtle had something there. You could see the resemblance, though the guy on the wanted poster was clearly chubbier and well-kempt, while this guy definitely ran toward the gaunt side. They took it back into the other room where their guy was. They were all in there, and finally Bandy said, "You aren't Jerry Wilson. Just who the hell are you?" The guy gave a cold laugh and said, calm as all get out, "Eric Rudolph." He paused a minute and said to the stunned cops, "I'm relieved."[6]

Holy shit. Eric Rudolph? Eric Rudolph! Popped by a rookie cop. Wasn't he dead or something? Jeff Postell got a prickly feeling at the back of his neck. It all added up, what the guy said, and comparing him to the wanted poster. Turtle had nailed it. Now, Postell realized, he was getting nervous. They all were. What to do? Call their bosses, of course. This guy could still be messing with them, doing his version of my name is Elvis, but it sure didn't seem that way. That's it. Call the bosses. Get them in. Let them confirm this. Holy shit, indeed.

Postell went off to phone his boss, Chief Mark Thigpen. Sheriff Keith Lovin, a former state trooper who replaced Jack Thompson after the last election, got called by his dispatcher sometime around 4 A.M. There was a 409, he was told, which meant urgent traffic, and that was never good, especially not at 4 A.M. on a Saturday morning. Usually it was a gruesome road accident, some drunk reenacting the irresistible force meets immovable object experiment in his pickup truck and losing. Not this morning. "We got this man," the sheriff was told, "and he says he's Eric Rudolph." Lovin hung up, called back, and got Turtle on the line. "What in hell is going on, Turtle?" "The man's back in booking here at the jail, Sheriff. And I swear, he says he's Eric." Lovin was stunned, just like the rest of them, but he had his wits about him enough to say, "Don't ask him any questions." (That could get them into some awkward legal ground.) "Wait 'til I get there. I'll be there in just a bit." Shit! This may be a hoax, but that's not the way everyone at the jail was acting. Lovin got himself to the jail in a hurry. So did Thigpen.[7]

It turned out there actually was a plan. What to do if Eric Rudolph was actually caught. It said so right on some folders someone in the Task Force had provided a long time ago. Sort of like those nuclear launch codes for the president. OK, maybe not quite on that scale, but one of those things you hear about and never, ever expect to open, especially not at 4 A.M. on a Saturday morning. And there was one more problem. No one had ever shared the folder with Sheriff Lovin. The best he could figure, now that he was looking for it, his predecessor must have kept the county's copy. But Chief Thigpen had a folder, and they quickly went through it before going back and talking to the man sitting back in the jail. Rudolph's physical description was included—the main thing aside from his height, weight, and hair and eye color was the distinguishing scar on his chin. There were also a few questions they could ask that might help with this verification process.

Right now, the man was being held in the booking area, which was an elongated room, nothing fancy, where the jailers kept a few chairs (including one with straps where someone could be restrained, if need be). Over in one corner was a specialized computer terminal called AFIS, which stood for Automated Fingerprint Identification System. Lift a good set of prints, load them into that machine, and you had not exactly the world at your fingertips, but just the reverse. You were immediately online with the FBI's database and you could get an ID just as soon as the computer ran a match. Over against one wall was the height chart where you stood if you were going to get a mug shot and where, if this really was Murphy's most famous resident, the man Lovin was about to see would pose for the mug shot seen round the world.

Sheriff Lovin and Chief Thigpen walked back into the booking area. The sheriff began asking questions, while the chief stayed behind him, hidden so he could look at the answers in the folder and see if they were correct. This could still turn out to be some sort of elaborate hoax. They started with the same question: Who are you? I'm Eric Rudolph. The man was nervous but seemed at the same time to be nonchalant about all the hubbub that was now going on around him. Lovin looked him over. The hair and eyes were the right color (brown and blue). He was about five feet eleven inches, which was the right height. They put him on the scale, and he weighed 140 pounds, which was considerably less than the 165 to 180 pounds it listed on the wanted poster. But again, no surprise if he really had been hiding in the woods, especially if he was Dumpster diving. It was a wonder he weighed that much. The sheriff took a look at the man's chin. Yep, there it was, under the stubble, your basic distinguishing characteristic—a noticeable scar.[8]

OK, thought the sheriff, *this really could be him*. "You understand we might be skeptical, so we have a few questions to ask you. Where did you leave your truck when you took off?" The man looked at him like he was nuts and said, "I ain't answering that!" Which told Sheriff Lovin right off the bat that this guy was probably not only Eric, but he was also on the ball. "What is your driver's license number? What is your hometown?" Most-likely-Eric gave all the right answers. Then the sheriff took a picture of him from the file and had him sign it on the back. The signature seemed to match. If this man was a fake, he had gone through incredible trouble. We're going to fingerprint you now, said the sheriff. And they lifted off a set that they put on the machine. Right away you could see that there were three clean matches, but they knew that everyone in the world was going to want this one locked tight, so they sent the sheet off to AFIS and then faxed off a set to the FBI for good measure.[9]

One of the first things that Sheriff Lovin had done when he got to the station was call the FBI. Now, things had changed mightily when it came to the Task Force and the FBI. Todd Letcher wasn't running the Task Force anymore; he was up in New York as the assistant special agent in charge. The fugitive part of the investigation, which at this point meant just hoping and waiting for a call like this one, had been transferred to the North Carolina field office in Charlotte, which had in turn assigned it to the office in Asheville, where it ended up being handed to a couple of young agents, Chris Lando and Andy Romagnuolo. That gave you an indication of the resources being put into the manhunt five and a half years after Rudolph had disappeared. No command posts, no Task Force. Just two agents in North Carolina and some folks down in Atlanta and Birmingham in charge of the case files. Needless to say, these agents hauled ass from Asheville, while calling over to their boss in Charlotte.

It was getting on past 6 A.M. by now. The way AFIS worked, all the information from the various fingerprints was turned into blocks of digital information, and there was a point-by-point comparison of each fingerprint to what was on file. They had fingerprints from criminal databases, fingerprints from military records (which was where Eric's were), and fingerprints from everyone who applied for a civil service job. All told, there were more than 80 million sets of fingerprints on file and every day there were 7,000 new sets.[10] AFIS ran around the clock, up at an FBI center in Clarksburg, West Virginia, and they promised results in under two hours. Given that it was an early Saturday morning and this was one big deal, someone got on the line with Clarksburg and asked that they move quicker than that.

The phone calls were already starting to come. Every fifteen minutes, someone from the FBI would call. What do you know? What do you have? IS IT HIM? Then CNN called, wanting confirmation they were holding a man who claimed to be Eric Rudolph. Same question: Is it him? How the hell did CNN know so quickly, Lovin wondered? They seemed to be more on the ball than the Feds. Sheriff Lovin tried to dance around the issue with them, but they seemed to have it nailed. He warned them there was no complete ID, which was the truth since the final word from AFIS hadn't come back yet, and he tried not to give anything away.

Then CNN went with the story—that there was a man in custody in Murphy who said he was Eric Rudolph and matched his description, but they were still waiting for the final fingerprint check. The calls really came pouring in after that. Lovin got another call from the Feds. We want to be sure, we have to be sure. We want to tell Attorney General Ashcroft, and Attorney General Ashcroft wants to tell the president, and we're all seeing this on CNN so what the hell is going on down there?[11]

When the prints finally went to AFIS, they confirmed what was already pretty obvious. This was Eric Robert Rudolph! He was alive. Not in Mexico. Not in Europe. Not in Moscow or California. Not on some Greek island with JFK or partying with Elvis at Graceland or hanging with D. B. Cooper in the wilds of the Pacific Northwest. Not dead down a cave or mine. Not eaten by a bear. Right there in the Cherokee County Jail, nabbed by a rookie cop on a routine patrol at 3:27 A.M. near a Dumpster while Eric was getting ready to search for food. After five and a half years of searching, almost seven years after the Centennial Park bombing, here he was with a few days' growth of beard in dirty, but not too dirty, work clothes and jogging shoes and a camouflage jacket, eating the first of two breakfasts this morning—eggs and bacon and milk—looking hungry and skinny but, once you cleaned him up a bit, not at all like a man who was supposed to have played Jeremiah Johnson or Grizzly Adams for the past sixty-five months.

"Bullshit!"

"No, really! We've got him."

Chief Thigpen was trying to convince Murphy Mayor Bill Hughes that he wasn't calling this early on a Saturday morning to yank his chain. When Hughes finally got over his shock, the former elementary school principal realized what Chief Thigpen and Sheriff Lovin had already figured out. Murphy was about to become the center of the known world again, at least for as long as Eric Rudolph was there. It had been a long time since the media circus had come to town, and that was only going to be a warm-up for this occasion. As far as Mayor Hughes was concerned, the best thing that could happen was the Feds would take Mr. Rudolph away in the next ten minutes, get him out of there and over to Asheville—which was the closest federal court—before the first satellite truck showed up.[12] He flipped on his TV. CNN was already going wall-to-wall with this. *And this had been shaping up to be such a nice summer,* he thought. There had been lots of rain and snow during the past winter, the Nantahala was running, and the lake was up to capacity. Oh well, maybe he could use this as an opportunity and let the world know that this area was more than Eric Rudolph.

Hughes put on a coat and tie and headed over to the jail. He wanted to find out what was going to be done in the way of crowd control. But Mayor Hughes had to admit he was curious and wanted to get a peek at Eric Rudolph. Which was only natural, and Lord knows he would be doing enough interviews in the next couple of days, so it made sense for him to get a briefing. Which was what he tried telling the guard with the black pants who was already standing outside the jail. I'm the mayor. Eventually this guy—he wasn't a local deputy or officer, let him in, and he went down the hall, took a right and a left, which put him into the booking area.

And there he was. Eric Rudolph. Since the jail was already fully booked and it made little sense from a security standpoint to put Rudolph in with the rest of the prisoners, he had been moved into a small room off the booking area. The sign outside read Breathalizer Room (it was misspelled). There were a couple of desks and chairs inside, so that on a normal day—or weekend night—one of the jailers or deputies could use a breathalyzer to test if someone was indeed as drunk as they appeared to be when they were stopped for DUI. Like everywhere else inside the jail, the walls were yellowish cinder block and the floor a pale yellow speckled linoleum. Later, the jailers would bring in a couple of thin green mattresses that were normally in the prison cells, stack one on top of the other, and put them between the desks, so that Eric could sleep in the room for as long as he was a resident of the Cherokee County corrections system. There was a one-way mirror where you could look from the booking area into the room, and Mayor Hughes took his peek. What he saw was a younger man wearing a dirty black T-shirt and black pants, who looked grungy. This wasn't a guy who had just walked out of Brooks Brothers. There he was, on the other side of the mirror, drinking coffee and chatting with two officers.[13]

Having satisfied his curiosity on that score, Mayor Hughes turned to the gaggle of law enforcement folks crowding the room and asked just how they were planning on dealing with the media madness headed their way. "We're formulating a plan," said one FBI agent who had already made it there. "In the meantime, we suggest you block off some streets, just in case." Eight months later, the mayor would still be waiting to hear the plan. He did see the gunmen start popping up on the roof of the courthouse, the jail, and some nearby buildings, which made it clear enough that Chief Thigpen, Sheriff Lovin, and the Feds were taking no chances that Eric would get away again or that anyone would be able to get to him. Mayor Hughes kind of wondered about that, but it was out of his hands.

The good-old-boy network was alive and well. Charles Stone got the call from North Carolina by 6 A.M., letting him know just exactly what was taking place at the Cherokee County jail. It said something that he would get called as soon as the FBI agents on the ground—and well before any of the FBI higher-ups. He got the whole story and started to spread the news. The first call was to me, which is how CNN first learned of the story, and we began to make our own calls as I raced into the office.

By the time we were ready to go to air, Stone had already made some other calls. He called the original FBI case agents, Tracey North and John Behnke, so they could spread the news. North worked in Washington these days, had a big-time job in the counterterrorism department, and she would certainly want to know. Behnke had stayed in Atlanta, a dedicated street agent, and these days his biggest battle was with cancer. He'd get chemotherapy one day and somehow manage to get into the office the next. Stone had to leave him a message, and he did the same for Sally Yates, the federal prosecutor who ran the Atlanta case.

Stone was lighting up the phones, reaching out to folks at the ATF and FBI who had worked on the Task Force. He woke up Pat Curry, who had been the Birmingham police captain who led his department's investigation into the death of Officer Robert Sanderson. Stone made some calls to folks at his old agency, the GBI, and everyone he reached had a similar reaction: No shit! Hot damn! Bullshit! (That one seemed particularly popular.) Verbal high fives all around. This being the South, there were going to be more cold ones raised than champagne corks popped, but no doubt there was going to be some partying today.

Stone had one more call to make. He had made a promise five years earlier to Patricia Rudolph, and he intended to keep it. If anything significant happened to her son, Stone had vowed he would let her know. He wasn't sure what sort of reaction he was going to get from her, but it wasn't likely to be what he had been hearing from his previous calls.

"Miss Patricia," he said in very even tones as she answered the phone, "this is Charles Stone calling you from Georgia. I promised I would keep you informed if anything happened to your son, and I just wanted to tell you that he was arrested this morning in Murphy, North Carolina. He is safe, and he is in the county jail up there." Stone paused, in case she had any questions, also to give her time to get over the shock. No one expects these early morning calls, and it takes some time for the mind to catch up.

Patricia Rudolph paused for barely a second or two before she replied. "I bet you folks are just dancing a jig up there, aren't you?" Then she hung up on him.

Sheriff Lovin was doing something of a slow burn inside. The FBI had shown up and started its we're-greater-than-God routine. Individually, he liked most of the agents, but once they started flashing their credentials, they wouldn't stop with the institutional arrogance. He'd had his fill of it back during the manhunt, when he was still in the state patrol and the FBI just completely blew off his guys. And it wasn't like Mr. Hoover's boys had caught Rudolph, after all, but here they were acting like it. Right now, Rudolph belonged to Murphy and Cherokee County, and it was pretty clear, this being a weekend, that it was going to stay that way until Monday, when federal court opened up in Asheville and he could be transported over there.[14]

Just to get it all straight in his head, Sheriff Lovin decided to step outside for a few minutes and take a walk. He asked C. J. Hyman, the ATF agent who had come over to Murphy that morning, to come with him and be a sounding board. Hyman—and the ATF in general—he liked. No bullshit with these guys, even back during the manhunt. When they said they'd help, they would actually help, and if you were stuck on a case, you could kick it up to them, and they might be able to make something work in federal court, especially when it came to drugs and guns, which were pretty much the problem in Cherokee County as they were just about everywhere else. C. J. had worked a bit with the Task Force, but he didn't get up Sheriff Lovin's nose like the FBI. Far from it. "Did we make the arrest?" he asked C. J. "You made the arrest." "Is he our prisoner?" "He's your prisoner." "Do I run the show until they're ready to move him?" "You run the show, Sheriff."[15]

By the time he got back to the jail, Sheriff Lovin had formulated his plan. He'd let the Feds help his guys with crowd control. It was a weekend anyway, so it wasn't going to be too bad. More a question of local folks staring at the satellite trucks and vice versa. And the Feds were right, there was no reason to take security lightly. Sheriff Lovin hadn't bought the line that Eric was on his own, not getting help, and there was nothing he saw from his first meeting with Eric that convinced him otherwise. He was dirty, but not too dirty, and he sure didn't have the skin or smell of a man on a five-year camping trip. So maybe he did have some helpers out there who might try something if he was caught.

But that was getting ahead of himself. Here was the plan. They'd bring the mattresses into the "Breathalizer Room" and set Eric up to stay in there. There would always be someone with him, either a jailer or a deputy. That person wouldn't be there to question Rudolph formally, especially about the case, but he'd just listen, and if Eric felt like talking, then they'd talk. If Rudolph ever said he wanted to lawyer up, then they'd do that for him. It was the law, and there was no point screwing it up at this point. The rule of thumb was simple and a bit tricky at the same time—if Eric ever said clearly and unequivocally that he wanted a lawyer right then and there, then they had to get him one. But it had to be a clear statement—I want a lawyer now. Until then, well, they would just see where the conversation would go. This was a man who maybe hadn't talked to anybody since he saw George Nordmann five years before. He ought to be willing to chat. Maybe they would learn something.

Ironically, without the benefit of any memos like that infamous one written by the FBI's profilers back in the summer of 1998, the sheriff was making the right moves. He was keeping the Feds out of the picture. He was setting it up so that his folks could create a rapport with Eric. And he had Eric in a comfortable place, relatively speaking. Eric was going to get three home-cooked meals a day (he got an extra breakfast that first morning), which was a trademark of the Cherokee County jail, the one touch that did make it seem just a bit like Mayberry. They had a couple of older women—not Aunt Bea—who prepared the meals under contract. The one who cooked the weekend meals, Elizabeth Swanson, couldn't stand the thought that he might not have had a decent meal in so long and made sure he got the extra fruit and vegetables he asked for (apples, bananas, oranges), along with her homemade grape jelly.[16] For a man who had apparently been getting ready to Dumpster dive in search of food, this was almost as good as it got. If all went according to plan, Eric wouldn't know the rest of the world was pressing in on him, that there would soon be twenty-seven satellite trucks parked a couple of blocks away.[17] It would just be him and his minders, a couple of locals, for as long as they could get away with it.

The sheriff and the jailer had a couple of candidates in mind. One was Lester White, a sergeant at the jail. He was a good old boy, hair running to gray, a bit beefy, and very sympathetic. Easy to talk to, which was important. The other was a senior investigator with the sheriff's department named Jerry Crisp. Crisp brought a lot to the job. He'd been doing this sort of work for twenty years, over in Graham County, then with the TVA. He'd spent some time with the Andrews Police Force before coming over to the Sheriff's Office when Lovin had been elected.

Crisp was tough, but you didn't get that when you started talking with him. What you got was quiet and easygoing, which might make you miss some underlying traits. He was a great listener. And he was patient. He'd always bring you back to where he wanted the conversation to go without you ever realizing it. One case, he had a guy he was sure killed his wife. He didn't have a body, and he really didn't have the guy, who could have gotten up and left any time, since there wasn't any evidence to speak of. But he kept working the guy and working the guy, not hard but more like establishing a bond, and six days and nights later, the guy gave it all up, including his wife's body. That guy had been executed just a year before.[18] Just keep them talking, was Crisp's motto, and sooner or later they all slip up.

As if that wasn't enough, Crisp had another side to him. Crisp was in the Naval Reserves and had just done survival school a couple of years earlier. You usually do this particular type of survival school, which is an advanced course called SERE (Survival, Evasion, Resistance, Escape), when you are in your twenties and a hotshot. But Crisp did it when he was forty, which is somewhere between crazy and absolutely nuts, and he did it at the navy's facility in Brunswick, Maine, which meant he was doing the cold-weather course. Not to mention that after your wilderness survival portion of the training, where you were out in the woods for a couple of weeks with little else but your wits, you were picked up and put in a mock POW camp, which didn't feel mock to you, and you were interrogated and yelled at and treated like dog shit, all with the idea that you were being trained to come back alive if you got behind enemy lines. So Crisp could make that military connection with Eric and talk with him about being in the woods. Plus, he was the perfect bullshit detector. He'd know the difference between a real snake-eater and someone who just had a cover story.

Like just about everyone else, Crisp had gotten an early morning call that Saturday. It was from the chief deputy saying, I need you to come in 'cause we got Eric Rudolph here. Of course, Crisp thought he was being screwed with; they wanted him to work a Saturday and were just playing games to get him in. On the way in, he got a call from his wife, who was a sheriff's deputy over in Graham County, wanting to know if the story she was hearing about Rudolph being in custody was true, which made him believe for the first time that maybe he wasn't being yanked around after all. When he got in, damned if it didn't turn out to be 100 percent legit. Everybody was in. But he didn't see Rudolph at that point. Instead, he was sent out to investigate a campsite that someone thought might have been Eric's. That turned out to be just a bunch of kids with a site right in the middle of a field, not likely to be where Rudolph had been hiding, so he was pulled off that and brought back to help set up a secure perimeter around the jail.

Crisp did that for a bit, then he got the call to come back inside and sit with Eric. Here was the assignment: Eric doesn't want to be anywhere near the Feds. You just stay with him. Don't question him, in case he decides to lawyer up. Just talk with him, get what you can. Federal agents were standing by, sort of like phone operators, ready to talk to Crisp every time he came out of the room. If he had any questions, there was an assistant United States attorney named Jill Rose from Asheville standing by in the jail (unlike the FBI, she quickly won over the local law guys;

she had also been the prosecutor of the guys who fired into the command post back when the Task Force was up and running).

One of the first things that Crisp did when he met Eric that morning was to get him another plate of eggs and biscuits. A nice touch, one which put the other guy in your debt right off the bat. Crisp knew he was being looked over, but he also was doing his own visual scan. Eric was still in his own clothes; he hadn't changed into the ubiquitous orange jumpsuit worn by prisoners at county lockups around the state and most of the country. Prisoner 7445, as he was soon to be officially known on his booking report form, looked pretty good to Crisp. He was clean-cut, didn't have any body odor that Crisp could tell. His hair was trim, and so was his mustache. His pants and shirt were dirty, but to Crisp it only looked like a couple of days' worth of grunge, not weeks or months or years. The bottoms, below the knees, were darker, as if he had been wading in a river (which it seemed he had been doing just before Officer Postell had spotted him). His skin looked pretty good, not at all weathered, and his teeth also looked pretty good. He did look thin, to be sure, as if he hadn't gotten many square meals lately, which was what led Crisp to order in a second breakfast for him. Knowing full well that it might also win Eric over just a bit.

It wasn't until Rudolph smiled that Crisp recognized him. All he had to go on were the images from the wanted poster, where Eric looked if not chipmunk-cheeked, at least fuller in the face. But that smile, which also lit up the eyes a bit, that did it. Now he could see where Turtle had made the connection. Which was the difference between a photo and a living face. It was hard to see how anyone else would have made the connection between this guy and Eric Robert Rudolph. What else do you talk about first but the weather? Which led naturally to them talking about living out in the weather, which gave Crisp a chance to introduce a bit of his own story about SERE school and survival training. No questioning, just a conversation. Crisp making his own observations but letting Eric take the lead mostly.

They ended up covering a lot of ground during their time together. From survival courses to the Bible. Eric seemed to want to talk, and Crisp was there to listen. It was like being on a five-and-a-half-year camping trip, Eric said. At first I moved around a lot, sometimes every day, sleeping only a few hours at a time. I began up in the area of Snowbird Mountain. It was tough that first winter and first year. Agents literally almost tripped over him a couple of times while they were out on patrol, he said. Bear hunters would walk right by him. It got to be that out there he felt like his senses of hearing and smell tripled. Crisp knew what that was like from his survival course.

Then Eric laughed. He told Jerry—they were getting informal here—that every move the FBI made was broadcast. Crisp knew he had a radio, that had been public knowledge for years. But Eric said something curious, may not have even realized what he was saying, that one time he saw the head agent on the news talking about moving the hunt to a different location. Saw? As in TV? Jerry wanted to ask him about this, but held his tongue, hoping there would be more where this came from.

What he got instead was more talk about life on the run. Especially that first year, Eric would eat salamanders, grub worms, and creek lizards. Just about anything he could find that was edible and had protein. Acorns rounded out his menu. You didn't have to cook that sort of food. He was running up through creeks all the time, but he didn't like to fish. That made him nervous because the sound of the running water would cover up the sound of approaching footsteps.

Eric and Jerry talked about how survival school and boot camp were important. The military trained him, Eric said, so that he could function in the woods. He told Crisp how during his time in the service, he brought one of his military buddies over from Kentucky, and they went rappelling over at Nantahala Dam. He also talked about how he began to settle down some in the woods, fixing up campsites. He got plastic trash bins and buried them in the ground, after hauling up grain and soybeans from a silo that was along the main Andrews-Murphy road. That was one way of getting food, and nobody seemed the wiser that he made forays down there. Eric began to hunt, using a .223 caliber rifle. He shot deer, turkey, even a bear, he said. Sometimes he would dress and cook the meat, sometimes he would dry it out in the sun, make jerky. You could do that if you sliced it real thin, used something like newspaper to separate out the layers. He got his hands on fruits and vegetables (you could also dry out the fruit in the sun, if you were careful). But Crisp wondered about that bear and cooking it. He'd had some and knew it was pretty tough stuff unless you boiled it for nearly forever. Eric's teeth didn't look chipped off or even particularly bad.

There were lots of inconsistencies like that. Eric never got sick in five and a half years? No dental problems? No flu? No colds? He wasn't Superman or Super-Survivalist Man. Eric talked about worrying he would get sick or injured to Crisp , but never that he did. He didn't seem to realize or just wasn't letting on that all those folks who didn't think he was hiding out in someone's basement thought that's what happened to him—that he got sick or hurt, then crawled off and died somewhere. Eric did tell one person in the jail that weekend that he had hurt his leg at one point and was afraid he'd die, that it took him three weeks to get to the point where he could recover. This went on for a while before finally Jerry said, You don't look like you were in the woods for all that time. Look at you. Look at your clothes. I was in the woods for two weeks and looked like warmed over shit afterward. Eric came back at him, started in with his line that he just lived in his sleeping bag (*The same one all that time?* Crisp wondered) and pulled leaves over himself. That was his hooch, and that was also his story. He'd do the basics, like keep his boots in the sleeping bag, so the leather would stay dry. *That's bullshit*, thought Crisp to himself. *I've been in blue blowing snow on the Canadian border and understand miserable. I was ready to give up. This story just doesn't make sense. This guy ain't Superman.*

Eric said he eventually settled down into more permanent camps, especially after the Feds eased off on their search, when they seemed to give up and go away. He had a winter camp and a summer one, or that's the way it sounded. When they brought in a state game warden into the Breathalizer Room, Eric pointed out his campsites on a topographical map. One, sure enough, was just up the hill from where he was arrested. You just crossed the river and did a short but very steep climb up toward the ridge. It took you past the high school and then right near former Sheriff Jack Thompson's place, although it wasn't clear if Eric knew that part. The other campsite was farther up the valley toward Andrews, overlooking the Fires Creek Recreation Area. This one was much more out of the way, up around 2,800 feet. Eric had the high ground there, and that's where he said he buried the food. What struck you almost immediately was that you could draw a line on the map and connect the two campsites, using that ridgeline as your roadway.

Eric told Crisp he had grown more daring, especially once the Task Force was all but gone. He was coming into town more and more. It was so easy from right there up on the ridge and so tempting. The town was literally at his feet. He would come in at night and learned to avoid the police officers. There were all sorts of stores and fast-food places right there, once you worked your way down past the high school (Home of the Murphy Bulldogs) and the work area run by the Department of Transportation. You had the Burger King, where he had that last meal before going on the run. There was a Taco Bell, which Eric liked to hit after hours, to see what food they threw away at closing time. Turns out they threw away more than food. At one point, Eric was able to walk off with one of their uniforms, which was found at one of his campsites. Embarrassed, Taco Bell would later say it was a mistake that it got tossed out. It had probably been sometime in April or May, about a month before Eric was caught. Welcome to Taco Bell, my name is Eric, may I take your order?

There was the Wal-Mart and of course the BI-LO. Jerry kept coming round to the idea of what he was taught about surviving. You improvise, use whatever you have. If that means Dumpster diving, then you Dumpster dive. When he was on his survival course, he had knocked over a cabin belonging to his instructors for supplies. Not in the rules, but the point was you made your own rules. That's what Eric was doing. He said he especially liked the Save-A-Lot. The other grocery stores would throw out their meat and vegetables when they were really going bad. But Save-A-Lot was a godsend, or at least its Dumpster was. You could get a couple more days off their meat sometimes, the beef was the safest, which made it just about his favorite spot, one that he took to visiting often. It was like going grocery shopping, just in the middle of the night.

Eric could spot the police officers making their rounds. It was pretty easy, because they went in regular patterns, had their lights on as they circled through and did their checks. "That's how that little shit, Postell, got me," he said. "He cut his lights! He was able to get right on top of me." But even when he was stopped, Eric was confident he wouldn't be arrested, that he would just be run off. Treated as a vagrant. Crisp wasn't sure why he felt this way, but even the sheriff admitted that it would have been easy enough to see him just taken to the county line if no one had figured out his identity.

In a way, Eric was amused. He was glad that if he had to be caught, it was by Postell, even if he called him a little shit. The truth seemed to be he had more of a sneaking admiration for him. Better him than the FBI. They'd been trying to catch him for five years. He hated the Feds, that much was clear. They tried to brainwash you, he told Crisp. At one point when Jerry was in with Eric, an ATF agent wearing a windbreaker swung open the door to the room. He just stood there and tried to get Rudolph into a stare-down. "Well look," Eric said with sarcasm dripping from his voice, "the mighty ATF has arrived." Crisp slipped out of the room as soon as he could after that to have a word with the sheriff. "We can't have any more Feds in here. Eric got all hinked up. That sort of bullshit could screw everything up."

Eric always seemed eager to talk. And that was another thing that Jerry found curious. Not that he wanted to talk, but that he could talk. If he was off on this extended camping trip, on the lam, who did he talk to aside from that one conversation with George Nordmann? He didn't seem to have any trouble. No scratchy vocal cords or anything like that. That was easy, according to Eric. I read aloud to myself or reasoned aloud, thought through my arguments and my philosophy.

Which was something else that Jerry Crisp heard a lot about that weekend: Eric's view of the world. Not just about the government, which Eric made pretty obvious he despised. There was also a fair portion of Jew-bashing. He called abortion a sin, committing murder. But Eric really harped on homosexuality, how wrong that was. He tried not to come off sounding like a racist, but Eric said the Bible was plain on that score. White men were in charge. Simple as that. Women were supposed to follow. Everyone else was, well, everyone else. Sooner or later, he would relate all his views back to the Bible, and he would quote Scripture at length to Crisp (remember that he took a book of readings from the Christian Bible from George Nordmann). When his jailers asked Eric if there was anything they could bring him, one of the first things he had requested was a copy of the Bible.[19]

Crisp made it clear to Rudolph that he was no Bible scholar, which seemed to get Eric going even more. Eric wanted to teach Jerry, and Jerry was willing to listen. Always build rapport. When Jerry got out of the room for a break on Saturday night—it was time for both of them to sleep, and Jerry wasn't going to bunk with Eric, that would have been a bit too obvious—he went home and read up on some of the passages that Eric had quoted. Eric wrote down one passage, from Job or John, that Jerry looked up. He still couldn't make much sense out of it, so he went to the prison chaplain, who told him that it was on the subject of protection (Lester White had asked Eric if he wanted to speak with the chaplain, but he didn't seem interested). Eric later told him it was about having protection for Jerry. Eric was definitely intelligent, there was no denying that, even if his arguments were way out there.

Eric did have some sense of the frenzy that must be gathering outside the jail. He asked Crisp what the media was doing and started in on them. They were as bad as the government. They painted him as a terrorist. Another revealing statement, perhaps. It wasn't like Eric had been front-page news or back-page news or any sort of news for years. Was this all based on the early days, when he was on the run? Was it all from the shortwave radio, or was he reading newspapers, watching TV, even looking at the Internet?

Every so often, like when he was talking about the media and how it portrayed him, Eric might say something like, Well maybe I should talk to a lawyer first. Jerry would jump in and change the subject, talk about the weather or something else. That was fair, under state and federal law. You told the guy early on he had a right to an attorney, but it was up to him to make the request, not just wonder aloud about getting one. There had been one short, formal interview done by Sheriff Lovin, but that hadn't yielded much. Just hanging out seemed to be working a lot better.

Not that Eric ever said why he ran in the first place, for example, which was such a big question. But when his jailers wondered why he had still been living in the area, he said he had no place else to go![20] At one point, he did tell Crisp that the case against him was mostly circumstantial, which showed a pretty keen grasp of affairs for someone who was supposed to have been in a news void, but Crisp didn't want to cross the line and ask him what he meant by that or which case he meant by that, Atlanta or Birmingham. Eric did get started down one track, however, when all of the sudden he started talking to Crisp about the Unabomber along the lines of where he thought the Unabomber might have gone wrong.[21]

A lot of the jail conversations that weekend were innocuous stuff, and they took place between Eric's frequent naps. He'd sleep for a couple of hours at a stretch. With jailer Lester White, he played country geography. Lester was a few years older than Eric, so he hadn't known him at school, but they figured out folks they knew in common. Interestingly, that was as far as it went. Eric didn't ask after these folks nor did he talk about his family, never requesting a chance to talk with any of them.

When Lester first went into the room and met him, it was silent for twenty minutes, then Eric also started telling Lester about that first year on the run, eating salamanders and acorns, moving every day, trying to think of it as one long camping trip. He told him some of the same things he told Jerry Crisp—how later on he shot bear, deer, and turkey, how he started taking grain from the silos by Andrews-Murphy Airport, how he set up more elaborate camps, how he used leaves to cover his sleeping bag for an extra layer of warmth. He mentioned having a cardboard box that he broke down and used as a mattress pad because the ground was real hard, not like the jail cell. He never left the area, he said. He had a topographical map for a while that he used.

Others who met him that weekend said Eric Rudolph was relieved at being caught. That's not the way it appeared to Lester White. Eric never said so, either way, nor did he mention whether he ever got lonely. Sometimes it seemed to Lester that he wanted to talk, but other times he would just keep to himself. Mostly he kept his own counsel, White told CNN, was real respectful, and seemed like a polite young man, saying thank you when he was brought food or allowed to take a shower.[22]

Someone finally asked Eric the question they were all dying to ask. "How did you go that long without a woman?" Either Eric was being the ultimate gentleman or he was simply telling the truth when he laughed and said, "You get used to it" (although he would later tell Lester White who would later tell *Newsweek* that Eric had been without a woman so long he was starting to look at the bears kind of funny). Jerry Crisp, with his survival training, thought it might be more a function of having the energy as well. If you were just getting by, then sex stopped being at the top of your list of wants. Though Eric was sober when he was picked up, Jerry suspected he was still getting his hands on marijuana out in the woods.

Eric did have a visitor that weekend. Kenny Cope, the deputy sheriff from Macon County, who went way back with Eric, came in to look on Eric. Cope didn't just know Eric from growing up in Topton, he was also the person that George Nordmann called to say that Eric had visited him. Someone at the jail who witnessed the encounter said Rudolph was asleep, and Kenny went pssst, trying to wake him. Eventually, Eric came to, and the first thing Kenny asked him was, "Did you steal my blueberries?" He was half-joking, but now that Eric was behind bars, folks were going to be curious whether Eric had been foraging off them. One of the jailers asked Eric, "Do you know this crazy SOB?" Eric nodded. The two men visited for a bit, then Cope left.

Sunday night, as Crisp and Rudolph were talking, Eric finally came out and said, "When can I get one of them lawyers? I would kind of like one now." That was unequivocal, even with the "kind of like" phrasing thrown in. Crisp got up, left the room, and told Jill Rose, the assistant U.S. attorney, that Rudolph was lawyering up. There would be no more talk until he left the next morning for Asheville and his removal hearing. *I just didn't have enough time with him*, thought Crisp. *He would have laid it out for me sooner or later. They all do.* Crisp was sure that Rudolph was guilty but thought that no one would ever get the full story from Eric, certainly not his own lawyers. There was so much unanswered—about the bombings, about why he did it, about who might have helped him, about where he kept his bomb-making tools. But the only way Crisp thought anyone would ever get the story is if they talked to Eric after his trials. Maybe right after he had been sentenced to death for what Crisp was sure he did in Birmingham and Atlanta. Maybe then someone would get the full story from Eric Rudolph.

Saturday morning, most of the world was just waking up to the news. By late morning, the official confirmation of Rudolph's identity had worked its way up the food chain, and Attorney General John Ashcroft put out a statement. There were even rumors that he wanted to fly in for the news conference that was about to be held in Murphy but couldn't because there would be too many weather delays. The FBI's agent in charge for North Carolina did make it over from Charlotte. There was no way he or his agency was going to miss this. Chris Swecker was actually a native, having played backup quarterback at Appalachian State before being a prosecutor in the eastern part of the state, then ultimately going on to the FBI. Like the quarterback he had once been, he naturally took center stage when the announcement was finally made. The tableau at the front of the room during this news conference was reminiscent of so many during the early days of the Task Force, except the faces had mostly changed, and the news was for once good. There were local, state, and federal officials up on the podium—many of them wondering why it was the FBI was trying in effect to claim credit for an arrest it didn't make. Reporters were eager for every scrap: What was Eric doing, what was he saying, what was he wearing, and what was he now eating? Lovin and Thigpen handled most of the details. Someone zinged Swecker about the multimillion dollar price tag of the manhunt, and he responded easily about how it was mostly loaded on the front end of the investigation, which is to say before he was involved, and how this—meaning the capture—was all part of the low-key plan that had been put in place after the manhunt was scaled back. Instead of busting a gut at that one in public, Sheriff Lovin covered his back, saying that none of his officers ever got together without talking about Eric Rudolph, not in the five and a half years since he had disappeared. The more likely truth was that none of the officers got together during that time without bitching about how they could have brought him in so much sooner if the Feds, by which they meant the FBI and not the ATF, hadn't messed up at every turn. Which even they had to admit was harsh, but once the FBI had arrived that morning, all the bad memories of being treated like stepchildren and watching as the Feds trampled through their community without showing any signs of knowing what they were doing had come flooding back. Now here they were, and the FBI was doing the same thing, saying, Yeah, a sheriff's deputy got him, but really it was our plan that made it happen.[23]

The reporters wanted to know what America wanted to know and what Jerry Crisp was slowly, carefully, trying to find out. Where was Eric this whole time? How did he survive for five years? Was anyone being investigated, and would they be prosecuted? And one more—which no one had the answer to—would Officer Postell get that million dollar reward? All good questions, but all forgotten once the man of the hour showed up. Jeff Postell may have dreamed many things when he was a kid thinking about going into law enforcement, and this might have been one of them. Just him, bringing the villain to justice. Yet the reality was so much more amazing. Rookie cop, twenty-one years old, standing before the national media, live! Answering questions about how he caught one of the Ten Most Wanted! Short of nabbing Osama bin Laden, another one of the Top Ten, this was about as big as it was going to get.

Slowly, maybe a little nervously, Postell laid out the details. How he had been doing business checks, how he spotted the man, how he stopped him, how he wasn't aware until Deputy Matthews told him that the man might be Eric Rudolph. Yes sir, no sir, always polite. "This was just a day's work," he answered, although it clearly wasn't, or they wouldn't have been there throwing these questions at him. The way he answered was reminiscent of the rookie who fielded questions after winning the big game. You could strut your stuff or you could go the justhappy-to-be-here, one-game-at-a-time route. Except there was no pretense with Jeff Postell. He was truly the local hero, and he was probably the only one who didn't realize it. "I think I put a lot of people's feelings at ease," he said, "when asked about capturing Eric Rudolph. A lot of stress was involved in this situation. This is closure. And that's about it. I was just glad I was out there doing my job and was glad I was in the right place at the right time." From anyone else it might have sounded scripted. But from Postell, who must have been running on nothing but leftover adrenaline at this point, it was the truth. He didn't much mind if he sounded like a cliché.[24]

Out in media-land, reaction was coming in to the big news. Emily Lyons went on CNN and a number of other outlets to say yes, she was happy, and she would be celebrating the capture of the man accused of maiming her with a bomb. Mike Rising, the FBI agent who was injured in the Sandy Springs bombing, was down in Centennial Park doing an interview on CNN. So was the former U.S. attorney for Atlanta, Kent Alexander, who had lived through the bombings in his city. His counterpart in Birmingham, Doug Jones, was overjoyed at the news and when asked on the air if he would like to come back and prosecute the case, he said, "Of course. What prosecutor wouldn't?" Not that it was going to happen, but it was a sign of the emotions that day.

John Hawthorne sat out the media circus that day, except for a couple of brief conversations with reporters. He didn't believe it when a friend called early that morning and said Eric Rudolph might have been arrested. He wanted to believe it, but he couldn't stand to have his hopes dashed. He drove over to see his mother in Alabama, and by the time he got there, the arrest was confirmed.[25] There, the man who had held so much anger in him—not at Eric Rudolph directly, because he knew that Rudolph had never even known his wife and wasn't trying to kill her per se—finally let go and cried.[26] It was like a weight finally being lifted from his shoulders. What would he like to see happen to Rudolph if he was found guilty? If you had asked him six years earlier, he said, his answer would have been the death penalty. No doubt. Now, a life sentence without parole might suffice, provided he lived long enough and hard enough to reflect every day on the unnecessary killings he had done. One hundred seventy years seemed about right.[27]

From Richard Jewell, the man who discovered the backpack in Centennial Park and then suffered so grievously at the hands of the FBI and media for his heroism, there would be a simple "No comment" through his lawyer. He was just trying to keep a low profile, make his way in the world of law enforcement. Over the years, he'd finally begun to get the recognition he deserved, but there were still the whispers and the jokes.

The first glimpse of Eric Rudolph came that night. Not from the perp walk, where a soon-to-be defendant gets paraded before the media. Instead, the Cherokee County Detention Center released a mug shot (not the official one, which came later, where he was showered and clean-shaven, dressed in the orange jumpsuit, holding up a little card that said prisoner 7445). As advertised, this was Eric Rudolph with short hair, a dark T-shirt, a mustache, and stubble, shortly after his capture. His chin puckered at the bottom, where the telltale scar revealed itself. His mouth was shut, lips set across, so you couldn't see the teeth, see whether they were worse for the wear. Even with the poor quality of the digital image, you could see the skin wasn't coarse, not roughened by the exposure to sixty months of living in the elements. What stood out were the eyes. Slightly reddened, although that could have been from the flash, but intense, staring straight ahead, punctuated for emphasis by his eyebrows.

Deputy Matthews had done his work. Those eyes were the only give-away. Maybe it was also having seen Eric in person once before, because the man staring at the camera in the Cherokee County lockup was not the man on the wanted poster or on the ponytailed sketch made after he showed up at Nordmann's. Not if you just walked by him. He was considerably thinner, dramatically thinner in the face. It would have been all too easy to miss, yet years of thinking about him kept the image fresh in Turtle's mind, so that he was able to spot Eric almost immediately. How many others had missed him? Walked right by him? Answered a knock on the door from a stranger and given him food?

There was one drawing that did seem to match this new Eric Rudolph. But you had to have done your time on this case. Charles Stone knew he had seen something that bore resemblance to the mug shot and so did I. The night of the capture, after hours spent on CNN talking about Eric, we went up to my office and went through the files. There it was! Goatee man, the sketch made all those years ago after the Centennial Park bombing. This was the man that the Speedo boys, the rowdy young men, had seen sitting on the park bench by himself. When he got up, they said, that's when they saw the backpack. This was the sketch of the Blobman, the man on the bench from the photo that NASA blew up but could still never get a face from.

If you put goatee man and Eric's mug shot side by side, you could find a lot of points in common. The eyebrows, the eyes, the ears, the ridge of the nose. The mustache was striking in its similarity, and if you darkened up the stubble from the mug shot, you could see the outline of the goatee. And if you had a noticeable scar, then a goatee was a clever way of hiding it. The cut of the face, especially the cheekbones, was a bit wider on the goatee man and the nostrils less prominent. But side by side, they suggested an interesting comparison, one that wasn't evident from any of the other photos of Eric. Jack Daulton, the former head of the Atlanta office and the Task Force, was stunned when he saw them together. Maybe there were eyewitnesses from Centennial Park after all, Stone thought.

The perp walk ritual was scheduled for Monday morning. Outside the jail, heavily armed police were patrolling. The media was back a little ways, cameras at the ready, forming an electronic gauntlet (this wouldn't be a New York style scrum, known in the trade as a gang bang, where everyone crowded in and questions came flying). The plan was to take Eric by car to the local airport, where he would be put on a National Guard helicopter and flown to Asheville. There he would meet with his duly appointed public defender, having signed the proper forms, and face what was called a removal hearing. After that, the decision had been made to take him to Birmingham, where he would be arraigned for the bombing of the New Woman, All Women Health Care Clinic.

Inside the jail, a strange sort of leave-taking was going on. Eric had made something of an impression on many of those who were at close quarters with him that weekend. Willing or not, he carried the aura of celebrity, though his putative folk hero status may have actually been diminished once it turned out he was a flesh-and-blood figure, now wearing the jumpsuit of the captured. Eric had signed more than one Wanted poster that weekend, as a few of the folks tried to get mementoes of that historic weekend at the Cherokee County jail. Just imagine what a shit storm that would cause, if any of the posters showed up on eBay! The FBI was busy confiscating every potential piece of Rudolph memorabilia it could find—even the photo of Eric that he signed for Sheriff Lovin when the sheriff was trying to identify him at the beginning and wanted to get a handwriting sample.

Lester White shook Eric's hand and told him he would remember him in his prayers. Joe Morris, the former state trooper who ran the jail, told Eric he would need to wear a bulletproof vest. Eric didn't want to, but he wasn't in a position to argue. As Morris bent down to put chains on Eric's legs, in the unlikely event he was able to ditch his armed escort, the jailer couldn't help feeling like he was sending his weekend prisoner off for an execution. He knew Eric was charged with serious crimes, but the thought that this was the last time Rudolph would see the hills where he had stayed for so long, his beloved hills, well, that just got to him a bit.[28] Jerry Crisp wasn't the sentimental type. What he thought was that if he'd just had more time with Eric, well, sooner or later they all slip up.

Others who witnessed the preparations for the perp walk say that to the last, Eric made it a point to ignore the Feds as best he could. C. J. Hyman, the ATF agent, had tried to tell Eric what would take place when he left, why he was wearing the shackles, and where he would be going. But Eric would have none of that. He just went mute. Ignored the ATF man, much in the way he had stopped his conversation the day before when he spotted a Fed looking in on him. Perhaps in his mind, once the Feds got ahold of him, he was a prisoner of war, which he had trained for all those years ago in the military. It was clear to everyone in the room as he was about to leave that Rudolph planned on having nothing at all to do with the Feds.

The whole strategy of getting Rudolph out of town and over to Asheville had been planned to within an inch of its life. Should we take him this route to the airport or that route? How many cars in the convoy? Helicopter or plane? Finally the sheriff and chief of police had enough of the constant back and forth—they weren't expecting some huge ambush—and just told the FBI and ATF (which were still playing games with each other) to let them know. In the end, perhaps more for political cover rather than actual security, Sheriff Lovin and Chief Thigpen were asked to drive Rudolph to the local airport. But if the Feds were expecting to get any final words out of Eric, they screwed the pooch by having an ATF and FBI agent ride in the back on either side of him. Once again, Eric shut down.

The perp walk itself didn't disappoint. Every one of these got measured by the granddaddy of all perp walks, Lee Harvey Oswald on display in Dallas when Jack Ruby came up and put a pistol in his gut. Tim McVeigh was the more modern counterpoint, dressed up like Rudolph in jumpsuit and Kevlar vest, surrounded by a phalanx of lawmen, as he was taken from a small-town jail back to Oklahoma City, looking impossibly young and clean-cut. When it came time for Rudolph's perp walk debut, he went for the cold-eyed look. As Eric came down the steps in his shackles, surrounded by security, but apart enough so that America could get a glimpse of him in motion, he put on what in the military is called the thousand yard stare, the look out into the distance. Truth was, his was more of a hundred yard glare, as those eyes, which first twigged Sean Matthews that this might be Eric Rudolph, burned toward the waiting crowd of media and security.

There seemed to be a mixture of contempt, disdain, and disinterest all rolled into that look. One of the jailhouse crowd thought it might have been aimed at Officer Postell, who was standing guard and would drive out to the airport to see him off. But others thought the look was for the media, Eric's electric Jew, which he felt had already tried and convicted him as a terrorist. There didn't seem to be any longing in his look for the hills and mountains that rose up behind the parking lot, a strong and silent reminder of the Appalachian splendor that brought folks—including the Rudolph clan—to western North Carolina in the first place. He shuffled down the steps as the chains pulled at his legs, staring and glaring, then just like that, he was in the backseat of the sheriff's car, flanked by those FBI and ATF agents. Sheriff Lovin himself drove the car with Chief Thigpen riding shotgun. They were headed to the Andrews-Murphy airport, where Rudolph was going to be flown by National Guard helicopter to Asheville, where he would appear before a federal judge and have what was called a removal hearing to decide if he was going to be sent off to Birmingham to stand trial.

If someone had a sense of humor, he could have totally messed with Eric and just about everyone on the extreme Right at this point. A coat of paint to the National Guard helicopter could have turned it to the dreaded color black, as in the legions of black helicopters which patrolled the paranoia of the militia movement, ready to invade America at any pretext. Of course, the reservists would have had to change uniforms, putting on the mythical blue helmets of United Nations peacekeeping troops, another part of the far-Right paranoid fantasy that America was under attack by agents of the New World Order. There's no telling how that would have played with Eric. Instead, it was a mundane parting at the airport as Eric was escorted onto the waiting helicopter and flown off to Asheville to begin his life in the federal system. Jeff Postell watched as the helicopter took off and headed over the mountains. Eric Rudolph had left North Carolina, possibly for the last time in his life.

13.

JUST ONE LONG CAMPING TRIP

THE MEDIA WAS on hand to witness Rudolph's arrival in Asheville. Once Eric was taken into the courthouse and unshackled, he signed a form that said he was destitute and in need of a public defender. Then Rudolph briefly met with a local attorney named Sean Devereux, who explained what was about to happen in the courtroom. Once they went in, Judge Lacy Thornburgh asked the man in orange at the defense table if he was indeed Eric Robert Rudolph, and he said yes, he was. Assistant U.S. Attorney Jill Rose, who had spent the weekend at the jail in Murphy, monitoring events there, read the charges against Rudolph—and he appeared to read along. Neither Rudolph nor his attorney objected to the point of the hearing, that he be removed to Birmingham to face arraignment, though Devereux made it clear that Rudolph had no intention of pleading guilty then and there. The hearing lasted thirty minutes. The next stop would be Birmingham, this time via small plane, where Rudolph would be formally arraigned in federal court the next day.

Devereux had his fifteen minutes of fame on the courthouse steps, jokingly encouraging the media to bring him other business. He said his client was not a zealot, even though he had been portrayed as one (which meant that Eric must have expressed the same sentiment to him about the media that he did to Crisp) and that he was "not an uncaring man." "He is a reflective individual and he has a lot to think about," Devereux said. It was his duty, even if was just for a matter of hours, to make sure that a man in such trouble had access to an attorney. Devereux did say he had not asked Rudolph about any of the facts of the case.

There had been about a hundred people in the Asheville courtroom waiting to see Eric Rudolph, but for one woman it was a chance to bear witness after sixty long months, to see the man accused of killing her husband. Felecia Sanderson had gotten the call Saturday morning from Don Bell, who had been the ATF supervisor up in Andrews. Her first question after hearing about Eric Rudolph's arrest: Was anybody hurt? She feared that Rudolph would be armed and dangerous, and she didn't want to think that he'd get into some sort of gun battle with the police.[1] Felecia Sanderson had spent five and a half years cajoling and inspiring the Task Force, while suffering the loss of her husband. She hadn't wanted to let herself believe that Rudolph was dead, that there would be no justice. There was no way she was going to miss this. She was sure the right man was about to face trial. Now, she was determined to get to Asheville and lay eyes on him.

What she hadn't expected was to feel a brief, small surge of sympathy when she first saw him in the Asheville courtroom. He looked pitiful, she thought. But then she said she pictured her own husband, his body ripped apart, lying in front of the Birmingham clinic. That did it. She saw Rudolph for the monster he was, she said, and when the handcuffs closed back over his wrists at the end of the hearing, the word that flashed through her mind was *Gotcha!*[2] No more running for Eric Rudolph.

Felecia Sanderson made it a point to be at federal court in Birmingham the next day when Rudolph was formally arraigned. But in between Asheville and Birmingham, she made a stop in Murphy. She wanted to meet and thank the young man who captured Eric Rudolph. Felecia worried that she hugged him so tight she might have squeezed the very breath out of Jeff Postell. "That's some young man," she said.[3]

Felecia Sanderson didn't like giving news conferences or doing interviews, especially on TV. They made her nervous. But she stood on the courthouse steps in Birmingham after Eric Rudolph's arraignment and read a statement. She talked about justice being done and what it was like to see the man accused of killing her husband finally arraigned. For all her protestations, though, Felecia Sanderson was tough. By her own count, she had visited North Carolina several dozen times, a living reminder that this wasn't about Eric-as-folk-hero or abortion, that this was about killing a police officer, a husband and a father, and that it was about killing a mother and a wife in Atlanta. She said she couldn't understand how anyone could commit such crimes. She was sure the right man was facing trial.

The arraignment had been almost an anticlimax after the five-plus years of waiting. Rudolph was asked several questions by Magistrate Michael Putnam during the twenty-minute hearing. He answered politely and followed along intently, as he did in Asheville. He had lawyers on each side of him. Richard Jaffe was a well-known Birmingham trial lawyer, appointed by the chief judge of the federal district court just the day before to represent Rudolph. He was Jewish, made no secret of it, certainly an ironic twist given Eric's beliefs. Bill Bowen was a former assistant state attorney general and a former judge, now back in private practice. He'd been watching the news on CNN Saturday morning, while visiting his son in Washington. *Hmm, this should make an interesting book someday*, he thought. Then, on Monday morning, he got a call from the chief judge asking him to come over to his chambers, where he, too, got the word that he was wanted for the job of giving Eric Rudolph the best defense possible.

Both men knew that while it would take months for the government to make it official, this was going to be a death penalty case. There was no federal public defender's office in Birmingham, so they were it. Later, they would add a third lawyer, along with several associates, to their team. Judy Clarke was a federal public defender based out of San Diego, who already had one very important client now serving a life sentence at the federal high-security prison in Colorado. She had worked out the deal that had saved Ted Kaczynski, the Unabomber, from the death penalty. There had been talk for a long time about the parallels between the Rudolph and Unabomber cases. This would be another.

Felecia Sanderson knew what she was doing that afternoon, standing on the courthouse steps. She knew that Richard Jaffe would come out and talk about how his client deserved the presumption of innocence, how the facts needed to be examined, how proof should be sorted out from hearsay. All fair words and true. She didn't want a kangaroo court, either. But she didn't want the news coverage to be dominated by the defense attorneys that night or any night. So Felecia Sanderson stood up before the cameras and spoke her mind. She was willing to be the victims' sound bite, the sort which TV news craves. Just in case anyone didn't have a picture of her husband, she brought one and held it up. This was going to be about him and the other victims, be they in Birmingham or Atlanta. Rudolph, through his attorneys, wouldn't go unchallenged.

Emily Lyons wasn't in court that day. She was still in New York, doing a round of television interviews, her way of reminding the American public that this wasn't some romantic tale of an outlaw spending his life on the run, but about a crime with victims and scars. She would finally get her chance to lay her one damaged but still functioning eye on Eric Rudolph a few weeks later at another hearing, when he would be reindicted, this time in such a way as to make death penalty charges apply. Emily and her husband Jeff had already won one victory against Rudolph, though it was likely to be one that was never enforced. She sued him in civil court in Birmingham for damages and won $115 million. Needless to say, he had never appeared to defend himself, though that was part of the idea behind it. Despite all the laws, Emily also wanted to make sure, if Rudolph was ever caught, that he wouldn't profit from what she was sure was his crime.

There were no revelations when Emily and Jeff went to court and finally saw Eric Rudolph. He looked much like that first mug shot and perp walk; he was still thin after his first few weeks in the Birmingham jail. It was hard to match that face with the wanted poster. They were struck by how involved he was with court procedure. He wasn't at all detached, the way they expected. But if Eric Rudolph saw Emily Lyons in the courtroom, he gave no indication. Instead, he looked away, back toward the judge. There was one thing that did strike Jeff Lyons that day.

It was simply this: Eric Rudolph didn't look like a man who had spent sixty months in the wild. He wasn't going to speculate, but he'd heard the same rumors as everyone else. Rudolph's condition didn't surprise Emily; all along she'd been convinced that someone was probably helping him.

If you had been in Murphy during the days after Eric's capture, there was no way you could miss the sign outside of the Peachtree Restaurant, which was over near the hospital and community college on one of the roads leading out of town. CNN certainly didn't. Neither did the *New York Times*, which had a photo on its front page the Monday morning after Rudolph's capture, the same morning he began his journey from Murphy to Asheville to Birmingham. PRAY FOR ERIC RUDOLPH, it said. To the invading media it bespoke of a secret sentiment, suddenly revealed, that this area was a haven for hillbilly terrorists and their legions of sympathizers, all suddenly unmasked in front of the world. At least that's the way Mayor Bill Hughes saw his town and region being portrayed. He was like Canute, valiantly but fruitlessly fighting the media tide, doing dozens of interviews in his blazer and tie, throwing in a few rhetorical flourishes, trying to convince the global village that his town wasn't about Eric Rudolph, that this man was a lone actor, and that the media was overstating support for him (Hughes had been a hot interview from the start, since he was one of the first people to lay eyes on Eric Rudolph and had been willing to talk about it, live, that Saturday morning).

He was fighting a losing battle. Not after Betty Howard put up that sign and especially not after the *New York Times* ran its story. It was like the manhunt all over again. The way Hughes saw it, the media was looking for the negative. There was no proof that Rudolph had help. Sure they could find sound bites with one-toothed hillbillies, which were about all they seemed to find, he thought, but that wasn't the real Murphy; that was some cynical game of rent-a-hick.[4] Later, the mayor would take some grim satisfaction in pointing out after the fact that Betty Howard's restaurant, the one with the sign about praying for Eric, shut down just weeks after Rudolph's capture.

The truth was a whole lot more complicated, and the media may have missed some but not all of it. There was still sympathy for Rudolph—that us versus them thing—and there was still some belief that this was about abortion (on the road out from Andrews toward Topton you could still see a big cartoonish sort of sign attacking abortion). Not a few kept coming back to the notion that the federal government had no cause to be sticking its nose into folks' business. Five years hadn't changed that. There was a new ballad that came out, another "Run Rudolph, Run," another paean to a fugitive on the run, this one written by a Baptist minister, and it got some airplay around Andrews and Murphy.[5] There were a number of folks who came forward and said very plainly, whether to the *New York Times* or *Atlanta Journal-Constitution*, yes, they would have helped Eric if he ever came to their door. That was an easy quote to get this week, although it was unclear just how much these folks meant it. If you wanted the best one, all you had to do was go out and see Steve Cochran, Randy's brother, and get a shot of him tooling around on his four-wheel ATV, as CNN's Art Harris did, revisiting a man who was still angry after all these years at the way he felt he and his brother and grandfather had been harassed for knowing Eric. "I think he acted alone," Steve said, "but if he'd have shown up at my back door, I'd have thrown a slab of meat on the barbecue and welcomed him. I'm in hock up to my eyeballs, but I wouldn't have touched that million dollar reward."[6]

How much of that was genuine, a mixture of bluster and defiance, a way of telling the media, the Feds, and even the outside world screw you? How much of it was a little country bullshitting, like when the CNN reporter looking for man-on-the-street reaction went into the local barbershop and asked a man if he'd seen Rudolph. Sure, he said, "we played golf together recently." Some of it, like the Rudolph T-shirts and bumper stickers from earlier years, was simply cashing in, American style. Up in Andrews, Peggy Ellison wasn't upset to hear of Eric Rudolph's capture. She just wished it had happened up there, so Andrews could maybe rake in a bit from the media circus, bring a little business back to what was now an economically struggling town. You didn't just have the sign in front of the Peachtree Restaurant. You also had signs in downtown Murphy at one coffee place advertising, CAUGHT CAPPUCCINO, LAST LATTE, CAUGHT YA' COFFEE, and ERIC ESPRESSO. When

Rudolph went on the run back in 1998, you would have been met with blank stares or a laugh if you asked for latte in Murphy. So maybe things had changed.

Here's the irony. Despite what the mayor said, the folks who were most convinced that Eric Rudolph had help were the same folks who were convinced all along that he was getting help. It was the locals, particularly the local law enforcement community, who thought the Task Force had always looked a bit the other way on this subject. Every bit of his own training convinced Jerry Crisp that Eric Rudolph had help along the way, not necessarily for the bombings, but during his time on the run. Just about every local lawman who spent time with Eric that weekend felt the same way.

They couldn't understand why the mayor or the Feds seemed so intent on saying he acted alone. Their eyes told them something different; so did their noses and hearing. This wasn't a man who spent five and a half years on a camping trip, as he put it, only revealing himself to George Nordmann. He was just in way too good shape. Thin yes, but well-groomed. The way Jerry Crisp put it, part of the survival training they taught in the military was making contact with friendlies, just like part of it would be breaking into cabins and using them. And he was sure that Eric was getting help from friendlies, whether they knew who he was or not. Which is not to say that Chris Swecker of the FBI necessarily thought Eric acted alone, either. Even at that first news conference the day Eric was caught, he expressed skepticism about Rudolph's skills as a survivalist. Swecker warned that day that the FBI would be launching an investigation, and anyone involved in harboring a fugitive faced prosecution.

There seemed to be an easy way to sort this out. Just visit the campsites that Eric told them about, see for themselves what the evidence showed. Even as investigators began doing that, they were deluged with other calls—from people around Murphy who suddenly were convinced they had seen Eric Rudolph in the days and weeks before he was captured. The mother of one of the jailers remembered seeing a young man in a camouflage jacket walking near her house about four days earlier. Ironically, she lived over near where Eric abandoned his truck the night

after the Birmingham bombing. A man over in Andrews shooed someone away from a picnic table a few days before the capture. He, too, was
sure it had been Eric, but he said he wouldn't have turned him in even if
he had known.[7]

No such compunction from the young woman who took out the
trash at the Save-A-Lot hours before Eric was popped. It was creepy that
he might have been out there day after day, she said, but she would have
taken the reward, no question. The produce manager at the store was
still wondering about fifty-four milk crates he said were stolen from the
delivery area, the same sort of milk crates that Eric hid behind after running from Officer Postell. He said he'd heard there had been a homeless
person living back behind the store for about a month, and while he
wouldn't eat the broccoli or squash he threw away, who knew if someone
else did. And the owner of the Save-A-Lot was sure he'd seen Eric, right
there in the parking lot in front of the store, just a few days earlier. He'd
been pushing in a bunch of shopping carts when a man walked in front
of him. Said he even told his wife he thought it was Eric Rudolph, but
she told him no way, he was dead.[8]

Each and every report was investigated, but Sheriff Lovin could
never verify any of them. Looking at the campsites was a different matter. Early on, in the hours following his capture, Eric had given up the
location of his first campsite, the one up above the high school. Later in
the morning, during that short formal interview with the sheriff, Eric
mentioned the location of the other place where he was living, up by
Fires Creek, which was farther away from town and much more remote.
The first order of business was to locate these sites on a map, so they
brought over Edwin Grant, the state game warden for Cherokee and
Macon County, and got Eric to point the locations out on a map.

Then there was the matter of getting folks out to the sites without
being followed by the media, which was no small feat, since the hordes
were beginning to arrive. And each of the campsites first had to be secured by a bomb tech, just in case Eric had booby-trapped the sites or
had some explosives cached. The bomb tech would also check for obvious signs of explosive residue, much as they had found in George Nordmann's truck after Eric took it way back when. Once the campsites had

been secured, the plan was to send in teams to examine them and collect evidence. There would be FBI folks in charge, because of course Rudolph had been a federal fugitive, but also in the words of the locals because the FBI couldn't stand not to be in charge. As usual, there was an acronym for this unit: ERT for Evidence Response Teams. Because the FBI was there, the ATF wanted a piece of the action. Since the second campsite, at least, appeared to be on Forest Service land, the Forest Service was going to send at least one of its folks—who of course also had to lay out a trail for the others so they wouldn't get lost in the woods. The state wanted a piece of the action, so it sent investigators along with the game warden, and the sheriff's department wanted to have someone there because nobody was going to tell them what was going on otherwise.

The investigators actually caught a bit of a break from the media that first day. Most of the reporters were hunkered down by the jail waiting for any morsels there. Those who did have time to wander off mostly headed for the Village Valley shopping center to see where Eric had been captured. They would have seen one of the ERTs in action nearby, trying to collect possible evidence over by the river and the base of a nearby bridge. They wouldn't try to make their way to the campsites—or even get word of their possible locations—for some time yet.

The investigators made it to the first campsite pretty quickly. It wasn't but a few minutes' hike up the hill near the high school, skirting past the edge of Jack Thompson's property. What they found when they got there jibed with what Eric had been saying, at least in part, about that site. It was obvious he hadn't been living there too long. Weeks, if not a couple of months. There simply wasn't that much evidence of firewood or ashes, although he could have buried or scattered the cinders. More importantly, there wasn't the damage to the surrounding area that a long-term stay would have caused. It wasn't badly stripped of firewood, there were no signs of trash being scattered or buried, not much evidence of any sort of construction. The soil and trees around the campsite would have looked a lot different and worse for the wear if Eric had spent a considerable length of time there.

There were some vegetables lying around, that was one of the first things you noticed. Onions, apples, and tomatoes. Some were rotting, but others looked like they had been sliced up, prepared in such a way that they would dry in the sun. There were several pieces of plywood, which might have come from the nearby high school, which had been doing some construction. A window blind was laid out across the area, and it might have been used as an improvised sleeping mat to protect against the ground. There were scraps of magazines and small pieces of wood, to be used for a cooking fire. A somewhat crushed beer can lay over to the side. There were leaves, which had been pushed down into a bedded area. Some welded wire that looked like a stronger version of chicken wire and black plastic tarp, which indicated that Eric was storing food or getting ready to store food. The team dug underneath that, looking for indications that he had started to bury things and settle in for the long haul.

There were other clues at the campsite. Part of the Taco Bell uniform was immediately evident. There were also the remnants of a big bag of shredded cheese, again with Taco Bell markings, the sort of thing that would be used to prepare the tacos and other dishes for customers. Either Eric was somehow making his way back into the kitchen area of the restaurant or, more likely, he had retrieved these items from the Dumpster. To the investigators, it looked like Eric had only been at this site for a short while. This campsite was organized, but it didn't appear to be built out in any significant way. Former sheriff Thompson, who had been up around the edge of his property not too many months before that, said he hadn't spotted anything back then. Although he wouldn't have been surprised if Eric had been making off with any items from his vegetable garden or taking any trout out of his small pond. But with the temptations of the various Dumpsters just down the hill, Rudolph might not have needed to play Peter Rabbit sneaking into Mr. McGregor's vegetable patch.

The other site—the one up by Fires Creek—was much more elaborate. Getting there was also a bit more involved. If you had a vehicle, which the investigators certainly did, you could drive out of town by a couple of different routes. Eventually you made your way over to the Fires Creek Recreation Area, down a winding road past the creek, and up past the Fly Shop, where you could tend to your fishing needs. Then the road changed to dirt and gravel, and there was a series of gates, sometimes locked, sometimes not, that the Forest Service controlled. If the right gate wasn't locked, you could drive to within about a half mile of the second campsite. Then you had to hump up a pretty steep slope. It took about twenty to thirty minutes, but unless you were an experienced hiker or guide, you were going to put some serious wear and tear on your hamstrings on your way up.

Which was what was going on with the ERT that hit the Fires Creek campsite. The Forest Service guy didn't have any trouble making it up there, but he was known in those parts as being able to walk the legs off a billy goat. Some of the FBI agents were huffing and puffing in a big way by the time they made it up to Eric's location. This wasn't easy work, even if you followed the pieces of tape tied to trees that marked off the trail the first folks to the scene had set up. But once they got to a clearing, which matched the location Eric had given back at the jail, they knew the climb was well worth it. This camp was considerably more sophisticated than the site near the high school.

All you had to do was look up in the air. Not that your average camper would do that—nor was it likely that your average camper would even make it to this spot. But if you looked up, you would see an extraordinary sight. Huge wheeled trash cans dangling by yellow nylon rope from the trees! A sort of backwoods version of an art installation, except this had a serious purpose that any woodsman understood. This was bear country, in fact this was pretty much inside a bear sanctuary, and if you didn't want visitors to your campsite, the first thing you were always told heading into the woods is place your food (and trash) out of reach. That meant, practically speaking, that if you spent any time out in the woods, you hoisted your food, your cooler, and your trash bags high enough off of a branch to keep your site from being overrun.

But this was one step beyond. These were those big wheeled sixty-eight-gallon trash cans, curbies they were called, and when the ERT finally got them down, and they listened to one of the locals with them, they understood where these might have come from. The curbies were marked Property of Andrews and could be found at homes and businesses all over town. The town had switched over to this sort of garbage pickup system in the 1980s, much in the way many cities and towns, large and small, had done over recent years. When that happened, these curbies were distributed. Sometime between then and now, Eric had made off with several of them and wheeled them up here to this campsite.[9]

Not all of them were dangling in the air, and not everything up in the air was a curbie. There was also at least one smaller, more conventionally shaped cylindrical wheeled trash can, the kind you can buy at Wal-Mart or Home Depot, dangling from the trees, and packed in part with gear. Another had been sliced up and placed around a tree trunk, a few feet up, in such a way that if a bear tried to climb up the tree to reach the other cans, it would have trouble gaining purchase on this plastic sort of guard.

Even as the team worked to cut down the trash cans, they were surveying the rest of the scene. It was well hidden. Again, the mountain laurel provided one layer of protection, even from the sky, that would have been there even during the winter, when Eric said he lived there. Hardwoods towered over the mountain laurel, providing the double canopy effect, which offered so much camouflage. If you turned yourself back around, you could look out across a good portion of the Fires Creek Recreation Area. If someone or something was coming up your way, you'd be able to hear them (again, they'd have to move through the mountain laurel, which would be noisy). Plus, you had a good view. You could see, but not be seen; hear, but not be heard. Eric clearly had taken the high ground and would have seen anyone approaching, an unmistakable sign of his military survival training.

The campsite was effectively a series of levels, though you'd have to look closely to spot that. Most of the area was steeply sloped, but there were small patches where it leveled off, making it possible for someone to sleep or set up a campfire. After all, one of the things you don't want to do is set up your sleeping bag in such a way that you end rolling down a hill! It isn't clear that the investigators would have ever spotted these areas or exactly what was in them if they hadn't gotten some information from Eric. As it was, as they looked across the ground, they saw some other traces of habitation aside from the dangling trash cans. There was an old World War Two–era Army mess kit on the ground. There was a small built-up area of rocks, which some described as akin to a patio, where there were traces of a fire. Clearly this had been used as a cooking spot, but there weren't that many ashes, which meant Eric had been using a small fire for cooking, which also reflected his army training. If he set up his sleeping bag by here, then he would have some degree of radiated heat as well as a flat spot to lie out in.

There were other signs that this had been someone's campsite. An old towel draped across a branch. Looped over another branch was an old-fashioned barrel hoop, although it isn't clear what its purpose was. Another tree branch had been taken down and tied across, almost making it parallel to the ground but a few feet up, which would have been a good place to drape a tarp over in case it was raining (it ran over the area where stones had been arranged with a small area for the campfire). It might also have been a good place to throw over a deer carcass after you bled it out, so you could dress it, cutting up the meat into portions. If Eric had sliced the deer meat to make jerky, as he had told Jerry Crisp, this is likely where he would have done it. That Eric had killed at least one deer was obvious, not just because of what he told folks back at the jail. There was a rack of antlers, belonging to what was probably a hefty buck, that had been turned upside down and used along with some rope as a way of lashing together a couple of branches. Again, this would have probably been a place he could have used to hang things, including a tarp when necessary.

There were other indications this was a camp where some hunting had been done. There were small turkey bones scattered near the rocks, which he could have ground up and put in his food as a source of calcium. There were turkey beards, which are the matted beards that you see growing on male (and a few female) wild turkeys. Eric had saved a few of those, which is something that hunters tend to do as a sort of trophy. Most importantly, hanging up in the trees, in one of those cans, was an FLAN .223 rifle and plenty of empty magazines. This was a semiautomatic rifle, with a padded and well-worn olive-green shoulder strap. Not your ideal hunting gun, but it would certainly do the trick since it had enough firepower to stop just about any animal with two or four legs.

There were other things in the barrels hanging from the trees, including topographical maps and a toothbrush.

But what was in the trees and on the ground was only part of what the evidence team found. As they walked around, still mindful of traps, they began to realize there was something underfoot. Here's where it got to be part evidence collection and part archaeology. In at least two places, under a coating of flat rocks and matted leaves, there was more of the welded wire that had been at the other campsite. It was like a grid, hidden by the leaves and dirt that were layered under the rock. So they moved the rocks, pushed away the leaves, and rolled the wire up. Underneath that was even more dirt and leaves. They kept digging.

Pretty soon, they hit plastic and realized there were curbies buried in the ground. When they pulled back the lid on one, there were big wooden sticks that were on top of some sheeting. Underneath that were more flat rocks, some plastic, and newspaper (including some coverage of a graduating class from Murphy High School). Once they pulled away that layer, there were black garbage bags. Inside them were grain, soybeans, and kernels of corn. Eric's version of a silo, just underground. There were enough layers to keep it hidden from the view of both casual hikers who might stumble upon his campsite and also from bears and other varmints, which would have a hard time picking up the scent of food so carefully wrapped and find it just wasn't worth the effort of digging through welded and barbed wire.

There were other finds. Eric had buried trash, which is something you have to do as well to keep the bears away unless you are planning on hauling it off somewhere. Collectible caps that had been handed out by Taco Bell to mark the release of the Star Wars movie, *Attack of the Clones*, were found at the site. Those would have been dated from around May of 2002, indicating that Eric must have been over to Murphy, which was no easy hike, and back sometime between then and a year later (he had claimed he spent the winter at this campsite, but he wasn't exactly clear just how many winters he meant). There was also a big bag of marijuana, hardly surprising given Eric's past. This wasn't processed and cleaned, as it would be for sale on the street. This was old, a collection of dried leaves, stems, and buds, although presumably of the quality that Eric had aspired to cultivate. Clearly this had been homegrown, at a time now uncertain, on hand for recreational purposes, and a reminder that the woods had been his home for a long, long time.

There was one other setup that the searchers found, at a creek bed near one of the campsites. Rudolph had buried some food in a container into the mud and silt. Cooled by the nearby running water, it was in the words of one investigator a natural sort of refrigerator. There was yet another indication that Eric had a weakness for Taco Bell; there were crumpled-up wrappers from the store in the container. Maybe, you think, he was angling for some sort of endorsement deal since this was, after all, the fast-food chain which made a Chihuahua dressed up like Che Guevara famous. *Mi llama Eric Rudolph. Yo quiero Taco Bell!*

How did these archaeological and forensic clues all add up? Was this proof positive that Eric had been out in the woods for all this time, one long camping trip, or did it suggest by the absence of so much else that there were other places, other options? And how in the hell could anyone have missed these dangling curbies? Which of course raised another question: How long had they been there?

It was easy enough to say that the other camp, the one overlooking Murphy, had only been there for a short time. It was there obviously during the spring of 2003, a time when no one was out looking for Eric Rudolph anymore. No one really had been for the better part of three years, maybe four, if truth be told. You could, if you wanted to, hike a route from the recent camp back to Fires Creek. It would take about ten miles and a strong pair of legs. Some of it, if you looked on a topographical map, was on a marked trail called the Fires Creek Rim Trail, which was what former Sheriff Thompson had been talking about. Some of it would require a more intimate sense of these woods and a fair amount of experience at bushwhacking. You could get there from here, or rather you could get there—to the summer camp—from the other there, being Fires Creek.

So you're back at Fires Creek, and that raises the question of just how long Eric had been there. The Taco Bell collectible caps, if they are Eric's, mean that at some point, most likely during the spring or summer of 2002, unless he picked them up from someone who dumped them along the trail, Eric had been back over by Murphy. And that maybe he migrated to Fires Creek for the winter, at least the winter of 2003. He certainly wouldn't have said, I feel like a taco, I'm going to hike over to Taco Bell for lunch. So, did he have another summer camp in 2002 that might have been somewhere near the one he used right before he was caught?

With so many questions being begged, here is another one that is pretty big: Just how did searchers miss the Fires Creek campsite in the first place, especially with those dangling curbies? Woody Enderson told a reporter that he remembered being flown over the area back when he was running the Task Force in 1998 and that someone pointed out Fires Creek. But he couldn't see anything from the air.[10] Even during the winter, when the hardwoods are barren, the mountain laurel still makes it difficult to see, either from the air or when you are hiking. The Task Force did send folks through Fires Creek during that first year, but that is when Eric said he was still constantly on the run.

Even if they came through, with so many acres, it isn't clear if they ever got near this particular ridge, nor is it clear anything there would have captured their attention. There is no way of knowing if the dangling curbies had been up there back then or even whether any other hikers had ever walked by. Even if they did, would they have made the connection to Eric Rudolph? They might see a site that had a couple of stone terraces, but even that wouldn't necessarily cause them to think Eric Rudolph, especially if it didn't look otherwise like anyone had been staying there. Another thing to consider was this was a bear sanctuary, which is one way of discouraging folks from spending too much time there, particularly when it isn't cold enough for the bears to be hibernating.

So there are a lot of reasons why this campsite would never have been spotted or, more importantly, why no one would have made the connection with Rudolph. How long he had lived at the campsite was another question that couldn't easily be answered either. There wasn't anything to indicate that he had been there recently, except common sense suggesting that he would only have left his rifle there if he knew he was headed to a place where it was possible to live without having to hunt for food (except possibly from Dumpsters). But ask the question another way: How did he get food up to this campsite, and what was he using it for? Those curbies could have been up there from the mid-1980s, when Andrews started using them. And remember that one of the first things that Joel Rudolph told investigators right after Eric went missing was that Eric had talked about burying food out in the woods as far back as the '80s. It had also been talked about that this might have been one of those survivalist techniques that Nord Davis was suggesting—having your caches of food stored out in the woods.

Getting the curbies up there before he went on the run might have made sense from another standpoint. More than one memo about Eric and his personality put out by the Task Force harped on the belief that he was lazy. In fact, the only mention of him exerting himself was in one of the interviews where someone told how he hiked jugs of water out to his marijuana plants. This seemed to stand out as something exceptional. Which made more than one investigator wonder how and when these curbies made their way up the side of that steep hill. Fear certainly is a great motivator, but if you think someone is looking for you, do you push these carts up the side of a hill?

Some law enforcement officials suggested an alternate scenario. That either back before he went on the run, or even afterward, if he had access to a vehicle, that Eric drove those curbies up to the end of the old logging road, just as close as you could get to that campsite, then pushed them up empty. Even that would take a full day of straining at least to go back and forth that last half mile up that steep incline. Add in the marijuana, and it made you wonder whether Eric had set this camp up years before he disappeared into the woods. It went back to that whole notion Charles Stone and others had that this was a man who spent a long time preparing, who for some reason thought there might come a time when he would go on the run.

Then you had the notion, which Eric was putting about to the folks at the jail, that he was sneaking down to the small cluster of silos near the airport with a backpack and taking out shelled corn or soybeans a pack-load at a time—and that he had almost been discovered in the process. Your first obstacle would be getting into the silo. It was easy enough to sneak up to them and not be seen, but physically trying to get the food out of the silos would not have been easy (Sheriff Lovin suggested that Rudolph might have been stealing shelled corn out of some other bins that the family who raised corn near the airport kept out separately because it would simply have been much easier than dealing with the silos). Then you had the long, long walk back. Unless of course this wasn't the only campsite he had where he was storing food and supplies. It is worth noting that the reason Charles Stone and the Task Force first brought up Duke Blackburn and the team from the Georgia Department of Corrections back in April 1998 was because a woman had seen a young man out trying to cross the road, which in retrospect was quite near where both the cornfields and the silo were.

There was no doubt that there were packed-up garbage bags full of corn and soybeans at the campsites, buried in the curbies. So Eric got them there somehow. And there were newspapers, used as layers, which also indicated he had been at this while he was on the run, even if he might have set up his caches there and at other sites at any time. But what was he using the corn for? He could have soaked it and boiled it, making some sort of mash, but that took time. Or he could have tried to mill it, grinding it into meal with a stone, making something more edible and nutritious, although the evidence team never found any evidence of milling (though he could have cleaned up after himself when he moved away from the winter camp). In a pinch, Eric could have eaten the kernels and soybeans raw, if he was down to worrying about subsistence. But if you put raw corn into your body, raw corn is going to come out of your body. It isn't the most easily digestible food, to put it mildly. The hunters and woodsmen among those who've pondered what was at the Fires Creek campsite think the corn and other buried food were there in part at least as bait, especially to attract wild turkeys. The turkey bones and beards certainly showed that Eric had some success on that score, as did the rack from the buck.

As built out in its own way as the Fires Creek campsite was, there wasn't a person connected with the case who believed that this was Eric's only place of residence. They simply couldn't buy the notion that just because he had a towel and a toothbrush there, along with a bag of pot, that this was home. For Charles Stone and others, there were too many things missing. Where were any explosives? Where was the generator? For that matter, where was the honey? The honey, that five-gallon jar he got from George Nordmann, was one of those enduring mysteries. It weighed more than sixty pounds. Where did Eric take it, especially if he was too lazy in the minds of many to go very far with it, and whatever happened to the bucket?

There were so many loose ends, even when you took what Eric said during the weekend in the Murphy jail and what investigators found at the campsites right after Rudolph's arrest (they did go back, one more time, in March 2004, to make another sweep of the area, walk the trail from the Fires Creek site to the summer camp, just to be sure they hadn't overlooked anything; but they didn't turn up anything of significance). In fact, there seemed to be as many new questions raised as there were answers found. The great white whale in all this would have been the evidence they were hoping to find, particularly explosives or a bomb factory, linking Rudolph in a much more direct way to the Atlanta and Birmingham bombings. But they didn't find that nor did they find enough evidence at these two campsites to convince them that Eric had lived just in those places for his sixty months on the run, even though searchers returned to the campsites and the surrounding area months later for a second look.

So it got back to the questions they were still chewing over around town in Murphy months after Eric's capture. What was Eric up to all that time, and who might have helped him, wittingly or not? After months of investigating, Chris Swecker of the FBI said there wasn't enough evidence to prosecute anybody for either aiding or abetting or for harboring a fugitive. Not that nobody had helped him, just that they couldn't prove it. Swecker had heard the rumors, along with everyone else.[11] His folks were still investigating, but hard proof was in short supply.

Ironically, the one person who actually said she expected to be arrested and indicted for helping Rudolph turned out to be the one person that investigators discounted. Brenda Kay Phillips had raised some eyebrows back in February, before Eric was ever found, when she first made her claims about helping him. She'd been a nurse, living in Murphy since 2001, when she quit her job at a local hospital, then took a shotgun and tried shooting up an abortion clinic in Asheville (no one was hurt). After being arrested, she made statements about aiding Rudolph. Once he was arrested, Phillips told a newspaper reporter from the *Atlanta Journal-Constitution* she expected to be indicted.[12] Her story didn't add up—she said she hadn't known Rudolph before moving from Indiana—and investigators blew her off.

But the rumors were out there, and months after Eric's capture, they were as strong as ever. You asked local law enforcement folks, and they would tell you they thought George Nordmann was one of those helping Eric. Maybe it meant turning a blind eye when he came calling, or letting him stay in his basement. That Eric had been coming and going from there for a lot longer before the bombings than George admitted. The problem with that being that Nordmann had passed a lie detector test when he said he hadn't been helping Rudolph. And that after he did call Kenny Cope, the Task Force had put cameras in and around his house, just in case Eric did get it in his head to return. Still, more than five years on, there were a lot of folks who still thought George Nordmann figured in there much more than he ever allowed. They just couldn't prove it.

He wasn't the only one under suspicion. The most persistent rumor went this way. There were two other men, folks living back up in the hills. They let Eric have run of their trailer. One of the men killed himself, the other later died. While both were alive, Eric had a place to come and go, clean up and get food. All this talk of acorns and salamanders was just talk. Or maybe not, maybe it took him a while to hook up with these guys. Why, if you believed one part of the rumor, then Eric actually showed up at the funeral of one of these men. Although one member of the Task Force, who certainly gave great credence to the theory, said he was sure that Rudolph never went to the funeral, hinting broadly that it had been staked out. Another variation on this theme had a third man involved, who left town right around the time that Eric was captured. The point was, according to the rumor, that Eric had his supporters, but at some point he was forced back into the wild when the two men died.

Nobody could ever prove any of it. That was frustrating and maddening, especially to the local guys, who on a daily basis dealt with the guns and drugs and militia guys out there. They were still bitter and thought the FBI had been on the wrong track the whole time. The insults came easily. That the FBI couldn't catch a cold if they tried. That you can't find what you ain't looking for. Eric had his friendlies, they were sure of that. If you believed the suspicion of local investigators, some of those friendlies knew Eric and knew exactly what they were doing when they might have left food out or a back door open. Others might have had their suspicions. There were yet others who probably never knew that the stranger coming to their door was Eric Rudolph.

After all, who would have recognized him? The Eric Rudolph from that mug shot—the one with close-cropped hair who was forty pounds lighter than on his wanted poster—could have put on that Taco Bell uniform and become invisible. Or, as one federal investigator put it bluntly, you drop forty pounds, get a buzz cut (and how exactly did he do that?), pull a cap over your head, and wear shades to hide those intense blue eyes, and for all anyone knows, Rudolph could have been shopping at the Murphy Wal-Mart anytime he wanted to, especially in more recent years.

The hardest man to catch, admitted Sheriff Lovin, was the one hiding in plain sight. Maybe the one walking through the parking lot of the Save-A-Lot. Murphy and Andrews were big enough so that you might not recognize everybody, but you also might get used to seeing a face and just letting it walk by. There might have been some women who helped the handsome young man, some of the investigators thought, never knowing exactly who the blue-eyed stranger was. Which harkened back to what the ATF's Jim Cavanaugh thought, that Eric was a lot more public than they might have expected, hiding in plain sight. Charles Stone could buy the idea that Rudolph had help. He just thought it was of the unwitting variety. He stuck to the notion that what happened during the Nordmann incident had taught Eric a lesson: trust no one. Rely on yourself. Look for targets of opportunity. Pass the winters by breaking into cabins, staying there as long as you could, covering as many traces when you left. Take what you need and leave the rest, as the song went. There were certainly cabin break-ins every time of the year, and it was impossible to explain all of them.

But there was another man who reckoned that one important fact was overlooked in all the commotion since Rudolph's capture. None of this, former Sheriff Jack Thompson thought, need have ever happened—not the five-plus years of the fugitive hunt; not the need to investigate the campsites and try to figure out after the fact how Rudolph lived on the run; nor looking at who might have helped him. He didn't want to talk too much about this before the trial because he didn't want to distract from the case, but he'd been doing a lot of thinking over the years, and he kept coming back to the afternoon of January 30, 1998. He and his folks had located Eric Rudolph's trailer, and they were ready to go pick him up. But the FBI never told him that Rudolph was anything more than a material witness. Instead, they told him to wait. After Rudolph had been named publicly by the U.S. attorney in Birmingham and after Rudolph went for his last meal at Burger King and his shopping expedition at the BI-LO grocery store, that's when the FBI finally showed up at Eric's trailer. By then Eric Rudolph had disappeared. If they hadn't screwed that up then, he thought, then nothing that followed need ever have happened.

As for the only man who knew the full story, he was sitting in the Birmingham jail, and he sure wasn't talking. Eric Rudolph said what he'd said that weekend in Murphy, and the only real talking he'd be doing from this point on was to his lawyers.

EPILOGUE

THE JAILER WANTED his orange jumpsuit back. Not because Cherokee County couldn't afford for one to go missing (though they certainly didn't want to let every prisoner walk out the door with one), but this one belonged to inmate 7445. Eric Robert Rudolph. Currently resident of the Jefferson County Jail in Birmingham, Alabama. Last seen wearing said jumpsuit on national television as he made his escorted trek from Murphy to Asheville to Birmingham. There were plans, big plans, to build a new jail up in Cherokee County, take in prisoners from neighboring jurisdictions, maybe boost the local economy, which had been in a bit of a funk lately. There'd been a taste of a law-enforcement based economy during the manhunt, and it got some of the folks thinking about how to make the area recession proof. Now, if only the jailer could get that jumpsuit back, it would make a nice display for the new jail.

Prisoner 7445 got a new inmate number when he went to Birmingham. Even though he was technically in the federal system, he was still being housed in a county jail. It was closer to his lawyers than the federal prison over in Talladega, and Rudolph could live in not-so-splendid isolation—which tended to be called solitary in jail terms—while awaiting his first trial. The Jefferson County sheriff visited his new prisoner shortly after Eric arrived and pronounced him frustrated. Rudolph didn't appear to know what was happening to him, said Sheriff Mike Hale, and although he was polite, the sheriff sensed the frustration.[1] The sheriff explained the house rules, told Eric that his issues were with the court, not the jail, and what would be expected of him so long as he was an inmate at the Jefferson County Jail. Which could be quite a while, as Rudolph awaited his first of two federal trials.

Eric's new world, barring the occasional trip to court, was reduced to 180 square feet. A cell area, normally intended for five prisoners, and what was called a day space, a sitting area with a table. A toilet and shower. The sheriff decided the safest course was to keep his most prominent prisoner, a dubious accolade whether you were in Murphy or Birmingham, separate from the rest of the jail population. It wouldn't do to have him knifed or beaten by one of the other inmates, particularly since he hadn't even stood trial.[2] And his attorneys had less to worry about with Rudolph in isolation, since a favorite jailhouse tactic by prosecutors the world over was to get another prisoner to cozy up to the inmate and hope he spilled his guts.

It wasn't a campsite or a cave or a mine or a cabin or a trailer or someone's root cellar or wherever the hell Eric had been. And there were no woods to roam in. Then again, there was no need to scrounge around in Dumpsters either. Eric was getting three squares a day, the trays delivered by the staff, but he wasn't putting the pounds back on (although Eric must have eaten well that first weekend in Murphy, since by the time he weighed in at his new home in Birmingham, he was up to 150 pounds). He got a complete physical when he arrived at the jail and was pronounced fit, in surprisingly good shape for a man who had supposedly been out in the wild for the last five and a half years.[3] There were no outside privileges for Eric, no trips to a protected courtyard, so for exercise he walked the twelve-by-fifteen-foot space or did sit-ups and push-ups. Surprisingly, by all accounts, he wasn't adding on many more pounds either, in spite of the carb-heavy jail meals.

The day space was also where Rudolph would meet with his lawyers. Or watch TV, if he wanted. Basic cable, the same as the rest of the inmates, provided by Charter Communications. There was also a pay phone for collect calls.[4] He could write and get letters, and he was getting a few. Anything that wasn't to or from his lawyers would be monitored, of course, same as it was for any inmate. A mundane and solitary existence, one deputy called it. Up at 6 A.M., lights out at 10 P.M. Just Eric and occasionally his attorneys, except for the single visit from his mother, Patricia, and his brothers Daniel and Joel. There was a surveillance camera, an unblinking eye, to make sure everything was on the up and up.

Eric was allowed a copy of the Bible and took advantage of that privilege. Visitors were not allowed to bring copies of books, although he could have a couple. He asked for Oswald Spengler's *Decline of the West*, one of his favorites and one of the many books that had made up his personal library in North Carolina. So there he sat and read and walked and thought and met with his attorneys. It is doubtful that he would ever be given a copy of the book he recommended to others, *Imperium*. Filled as it was with racism and hate, it wouldn't have made it on the approved list at the jail. But did Eric ponder that its author, Francis Yockey, killed himself while in the San Francisco jail? Perhaps, but Eric Rudolph showed every intent of fighting.

Rudolph had a first-class legal team. Because this was such a high-profile case and because Birmingham didn't have its own federal public defender, Eric was going to get the best defense the taxpayers of the United States could buy. By the time it was all over, the costs were going to run in the millions. Just putting the evidence together and onto CD-ROM was running well over a million dollars. There were expert witnesses, investigators, and all sorts of other expenses for the defense—and that was just in Birmingham. Paying the legal team of Jaffe, Bowen, and Clarke (she at least was already on the Federal payroll), was also going to cost millions. Jaffe left the case in the summer of 2004 and Clarke took over as lead attorney.

And that was just for Birmingham. Whatever the verdict there, whenever the trial was over, there would be another one in Atlanta. That was the plan, even if Rudolph was sentenced to death. This, too, would also be a death penalty case, whether Alice Hawthorne's husband was committed to such an outcome or not. Justice would be served, no matter what the cost. After spending more than thirty million dollars on the hunt for Eric Rudolph, this might be considered small change. Emily Lyons, who had recently had her nineteenth operation (that didn't include countless minor procedures), this time to fuse the bones in one of her fingers, would be there, wherever the Birmingham trial was held. So would Felecia Sanderson. Both were sure to testify. Even though Emily retained no memory of what happened that morning, she could eloquently testify to the effects of the bombing. By the time she took the stand, perhaps she would have been through yet another procedure, as the bomb continued to wreak its daily havoc on her body.

The government's case would be clear enough. That sometime on the morning of January 29, 1998, Eric Rudolph planted and detonated the bomb outside the New Woman, All Women Health Care Clinic in Birmingham. That as he was leaving the scene, he was spotted by a witness who followed him. That the witness, while attempting to call 911 after having lost the suspect, spotted him again. That the witness and a second man spotted Rudolph as he was leaving Birmingham in his gray Nissan truck. That elements of the materials found in Rudolph's trailer, storage unit, and truck appeared to match elements of the bombs (the defense challenged the legality of those searches).

The Atlanta case—that he planted the bombs at Centennial Park, the Northside Family Planning Clinic, and the Otherside Lounge—would be much more driven by forensic evidence. Cut nails, plastic containers, smokeless powder, the pole sander. All these were to be introduced in evidence. There might be eyewitness accounts, in the form of the Speedo boys at Centennial Park and the man outside the Sandy Springs clinic, but this was a case built on painstaking layers of forensics and probabilities. How likely was it that anyone else other than Eric Robert Rudolph had a pack like the one used, had the training he did, had the same sort of cut nails, access to the same smokeless powder, had a pole sander head whose handle was missing but part of which matched the handle of the pack used to hold the bomb AND had access to all the other components, elements of which appeared to be in his possession back in North Carolina. That would be the prosecution's argument.

And of course there was the other issue. If he didn't do it, why did he run? That admittedly for his attorneys was perhaps the hardest question to answer. How do you quantify paranoia? If you admit that he feared the government and held extremist views, and throw in the example of what happened to Richard Jewell when he was falsely accused, how do you still get around five and a half years on the run? And once you start admitting of such intense paranoia, then does that lead you down the slippery slope to where a juror or a prosecutor is going to say, well if he's that paranoid, then why wouldn't or couldn't he have been the bomber?

The defense—at least in Birmingham—had the chance to do what defenses often do, sometimes quite rightly so. Ladies and gentlemen of the jury, someone else did it. Not our client. And they would poke holes in the prosecution case. Take the jury on the same improbable path that the chief eyewitness took, from Rast Park to the McDonald's and beyond. Point out the man never actually saw Rudolph near the clinic or detonating any sort of device, just that he saw a man walking away from the area. Point out that every time the witness tried to find the man, from the time he ran out of the dorm and got in his car, to the time the man disappeared down the alley behind the apartment only to reappear, and the time he saw him many minutes later across the street from McDonald's AND later when he saw him again in the truck, that there were differences in description—either in the hat or the hair or the shirt. How did he spot him driving down the street, when Rudolph was supposedly in the truck driving the other way? How did he make a U-turn, pull up beside him, and then lose him again? How did he come up with the license plate number? That same improbable journey, from the dorm room to the McDonald's and beyond, would look considerably different once a defense attorney worth his or her salt got through with the witness.

But you can't just poke holes in the prosecution case, despite all those shows on TV from Perry Mason on. You need other candidates who could fit the same suit the government was tailoring for your client. You can't just say, it wasn't me, Your Honor! You have to come up with at least one good alternative. Hence the Army of God letters and the Army of God. You actually didn't need to show a real army, but you could point to the manual, which clearly wasn't written by Eric Rudolph and the number of abortion clinic bombings solved and unsolved around the country and raise this issue of, if not an army, a network of confederates all committed to the cause.

Lord knows, there were characters even in Birmingham who the defense could throw in for good measure. There was Jeff Dykes, a local antiabortion activist. He lived only a couple of blocks from the clinic. Early on in the investigation, he came into the frame, which was only natural, given his proximity and his rhetoric. He was one of the earliest people on the scene, and he was quoted the next day in the *Birmingham News* as saying, "I don't like to see anybody die, but they're in a business of death. You live by the sword, you die by the sword. We've told them that they're in a grisly business—the flesh trade. You never know what's going to happen to you." While he regretted the death of Officer Sanderson, "There are 200 to 300 people killed a week in those clinics. That's a much more tragic loss of life."[5] There were all sorts of rumors about Dykes—and about David Lackey, the local leader of the antiabortion group Operation Rescue, who had, unlike Dykes, condemned the bombing. But Dykes agreed to let his apartment be searched, and the ATF could find no forensic links to Rudolph, and despite the lack of evidence, the rumors would persist among the more conspiratorially minded that somehow he was involved. For a defense attorney, that might be as good as it got, although Tim McVeigh's defense, for example, never got far on the "some other dude did it" track.

Then there was the whole issue of Atlanta and Birmingham. The cases weren't being tried together, deliberately so, even though for example all the Unabomber cases were brought under the same prosecution. Which side, if either, wanted to bring Atlanta into Birmingham, even though he was charged in both cases? If the prosecution didn't tie the cases together, then it made it harder for the defense to bring in Atlanta. You couldn't exactly show that someone else might have done one of the Atlanta bombs when the prosecution in Birmingham never brought it up in the first place. But Atlanta was there, looming, in the event that Rudolph's defense team got an acquittal. And if they somehow walked away with just a life sentence in the Birmingham trial, then the state of Alabama would look long and hard at how it might try Rudolph on murder charges and go for the death penalty, if it could figure a way around the double jeopardy issue.

It is a sign of how you have to prepare for a death penalty case that even as Rudolph's attorneys were getting his defense ready, they were also planning for what is called the penalty phase of a death penalty trial. That is to say, if he was found guilty, there would be a whole separate hearing on whether he should live or die. As his lawyers put in one of their motions, there really were only three outcomes to this case: acquittal, life in prison, or death by lethal injection. Barring an acquittal, you had to be ready for the next step in the trial. Here, the defense could try to prove mitigating circumstances if it got that far. The family upbringing. Lay it off on the mother and the father figures. Again, shift responsibility. The defendant can testify in the penalty phase, just as he can during the regular part of the trial. There's only one catch: if you're facing another trial, then anything you say, whether it is in the regular part of the trial or the penalty phase, can and will be used against you in a court of law, which means don't count on getting an explanation at least until the end of the Atlanta trial.

So will the why of it ever get answered? Can any big what-it-all-means conclusions get drawn from the Eric Rudolph story? Patricia Rudolph had her explanation, which appeared during an interview with *Rolling Stone*. It can't necessarily be considered Eric's view, but it gives some sense of the world according to the Rudolphs and the infinite capacity for rationalization:

> Pose this question to yourself [said Patricia]. Why is the government spending money out the yin-yang on one man, who supposedly killed one man and a nurse, for God's sake? Does the government think we're all that dumb? I mean you don't have to be a quote Christian Patriot or a militia mobster or whatever the hell they call them to know something's going on with this government. That's what the whole invasion of the western Carolina mountains is all about. My son's just an excuse. They want to see what these mountain people are up to. And believe me, there's people out there

who know what the government's up to to. And they are fed up. I hope they kick ass, because I don't know what else can be done.[6]

What can be done? A title, ironically, of one of Lenin's more famous essays. Patricia made it clear in the same interview that she thought her son was innocent, used the same line that Daniel had used with Charles Stone so many years before. That if any of her sons was likely to have been a bomber, it would have been Daniel, not Eric. Still, she said something else that could only leave you wondering: "Eric knew the mess this country's in, the same as I do, and anybody else's awake. Most people aren't."[7]

It is clear that Patricia Rudolph retained the core of her antigovernment beliefs. She described herself as a pacifist and anarchist. And it is clear that she had a profound influence on her son and she realized that others would see her as the person who might have set her son—who again she believed was innocent—on his path.[8] Whether she had moved on from Christian Identity isn't clear. But from his jailhouse conversations with Jerry Crisp and others, it is clear that Eric remained resolute in his beliefs—that the Bible said white men were to lead, that others were to follow. That abortion and homosexuality were wrong (he didn't spell the out the reasons why in jail, but he had certainly made it clear earlier how these beliefs came from Christian Identity and not the right-to-life movement, especially that abortion was a plot to destroy the white race).

The paradox remained. How could a man who by his entire family's account loved his gay brother, allegedly plant bombs at a gay nightclub? His family certainly didn't hear what he said that weekend in the Murphy jail about gays, which made it quite clear what he believed after five and a half years on the run. But put that aside for a moment and add a second paradox: how could a man who believed that Jews were mud people, that they were Satan's seed and all that was evil in the world, how could a man who believed that have a Jewish lawyer defending him (at least until Jaffe quit the case)? Was it a clever trick in his mind, using evil to fight evil? Or was it simply this: Could he love the sinner but hate the sin? That he could hold impersonal hatreds, but not personal ones? Until Jaffe, had he ever even known any Jews personally?

There is another reason to ask this question. If Eric Rudolph was the bomber, what sort of bomber was he? Was he a terrorist/patriot? Was he a serial bomber? Was he a serial killer who used bombs (two out of the four bombings killed, and the others weren't for a lack of trying)? If it was him, and he was a serial bomber or a serial killer who used bombs, then again ask why. There are two commonly held reasons for bombers who kill (and not all do): one is that they want to kill a lot of people. It is easier to do that with bombs, especially if you are planning on doing it more than once. Spraying a crowd of people with a gun would make you a mass murderer, but not a serial killer. The other reason, which comes back to the paradox of how a man with a gay brother and a Jewish lawyer can hate gays and Jews as groups, holds that bombers use their devices because they are an impersonal method of killing. You don't view your target in your sights, then squeeze the trigger. You don't look the person in the eye. Plant, leave, boom. You have the distance, emotionally and physically, to kill. Where this theory runs into a bit of trouble is that at the Birmingham clinic, whoever was behind that tree made a conscious choice to detonate the bomb at that particular point, knowing it would kill a particular person, perhaps two. But no theory is perfect.

Could Eric have done it? Back when he showed up at George Nordmann's, he told George that he was being framed. But even Nordmann says Eric certainly had the skills to do it.[9] If he did it—and his mother remained adamant that it couldn't be him—Patricia Rudolph had an idea where he might have learned those skills because she had certainly been a pacifist all her life. She told *USA Today*, "I don't think the Army is the best place to go. Why he went, I have no idea, but when you go there, you learn how to kill. That's their job. I don't think that was a good choice of his."[10] The most interesting take comes from one of his brothers. When asked to listen to the 911 tape from Centennial Park as many close to Eric had been, he said, sure that's him but that doesn't prove anything!

Could he have done it is still a different question than why Eric might have done it. It isn't enough to say he was steeped in Christian Identity beliefs, since even such a fervent apostle of CI as Dan Gayman believed that violence was the wrong course of action. Then there is the question of why Eric and not Daniel, or even Jamie or Joel, all of whom were exposed to the same beliefs—although Eric was the only one to join the army. Kerry Noble, who was "converted" to CI and became one of the leaders of the CI-based group, the Covenant, the Sword and the Arm of the Lord (CSA) has some ideas. Remember that Noble went to prison on illegal weapons charges, after the federal government, its archenemy, cracked down on CSA. Now Noble, who rejects CI, studies and monitors the movement he once embraced. You get to a certain point where you've heard the rhetoric long enough, you don't see anything changing, and because of your zeal you cross the point to where you have to do something, he says. If you back off, you would betray God. Your options are limited. You are taught for so long in the movement, you start out with God's timetable, that you can end up waiting for God to do something. Noble says the teaching is really: "Why should we be waiting on God, when God is waiting on us?" So then you say, "OK, maybe God's waiting on me to act. Now, I feel the burden of this." If that's what Eric was going through, says Kerry Noble, that could set him off.[11]

Kerry Noble has an interesting idea on how homosexuality figures into this. That seeming contradiction between Eric's alleged actions and his relationship with his own brother. "In Christian Identity," says Noble, "you are taught the Jews push the idea of homosexuality. You don't see Jewish queers. We were programmed with this thing that the Jews were doing to get rid of the white race and that they were doing it through homosexuality and abortion." So what might happen if Eric found out his own brother was gay, or knew it in his heart but was also brought face-to-face with it when he visited him in New York? "Typically," says Kerry Noble, "the normal interpretation is that if God is taking care of you, then judgment is coming, and it will be favorable. But if something like homosexuality comes to a member of your family, it is an obvious sign. Eric could interpret it that God is displeased with him and that he has to act."[12]

There are other questions to be asked, even if the why of it may never be answered. Two are particularly relevant in a post-9/11 America. What makes someone like Eric Rudolph, whether he did the bombings or not, different than a member of al Qaeda? And is the domestic terrorism that Eric Rudolph or Tim McVeigh are supposed to represent really a thing of the past, or will there be a time in the future when the enemy once again becomes us? There may be a third question, growing out of the other two: Can you ever stop a lone wolf if he (or she) is determined to carry out an act of terrorism?

It was charged, primarily in the Moslem world, right after 9/11, that America had no room automatically to condemn the attacks on the World Trade Center and Pentagon as religious violence, particularly as Islamic fundamentalism, when America had its own terrorists like McVeigh and Rudolph (it was usually just McVeigh, since he had been so striking in his body count at Oklahoma City). Now, that argument was usually aimed at saying it wasn't al Qaeda followers who were responsible for 9/11, an attitude that persists in some segments of the Islamic world even to this day, even in the face of overwhelming evidence and particularly since bin Laden and others involved in the planning have directly and indirectly claimed responsibility. But let's say you wipe away all the nonsense associated with that argument—that al Qaeda didn't do 9/11—and come at the question again; then you frame it in a much more relevant way. Is there any difference between a Mohammed Atta, who piloted one of the planes that flew into the World Trade Center, and an Eric Rudolph or Tim McVeigh?

Yes, you start to answer, of course. Atta knew he was going to die for his cause; he was part of an organized plot, one of the leaders of it; he had been to Afghanistan, trained in the camps run by al Qaeda; had fully embraced his cause. He viewed the Jews and Crusaders (Americans) as the root of all evil. He was on a jihad, a holy war. How could you even begin to compare him to McVeigh or Rudolph? First of all, they were lone wolves—or in the case of McVeigh, part of a very small cell. Tim McVeigh didn't stay in the truck that was parked at the Murrah Federal Office Building in Oklahoma City. Eric Rudolph, it if was him, didn't strap the backpack to his chest and detonate it in the middle of the crowd at Centennial Park. Christian Identity would surely classify all of the Islamic nation as mud people, alongside Jews and blacks. So how could there be any similarity, any commonality?

You could probably start with McVeigh on a gurney at the federal prison in Terre Haute, Indiana, as the needle was being slipped into his arm and he was being given a lethal injection. It is the same fate that could await Eric Rudolph as well, should he be found guilty on one or all of the charges against him in Birmingham and Atlanta. The consequences of their actions, whether they were caught almost immediately, like McVeigh, or after a long time in hiding, like Rudolph, would surely, inevitably lead them to the likelihood of dying for the cause and their own version of God, even if they weren't chanting *Allahu akbar*, God is great, as they crashed a plane into a building. Arguably, Eric Rudolph had far more exposure to his fundamentalist world than a Mohammed Atta, as his mother took him from Florida to North Carolina to Missouri and back. He was already converted to the worldview.

Actually, if there is someone who can see the comparison, it is Kerry Noble, who lived at the CSA compound in Missouri and was ready to take up arms against the government. Who trained with the weapons. Who sees how the ideology of both causes, Christian Identity and Islamic fundamentalism, share elements in common. The first part is easy enough to spot, since it is unfortunately what so many belief systems share—that the Jews are the root of all evil. The Jews and Crusaders is usually the phrase that Osama bin Laden uses, and he sees the war in Iraq as one example of America doing Israel's bidding.

Which of course is the same argument you get from the extremist Right in America (and sometimes others on the Left and Right), which refers to the government in Washington as ZOG, the Zionist Occupation Government. Hard to miss it. Hate the Jews. Kerry Noble likes to point out the phrase—the enemy of my enemy is my friend—has as much resonance in extremist America as it does in the Islamic world. And should you really want to indulge in conspiranoia, which is a favorite pastime of both movements, consider the case of Ahmed Huber. He is a Swiss convert to Islam, an acolyte of the Nazis who found Allah and reveres the Ayatollah Khomeini, who was on the board of a company singled out as a front for laundering money to al Qaeda and who sees it as his life's work to bridge the gap between the extreme Right, particularly neo-Nazis, and Islamists.[13]

On matters of religious doctrine, too, Christian Identity and Islamic fundamentalism share the same tendency to pervert accepted beliefs. Hence, in Islamic fundamentalism, one of the pillars of Islam becomes a duty to jihad, even though that is not one of the five pillars of the faith laid out by the Koran. In Christian Identity, you have the two-seed theory propagated by Dan Gayman, that there are the true Israelites and Satan's spawn, that there are white Anglo-Saxons and the Bible is their history. This is all inexact. The two perversions of belief share another trait. Both see their followers as defenders of a faith under attack. Osama bin Laden's frequent calls for jihad are always couched as part of claims that the Moslem nation, the *ul'ma*, is being threatened. Just as CI is preaching that ZOG is controlling Washington and the dreaded United Nations is somehow poised to take over America. There is no exact one-to-one correlation where you can say Islamic fundamentalism equals Christian Identity, but there are more than enough similarities to make the comparison disquieting for anyone who labors under the illusion that the beliefs which spawn religious terrorism lay far beyond America's shores.

Which cuts to the heart of the second question: Does Eric Rudolph represent the end of domestic terrorism as we know it? There is little doubt that the extremist Right, which clearly nurtured both McVeigh and Rudolph, is at a historical low point. The reasons are varied: some of the leadership of major groups, including the National Alliance and the Aryan Nations, have passed out of the hands of their founders. William Pierce, the man who wrote the hate-filled *Turner Diaries* and founded the National Alliance, is dead, and his successor simply doesn't have the charisma or the ability to keep the group from fracturing. Even Dan Gayman had a group led by a dissident minister that broke off from his Church of Israel. There is no doubt that the government crackdown in the 1980s against groups like CSA and The Order also worked. And eventually, in the 1990s, after the Waco debacle, the FBI learned how to end a standoff without bloodshed. The Montana Freemen siege ended quietly, thus depriving the movement another cause célèbre.

It seemed in the wake of Oklahoma City that everywhere you turned, there was a citizens' militia, marching and making statements about the direction of the country. But that, too, was in a sense illusory. The bombings at Oklahoma City and the Olympics did not spark further action or inspire others. If that was the aim, it failed miserably. Interestingly, the argument was put about by many on the fringe that Tim McVeigh was really a government stooge or a patsy, who was set up by a federal government intent on using the excuse of Oklahoma City to crack down on the far Right. There were no violent acts of protest to mark McVeigh's death. Few, with the possible exception of Eric Rudolph, viewed him with any sort of sympathy.

The movement foundered for all these reasons. But of course it declined for another: 9/11. There was some initial common cause, the sort that would make a man like Ahmed Huber proud. William Pierce, before his death, pointed the finger of blame at, of course, the Jews and Israel for causing 9/11 to happen.[14] Others, in the initial stages, seemed to parallel both the arguments about McVeigh and the theories in the Arab world, that someone else rather than al Qaeda was responsible. That it was either another plot by the federal government or that the Israeli Mossad must have done it. But for most Americans, even those on the extreme Right, this was too much to take. The enemy of their enemy was not their friend. America was under attack, and the attackers, at least the one in charge, had a recognizable face.

Consider, of all people, George Nordmann—the very man at whose house Eric showed up at all those years ago—as an example. These days he's busy packing up the remnants of his health food store, selling off the last of his stock, ready to retire back to his home in Topton and collect his Social Security but still willing to part with some homeopathic advice. He spends his days listening to the shortwave radio (no Internet for him) for word of the conspiracies that still come through loud and clear on his personal frequency. But the world is a more complicated place. There are the usual plots, the conspiracies that control the government and prevent the real news from ever getting out; the group that controls the Vatican and has made the Church defunct since Vatican Two. And there are the new plots, from the other enemies of America, the ones who live on foreign shores and worship Allah, the ones it seems that so many in government are blind to. But fortunately he listens to the people who know. And they tell him, they warn him about the terrorist threats from abroad.

It is tempting to think because domestic terrorism is at a nadir that it will pass from history altogether. There are days when members of the FBI's Joint Terrorism Task Forces who are assigned to monitor domestic terrorism (it is called DT to distinguish it from IT, international terrorism) have little to do because they can't find cases to make.[15] But history does seem to move in cycles. Just ask Eric Rudolph, and he'll tell you that's what his man Oswald Spengler writes. Those who are ready to forecast an end to history or an end to the cycles of domestic terrorism are akin to those who in the late 1990s were ready to declare an end to business cycles. Go back now and ask them how much money they lost in the stock market when it crashed.

If you don't confuse a movement at its low point with a movement gone forever, does that mean America is due for a vicious comeback anytime soon? Todd Letcher, the last man to head the Southeast Bomb Task Force, who later returned to oversee the evidence as it was prepared for trial, raises an interesting theory. If you look at Tim McVeigh and Eric Rudolph in the context of the Gulf War of 1990-1991 (McVeigh fought in it; Rudolph was already out of the army) and you look at what is happening in the Iraq War and postwar occupation, then maybe a whole new group of people are potential candidates to come home disillusioned. There are certainly easy holes to poke in that theory—that perhaps the economic situation will be different; that you didn't see World War Two veterans or Vietnam vets resorting to domestic terrorism; that America is at a different place than it was in the late 1980s and early 1990s; and most of all, that McVeigh looked at Waco as the event that triggered his rage. Rudolph, according to some of those who knew him, also looked to Waco. Whoever signed the Army of God letters in Birmingham and Atlanta used the date of Waco burning as the secret code. So even if the theory were true, there would still need to be a trigger. As imperfect as Letcher's theory is, it is not discounted by people in the veteran's movement, who do share concerns. Nor does Kerry Noble, who once walked the walk, take the theory lightly, although he, too, holds that there would still need to be a triggering event on the order of Waco.

Even as the agents investigating domestic terrorism look over the landscape and try to figure out where to focus their energies, one thought does haunt them. How do you stop a lone wolf? For that matter, how do you detect him (and so far it has always been a him) in the first place. Lone wolves aren't suicide bombers, at least so far, but they still have a lethal capability. It is important to realize that suicide bombers don't act in a vacuum. They have support cells. They either go off to Afghanistan and become, if they aren't already, willing converts as in the case of the 9/11 hijackers. Or in places like the Middle East, they have minders and trainers and people who supply them with their weaponry and targets. A lone wolf doesn't necessarily show up at any public meetings or even with a cell. Tim McVeigh did have Terry Nichols (and another man Michael Fortier). But what would have marked Eric Rudolph for investigation, even if someone was looking in his direction? It isn't a crime to hate the government or blacks or Jews or gays or abortion. He wasn't talking loudly or publicly about any plans.

It has been a tenet of the far Right to believe in something called leaderless resistance. That was, in fact, the name of an essay written by Louis Beam that first appeared in 1992, after the federal government cracked down on The Order and CSA. The government can't penetrate a command structure that doesn't exist, he argued:

> It is clear, therefore, that it is time to rethink traditional strategy and tactics when it comes to opposing state tyranny, where the rights now accepted by most as being inalienable will disappear. Let the coming night be filled with a thousand points of resistance. Like the fog which forms when conditions are right, and disappears when they are not, so must the resistance to tyranny be.[16]

The lone wolf—or the leaderless resistance—of course has its limits. As devastating as Oklahoma City was and Centennial Park could have been, they were not followed by hundreds of other attacks in sympathy. But a lone wolf can still strike fear. The Washington-area snipers (OK, this was two instead of one) terrorized that city and by extension a good deal of America for a period of weeks. Whoever sent the anthrax letters did the same.

Eric Rudolph's arrest apparently sparked one man into action, a reminder that what can be called domestic terrorism remains a live threat. Stephen John Jordi was arrested in Florida and charged with planning to firebomb gay bars, abortion clinics, and churches. Prosecutors said he was a former Army Ranger who was allegedly planning on using his survival skills to help him hide out from authorities. Jordi was arrested after a sting operation, when he was trying to buy supplies to begin his firebombing campaign from a government informant. Relatives said Jordi became determined to carry out his plans after Rudolph's capture. Jordi ended up pleading guilty to one count of attempted firebombing.[17]

So what does it all mean? Don't count out domestic terrorism, even when it is seemingly at its weakest point. If "You can't find what you ain't looking for" was the sarcastic rejoinder of some local law enforcement to the FBI during the hunt for Eric Rudolph, maybe here it is more appropriate to say you may not even find it if you are looking for it, at least beforehand, when you start talking about lone wolves. The question is whether catching Jordi was the exception or the rule. But circumstances change and five or ten years from now, the war on terrorism may look completely different than it does now, just as it looked different ten years ago.

What about Eric Robert Rudolph, and where does he fit in? Whether he is found guilty or not through all his trials, it is easy to place him into an era when America was at war with itself, an era that has passed but may soon return. An era that changed during the time he was on the run. That's what happens when you disappear for five and a half years. The world changes, you become an artifact, a curiosity. No less dangerous for becoming a T-shirt or, God forbid, something of a folk hero.

At the end of the day, in the hunt for Eric Rudolph, there is still the question of why. If he was the bomber, why did he do it? Whether he was or wasn't, why did he run? There are those other questions, too: How did he live? Who helped him? Did they know who they were helping? If he did it, where is his bomb factory? His real hideout?

When he sat with Eric during the weekend of his capture, Deputy

Jerry Crisp got a few answers, but they only seemed to lead to more questions. He believes that Eric Rudolph may answer those questions eventually, but only at a time of his choosing. Ask him once he's been through all his trials, says Crisp. Ask him when he's been sentenced to death (for Crisp believes Rudolph is guilty). Ask him before the needle goes into his arm. Maybe that's when we'll get answers.

NOTES

Chapter One

[1] Transcript of call released by Atlanta Police Department

[2] Interview with Fallon Stubbs and John Hawthorne, May 2001

[3] Interviews with Robert and Nancy Gee, May 2001; author interview October 2003

[4] *Atlanta Journal-Constitution*, 1993, requoted 9/18/95.

[5] *Atlanta Journal-Constitution*, 9/18/95

[6] *Atlanta Journal-Constitution*, 9/18/95

[7] Kennedy School of Government report. *Security Preparations for RA 1996 Centennial Olympic Games*, Kennedy School of Government Case Program, C16-00-1582, 1998.

[8] The Georgia State Patrol even brought over the head of the Israeli National Police's antiterrorism squad for an entire year to train state and local law enforcement.

[9] Kennedy School of Government report. Author Ben Sherwood, who spent time observing security preparations, used the premise of a small plane crashing into the Olympic Stadium as part of his thriller about the Atlanta Games, *Red Mercury*.

[10] The families of the Israeli athletes were in Atlanta during the Games, making their case for some sort of memorial after the IOC had virtually ignored them for the past 24 years.

[11] The official cause was eventually ruled to be a problem with the center fuel tank on the Boeing 747, but the terrorism angle was investigated exhaustively for months.

[12] Author interview with K. P. S. Gill, Indian field hockey federation, July 1996. Gill was hated by Sikh militants for leading the government crackdown on them. They

charge he was responsible for up to 50,000 killings during the security sweep; he said the number was closer to 500.

[13] CNN.com, "Witness: Pipe bomb defendants talked of bombing Olympics," October 29, 1996; *Washington Post*, November 3, 1996. Defense attorneys contended the informant invented the Olympic link. Robert Starr III, Troy Spain, and Jimmy Mc-Craine were later convicted of conspiring to stockpile pipe bombs and sentenced to prison, but the Olympics charge was never proven in court.

[14] Kennedy School of Government report

[15] Gee videotape, interviews with author

[16] Interview with Tom Davis, May 2001; Richard Jewell FBI interview, October 1996

[17] Interview with Tom Davis, May 2001; author interview with FBI bomb tech Bill Forsyth

[18] Richard Jewell FBI interview, October 1996

[19] Atlanta Police Department recording of the tape, released August 1996

[20] CNN and other news reports; Interview with Tom Davis, May 2001; KSG report.

[21] Interview with John Hawthorne and Fallon Stubbs, May 2001

[22] SE Bomb Task Force time line

[23] Task Force time line. Everyone's watch seemed to be set to a different time. Later, 1:20 a.m. would be the commonly accepted time of the explosion because an Atlanta Police dispatcher logged a reort of the bombing then.

[24] Interviews with Fallon Stubbs, May 2001

[25] Interview with Tom Davis, May 2001

[26] Interview with John Hawthorne and Fallon Stubbs, May 2001

Chapter Two

[1] Surprisingly, all but one was brought back. That one was broadcast by French television, which gave a copy to CNN.

[2] *Atlanta Journal-Constitution* broke the 7/28/96 story, then CNN reporting.

[3] Department of Justice OPR report

[4] Author interviews with unnamed FBI agents, week of July 28, 1996

[5] OPR report

[6] Author interviews with principals in the case and other agents, done from 1997–2003. Few take issue with the chronology; most are critical of the findings, especially as they concern the role of FBI Director Louis Freech and the role of Washington in leaking information about Richard Jewell.

[7] The author personally directed that search for Jewell, and Karen Klaus, a producer on temporary loan from the CNN Medical Unit made contact with AT&T, which agreed to provide Jewell.

[8] OPR report, page 9

[9] OPR report, page 9

[10] OPR report. Others would be suspicious about another remark Jewell made during the interview, that he helped clear people from in front of the tower, when in fact he

had gone around to the other side to help evacuate the people inside the sound and lighting tower. This placed him out of view of the officers and GBI agents for a few seemingly crucial minutes.

[11] OPR report

[12] Art Harris, CNN, August 28, 1996, to author, immediately after this happened. Harris would mention this several times on air during the ensuing days.

[13] Tom Johnson remarks, March 23, 2004

[14] As the days dragged on, certain TV networks even formed a media pool to do the stakeout so they could cut down on their costs by sharing the duty.

[15] OPR report

[16] OPR, page 22

[17] Author interviews with FBI investigators, 1996–97; Charles Stone observations from Task Force

[18] That took place at an FBI press conference on December 9, 1996.

[19] FBI Deputy Director Weldon Kennedy, December 9, 1996

[20] Same LAT article

Chapter Three

[1] Criminal complaint affidavit, FBI agent Tracey North, 10/14/98

[2] Scott was interviewed by Task Force agents shortly after the blast reinterviewed in February 1998.

[3] *Atlanta Journal-Constitution*, January 17, 1997

[4] CNN live interview, May 31, 2003

[5] Park Dietz report, April 14, 1997, p. 2

[6] Park Dietz report, April 14, 1997, p. 2–3

[7] Park Dietz report, April 14, 1997, pp. 2–7

[8] Park Dietz report, April 14, 1997, pp. 4–5

[9] Tracey North affidavit, October 1998. They also checked EXIS for plastic containers since all five bombs used those and came up with only 148 incidents out of 40,000 where plastic containers were used.

Chapter Four

[1] Interview with Emily and Jeff Lyons, May 2001

[2] Interview with Emily and Jeff Lyons, May 2001

[3] *Boston Globe*, January 31, 1998

[4] ATF affidavit

[5] Feminist Majority Foundation report, February 5, 2001

[6] *Boston Globe*, January 31, 1998

[7] Felecia Sanderson interview with *Sarasota Herald-Tribune*, Feb. 17, 1998

[8] Felecia Sanderson interview with *Sarasota Herald-Tribune*, Feb. 17, 1998

[9] Felecia Sanderson interview with *Sarasota Herald-Tribune*, Feb. 17, 1998

[10] *Atlanta Journal-Constitution*, June 5, 2003 and various news reports, plus interview with Officer Morro

[11] *Atlanta Journal-Constitution*, June 5, 2003

[12] *Atlanta Journal-Constitution*, June 5, 2003

[13] Interview with Emily and Jeff Lyons, May 2001

[14] Interview with Emily and Jeff Lyons, May 2001

[15] *Atlanta Journal-Constitution*, June 5, 2003

[16] *Atlanta Journal-Constitution*, June 5, 2003 and other news accounts

[17] Application for Search Warrant, 2/3/98, plus witness interviews (the remainder of this account is based on various court papers and investigative reports) 17 interviews with Doug Jones, May 2001

[18] Antiabortion advocates would say, of course, that millions more were victims of abortion violence, but that is not the subject of this particular story.

[19] As a result of the Atlanta bombings, the Task Force and the GBI had been trained by a team from Sandia National Laboratory led by Chris Cherry in new techniques on how to render bombs safe.

[20] Transcripts from various local and national news programs show the news conference happened before 6:00 P.M. ET (Birmingham was on central time)

Chapter Five

[1] Search warrant affidavit, 2/4/98

[2] Search warrant affidavit, 2/4/98; although it is possible that the neighbor saw Rudolph returning from the video store

[3] The time comes from Plaza Video's records, search warrant affidavit, 2/4/98. The timetable for Rudolph's movements is based on search warrant affidavits and interviews with investigators.

[4] Interviews with Sheriff Jack Thompson, 2001 & 2003; also search warrant affidavit, 2/4/98; Russell's account comes from court testimony 11/2/04.

[5] Search warrant application for trailer, 2/3/98

[6] Search warrant application for Cal's, 2/1/98

[7] Search warrant application for Cal's, 2/1/98

[8] Criminal complaint affidavit, Larry Long, et al., 2/14/98

[9] Search warrant return, Cal's 2/2/98

[10] CNN producer Mike Phelan was driving by Cal's when he saw the agents. He took out a Sony Handy-Cam and recorded the events from outside the fence.

[11] Criminal complaint affidavit, Tracey North, 10/98

[12] Search warrant return for Caney Creek trailer, 2/4/98

[13] Search warrant return, Nissan truck, 2/9/98

[14] Search warrant return, Nissan truck, 2/9/98

[15] Criminal complaint affidavit

Chapter Six

[1] Eric Robert Rudolph, *A Biographial Dossier*, 1st Edition, February 14, 1998

[2] Rexford Vernon and David Booth affidavit, 2/1/98; also Larry Long affidavit, 2/14/98 SE Bomb Task Force Fugitive Investigation memo, 6/8/98, p. 3

[3] Larry Long affidavit, 2/14/98

[4] That includes the cover, which bears the title Eric Robert Rudolph, *A Biographical Dossier*, 1st Edition, February 14, 1998

[5] Table of contents, Eric Robert Rudolph, *A Biographical Dossier*, 1st Edition, February 14, 1998

[6] Eric Robert Rudolph, *A Biographical Dossier*, 1st Edition, February 14, 1998

[7] Eric Robert Rudolph, *A Biograhpical Dossier*, 1st Edition, February 14, 1998

[8] Eric Robert Rudolph, *A Biographical Dossier*, 1st Edition, February 14, 1998

[9] Eric Robert Rudolph, *A Biographical Dossier*, 1st Edition, February 14, 1998 This story certainly changed on closer examination by the Task Force.

[10] Eric Robert Rudolph, *A Biographical Dossier*, 1st Edition, February 14, 1998

[11] Eric Robert Rudolph, *A Biographical Dossier*, 1st Edition, February 14, 1998

[12] Eric Robert Rudolph, *A Biographical Dossier*, 1st Edition, February 14, 1998

[13] Eric Robert Rudolph, *A Biographical Dossier*, 1st Edition, February 14, 1998

[14] Eric Robert Rudolph, *A Biographical Dossier*, 1st Edition, February 14, 1998

[15] Eric Robert Rudolph, *A Biographical Dossier*, 1st Edition, February 14, 1998

[16] Interview with Deborah Rudolph, May 2001

[17] Eric Robert Rudolph, *A Biographical Dossier*, 1st Edition, February 14, 1998

[18] Charles Stone interviews with Deborah Rudolph, beginning Feb. 1998; also interviews, including May 2001

[19] An FDA notice from 1987 gives some flavor of the debate over laetrile: "U.S. drug laws require that the safety and effectiveness of drugs be scientifically established before they can be marketed to the public. Laetrile had never complied with these requirements and animal studies had shown no anti-cancer activity in Laetrile." A federal judge in Utah for a time had ruled that laetrile could be imported, but most doctors, mindful of the lack of proof about laetrile's efficacy, refused to administer it.

[20] Charles Stone interviews with Deborah Rudolph, beginning Feb. 1998; also CNN interviews, including May 2001; it should be noted that Tom Branham offered a different take. He said the family had obtained laetrile and administered it to Robert, but when that didn't work, they wanted the doctors to inject him with potassium, but the doctors refused to do that.

[21] *The Thunderbolt* started as a publication of the National States Rights Party; it later changed its name to *The Truth at Last*, and was put out by former NSRP member Edward Fields, who ran a racist group, called the America First Party, according to Chip Berlet's Political Research Associates. Berlet is a leading researcher into extreme Right-wing groups.

[22] Interview with Deborah Rudolph, May 2001

[23] Charles Stone interviews with Deborah Rudolph, beginning Feb. 1998; also CNN interviews, including May 2001

[24] Charles Stone interviews with Deborah Rudolph, beginning Feb. 1998; also author interviews, including May 2001

[25] Charles Stone interviews with Deborah Rudolph, beginning Feb. 1998; also author interviews, including May 2001

[26] *Atlanta Journal-Constitution*, February 18, 1998, p.1

[27] *Atlanta Journal-Constitution*, March 22, 1998

[28] *Atlanta Journal-Constitution*, March 22, 1998

[29] *Atlanta Journal-Constitution*, March 11, 1998

[30] *Atlanta Journal-Constitution*, March 22, 1998

Chapter Seven

[1] Search warrant return, Caney Creek trailer, 3/5/98

[2] Search warrant return, Cal's Mini-Storage, 3/6/98

[3] Search warrant return, Cal's Mini-Storage, 5/98

[4] Tracey North affidavit in support of Atlanta indictment, 10/14/98

[5] Tracey North affidavit in support of Atlanta indictment, 10/14/98; CNN obtained a copy of the same tape from Frank and Sandy Sauer. On it, there is something that appears to be a pole sander, but the picture is blurred.

[6] Park Dietz profile, April 14, 1997, p. 5

[7] ATF report on Tom Branham

[8] Eric Robert Rudolph, *A Biographical Dossier*, 1st Edition, February 14, 1998

[9] Eric Robert Rudolph, *A Biographical Dossier*, 1st Edition, February 14, 1998

[10] One of those interviewed by both the FBI and the author admitted that his recollections of exact dates was hazy because he had spent so much of the 1980s stoned, some of it on what he claimed was Rudolph weed.

[11] Interview with Deborah Rudolph; also information from search warrant application, May 1998

[12] Interview with Deborah Rudolph, May 2001

[13] Rudolph also owned the *Black Book Companion*, which covered state-of-the-art improvised munitions.

[14] Interviews with Deborah Rudolph

[15] Eric Robert Rudolph, *A Biographical Dossier*, 1st Edition, February 14, 1998

[16] Author interview with a source, May 2001

[17] Author interview with a source, May 2001

[18] Interviews with Deborah Rudolph

[19] Eric Robert Rudolph, *A Biographical Dossier*, 1st Edition, February 14, 1998; Army records

[20] Eric Robert Rudolph, *A Biographical Dossier*, 1st Edition, February 14, 1998

[21] Eric Robert Rudolph, *A Biographical Dossier*, 1st Edition, February 14, 1998. By contrast, Eric's reading of explosives manuals would have seemed far more in keeping with the army way.

[22] Eric Robert Rudolph, *A Biographical Dossier*, 1st Edition, February 14, 1998

23 Eric Robert Rudolph, *A Biographical Dossier*, 1st Edition, February 14, 1998, plus author interview with Deborah Rudolph

24 *NY Times*, David Johnston with Devin Sack, 2/27/98

25 Interview with Deborah Rudolph, 2001

Chapter Eight

1 Nordmann interview 2/2/04. Nordmann mentioned the connection to Nord Davis, who became a key figure in the lives of the Rudolphs (see the next chapter) during the course of a conversation. This link had never been previously disclosed to the Task Force.

2 *Atlanta Journal-Constitution*, 7/16/98

3 *Atlanta Journal-Constitution*. 7/16/98

4 Tracey North affidavit in support of Atlanta indictment, 10/98

5 Information from the group's Web site: http://www.sovorderofsaintjohn.org/

6 Years later, in 2001, when Stone visited Nordmann with a journalist, Nordmann was still complaining that the government hadn't given him $500!

7 Tracey North affidavit in support of Atlanta indictment, 10/98

Chapter Nine

1 Remember that Nordmann told the Task Force Eric had visited his church much more recently and without his mother; instead, this took place as a result of a conversation between Eric and Nordmann.

2 *Birmingham Post-Herald*, 2/5/98. The article said that a doctor who performed abortions at a clinic in Asheville lived in the complex—and the same family that owned the Asheville clinic also owned the property where the Birmingham clinic stood. During 1997, an antiabortion group did picket the apartments. They also had been circulating brochures originally put out by the group that owned the Asheville clinic. On it, the predecessor to New Woman clinic, at the same address, is listed. While all of this may be coincidence, it could also explain why and how Birmingham was chosen as a target.

3 Patricia Rudolph would give a far more extensive discussion of her own beliefs and Eric's family history in an interview with Peter Wilkinson for *Rolling Stone* after Eric's capture.

4 This was the same explanation that Eric's brother Damian gave for why Eric left the army when FBI agents interviewed him in February.

5 Despite this agreement, the FBI asked them a year later to write up their notes for the file.

6 Associated Press, July 25, 1998

7 Though he did feel bound by his promise and called her five years later, the morning of Eric's capture.

8 Interview with Mark Pitcavage, *ADL*

9 *News and Observer,* Raleigh, NC, April 11, 1996. The rocket launcher was inert, according to the ATF, and not illegal, but agents warned of militia and extremist activity in the region.

10 *News and Observer,* Raleigh, NC, April 11, 1996. Klanwatch Intelligence Report, Summer 1997, from the Southern Poverty Law Center.

11 Author interviews with Deborah Rudolph, May 2001

12 Salon.com, January 29, 1998, in an interview with Jeff Stein

13 *Rolling Stone,* July 10, 2003, in an interview with Peter Wilkinson

14 Salon.com, January 29, 1998, in an interview with Jeff Stein

15 Angie Bateman. Bateman was Eric's ninth grade teacher at the Nantahala School. She told her story to the FBI and news media.

16 *Atlanta Journal-Constitution,* May 26, 1996

17 *New York Times,* March 1, 1998

18 *Rolling Stone,* July 10, 2003, in an interview with Peter Wilkinson

19 All but one. Dorothy Day was antiabortion, and some of the debate by her followers about whether they should try to have her canonized revolved around how the Vatican might embrace her antiabortion message while rejecting her other political and social beliefs.

20 Mark Pitcavage, *ADL/Militia Watchdog,* May 1996. The man was Gordon Kahl.

21 *USA v Thomas Wayne Branham* court papers

22 David Lance affidavit, *HJ Heinz Company v Thomas W. Branham,* B-C-84-95

23 Thomas Branham motion for continuance, *HJ Heinz Company v Thomas W. Branham,* B-C-84-95, March 29, 1984

24 *Rolling Stone,* July 10, 2003, in an interview with Peter Wilkinson; Bail surety notice for Thomas Wayne Branham, December 2, 1986

25 David Rossie, *Binghamton Press and Sun-Bulletin,* June 27, 2003

26 *Charlotte Observer,* July 26, 1995

27 Various Nord Davis publications, including *On Target*

28 *Greensboro News and Record,* June 25, 1995

29 *Asheville Citizen,* February 23, 1991. Despite that, Davis still complained that his group was being lumped in with Nazis and other groups.

30 ADL/Militia Watchdog, July 1996. The FBI had learned the lessons of Waco and the Montana siege eventually ended peacefully.

31 *Rolling Stone,* July 10, 2003, in an interview with Peter Wilkinson

32 The interview was done with Max McCoy of the *Joplin Globe* on December 7, 2000 for an investigative series McCoy did on Gayman's church, *"Ordained by Hate."* These notes are from the interview transcript, which was recorded on audiotape by McCoy and provided to me.

33 Tim and Sarah Gayman interview with Southern Poverty Law Center newsletter, 2001. The Gaymans also provided a similar account to Max McCoy for his series.

34 Tim and Sarah Gayman interview with Southern Poverty Law Center newsletter, 2001

35 ADL Intelligence Report, *Danger: Extremism,* 1996

36 Eric Robert Rudolph, *A Biographical Dossier*, 1st Edition, February 14, 1998; ADL Intelligence Report, *Danger: Extremism*, 1996

37 Tim and Sarah Gayman interview with Southern Poverty Law Center newsletter, 2001

38 *Fables vs Truth*, by Pastor Dan Gayman, Provided by the Center for Democratic Renewal

39 Tim and Sarah Gayman interview with Southern Poverty Law Center newsletter, 2001. From their account, they apparently never met Tom Branham, but were reflecting back where Eric had told them about him.

40 Tim and Sarah said that Joy later committed suicide after marrying someone else. Others, including Branham and Deborah Rudolph, also confirmed his relationship, although not his engagement, with Joy.

41 *Rolling Stone*, July 10, 2003, in an interview with Peter Wilkinson

42 Author interview with Deborah Rudolph, May 2001. Unfortunately, by May 2001, Deborah no longer had copies of the tape.

43 Eric Robert Rudolph, *A Biographical Dossier*, 1st Edition, February 14, 1998, p. 39. It isn't clear from the report whether this was Tim Gayman's address from when he was still living at his father's compound or after he broke off relations with him.

44 Deborah Rudolph, 2/07/04

45 Southern Poverty Law Center, various press clippings from February 1998 and follow-up interviews with Mark Potok of SPLC. It is important to note that SPLC, which has excellent sources of information inside the extremist community, made its claim about Davis and Rudolph before it ever interviewed Deborah Rudolph.

46 *Rolling Stone*, July 10, 2003, in an interview with Peter Wilkinson

47 *Basement Nukes: The Consequences of Cheap Weapons of Mass Destruction*, by Erwin and Edwin Strauss, Loompanics Unlimited, 1984.

48 Information from Southern Poverty Law Center; ADL; Simon Wiesenthal Center. The IHR Web site claims it does not deny the Holocaust, but the list of people it supports and publishes include prominent Holocaust deniers, such as David Irving and Ernest Zundel. Irving lost a well-publicized lawsuit against Emory Professor Deborah Lipstadt after claiming she libeled him by branding him a Holocaust denier.

49 *Denying the Holocaust*, Deborah Lipstadt, pp. 139–142. The man who offered the proof, Mel Mermelstein, lost several members of his family at Auschwitz and other death camps.

50 http://www.oswaldmosley.com/people/fjpveale.html. Oswald Mosley was the leader of the BUF and spent World War II in confinement for his support of Hitler and fascism.

51 IHR goes into great detail about his split with Carto, on his own Web site and also at http://homepage.mac.com/lsf/index.html

52 *International Jew*, by Henry Ford Sr., 2003 University Press of the Pacific

53 Yockey actually started out assisting the Nuremburg War Crimes prosecution but soon became disaffected and moved to the extreme Right. He committed suicide in 1960 in a jail cell in San Francisco, but his work and cause were picked up and championed by Willis Carto.

[54] *San Antonio Express-News*, February 26, 1999
[55] *Rolling Stone*, July 10, 2003, in an interview with Peter Wilkinson
[56] Frank and Sandy Sauer, interview; ironically, the Sauers said Patricia Rudolph would also do her own proselytizing, give them anti-Catholic pamphlets after finding out they were Catholic.
[57] Salon.com, January 29, 1998, in an interview with Jeff Stein
[58] *Rolling Stone*, July 10, 2003, in an interview with Peter Wilkinson
[59] Interview with Deborah Rudolph, May 2001
[60] Salon.com, January 29, 1998, in an interview with Jeff Stein
[61] Interviews with Deborah Rudolph, May 2001
[62] Salon.com, January 29, 1998, in an interview with Jeff Stein
[63] *USA Today*, June 2, 2003, in an interview with Blake Morrison and Laura Parker
[64] *Rolling Stone*, July 10, 2003, in an interview with Peter Wilkinson
[65] Interviews with Deborah Rudolph, May 2001. Eric divided the world between strong and weak people. He was a strong person; the weak were bloodsuckers.
[66] Kerry Noble interview, 2/2/04
[67] *Terror in the Name of God*, Jessica Stern, Harper-Collins, 2003
[68] Kerry Noble interview, 2/2/04
[69] The book, by Brandon Stickney, came out in late 1996 and was the first major book about McVeigh, written before his trial.
[70] The actual quotation from Thomas Jefferson to William Smith in 1787 was "God forbid we should ever be twenty years without such a rebellion . . . We have had thirteen States independent for eleven years. There has been one rebellion. That comes to one rebellion in a century and a half, for each State. What country before ever existed a century and a half without a rebellion?" *The Writings of Thomas Jefferson*, Memorial Edition (Lipscomb and Bergh, editors) 20 Vols., Washington, D.C., 1903–04. Jefferson did distinguish between rebellion and revolution, however.
[71] Frank Sauer, interviews
[72] He then exchanged that cashier's check for another one, which he later cashed, according to a time line put together by the Task Force.

Chapter Ten

[1] Report from WAGA television, Atlanta, 2/21/98
[2] Salon.com, January 29, 1998, in an interview with Jeff Stein
[3] If any of this sounds familiar, maybe it is because the author of *Cold Mountain*, Charles Frazier, grew up in part around Andrews.
[4] From an account entitled, *History of the Last Battle of the Civil War*, by John H. Stewart, 1st Lieut., 69th North Carolina Regiment, 1935
[5] Letter from Lou and Kathie Palladino, Green Pastures Farm, Murphy, June 14, 1998
[6] Lonnie Moore, quoted in *New Yorker* article by Tony Horowitz, March 15, 1999
[7] *Atlanta Journal-Constitution*, August 4, 1998

[8] Associated Press, July 21, 1998

[9] Associated Press, July 21, 1998

[10] Associated Press, July 26, 1998

[11] Grace Toney Edwards of Radford College wrote an essay on the ballad and its performance for *Newsday*, June 15, 2003. Another more local expert, Fred Hawley, was also quoted on the subject. Hawley was a professor at Western Carolina University and an amateur folklorist.

[12] E-mail from Grace Toney Edwards, January 2004

[13] Hawley in the *Ashville Citizen Times*, June 11, 1999

[14] Associated Press, August 4, 1998 and January 21, 1999

[15] Interview with Cherokee County chief jailer, December 2003

[16] Interview with FBI surveillance expert Bob Rolen, 1998

[17] Interview with former North Carolina state trooper, December 2003

[18] Interview with former Cherokee County Sheriff Jack Thompson, November 2003

[19] Agence France-Presse, August 4, 1998

[20] Associated Press, July 16, 1998

[21] *Behavioral Considerations Regarding Fugitive Eric Robert Rudolph*, by Thomas Neer and Ronald Tunkel, 7/26/98

[22] Later, Gritz would develop a link to the Church of Israel, where his fourth wife had personal connections. However, he had a falling out with Dan Gayman, who disinvited him to a church function, according to "Ordained by Hate," the series by Max McCoy in the *Joplin Globe*.

[23] *Atlanta Journal-Constitution*, 2/14/98. The Southern Poverty Law Center had put out a statement identifying Rudolph as a follower of Nord Davis, but both Ben Davis and his mother denied knowing either Eric Rudolph or his mother.

[24] All this comes from a release issued by Gritz entitled, "Let's Save Eric Rudolph."

[25] A local district attorney in Idaho attempted to try Horiuchi on manslaughter charges. After winning the right to do so in federal court, he eventually dropped the charges. Horiuchi said he didn't see Vicki Weaver, who was holding her ten-month-old baby, when he fired at another person in the cabin, Kevin Harris.

[26] *Kansas City Star*, March 14, 1999

[27] ADL Reports: *Extremism in America*

[28] Associated Press, August 21, 1998

[29] *USA TODAY*, August 18, 1998

[30] *Kansas City Star*, March 14, 1999

[31] Associated Press, August 13, 1998

[32] Southeast Bomb Task Force press release, August 13, 1998

[33] Task Force letter to Attorney General Janet Reno. The letter was dated August 20, 1998, and copies were also sent to the heads of the ATF, FBI, and GBI, along with the U.S. attorneys in Atlanta, Birmingham, and Charlotte. The head of the FBI field office in Atlanta, Jack Daulton, who had previously headed the Task Force, also signed the letter.

[34] Task Force letter to Attorney General Janet Reno

[35] Feldspar and quartz were used in TV picture tubes, but were also a common component in bath tiles and in abrasive cleaners. Depending on the type of mica, it could be used in products ranging from wall board to paint. Talc of course goes into many products, including talcum powder. North Carolina Department of Environment and Natural Resources, Ask a Geologist Program

[36] Darren Free interview, May–June 2001

[37] *Foxfire* started as a magazine in 1966, as part of a southern Appalachian cultural center founded in Rabun Gap, Georgia. It was aimed at capturing regional traditions and offering practical tips, based on the folkways of the area. The first compilation was published to great acclaim several years later and became a staple in southern homes, as did many of the succeeding volumes. See www.foxfire.org. Professor Grace Toney Edwards, an Appalachian expert at Radford College, says the Foxfire books would have been essential survival guides for someone trying to live out in the woods.

[38] *New York Times*, David Johnston, October 15, 1998

[39] *Washington Post*, October 27, 1998

[40] Interview with Bob Rolen, summer 2001

[41] Cox News Service, January 31, 1999

[42] E-mail from Joe Burton aka joe 6-pack, 12/4/98 and Web posting, http://www.uhuh.com/control/6pakand.htm

[43] Barton got his hands on some of the paperwork from the DOD and FBI, posting it on the Internet http: www.uhuh.com/control/6pakand.htm

[44] Associated Press, June 8, 2000

Chapter Eleven

[1] *The Anarchist Cookbook* was supposedly one of the books making the rounds of Eric's barracks, according to his commander. It is by far the most unbiquitous bomb-making manual for amateurs in print. The author of the original, William Powell, says he wrote it during 1968 and 1969, but that when it was first printed, the publisher retained the copyright. Powell now has a message on Amazon.com's Web site saying he is now much older and has become a confirmed Anglican. He adds the contents of the book now disturb him greatly, and he wishes the book would no longer be published, but that he has no control over the copyright.

[2] The scandals began when Frederic Whitehurst, a scientist at the lab and its leading expert on bomb residue, turned whistle-blower and made allegations of shoddy work and misleading testimony by his colleagues. He was suspended for a year, but an investigation into his complaints led to many changes at the lab. He was reinstated but resigned a day later after getting a $1.6 million settlement, CNN.com, 2/27/98

[3] Bill wasn't without problems; he admitted in his first interview with the FBI he would have trouble testifying before any grand jury about Rudolph unless he got some immunity concerning his marijuana dealings with Eric. He had teenage children, and he was worried his ex-wife could use his testimony or any problems resulting from it to get custody of them.

[4] Affidavit in support of Criminal Complaint, FBI Special Agent Tracey North, 10/14/98

[5] Affidavit in support of Criminal Complaint, FBI Special Agent Tracey North, 10/14/98

[6] Affidavit in support of Criminal Complaint, FBI Special Agent Tracey North, 10/14/98

[7] Affidavit in support of Criminal Complaint, FBI Special Agent Tracey North, 10/14/98

[8] Task Fore time line

[9] Task Force time line

[10] Task Force time line

[11] Task Force time line

[12] Affidavit in support of Criminal Complaint, FBI Special Agent Tracey North, 10/14/98

[13] Associated Press, July 21, 1999

[14] *Washington Post*, March 23, 1999

[15] Associated Press, March 16, 1999

[16] Bernazzani would later play a major role, post-9/11, in the FBI's counterterrorism efforts, particularly working with the CIA.

[17] Nordmann's comments were caught by a CBS producer using a hidden camera for a *60 Minutes* piece.

[18] Steve Cochran interview with CNN, spring 2001

[19] *USA Today* interview with John Magaw, December 14, 1999

[20] Interview with Deborah Rudolph, May 2001

[21] Interview with Emily Lyons, May 2001

[22] Knight-Ridder News Service, August 29, 1999. The poll of 913 North Carolina residents was done for the *Charlotte Observer* and WBTV.

[23] Interview with Jim Cavanaugh, spring 2001

[24] Interview with Todd Letcher, spring 2001

[25] Interview with Doug Jones, 2001

[26] *Charlotte News & Observer*, June 1, 2003

[27] NBC *Today Show*, October 29, 1999

[28] Gannett News Service, November 16, 2001

[29] *Charlotte News & Observer*, June 1, 2003

[30] *Birmingham News*, February 2, 2002

[31] David Hyde, *South Florida Sun-Sentinel*, February 10, 2002

[32] David Hyde, *South Florida Sun-Sentinel*, February 10, 2002

[33] Interivew with John Hawthorne, May 2001

[34] Interview with Emily and Jefrey Lyons, May 2001

[35] Interview with Emily and Jeffrey Lyons, May 2001

[36] The connection between Rudolph and bin Laden wasn't lost on Cofer Black, the man who led the hunt for bin Laden at the CIA immediately after 9/11. In the summer of 2003, when asked by CNN about the current hunt for Osama bin Laden,

Black brought up the case of Eric Rudolph, pointing to the difficulties and the time it took finding him.

Chapter Twelve

1. Interview with Jeff Postell, 2/2/04
2. Interview with Jeff Postell, 2/2/04
3. Interview with Jeff Postell, 2/2/04
4. Interview with Jeff Postell, 2/2/04
5. Interivew with Jeff Postell, 2/2/04
6. From Charles Kilby, according to Associated Press, 6/1/03
7. Interview with Sheriff Keith Lovin, 2/2/04
8. Interview with Sheriff Keith Lovin, 2/2/04
9. Interview with Sheriff Keith Lovin, 2/2/04
10. http://www.fbi.gov/hq/cjisd/iafis.htm
11. Interview with Sheriff Keith Lovin, 2/2/04
12. Interview with Mayor Bill Hughes, 2/2/04
13. Interview with Mayor Bill Hughes, 2/2/04
14. Interview with Sheriff Keith Lovin, 2/2/04
15. Interview with Sheriff Keith Lovin, 2/2/04
16. *New York Times*, June 6, 2003
17. Mayor Hughes made it a point to count them.
18. Interview with Investigator Jerry Crisp, 2/2/04 (most of the details that follow, except where noted, come from Crisp)
19. Interview with Lester White, 6/2/03
20. *New York Times*, June 6, 2003
21. Interview with Investigator Jerry Crisp, 2/2/04. Crisp declined to answer specifics on the Unabomber remarks, in case he had to testify to them in court.
22. CNN interview with Lester White, 6/2/03
23. Interviews with various local and federal law enforcement officials
24. Transcript of news conference, 5/31/03
25. John Hawthorne interview 6/4/03
26. *Atlanta Journal-Constitution.* 6/1/03
27. John Hawthorne, CNN interview 6/4/03
28. Interview with jailer Joe Morris, 12/2/03

Chapter Thirteen

1. Felecia Sanderson news conference, 6/3/03
2. *Charlotte Observer*, 6/4/03
3. *Charlotte Observer*, 6/4/03
4. Interview with Mayor Bill Hughes, 2/2/04
5. It was called "The Ballad of Eric Rudolph" by Gene Collett, and somehow it never

made the Top 40, but it did rate articles in the *Charlotte Observer* and *Atlanta Journal-Constitution*. The chorus ran: "Right or wrong in what he's done, his race is over / Now only in his mind are the sweet fields of clover / Eric Rudolph has run and where has he trod / Now he faces Caesar, but his final judge is God."

[6] Steve Cochran interview with CNN, 6/3/03

[7] *New York Times*, 6/3/03

[8] All of these people were interviewed by Linda Saether of CNN on 5/31/03 outside the store.

[9] The curbies were actually numbered, but according to interviews with local officials, it didn't appear that records were kept tracking the distribution of them.

[10] *New York Times*, 6/8/03

[11] *Charlotte Observer*, 12/24/03; Swecker held the same sentiments when we spoke to him in March 2004.

[12] *Atlanta Journal-Constitution*, 7/6/03

Epilogue

[1] CNN.com, 6/3/03

[2] Inmate security is always an issue. Serial killer Jeffrey Dahmer and the defrocked Roman Catholic priest John Geoghan are two examples of inmates killed in prison.

[3] Interview with Jefferson County Deputy Sheriff Randy Christian, January 2004

[4] At one point, the government asked for the records and tapes of those calls, but later withdrew the request.

[5] *Birmingham News*, 1/30/98

[6] *Rolling Stone*, 7/10/03

[7] *Rolling Stone*, 7/10/03

[8] *USA Today*, 6/2/03

[9] Interview with George Nordmann, 2/2/04

[10] *USA Today*, 6/2/03

[11] Kerry Noble interview, 1/29/04

[12] Kerry Noble interview, 1/29/04

[13] Interviewed by the author in Bern, Switzerland, in 2002

[14] A sample of one of his shortwave radio broadcasts could also be found on the Internet. In it, Pierce said, "As long as we continue to let the Jews control our country, one calamity after another will be inflicted upon us."

[15] Interview with JTTF member, February 2004

[16] "Leaderless Resistance," Louis Beam, printed first in *The Seditionist*, 1992

[17] *Miami Herald*, 2/14/04

INDEX